ON THE ROAD

The Original Scroll

Edited by Howard Cunnell

Introductions by Howard Cunnell, Penny Vlagopoulos,
George Mouratidis, and Joshua Kupetz

ON THE ROAD

The Original Scroll

JACK KEROUAC

VIKING

VIKING
Published by the Penguin Group
Penguin Group (USA) Inc., 375 Hudson Street, New York, New York 10014, U.S.A. • Penguin Group (Canada), 90 Eglinton Avenue East, Suite 700, Toronto, Ontario, Canada M4P 2Y3 (a division of Pearson Penguin Canada Inc.) • Penguin Books Ltd, 80 Strand, London WC2R 0RL, England • Penguin Ireland, 25 St. Stephen's Green, Dublin 2, Ireland (a division of Penguin Books Ltd) • Penguin Books Australia Ltd, 250 Camberwell Road, Camberwell, Victoria 3124, Australia (a division of Pearson Australia Group Pty Ltd) • Penguin Books India Pvt Ltd, 11 Community Centre, Panchsheel Park, New Delhi – 110 017, India • Penguin Group (NZ), 67 Apollo Drive, Rosedale, North Shore 0632, New Zealand (a division of Pearson New Zealand Ltd.) • Penguin Books (South Africa) (Pty) Ltd, 24 Sturdee Avenue, Rosebank, Johannesburg 2196, South Africa

Penguin Books Ltd, Registered Offices: 80 Strand, London WC2R 0RL, England

First published in 2007 by Viking Penguin, a member of Penguin Group (USA) Inc.

ISBN-13: 978-0-7394-9426-4

Printed in the United States of America
Designed by Carla Bolte • *Set in Iowan*

CONTENTS

Fast This Time

Jack Kerouac and the Writing of *On the Road*

Howard Cunnell

1

"I've telled all the road now," Jack Kerouac said in a May 22, 1951 letter he sent from New York west across the land to his friend Neal
Cassady in San Francisco. "Went fast because the road is fast." Kerouac told Cassady that between April 2 and April 22 he had written a
"125,000 [word] full-length novel . . . Story deals with you and me and
the road." He had written the "whole thing on strip of paper 120 foot
long . . . just rolled it through typewriter and in fact no paragraphs . . .
rolled it out on floor and it looks like a road."

Like everything else about him, the story of how Jack Kerouac
came to write *On the Road* became a legend. Certainly when I read the
book at sixteen my friend Alan knew all about it. He had read it first
and now he was wearing a white T-shirt and low-hipped Levi's and
listening to George Shearing. This was in a sun-washed white-and-
blue seaside town on the south coast of England twenty-five years ago.
Kerouac was high on Benzedrine when he wrote *On the Road*, Alan
told me, and he wrote it all in three weeks on a long roll of Teletype
paper, no punctuation. Just sat down with bop on the radio and
blasted it out and it was all true-life stories, every word, all about riding the roads across America with his mad friend Dean, and jazz,
drink, girls, drugs, freedom. I didn't know what bop or Benzedrine
was but I found out, and I bought a bunch of records by Shearing and
Slim Gaillard. *On the Road* be the first book I'd read or heard of with
a built-in soundtrack.

After I read *On the Road* and tried to find other books by Kerouac it was always the same story that I heard. On the dust jacket of my old English copy of *Visions of Cody* it says that *On the Road* was written "in 1952 in a few hectic days on a scroll of newsprint." The story goes that Kerouac grabbed the scroll and raced over to Robert Giroux, the editor at Harcourt, Brace who had worked with Kerouac on *The Town and the City*, the novel he had published the previous spring. Kerouac rolled the road out in front of him and Giroux, not getting it, asked Kerouac how could the printer work from *that*? A story that whether true or not perfectly expresses the collision of straight America and a new subterranean hipster generation come to tell you about IT. Books, if not exactly square, certainly didn't look like this. Kerouac takes the novel away and refuses to revise it and goes on the road again to California and Mexico, and he discovers Buddhism and spontaneous prose and writes more novels fast one after another in little notebooks that nobody dares publish. Years go by before Viking buys *On the Road*. Allen Ginsberg says that the published novel is not at all like the wild book Kerouac typed in '51. Ginsberg says that someday when "everybody's dead" the "original mad" book will be published as it is.

In his May 22, 1951 letter to Neal Cassady, Kerouac had explained that "of course since Apr. 22 I've been typing and revising. Thirty days on that," and Kerouac's closest friends knew he had been working on the book at least since 1948. Fifty years on from the novel's eventual publication, however, the defining images of Jack Kerouac and *On the Road* in the cultural imagination remain his apparent frenzied channeling of a true-life story; the never-ending roll of paper billowing from the typewriter like the imagined road, and the T-shirts Kerouac sweated through as he speed typed hanging to dry in the apartment like victory flags. Kerouac's clattering typewriter is folded in with Jackson Pollock's furious brushstrokes and Charlie Parker's escalating and spiraling alto saxophone choruses in a trinity representing the breakthrough of a new postwar counterculture seemingly built on sweat, immediacy, and instinct, rather than apprenticeship, craft, and daring practice.

We've known for a while now that there is much more to it than this, just as the novel is far more spiritual quest than how-to-be-a-hipster manual. *On the Road* does not appear out of clear blue air. From Kerouac's writing journals we know that during his travels through America and Mexico from 1947 to 1950 he collected material for a road novel he first mentions by name in an entry dated August 23, 1948. *On the Road*, Kerouac writes, "which I keep thinking about: [is] about two guys hitch-hiking to California in search of something they don't *really* find, and losing themselves on the road, and coming all the way back hopeful of something *else*."

The impossible romance of the three weeks in April continues to dominate the imagination when we think about Jack Kerouac. The original scroll version of *On the Road* is the key document in the history of one of the most enduringly popular and influential novels published in the last fifty years, and among the most significant, celebrated, and provocative artifacts in contemporary American literary history. Here I trace a compositional and publication history of *On the Road*. The story is about work, ambition, and rejection, but it is also about transformation. These are the years in which Kerouac transforms himself from a promising young novelist into the most successfully experimental writer of his generation. The key texts in this story are the original scroll version of *On the Road*, and *Visions of Cody*, which Kerouac began in the fall of the year in which he wrote the scroll. Because the scroll is the wildflower from which the magic garden of *Visions of Cody* grows, it is the pivotal text in the story of Jack Kerouac and his place in American literature. The story is also, of course, about Neal Cassady.

2

As Kerouac neared the completion of *The Town and the City* in the late summer and fall of 1948 he was already thinking about his second book. Kerouac worked on *The Town and the City* between 1947 and 1949, and the novel was published on March 2, 1950. In the latter half of Kerouac's first novel can be found many of the themes that will dominate his second, while in the original version of *On the Road* the reader marks the progress "Jack" makes in *The Town and the City*. If the style of *On the Road* can be read as a reaction to and a progression from that of the earlier book, then the original version of *Road*, which begins with the death of the father just as *The Town and the City* ends with that death, also shows how Kerouac's second novel should be read as a sequel to his first.

It would take a full-length book to do justice properly to the amount of writing Kerouac produced between 1948 and 1951 as he worked on his second novel. Writing most often late into the night he filled notebooks, journals, hundreds of manuscript pages, and letters, as well as conversations, with ideas for it. In October of 1948 Kerouac wrote in his journal that his ideas for *On the Road* "obsess me so much I can't conceal them." To Hal Chase on October 19 Kerouac wrote that his work plans "overflow out of me, even in bars with perfect strangers."

One way of navigating the material is through the three major proto-versions of the novel that Kerouac writes between August 1948 and April 1951. These are the fifty-four-page "Ray Smith Novel of Fall 1948," the Red Moultrie/Vern [later Dean] Pomery Jr. versions of 1949, of which the longest draft is also fifty-four pages, and "Gone on the Road," a thirty-page, heavily corrected seven-chapter version featuring Cook Smith and Dean Pomeray that Kerouac typed in Richmond Hill in August of 1950. These stories are where Kerouac gives formal expression to the ideas that fill his dreams and notebooks.

In them, Kerouac is consciously trying to write a novel the way novels had always been written, fusing what he remembers with what he can make. Things must stand for other things. Elaborate backstories and histories must be built to explain why his people take to the road. They are to be half brothers in blood, searching for a lost inheritance, for fathers, for family, for home, even for America. Maybe they'll be part Comanche to better illustrate what they have lost.* He accumu-

---

*In the cast of characters in a manuscript titled "'On the Road' as reconceived Feb 15, 1950" Chadwick "Chad" Gavin, Brooklyn baseball player, scholar, jailbird, and roamer, is half brother to Dean Pomeray Jr. Pomeray is a "hipster, hot-rod racer, chauffeur, jailbird, and teahead." The men are "half-brothers in blood; each 1/16th Comanche."

lates and rehearses set pieces in his notebooks. The myth of the rainy night. Versions of the dream of the shrouded stranger. The remembered horror of waking in a cheap Iowa hotel room not knowing who or where he was but only that he was getting old and death was getting nearer. Again and again he returns to the death of the father.

For and against Kerouac as he works is the sweet inviting world outside his window. The writing of the novel, begun before Kerouac first travels on the road with Neal Cassady in December of 1948, is tested, broken, and changed by the subsequent transcontinental trips Kerouac makes with him that will in the end become the story of the book and that Kerouac faithfully records in his travel journals. His focus widens as he moves from New York into the West, then back and farther on into the East and then West again and down into Mexico. The places where the imagined book and the lived experiences intersect are the places where what the book is to become are negotiated. What is being negotiated is the relationship between fiction and truth, where truth is understood by Kerouac to mean, "the way consciousness *really* digs everything that happens."

As Penny Vlagopoulos explains in the essay that follows, Kerouac is consciously writing against a monological and fearful cold war culture that encouraged Americans in self-surveillance and self-censorship and the transmission of politically acceptable levels of reality. Working on the novel in 1949 Kerouac often visited John Clellon Holmes and showed him his work-in-progress. Holmes writes,

> When he came by in the late afternoons, he usually had new scenes with him, but his characters never seemed to get very far beyond [what] . . . a well-made novel seemed to demand as a contrast to all the footloose uprootedness to come. He wrote long, intricate Melvillian sentences . . . I would have given anything I owned to have written such tidal prose, and yet he threw it out, and began again, and failed again, and grew moody and perplexed.

Excepting those writers, such as Melville, Dostoyevsky, and Joyce, who clearly influenced him, fiction, even and especially well-made

European fiction, was linked in Kerouac's imagination with both an aesthetic and political culture of self-censorship. The old forms of fiction obscured meaning; stopped you getting at what was underneath. *On the Road* is the beginning of a process in which Kerouac dismantles and then radically reapplies what he has learned as a fiction writer so that he can, as John Holmes writes, "free the whole range of his consciousness to the page."

In the "Ray Smith Novel of Fall 1948" Smith, who will reappear as the practiced hitchhiking narrator of *The Dharma Bums* (1958), barely gets on the road at all. Young Smith decides to travel to California from New York after finding out that his forty-year-old girlfriend Lulubelle has taken up with a man her own age. Ray gets stuck in the rain north of New York City at Bear Mountain because of his foolish dream of thinking he can ride Route 6 all the way to the West Coast. At Bear Mountain, Smith meets Warren Beauchamp, a blond, troubled, privileged Franco-American boy who persuades Ray to travel back with him to New York so that Beauchamp can get money from his family and continue the trip West. The narrative comes to a dead end in a drunken night in New York. Beauchamp's alcoholic father passes out, and the boys go to Times Square looking for Ray Smith's friends Leon Levinsky [Allen Ginsberg], Junkey [Herbert Huncke] and a place to stay. Smith meets Paul Jefferson, Lulubelle's half brother, and eventually Smith and Beauchamp tramp back to Harlem and sleep on Lulubelle's floor while Lulubelle's new lover sleeps in Ray's place in her bed.

In his journal Kerouac writes that he has "no idea where I'm heading with the novel." On December 1 Kerouac writes a chapter insert titled "Tea Party," typing the manuscript on December 8. In the story Smith and Beauchamp and various subterranean East Coast hipsters including Junkey and Levinsky meet at Peter Martin's sister Liz's apartment to smoke marijuana and inject morphine.

Here Kerouac writes the dream of movement, the journey stalled, and the compensation of drugs that would promote an interior voyage. So that the world might at least appear transformed, just as Liz

Martin disguises her apartment as a proletarian slum while the back room is decorated with black and red painted walls and drapes, candles, and "cheap Five-and-Ten Buddhas belching incense."

In *The Town and the City* Kerouac traced how the postwar generation had begun to disperse to places that William Burroughs in *Junky* called "ambiguous or transitional districts." A transracial, transgendered counterculture had begun to emerge among these small, interlocking New York subterranean communities of writers and artists, street hustlers and drug users, homosexuals, and jazz musicians, but Peter Martin and Ray Smith found only uneasy refuge enclosed and corralled in these transitional districts. They needed to *move*.

John Clellon Holmes astutely noted that the "the breakup of [Kerouac's] Lowell-home, the chaos of the war years and the death of his father, had left him disrupted, anchorless, a deeply traditional nature thrown out of kilter, and thus enormously sensitive to anything uprooted, bereft, helpless or persevering." To Kerouac, this personal sense of loss and restlessness recorded in *The Town and the City* led to faith in the possibilities of movement, and to a connection with the historic aspirational American belief in movement as the means of self-transformation. From Whitman's *Song of the Open Road* to Cormac McCarthy's bleakly radiant postapocalyptic novel *The Road* (2006), the road narrative has always been central to America's cultural representations of itself. When in a 1949 notebook Kerouac described his decision to set his second novel on the road, he said it was "like a message from God giving a sure direction."

The road would occupy Kerouac from the beginning to the end of his writing life. In 1940 he wrote a four-page short story called "Where the Road Begins" that explored the contending attractions of the open road and the joy of returning home again. *The Town and the City* is in part a road narrative, as Joe Martin, intoxicated by the perfume of spring flowers and "the sharp pungent smell of exhaust fumes on the highway, and the heat of the highway itself cooling under the stars," and embodying and anticipating a new American generation's questing need to *go*, feels himself fated and driven to take a "wild wonderful trip out West, anywhere, everywhere." In the month of his death Kerouac submitted reworked and previously discarded material from *On the Road* to his agent Sterling Lord as the novel *Pic* (posthumously published in 1971).

As Holmes writes, Kerouac, as Americans always have, "hankered for the West, for Western health and openness of spirit, for the immemorial dream of freedom [and] joy." The on-the-move outsider nation of *On the Road* dramatizes Kerouac's strong belief that this elemental American idealism, this faith in a place at the end of the road where you could make both a home and a stand had, in Holmes's words, "been outlawed to the margins of American life in his time. His most persistent desire in those days was to chronicle what was happening on those margins."

Kerouac writes from those margins. The love of America that so distinguishes *On the Road* and *Visions of Cody* came from Kerouac's own double sense of himself as both American and French Canadian. This idea of Kerouac as a postcolonial writer is confirmed most particuarly by his magic-realist novel *Doctor Sax*, in which Kerouac writes the French-Canadian experience into the American national narrative in a way similar to Salman Rushdie's inscription of the Anglo-Indian experience in *Midnight's Children*. Interestingly, Kerouac was working on both *Road* and *Sax* at the same time and considered merging the two novels. As late as the summer of 1950 he was using a French-Canadian narrator for *Road*, but only traces remain of *Sax* in that novel.

More than anything else the story of *On the Road* returns again and again to Neal Cassady. Cassady was Kerouac's lost brother returned; the longed-for adventuring Western hero made young again; and the living expression of the Dionysian side of Kerouac's own dual nature. Cassady, as Kerouac would write in *Visions of Cody*, was the one "who watched the sun go down, at the rail, by my side, smiling," but he was also a destructive presence from whose speed-freak con-man mystique Kerouac sometimes felt the need to escape. They met in 1947 but did not ride together until December of 1948, and with each new adventure Kerouac steered the novel further toward him. He was variously named Vern Pomery Jr., Dean Pomery Jr., Dean Pomeray Jr., Neal Cassady, Dean Moriarty, and in *Visions of Cody*, Cody Pomeray. In the scroll Kerouac makes the connection explicit:

> My interest in Neal is the interest I might have had in my brother that died when I was five years old to be utterly straight about it. We have a lot of fun together and our lives are fuckt up and so there it stands. Do you know how many states we've been in together?

Kerouac and Cassady made two trips in late December with LuAnne Henderson and Al Hinkle, shuttling family belongings from Rocky Mount, North Carolina (where Kerouac was spending Christmas with his family), to the Kerouac home in Ozone Park, New York. After New Year's celebrations in New York the four drove to Algiers, Louisiana, to visit Bill Burroughs and his family. Herbert Huncke and Hinkle's new wife Helen were also staying in Burroughs's ramshackle house by the bayou. Leaving Hinkle in Louisiana with Helen, Cassady, LuAnne, and Kerouac then proceeded to San Francisco. Kerouac returned to New York alone in February.

On March 29, 1949, Kerouac learned that Harcourt, Brace had accepted *The Town and the City*. A jubilant Kerouac continued work on *On the Road*, filling notebook pages with plans and writing to Alan Harrington on April 23 "I start work in earnest on my second novel this week." Kerouac reports the arrests in New Orleans of Bill Burroughs for drug and weapons possession, and in New York of Allen Ginsberg, Herbert Huncke, Vicki Russell, and Little Jack Melody after the police raided Ginsberg's apartment and found drugs and stolen goods. The arrest of his friends, the fear that he might be questioned himself, and the acceptance of his novel led Kerouac to write that he was at a turning point in his life, "the end of my 'youth.'" Kerouac was "determined to start a new life." In this new version of the novel there would be "no more" Ray Smith. Instead, Red Moultrie, a merchant seaman imprisoned in New York on drugs charges, will look for God, family, and home in the West.

In May, Kerouac traveled to Denver as a soon-to-be-published young novelist with a thousand-dollar advance. Hitchhiking to save money, Kerouac was "itching" to establish the family home he had dreamed about for years. On a late-May Sunday afternoon Kerouac writes that starting "'On the Road' back in Ozone, and here, is difficult. I wrote one full year before starting T & C, (1946)—but this mustn't happen again. Writing is my work . . . so I've got to *move*." On June 2 Kerouac's mother Gabrielle, his sister Caroline and brother-in-law Paul Blake, and their son Paul Jr. joined Kerouac at the house he had leased at 6100 West Center Avenue in Denver. On June 13 Kerouac writes that he is at "the true beginning" of *On the Road*.

By the first week of July, Kerouac was alone again. Gabrielle and Caroline and her family were unhappy in the west and had returned home. On July 16 Harcourt, Brace editor Robert Giroux flew to Denver to work with Kerouac on the manuscript of *The Town and the City*.

Kerouac typed and revised a twenty-four-page handwritten draft of the beginning of a new version of *Road* titled "Shades of the Prison House. Chapter 1 On the Road - May-July 1949." The manuscript is marked New York–Colorado, indicating that Kerouac wrote the handwritten draft in Ozone Park and brought it West. "Shades of the Prison House" is informed by Kerouac's trips with Cassady earlier in the year and the stories Cassady had told him about his boyhood, by Kerouac's hopefulness for the impending publication of *The Town and the City*, and by the arrest and imprisonment of his friends in April. Kerouac may also have been remembering his arrest and brief imprisonment as a material witness and accessory after the fact in Lucien Carr's killing of Dave Kammerer in August 1944. Above all, in this period of fragile optimism, the new version of *On the Road* was buoyed by Kerouac's abiding love of God.

In a cell in the Bronx jail overlooking the Harlem River, Red Moultrie leans against the worn bars and watches the red sunset over New York the night before his release. To "the cops [Red] was just another young character of the streets—nameless, anonymous, and beat."

Brown eyes "red in the light of the sun; tall, rocky, dogged, sober-souled," Red is twenty-seven and "growing older all the time and his life was slipping away." He plans to go to New Orleans and has ten dollars from "Old Bull" to get there. From New Orleans, Red will drive to San Francisco with his half brother Vern Pomery Jr., and from there Red will go home to Denver to look for his wife, child, and father. Pomery is to be a representation of Cassady, and he appears here for the first time in the projected novel as an idea, a phantom presence on the far horizon of the text.

Red is haunted by "the great realities from the other world which appeared to him in dreams like the dream of the shrouded stranger," in which he is pursued through "Araby" and seeks refuge in the "Protective City." Watching the splendid sunset Red decides to follow the direction he sees in the evening sky:

> The blushing sunset on this last night in jail was a hint from immense nature telling him that all things could very well return to him if he would only pray . . . "God make everything right," he prayed in a whisper. He shuddered. "I'm all alone. I want to be loved, I've got no place to go." Whatever that dark thing was he kept on missing . . . mattered no more. He had to go home.

In August, Kerouac closed up the house and left Denver to visit Neal and Carolyn Cassady in San Francisco. In *On the Road* Kerouac writes:

> I was burning to know what was on his mind and what would happen now, for there was nothing behind me any more, all my bridges were gone and I didn't give a damn about anything at all.

Kerouac arrived in California as the marriage of Neal and Carolyn seemed to be imploding. Pregnant, Carolyn threw Neal out, and Jack suggested Neal come back with him to New York. They traveled east where they visited Kerouac's first wife Edie in Grosse Pointe, Michigan. Kerouac writes that this "memorable voyage described elsewhere sometime. (In "Rain & Rivers" book)." The "Rain and Rivers" journal, a notebook given to him by Cassady in January 1949, was where Kerouac recorded the majority of the journeys and specific adventures that would come to make up the narrative of the novel. As Kerouac struggles to identify and articulate the themes of his novel in his notebooks and proto-fiction, the narrative is, perhaps unknowingly at first, recorded in these travel journals.

By late August, Jack and Neal had arrived in New York. The two friends walked all over Long Island because, as Kerouac will write in *On the Road*, they were so used to moving but "there was no more land, just the Atlantic Ocean and we could only go so far. We clasped hands and agreed to be friends forever." On August 25 Kerouac resumed what he calls his "ragged work" on the road novel while with Robert Giroux he continued preparing *The Town and the City* for publication the following spring. Kerouac typed a fifty-four-page revised double-spaced version of "Shades of the Prison House." The sunset now appears "goldenly" in an "opening in the firmament between great dark cloudbanks."

> The central joyous source of the universe was always there, and clear as ever, when at last some strange earthly confluence forced the clouds apart, and as if curtains were drawn by arrangement, revealed the everlasting light itself: the pearl of heaven flaming on high.

Red's long night ends in a list of names and images from Kerouac's travels and private mythology. Kerouac's incantation covers pages 49–53, and these pages are single spaced in contrast to the double spacing of the rest of the typescript, suggesting the book to come, the book still to write and imagined in reverberating fragments:

> Fresno, Selma, Southern Pacific Railroad; cottonfields, grapes, grapey dusk; trucks, dust, tent, San Joaquin, Mexicans, Okies, highway, red workflags; Bakersfield, boxcars, palms, moon, watermelon, gin, woman . . .

The typescript ends on the morning of Red's release. Red hears birds singing "and the Sunday bells at seven did begin to peal."

On the verso of page 54 Kerouac has handwritten "Foolscap for New Beginning '<u>On the Road</u>' Aug 25 1949 - Reserving back of these pages for opening of new Part Two - THE STORY JUST BEGINS." By hand Kerouac begins the new story set where he had just spent the summer, in Colorado. It is 1928. Old Wade Moultrie owns a two-hundred-acre farm worked by his son Smiley Moultrie and Smiley's best friend Vern Pomery. There was "a touch of the old West" in Old Wade, and when he pulls a revolver on some "young hoodlums" trying to steal his Ford he is shot and killed. This has nothing to do, Kerouac writes, "with our heroes Red Moultrie and Vern Pomery Jr." In a journal entry for August 29 Kerouac notes:

> Resuming true serious work I find that I have grown lazy in my heart . . . And why that is—for one thing, indirectly speaking, I cannot for instance as yet understand why my father is dead . . . no meaning, all unseemly, and incomplete.

By September 6 this same journal had become the "Official Log of the 'Hip Generation,'" as he was now calling *On the Road*. "I haven't really worked since May 1948," he writes. "Time to get going . . . Let's see if I can write a novel." The eighteen-page "Hip Generation" story Kerouac then begins to write continues the story he had begun on the back page of the August 25 version of "Shades of the Prison House," while cutting the jail material.

Red's mother Mary Moultrie has an affair with Dean Pomery and dies giving birth to Red's half brother Dean Pomery Jr. Wade Moultrie's farm has gone to ruin in the years after his death, a death Kerouac intended to stand for the passing of the values of the Old West and for the passing of a kind of moral compass, a north star certainty lost to Kerouac's fatherless travelers.

Still Kerouac is writing around the road. The road exists in future time, to be traveled *when* Red gets out of jail or *when* he and Vern grow up out of the backstory Kerouac constructs in place of the jail episodes. Kerouac is writing the why of the road, not the road itself. He is committed to the aspirational elements of the story even as the events that inspired those elements, bringing his family West, his status as a young novelist with a future, had either collapsed or been made to seem suddenly fragile again. If he could not successfully make a home in the West perhaps the novel might also fail. It was difficult to write about Red's leaving the prison of life to go back home to his inheritance and to his family when Kerouac was effectively homeless, his dreamed Western home collapsed; his marriage to Edie emphatically over; and the thousand-dollar "inheritance" from Harcourt vanished into the air.

For much of the rest of September Kerouac worked on *The Town and the City* manuscript at the New York offices of Harcourt, Brace. When this work was finished Kerouac wrote that he was "once more ready to resume On the Road," before confessing on September 29 that

> I've got to admit I'm stuck with <u>On the Road</u>. For the first time in years I DON'T KNOW WHAT TO DO. I SIMPLY DO NOT HAVE A SINGLE REAL IDEA WHAT TO DO

The next day, and writing that he was not a "hipster . . . Nor am I Red Moultrie . . . I am not even Smitty, I'm none of them," Kerouac claimed to have settled the problem of his inability to write:

> The world really does not matter, but God has made it so, and so it matters in God, and He Hath Aims for it, which we cannot know without the understanding of obedience. **There is nothing to do but give praise.** This is my ethic of "art" and why so.

On October 17, 1949, Kerouac writes that it is still "impossible to say 'Road' has really begun." "I really began On the Road in October of 1948," he writes, "an entire year ago. Not much to show for a year, *but the first year is always slow.*" Still, Kerouac thought, the novel was "about to *move.*" By the end of the month Kerouac writes to "hell with it; don't worry, simply do." He trusted that in the "work itself" he would find his way, but writes, "still don't feel On the Road is begun."

In November, and writing in the back of his "On the Road Readings and Notes, 1949" journal begun in the spring of that year, where he had made notes for episodes in the novel including "The Tent in the San Joaquin Valley" and "Marin City and the barracks cops-job," Kerouac writes a "New Itinerary and Plan." Above a drawn map of America marked with the names of the towns and cities where the action of the novel would take place Kerouac wrote "On the Road" and "Reverting to a Simpler style – Further draft + beginning - Nov 1949." The novel would begin in the New York jail and move through New Orleans, San Francisco, Montana, Denver, and back to Times Square in New York. The list of characters Kerouac notes includes Moultrie and "Dean Pomeray," "Slim Jackson," brother of Pic, "Old Bull," and "Marylou."

In notes and manuscript fragments written in the new year Kerouac returned to the themes of loss, uncertainty, and crowding mortality. A ten-page manuscript dated January 19, 1950, handwritten in French and translated by Kerouac ("On the Road ECRIT EN FRANCAIS") begins

> After the death of his father—Peter Martin found himself alone in the world, and after all what is a man going to do when his father is buried deep in the ground other than die himself in his heart and know that it won't be the last time before he dies finally in his poor mortal body, and, himself a father of children and sire of a family he will return to the original form of a piece of adventurous dust in this fatal ball of earth.

The running theme of the search for the father who is dead and the Father who is God gives us to understand that death, as Tom Clark has written, was "the ground bass of [Kerouac's] understanding of life, the undertow that moved the deep currents in his work and gave it what Kerouac himself called . . . 'that inescapable sorrowful depth that shines through.'" The deaths of his brother Gerard, his father Leo, his best friend Sebastian. His drowned dead friends among the crew of the SS *Dorchester* sunk by torpedo on February 3, 1943. War dead, Hiroshima dead. The bomb that had come, as Kerouac writes, was one which could "crack all our bridges and banks and reduce them to jumbles like the avalanche heap." And it is death, in the form of the dreamed figure of the shrouded stranger, who pursues the traveler across the land.

Long before his readings in Buddhism Kerouac was intuitively attempting to reconcile a worldview that saw his lived experience both as one made painfully meaningless by his hard-wired knowledge of mortality and as one to be celebrated in every detail and at every moment precisely because, as he writes in *Visions of Cody*, we are soon "all going to die." Kerouac escapes this encircling loss in the act of writing. To say what happened. To get it down before it is lost. To make mythology from your life and from the lives of your friends. This urgency pushes Kerouac to strip his writing of "made-up" stories. Life's impermanence and the inevitability of suffering inform and motivate Kerouac's heightened sensitivity and responsiveness to the phenomenal world. What Allen Ginsberg called his "open heart" and Kerouac himself described as being "submissive to everything, open, listening" results in a body of fiction in which the representation of the magical nature of entrancing and life-affirming fleeting detail is the outstanding feature.

In the early months of 1950 Kerouac anxiously looked forward to the publication of his first novel, asking, "Will I be rich or poor? Will I be famous or forgotten?" On February 20 he confesses, "I gloat more & more in the fact that I may be rich & famous soon." *The Town and the City* was published on March 2, 1950, and on March 8 Kerouac admits that the "swirl" of publication had "interrupted the work I was doing on Road." As it became clear to him that *The Town and the City* would not be a financial success he began again to worry about money and about his mother, who, he wrote, "can't work forever." These worries together with the "one-eyed" reception of his novel left him unable to write. On April 3 he writes, "BOOK NOT SELLING MUCH. Wasn't born to be rich."

At the invitation of William Burroughs, Kerouac traveled to Mex-

ico City from Denver with Frank Jeffries and Neal Cassady in June
1950. After Cassady left Mexico, Kerouac and Jeffries moved into an
apartment on Insurgentes Boulevard across from the house rented by
William and Joan Burroughs. Writing to his Denver friend Ed White
on July 5 Kerouac explained that he was intent on investigating "all
the levels" of "mile-and-a-half-high" consciousness promoted by
smoking Mexican marijuana, "particulary with reference to the many
problems and considerations of that second novel I have to write."
The sentences might crack open when he was high.

Kerouac wrote that because when he was smoking marijuana his
"deep subconscious thoughts" often came to him in his native Franco-
American French, he had created a hero, Wilfred Boncoeur, who was
French Canadian but whose ambiguous postcolonial status is suggested by his "English silliness." Referencing the foundation text of
the narrative tradition in which he was consciously working Kerouac
wrote that he intended to have Boncoeur travel with a companion
named "Cousin" who would act as "Panza to the hero's Quixote."
Kerouac makes notes for the Freddy "Goodheart" novel in the 120-
page "Road Workbook" he kept in Mexico that summer. Boncoeur has
been told his father Smiley is dead but "I did not believe it." When
he is fifteen Freddy is told his father was "really alive but nobody
knew where," and he and Cousin go on the road to find him.

Eventually worried that "Freddy" at fifteen would be too young to
tell the novel "right," Kerouac changed tack once more, writing that
the novel would still have a French-Canadian narrator but that the
"F.C narrator is me." Kerouac then rejected the idea of writing "auto-
biograph straight like Tom Wolfe" because it wouldn't be "archetypal."
His narrator would instead be the roaming French-Canadian "Cook"
Smith.

In his Mexican journal Kerouac wrote:

But you can go on thinking and imagining forever further and stop at
no decisions to pick up a bag for the thinkings. Turn your thinking
into your work, your thoughts a book, in sieges.

Enough of notes on all this Road business since Oct '48 (or a year and a half + more) and start writing the thing.

I am.

The Cook is the guy

Back in Richmond Hill in August Kerouac typed the "Private Ms. OF Gone on the Road—COMPLETE FIRST TREATMENT AND WITH MINOR ARTISTIC CORRECTIONS." "Cook" Smith, "not yet ready for the road, not at all," wakes up in a boardinghouse room in Des Moines, Iowa, not knowing who or where he is, realizing only in the void of his "hollowed mind" that he is growing older and death is growing nearer. At his job as a short-order cook Smith makes a free hamburger meal for an old black hobo who in return sings Smith a blues about the death of his father. After being in Iowa for months Smith determines to hitch home to his wife Laura in Denver, after God, "with a stroke of fleece upon my mind," tells Smith she is still his girl. For sixteen dollars traveling money Smith moves a box of mostly European books belonging to his German landlord. In the "sad, red, European light" of Iowa Smith fails to sell the books or even give them away.

On the road west Smith meets a young black man who is also hitchhiking. After watching the man, who may be Slim Jackson, walk out of sight, Smith is picked up by a Texan truckdriver who lets him sleep. Smith then dreams Red Moultrie's dream of being pursued by a shrouded stranger as he tries to escape from some "Araby-land to the Protective City."

Waking up Smith is let out by the truckdriver in Stuart, Iowa. There he meets a talkative, free and easy "license-plate thief" who is traveling east to a Notre Dame football game by hitchhiking in the day and stealing cars by night. The young man, whose name is Dean Pomeray, reminds Smith that they had met in Denver, at Welton and Fifteenth. The story ends as Smith and Pomeray sit talking in the waiting room of the telegraph office in Stuart.

"Gone on the Road" further dramatizes Kerouac's interior struggle to find his own voice and free his creative self from an imprisoning and intimidating European literary tradition. Watched by a bored waitress in a diner, Smith is showered by the old books that fall on his head through a hole in the box he carries them in. Standing under a waterfall of European literature Smith knows that he strikes "an awful pose" to the young American woman watching. This heavy symbolism is smoothed out in the published novel as Sal Paradise, whose own dream of not knowing where he is also takes place at the junction of the east of his past and the west of his future, sits on a bus reading the American landscape in preference to Alain-Fournier's great novel of boyhood friendship, love, and loss, *Le Grand Meaulnes*. As Cook Smith joins Dean Pomeray, Kerouac leaves behind the "sad, red, European light," and the pose of European books to travel "back to everybody" in America.

At the end of the story the frustration Kerouac was feeling after more than two years working on a novel still obstinately stalled boiled over in a direct appeal to God:

Pomeray was too excited to notice any of these things that norm—[Dear God please help me, I am lost]—ally drove him into excited explanations of all kinds.

On the verso of the title page Kerouac wrote his own self-criticism—"Prettifying life like a teahead."

Kerouac sent "Gone on the Road" to Robert Giroux, who, while not rejecting it outright, suggested Kerouac revise the story. In the fall of 1950 Kerouac was smoking "three bombs a day [and] thinking about unhappiness all the time." He had once imagined *On the Road* as one in an ambitious "American Times" series of novels to be "narrated in the voices of Americans themselves." The ten-year-old African American boy Pic would narrate "Adventures on the Road" while other books in the series would be narrated by "Mexicans, Indians, French-Canadians, Italians, Westerners, dilettantes, jailbirds, hoboes, hipsters and many more." But where was his voice? Rather than revise "Gone on the Road," he began again.

On Wednesday, December 20, 1950, Kerouac started handwriting a new version of his road novel titled "Souls on the Road." The five-page manuscript begins

> One night in America when the sun had gone down—beginning at four of the winter afternoon in New York by shedding a beautiful burnished gold in the air that made dirty old buildings look like the walls of the temple of the world . . . then outflying its own shades as it raced three thousand 200 miles over raw, bulging land to the West Coast before sloping down the Pacific, leaving the great rearguard shroud of night to creep upon our earth, to darken rivers, to cup the peaks and fold the final shore in—a knock came at the door of Mrs Gabrielle Kerouac's apartment over a drugstore in the Ozone Park section of Greater New York.

At the door is Neal Cassady. The images of the sun going down over the "raw, bulging land" of America, of night coming to "darken rivers, to cup the peaks and fold the final shore" are taken from "Shades of the Prison House," and will of course resurface in the final paragraph of the published novel. In rearranged sequence the episodes Kerouac writes here, in which "Jack Kerouac" recounts his first meeting with "Neal Cassady" in "an apartment in the slums" of Spanish Harlem and Cassady comes to Ozone Park to ask Kerouac to teach him to write, have all the elements of the opening chapter of the published book.

On the manuscript Kerouac has crossed out the name "Benjamin Baloon" in the line "And Benjamin Baloon went to the door" and replaced it with the name "Jack Kerouac." Kerouac had originally written that it "was Dean Pomeray" at the door, replacing "Dean Pomeray" with "Neal Cassady." From page three Ben and Dean become Jack and Neal.

3

Aside from this momentum, what led to the three-week burst of writing in April 1951? Key influences have to include Kerouac's mostly friendly competition with John Clellon Holmes (whose novel *Go*, published in 1952 and featuring portraits of Kerouac and Cassady, Kerouac would read in March 1951), Dashiell Hammett's locomotive prose, and Burroughs's own straight-ahead novel in manuscript (then called *Junk*). Central importance, however, must be given to the long "Joan Anderson and Cherry Mary" letter from Neal Cassady that Kerouac picked up from the front step of his mother's apartment in Richmond Hill on December 27, 1950. Kerouac's exuberant same-day reply to Cassady's urgent story of sexual misadventure, in which he said that he thought it "ranked among the best things ever written in America," suggests that the effects of the letter on Kerouac were immediate and complex (Joan Haverty also wrote to Cassady on the twenty-seventh, telling him that Jack "read [the letter] on the subway on his way into town . . . [and] spent two more hours reading it in a café").

"Souls on the Road" shows that Kerouac had already moved toward autobiographical fiction but had not yet made the critical switch to a first-person narrative. It was Cassady's long, fast, sexually frank and detailed first-person story, broken and interrupted by what Cassady called his "Hollywood flashbacks," that confirmed and encouraged Kerouac to push further in the direction he was already headed. What survives of the letter was published as "To have seen a specter isn't everything . . ." in Cassady's book *The First Third*. The fragment is interesting both for its mixture of confession and boastfulness and for what Lawrence Ferlinghetti called Cassady's "hustling voice," a voice brilliantly captured by Kerouac in the novel. Cassady's prose, as Ferlinghetti notes, is "homespun, primitive [and] has a certain naïve charm, at once antic and antique, often awkward and doubling back upon itself, like a fast talker."

"All the crazy falldarall you two boys make over my Big Letter," Cassady told Ginsberg on March 17, 1951, "just thrills the gurgles out of me, but we still know I'm a whiff and a dream. Nonetheless, tho I blush over its inadequacies, I want you to realize the damn thing took up the better part of three straight Benzidrene afternoons and evenings. So I did work hard at it and managed to burn a little juice out of me and if the fucking thing is worth any money thats great."

Kerouac's response suggests that what most excited him about Cassady's letter was what *he* might do with this method. Kerouac sounded at times as if he were talking to himself; as though he were writing rules for a new method he would soon apply. "You gather together all the best styles . . . of Joyce, Celine, Dosty & Proust," he wrote, "and utilize them in the muscular rush of your own narrative style & excitement . . . You wrote it with painful rapidity & can patch it up later."

In the ten letters he sent Cassady over the next two weeks, Kerouac took Cassady's method and amplified it until, as Allen Ginsberg notes, he had developed a style that

> was the long confessional of two buddies telling each other every-thing that happened, every detail, every cunt-hair in the grass included, every tiny eyeball flick of orange neon flashed past in Chi-cago in the bus station; all the back of the brain imagery. This required sentences that did not necessarily follow exact classic-type syntactical order, but which allowed for interruption with dashes, allowed for the sentences to break in half, take another direction (with parentheses that might go on for paragraphs). It allowed for individual sentences that might not come to their period except after several pages of self reminiscence, of interruption and the piling on of detail, so that what you arrived at was a sort of stream of con-sciousness visioned around a specific subject (the tale of the road) and a specific view point (two buddies late at night meeting and rec-ognizing each other like Dostoevsky characters and telling each other the tale of their childhood).

Kerouac's letters, most often read as spontaneous responses to Cas-sady, are in many of their episodes and details developments of notes and story fragments he had first made on December 13, 1950, also under the title "Souls on the Road." These notes include thirty-five numbered "memories," ranging from the story about Kerouac's moth-er's picking "worms from my ass-hole"; his "riding licketysplit" down a street near Lupine Road; and the haunted "One Mighty Snake Hill

Castle" on Lakeview Avenue, many of which Kerouac worked into the letters he sends Cassady. This is not to diminish the catalytic importance of the Joan Anderson letter to Kerouac. John Clellon Holmes remembers Kerouac saying, "I'm going to get me a roll of shelf-paper, feed it into the typewriter, and just write it down as fast as I can, exactly like it happened, all in a rush, the hell with these phony architectures—and worry about it later." In the scroll Kerouac writes that "in a few years [Cassady] would become such a great writer," and suggests that this is why he is writing Cassady's story. After reading the Joan Anderson letter and writing his own series of letters in reply Kerouac was convinced that *On the Road* should be written in a straight-ahead, conversational style and that he should "renounce fiction and fear. There is nothing to do but write the truth. There is no other reason to write." The novel would detail Kerouac's five trips across America since first meeting Cassady in 1947 and would end with the previous summer's trip to Mexico.

What were Kerouac's working methods like during those three weeks in April of 1951? Some years later Philip Whalen wrote an account that allows us to imagine the writing practice Kerouac first developed at that time.

He would sit—at a typewriter, and he had all these pocket notebooks, and the pocket notebooks would be open at his left-hand side on the typing table—and he'd be typing. He could type faster than any human being you ever saw. The most noise that you heard while he was typing was the carriage return, slamming back again and again. The little bell would bing-bang, bing-bang, bing-bang! Just incredibly fast, faster than a teletype . . . Then he'd make a mistake, and this would lead him off into a possible part of a new paragraph, into a funny riff of some kind that he'd add while he was in the process of copying. Then, maybe he'd turn a page of the notebook and he'd look at that page and realize it was no good and he'd X it out, or maybe part of that page. And then he'd type a little bit and turn another page, and type the whole thing, and another page, and he'd type from that. And then something would—again, he would exclaim and laugh and carry on and have a big time doing it.

Kerouac worked in what Holmes remembered as a "large, pleasant room in Chelsea." His notebooks and letters and a "Self-Instruction" list "sat at side of typewriter as chapter guide." The paper Kerouac used was not Teletype paper but thin, long sheets of drawing paper belonging to a friend, Bill Cannastra. Kerouac had inherited the paper when he moved into Cannastra's loft on West Twentieth Street after Cannastra's accidental death in the New York subway. When did Kerouac first flash on an image in his mind of the paper joined together? A long roll of paper like the remembered road that he could write fast on and not stop. So that the paper joined together became an endless page.

It is clear that the scroll is something consciously *made* by Kerouac rather than found. He cut the paper into eight pieces of varying length and shaped it to fit the typewriter. The pencil marks and scissor cuts are still visible on the paper. Then he taped the pieces together. It's not known whether he taped each sheet on as he finished it, or waited until he had finished the whole thing before taping the sheets together.

The scroll is, for the most part and contrary to mythology, conventionally punctuated, even to the extent that Kerouac presses the space key before each new sentence. It runs in a single paragraph. Like the published novel it's structured in five parts. As to the myth that his work was fueled by Benzedrine, we have what Kerouac told Cassady: "I wrote that book on COFFEE, remember said rule. Benny, tea, anything I KNOW none as good as coffee for real mental power kicks." By his own account Kerouac averaged "6 thous. [words] a day, 12 thous. first day, 15,000 thous. last day." In a letter to Ed White written when Kerouac estimated he had completed 86,000 words he writes, "I don't know the date nor care and life is a bowl of pretty juicy Cherries that I want one by one biting first with my cherry stain'd teeth.—how?"

Kerouac dramatically collapses the distinction between writer and narrated "I," all the while utilizing established techniques of fiction writing, including double-perspective narration, to control the progress of the text. Headlong, intimate, discursive, wild, and "true," with improvised notations—dots and dashes—to break sentences so that they pile upon themselves like waves.

There's an exciting difference here to most everything you've read before; the unmatched intimacy of what Allen Ginsberg called Kerouac's sincere and sweetly connecting "heart-felt speech." Maybe you're dazzled at first by Neal's incandescent energy burning up everybody and everything around him, but you also understand that at the heart of the novel is Jack's quest and that he's asking the same questions that keep you awake at night and fill your days. What is life? What does it mean to be alive when death, the shrouded stranger, is gaining at your heels? Will God ever show his face? Can joy kick darkness? This quest is interior, but the lessons of the road, the apprehended magic of the American landscape described like a poem, are applied to illuminate and amplify the spiritual journey. Kerouac writes to be understood; the road is the path of life and life is a road.

Kerouac does not hide the cost of the road either to those who will head for it or to those for whom, in Carolyn Cassady's words, a different kind of "responsibility mapped the course." What is electrifying about the novel is the idea that God, self-realization, and a transforming freedom are *out there*, through the window where you sit confined at school or at work, maybe where the city ends or just over that next hill. This makes the heart thump and the blood beat in your ears. A religious seeker and a writer of dreams and visions, Kerouac is a source in that sense, if you are fixed on seeking answers, and once that kind of light goes on in your house it's likely to stay on and you'll always be looking. He had told Cassady that "I aim to employ all the styles and nevertheless I yearn to be non-literary." In so consciously disrupting our understanding of what it is we are reading when we read the original scroll version of *On the Road,* Kerouac's claim to Cassady that the book "marks complete departure from *Town & City* and in fact from previous American Lit" seems justified. *On the Road* is the nonfiction novel, ten years early.

4

It would be more than six years before *On the Road* appeared, but remarkably nobody who was in a position to publish it ever read the scroll manuscript. Kerouac immediately began to revise the novel. As Kerouac biographer Paul Maher notes, "*On the Road* was now typed onto separate pages to make its appearance more conventional and thus more appealing to publishers. . . . Jack scribbled annotations on some pages, added typesetting instructions, crossed out passages, and proposed textual insertions. . . . His cuts to *On the Road* precede Malcolm Cowley's suggestion that he shorten the manuscript, contrary to previous biographers' assertions that Jack had insisted on maintaining the text as he originally wrote it in April 1951." On May 22, 1951, Kerouac told Cassady that he had been "typing and revising" since he finished the scroll on April 22. "Thirty days on that." He was, he told Cassady, "waiting to finish my book to write to you." Kerouac writes that Robert Giroux was "waiting to see" the novel.

There are two known subsequent extant drafts of the novel: a 297-page, heavily revised draft with numerous lines thickly deleted and handwritten inserts on the verso of some pages and a 347-page draft revised by Kerouac and an editor, probably Helen Taylor, from Viking. Both manuscripts are undated. More scholarship is needed to compare and interpret the relationship between the three drafts. While it seems most likely that the 297-page draft is the one Kerouac worked on after finishing the original scroll, it is less clear when the 347-page draft was written. There is evidence that Kerouac and Viking were working from this draft by the fall of 1955. Letters between Kerouac and Malcolm Cowley in September and October 1955 refer to "Dean Moriarty" "Carlo Marx," and "Denver D. Doll." These names are only used in the 347-page draft. Page notations in the libel report compiled by lawyer Nathaniel "Tanny" Whitehorn (a lawyer from Hays, Sklag,

Epstein & Herzberg who had been hired by Viking to review the manuscript) and submitted to Viking on November 1, 1955, also correspond to the 347-page draft.*

Kerouac also began writing *Visions of Cody* out of his revisions of *On the Road* in the fall of 1951, and the relationships between all of these texts are highly complex. While clearly readers will be interested in the differences between the original scroll version of *On the Road* and the published novel, to speak only about scenes in the original scroll version being "cut" from the published novel elides Kerouac's redrafting process and serves to marginalize Kerouac from the writing of his own novel. Certainly there are scenes and episodes in the scroll that are not present in the published novel, but that text is the result of a conscious process of redrafting and revision begun by Kerouac and influenced by a number of readers, editors, and lawyers, including Robert Giroux, Rae Everitt, Allen Ginsberg, Malcolm Cowley, Nathaniel Whitehorn, and Helen Taylor.

Significant scenes present here but absent in the published novel include a richly comic account of Neal and Allen's visit to Bill Burroughs in the fall of 1947; a poignant discussion between Jack, Neal,

---

*One side of the cover page of the 297-page draft of *On the Road* has the carefully written holograph title "The Beat Generation" crossed through and "On the Road" written less carefully above it. On the other side of the title "On the Road" is typed in caps and there is a thickly deleted five-word subtitle, the first three words reading "On the Road." Below the title Kerouac has typed "by John Kerouac" and deleted the "John," handwriting "Jack" above it in caps. In the lower-right-hand corner of this page Kerouac has typed his name with the "John" once again crossed through. Below this his address is typed as care of "Paul Blake," Kerouac's brother-in-law, with a partly legible address in North Carolina. This address is thickly deleted and by hand Kerouac has written "c/o Allen Ginsberg 206E. 7th St. New York, N. Y." On a separate page Kerouac has handwritten titles for the five books of the novel: "Get High and Stay High" (above a typed, deleted, illegible, alternate title), "I Can Drive All Night," "A Hundred and Ten Miles an Hour," "The Bottom of the Road," and "Can't Talk No More."

The double-spaced text begins with a heavily edited eight-page opening paragraph that begins "I first met Dean not long after [typed] my father died and I thought everything was dead [handwritten]."

The 347-page draft is typed, double spaced on nonuniform paper. The text is edited with additions and deletions by Kerouac and more heavily by an editor at Viking, possibly Helen Taylor. In the bottom right-hand corner of page 347 is typed "JEAN-LOUIS c/o Lord & Colbert 109 E. 36th St. New York, N. Y." The manuscript begins "I FIRST MET DEAN not long after my wife and I split up."

and Louanne as they pass through Pecos, Texas, on the way to San Francisco about "what we would be if we were Old West characters"; a wild, destructive party at Alan Harrington's adobe house in Arizona during the same journey that reinforces the sense of the speeding Cassady's out-of-control sexuality; Jack's second return trip from San Francisco "across the groaning continent" to New York; and Jack and Neal's visit to Jack's first wife Edie in Detroit toward the end of Part Three.

As detailed below, there were many reasons for the deletion of these and other scenes, including, as the years passed, Kerouac's increasing desperation in the wake of the success of Holmes's *Go* and Allen Ginsberg's *Howl* to see the novel published. By September 1955 he was telling Malcolm Cowley that any "changes you want to make OK with me." The second return trip to San Francisco was cut by Kerouac to streamline the story, while the Detroit section of the novel, in which Edie is represented as fat and wearing overalls, drinking beer, and munching candy, was among a number of scenes also cut by Kerouac on the recommendation of Cowley and Nathaniel Whitehorn, who were fearful of libel suits. Despite Kerouac's deletion of much of the sexual material and language, in particular the homosexual content, as part of the redrafting process, other scenes that survived into the 347-page draft, including the story of a sodomizing monkey in an LA whorehouse, were later cut for obscenity.

Interestingly, many scenes in the original version that were deleted by Kerouac in the 297-page draft find their way, reworked, into the 347-page draft and into the published novel. For example, early in Part 2 of the scroll, as Neal and Jack make ready to leave Ozone Park for the Christmas 1948 trip back to North Carolina to collect Gabrielle, they are visited by Allen Ginsberg, who asks, "What is the meaning of this voyage to New York? What kind of sordid business are you on now? I mean, man, whither goest thou?" Neal has no answer. "The only thing to do was go." Kerouac has lined through this 26-line scene in the scroll, and it is not present in the corresponding place (page

121) of the 297-page draft. On page 130 of the 347-page draft, however, the scene is restored, with Allen Ginsberg as Carlo Marx, Hinkle as Ed Dunkel, Neal as Dean Moriarty, and Jack as Sal Paradise. They are in Paterson, New Jersey, preparing to travel to Virginia to pick up Sal's aunt. After Marx asks the pivotal question, "I mean, man, whither goest thou?" Kerouac has added a handwritten line that, critically, makes the question politically representative rather than simply personal: "Whither goest thou, America, in thy shiny car at night?" Kerouac had made a note of this line in his "Rain and Rivers" journal; in the published novel the scene appears with the line added.

Equally important are those passages of rough lyricism in the scroll that Kerouac refines in the redrafting process. The famous image of Cassady and Ginsberg as "roman candles" is polished and reworked in subsequent drafts. In the scroll Kerouac writes,

> [Neal and Allen] rushed down the street together digging everything in the early way they had which has later now become so much sadder and perceptive . . . but then they danced down the street like dingldodies and I shambled after as usual as I've been doing all my life after people that interest me, because the only people that interest me are the mad ones, the ones who are mad to live, mad to talk, desirous of everything at the same time, the ones that never yawn or say a commonplace thing . . . but burn, burn, burn like roman candles across the night.

Kerouac has made some holographic corrections to the last four words of the text here, including placing the word "yellow" before "roman candles." In the scroll Kerouac caps and eroticizes the image by linking it to Neal and Allen's sexual relationship. Allen was "queer in those days, experimenting with himself to the hilt, and Neal saw that, and a former boyhood hustler himself in the Denver night, and wanting dearly to learn how to write poetry like Allen, the first thing you know he was attacking Allen with a great amorous soul such as only a conman can have." Jack is in the same room. "I heard them across the darkness and I mused and said to myself, 'Hmm, now something's started, but I don't want anything to do with it.'" Kerouac has lined through "but I don't want anything to do with it" on the scroll. On pages 4–5 of the 297-page draft Kerouac has typed the passage about Neal and Allen's sexual relationship but has then heavily deleted it. Dean is now simply conning Justin Moriarty (Ginsberg) to teach him to write. With Kerouac's deletions, the candle image has been amended to read:

> They rushed down the street together digging everything in the early way they had which has later now become so much sadder and perceptive, but then they danced down the street and I shambled after because the only people that interest me are the mad ones, the ones who are mad to live, mad to talk, desirous of everything at the same time, the ones who never yawn or say a commonplace thing . . . but burn, burn, burn like yellow spidery roman candles with the blue centerlight across the night.

By hand Kerouac has added, "What would you have called these people in Goethe's Germany?" On page 6 of the 347-page draft the passage has been redrafted and typed by Kerouac and then further corrected by hand, possibly by Helen Taylor. The corrections are shown below in brackets, and it is the corrected passage that appears in the published novel.

> They rushed down the street together[,] digging everything in the early way they had[,] which has later now become [which later became] so much sadder and perceptive and blank[. B] but then they danced down the street like dingledodies[,] and I shambled after as usual [as usual] as I've been doing all my life after people who interest me, because the only people for me are the mad ones, the ones who are mad to live, mad to talk, mad to be saved, desirous of everything at the same time, the ones who never yawn or say a commonplace thing . . . [,] but burn, burn, burn like fabulous yellow roman candles exploding like a [a] spider[s] across the stars and in

the middle you see the blue centerlight pop and everybody goes "Awww!" What do you [did they] call such young people in Goethe's Germany?

In this example of one of *On the Road*'s best-known passages, we can see how in the complex process of revision and redrafting it is Kerouac who begins tempering the sexual content of his novel. In this instance the excising of the sexual relationship between Neal and Allen serves to obscure the erotic aspect of the image Kerouac is simultaneously trying to refine. Also significant are the later editorial changes that break Kerouac's single long sentence in two. It is these changes to his sentences, rather than the cutting of scenes, which Kerouac would most strongly object to after the novel was published. He would blame Malcolm Cowley for making "endless revisions" and inserting "thousands of needless commas," though it is Helen Taylor who very likely made these changes. Prevented from seeing the final galleys before the novel was printed, Kerouac would say that he "had no power to stand by my style for better or worse."

Is the scroll the real *On the Road*? This is a natural question, especially as the novel trades so strongly in questions of authenticity, but it is perhaps the wrong one to ask. The scroll does not call into question the authenticity of the published novel but is in dialogue with it and all other versions of the text, including the proto-versions of the novel and *Visions of Cody*, so that Kerouac's road novel becomes a twentieth-century *Song of Myself*. The scroll version of *On the Road* is, however, a markedly darker, edgier, and uninhibited text than the published book. The original version of *On the Road* is also, of course, a younger man's book. Kerouac was still only twenty-nine in the spring of 1951. By the time the novel was published he would be thirty-five.

If the history of the novel from the fall of 1948 to the spring of 1951 is the story of Kerouac's struggle to access the intimate style of writing so powerfully expressed in the scroll manuscript, what follows is the story of how, in editor Malcolm Cowley's words, the novel became "publishable by [Viking's] standards."

5

By June 10, 1951, Kerouac's brief marriage to Joan Haverty had collapsed; Joan was pregnant and had returned to her mother after Kerouac denied he was the father of the child. In a letter written on that date, when Kerouac was moving from the apartment he had shared with Joan on West Twentieth Street to Lucien Carr's nearby loft on West Twenty-first, Kerouac told Cassady that the "book is finished, handed in, waiting for the word from Giroux."

Interviewed in 1997, Robert Giroux told the story of Kerouac's unrolling the scroll in his office. Giroux insisted that the manuscript would have to be cut up and edited. Kerouac supposedly refused to entertain any such idea, telling Giroux that the "Holy Ghost" had dictated the novel. Kerouac also retrospectively recounted versions of this episode. It is possible Kerouac retyped and revised the scroll after such a confrontation, but the story may well be part of the mythmaking surrounding *On the Road*.* If it happened the meeting would have taken place in the days immediately after Kerouac completed the scroll and may possibly have first occasioned or encouraged Kerouac's retyping of the scroll into more conventional form, though I believe Kerouac had already arrived at this decision by himself. On June 24 Kerouac reported that while Giroux had said he liked the book, formally submitted in a conventionally typed format, Harcourt, Brace

---

*Interviewed in the documentary *On the Road to Desolation* (David Steward, dir., BBC/NVC Arts Co-production, 1997), Giroux said: "I would say in the first half of 1951, I was at my desk at Harcourt, Brace, and the phone rang and it was Jack, and he said, 'Bob, I've finished it!' and I said, 'Oh great, Jack, that's wonderful news.' He said, 'I want to come over.' I said, 'What, right now?' He said, 'Yeah, I have to see you, I have to show you . . .' I said, 'Okay, come on, come over to the office.' We were on Forty-sixth Street and Madison Avenue. He came into the office looking . . . high, looking, you know . . . drunk, and he had a big roll of paper, like a paper towel like you use in the kitchen, big roll of paper under his left arm, and he was, you know . . . This was a great moment for him, I understood that. He took one end of the roll and he flung it right across my office like a big piece of confetti, right across my desk, and I thought, 'This is a strange manuscript. I've never seen a manuscript like this.' And he looked at me, waiting for me to say something. I said, 'Jack, you know you have to cut this up. It has to be edited.' And his face flushed, and he said, 'There'll be no editing on this manuscript.' I said, 'Why not, Jack?' He said, 'This manuscript has been dictated by the Holy Ghost.'"

had rejected it as "so new and unusual and controversial and censorable (with hipsters, weeds, fags, etc.) they won't accept." Kerouac was going south with his mother, he told Cassady, "to rest my mind and soul."

On July 6 Kerouac's then agent Rae Everitt at MCA wrote Kerouac care of his sister's address in North Carolina, praising what she called the moments of "sheer magic poetry" in the novel. She commented that she had read the book

> long before writing you this letter, but it took a lot of musing about . . . the musing came in trying to think whether this time I could speak honestly about my reaction to some of the rest of it without having you yank it away from me.

Everitt favored Books 3, 4, and 5 to 1 and 2 because there was a "shape and intensity to Dean and Sal's" travels. Everitt told Kerouac that the novel began too self-consciously, as if Kerouac were trying to accustom the reader to "this extremely specialized style of writing." As a result the novel was much too long,

> the manuscript pages as they are now are about a page and a half of regular pages, which brings your total page count to roughly 450. Do you want to do this now or leave it [?]

Everitt's assessment of the page count would indicate a manuscript of around three hundred pages.

On July 16 Kerouac sent a letter to Allen Ginsberg addressed to Allen Moriarty. Allen Moriarty, corrected by hand to Justin Moriarty, is the name Kerouac gives to Ginsberg in the 297-page draft. In the letter Kerouac writes that he is continuing cutting and writing insertions for the novel, and Everitt's letter may have occasioned these further revisions.

Kerouac fell ill with phlebitis in North Carolina, and from August 11 to the end of the first week in September he was in the Veterans Hospital on Kingsbridge Road in the Bronx. From there he wrote to Ed White on September 1 to make arrangements for White's visit to New

York. On the back of some rough inserts in both French and English and headed "On the Road" Kerouac has written, "Yes—Am completely rewriting Neal-epic." Kerouac's re-writing may have included some of the handwritten inserts to be found in the 297-page draft of *Road,* but this is also the time Kerouac begins to write *Visions of Cody.*

In October and using a new technique he would call "sketching," Kerouac began to fill the first of nine notebooks that would, when he was finished, amount to 955 handwritten pages. The first page of the first notebook is dated October 1951 and titled "On the Road. A Modern Novel." On the front of the first notebook is written "Visions of Cody." Kerouac tells Cassady on October 9, 1951 that he is sending him "these 3 now-typed-up-revised pages of my re-writing ROAD," and that "since writing that I've come up with even greater complicated sentences & VISIONS."

In the fall of 1951 Kerouac received an offer from Carl Solomon, then an editor at A. A. Wyn, to publish *On the Road* in their Ace imprint as the first in a three-book contract. Kerouac then traveled west again to visit Neal and Carolyn. He would stay in San Francisco until the spring, working for the Southern Pacific Railroad and continuing his labor on *Visions of Cody.* Stalling on delivering a manuscript that was becoming more radically experimental by the day, on December 27, 1951, he wrote to Carl Solomon that "I'm not gone off from A. A. Wyn. I'm only gone off to earn money on my own hook so that when I do sell my book it won't make any difference and anyway it isn't finished yet." On March 12, 1952 he told Ed White that he had finished the novel in Neal's attic. This novel was *Visions of Cody.*

On March 26, A. A. Wyn wrote to Kerouac care of the Cassady residence at 29 Russell Street, San Francisco:

> Enclosed your copy of the signed contract of ON THE ROAD. The first advance of $250 is being sent to your mother . . . We look forward to seeing the present draft of the manuscript.

On April 7, Kerouac replied to Solomon, suggesting that Wyn publish an abridged paperback version of *On the Road* that would include a 160-page "sexy narrative stretch" about Cassady that Kerouac planned to excerpt from his manuscripts. The narrative Kerouac refers to, "I first met Neal Pomeray in 1947 . . . ," corresponds to the last section of the published *Cody*. Kerouac may have been trying to prepare Solomon for what he knew would be the shock of the rest of *Visions of Cody*, writing that "my only fear is you wouldn't publish full ROAD [*Cody*] in hardcover . . . believe me, Carl, the full ROAD will make Wyn a first rate reputation." Telling Solomon not to worry about sacrificing reputation for profit Kerouac wrote, "Let's do 2 editions."

On May 17 Kerouac told Ginsberg that he had sent the manuscript to Carl Solomon and that he expected it to arrive by May 23. On May 18 Kerouac gave Ginsberg a high-spirited explanation of the "sketching" technique he had used to change "the conventional narrative survey" of *On the Road* to the "big multi-dimensional conscious and subconscious character invocation of Neal in his whirlwinds" of *Cody*:

> Now here is what sketching is. In the first place you remember last September when Carl first ordered the Neal book and wanted it . . . Sketching came to me in full force on October 25th . . . - so strongly it didn't matter about Carl's offer and I began sketching everything in sight, so that On the Road took its turn from conventional narrative survey of road trips etc. into a big multi-dimensional conscious and subconscious character invocation of Neal in his whirlwinds. Sketching (Ed White casually mentioned it in 124 the Chinese restaurant near Columbia, "Why don't you just sketch in the street like a painter but with words") which I did . . . everything activates in front of you in myriad confusion, you just have to purify your mind and let it pour the words (which effortless angels of the vision fly when you stand in front of reality) and write with 100% personal honesty both psychic and social etc. and slap it all down shameless, willynilly, rapidly until sometimes I got so inspired I lost consciousness I was writing. Traditional source: Yeats' trance writing, of course. It's the only way to write.

The novel, Kerouac told Ginsberg, was "all good":

> We can show Road to Scribners or Simpson or Farrar Straus [Stanley Young] if necessary, change title to Visions of Neal or somethin, and I write new Road for Wynn.

What Ginsberg then read and what Kerouac had sent Carl Solomon at Wyn was indeed the manuscript of *Visions of Cody* and not *On the Road*. Kerouac's attempts to prepare the ground for his revolution in prose went unheeded. In *Cody*, Kerouac's command of his adopted language appears magical. It is a novel in which, as Holmes would later write, "the words were no longer words, but had become things. Somehow an open circuit of feeling had been established between his awareness and its object of the moment, and the result was as startling as being trapped in another man's eyes."

At the time Holmes read the novel with a kind of angry disbelief. Writing that he sometimes wished Kerouac "would blunt the edge" of his writing so that it might be given the recognition it deserved, Holmes later remembered

> going out to walk by the East River, cursing Kerouac in my head for writing so well in a book which, I was firmly convinced, would never be published. . . . I recall that I cursed *him*, rather than the publishers, or the critics, or the culture itself that was excluding him. Some years later, I reread *Cody* with a feeling of amazement at my own confusion that was fully as great as my shame.

Allen Ginsberg also read the novel in the context of its commercial potential. "I don't see how it will ever be published," he told Kerouac on June 11. Some of the writing was "the best that is written in America," but Kerouac's book was also "crazy in a bad way." It was "mixed up chronologically"; the surreal sections refused "to make sense" and the "Taperecords are partly hangup" and should be shortened.

Solomon was even more horrified than Ginsberg. On July 30 he sent a blistering letter to Kerouac care of his mother's Richmond Hill address:

We've had a reading of ON THE ROAD and, though we understand it to be merely a "present draft," we are thoroughly bewildered by almost everything you've done since the opening 23-page sample and the prospectus. The subsequent 500 pages are so utterly unlike the novel you began and which we were expecting [after having contracted for it] that they seem to have no relation to each other. . . . At present, some ninety-five per cent of what follows page 23 seems to us a thoroughly incoherent mess.*

Kerouac added a handwritten note to Carolyn Cassady: "This is the reception *On the Road* [Cody] is getting – Ginsberg + Holmes are even more irritated – it's undoubtedly a great book." In reply to Solomon on August 5, Kerouac conceded that the "new vision" of *Visions of Cody* (which he was still calling *On the Road*) is "going to be considered unprintable for a while to come," but this was because of the shortsightedness of publishers. To label the book "incoherent is not only a semantic mistake but an act of cowardice and intellectual death."

This is what will happen: "On the Road [Cody]" will be published . . . and it will gain its due recognition, in time, as the first or one of the first modern prose books in America; not merely a "novel," which is after all a European form . . . And all you will have succeeded in doing is putting another cookbook on your list to fill the gap I leave. You can spin a thousand neat epigrams to prove that any cookbook is better than the wild visions of Neal Pomeray and the Road. But not when the worms start digesting, brothers and sisters.

I didn't write "On the Road" [Cody] to be malicious, I wrote it with joy in my heart, and a conviction that somewhere along the line somebody will see it without the present day goggles on and realize the freedom of expression that still lies ahead.

---

*The "Visions of Cody" revised typescript in the Berg Collection has the holographic title page: "Visions of Cody, Jack Kerouac '51-52." A second holographic title page reads "On the Road," written in ink and canceled, and retitled "Visions of Neal (Cody)" in pencil. The first page of the typescript is titled "Visions of Enal." The typescript has 558 leaves. There is no extant draft of *On the Road* in excess of 347 pages.

Solomon's reply to Kerouac's "masterful cudgelling" on August 5 accepted that "you may be entirely accurate in accusing us of lack of vision, and of tastes molded by television. However, we have never claimed to be prophets . . . [O]ur rejection of [Cody] in 1952 may well, as you feel, mark us for ridicule twenty-five years later." Writing that he was obliged to judge manuscripts by the standards of the day, Solomon wrote that the novel, "after the point when you discovered your 'sketching' technique, is simply an experiment we do not understand." *Visions of Cody* would not be published until 1972, three years after Kerouac's death.*

For Kerouac the years immediately after the failure to get *On the Road* or *Visions of Cody* published are marked by obscurity and ragged wandering between North Carolina, San Francisco, Mexico, and New York. In the summer of 1952 he left Mexico and returned to Rocky Mount, where he worked for a short time in a textile mill. In the fall he returned to the West Coast and worked on the railroad, living for the most part in a San Francisco skid row hotel room and saving to go back to Mexico. Remarkably, although he was rejected, alone, poor, and homeless, the flow of brilliant work that had started with *On the Road* and *Visions of Cody* continued. His writing flew. In Mexico in the summer he finished *Doctor Sax*. In the West he wrote "October in the Railroad Earth." Back in Richmond Hill in the New Year he wrote *Maggie Cassidy*. On his thirtieth birthday on March 12, 1952, Kerouac, on his way to Mexico from San Francisco, wrote to John Holmes:

> I have completely reached my peak maturity now and am blowing such mad poetry and literature that I'll look back years later with amazement and chagrin that I can't do it anymore, but nobodys going to know this fact for 15, 20 years, only I know it, and maybe Allen.

*Ginsberg contributed an introduction titled "The Great Rememberer," writing that "I don't think it is possible to proceed further in America without first understanding Kerouac's tender brooding compassion . . . Bypassing Kerouac one bypasses the mortal heart, sung in prose vowels; the book a giant mantra of appreciation and adoration of an American man, one striving heroic soul."

In July 1953, Malcolm Cowley began to take an active interest in Kerouac's work after receiving a letter from Allen Ginsberg. As Steve Turner notes, Ginsberg had worked in advertising and journalism for years, and his approach to Cowley was not accidental. A hugely significant and influential figure in the story of twentieth-century American literature, Malcolm Cowley had championed Hemingway in the 1920s and done much to recover the listing reputation of William Faulkner by editing *The Portable Faulkner* for Viking in 1946. Born in 1898 and enlisting, like Hemingway, in the ambulance service during the First World War, Cowley had been literary editor of *The New Republic,* succeeding Edmund Wilson, from 1929 to 1944, and would become president of the National Institute of Arts and Letters in 1956. A literary adviser to Viking, Cowley, who had been among the foremost literary historians of the Lost Generation writers of the 1920s and who would write that remembered writers "do not come forward singly . . . they appear in clusters and constellations that are surrounded by comparatively empty years," was in this sense a good man to have in Kerouac's corner. But Cowley never really understood Kerouac's work and was often patronizingly hostile to it, and he did not support Kerouac's plans for what Cowley called "the interminable" Duluoz Legend.

In his July 6 letter Ginsberg reported to Cowley that Kerouac had asked that Ginsberg try to "set his affairs in order." Ginsberg wrote that Kerouac "is well and working on another version of On the Road. (I understand you were not aware that he intended to continue work on this book)."

Calling Kerouac "the most interesting writer who is not being published today," Cowley replied on July 14 that the "only manuscript of his that I have read with a chance of immediate publication is the first version of On the Road. As much of the second version as I saw contained some impressively good writing but no story whatsoever." Cowley's reply suggests that what he had seen was the second draft of *Road* and sections of *Visions of Cody,* while Ginsberg's comment that Kerouac was working on "another version" of *On the Road* raises the possibility that Kerouac had begun work on a third draft. By the fall the second draft was under consideration at Viking. In his in-house memorandum of October 20 editor Malcolm Cowley wrote:

> On the Road is an account of some trips across the continent in the years 1947–9. It was written almost breathlessly by the author working day and night on a 100-foot-long roll of artist's paper. I think he finished it in three weeks, handed it in to his (then) editor at Harcourt, Bob Giroux, and had it rejected. Later he did a good deal of rewriting on this conventionally typed draft, and this summer he went through the draft making many small cuts and some additions. We have it now, with the author's permission to change it any way we please---though I think he is making a few additional changes of his own, especially cutting out the second return from San Francisco and moving one Denver chapter to the West Coast. These sound like good changes that will tighten the story.
>
> I think it is the great source document of life among the beat or hip generation. Faults: the author is solemn about himself and about Dean. Some of his best episodes would get the book suppressed for obscenity. But I think there is a book here that should and must be published. The question is whether we can publish it and what we can or must do to make it publishable by our standards. I have some ideas, all for cutting.

Viking rejected the 297-page draft of Road in November 1953.

On Cowley's recommendation, in the summer of 1954 Arabelle Porter, editor of New World Writing, accepted for publication Kerouac's "Jazz of the Beat Generation," a fusion of material taken from Road and Cody and credited with being selected from The Beat Generation, a novel completed in 1951. In his letter of thanks dated August 6, 1954, Kerouac told Cowley that On the Road was now retitled "Beat Generation." This was the title Kerouac would prefer until the fall of 1955. The book had been at Little, Brown for a "long time," he said, and had been rejected there. It was now under consideration at Dutton. In September, Sterling Lord, who had now become Kerouac's agent, told Cowley that "On the Road, or The Beat Generation, as he now calls it, is still unsold." On August 23 Kerouac told Ginsberg that he had called the novel "The Beat Generation," "hoping to sell it . . . Littleshit Little Brown Seymour Lawrence" had turned the novel down.

Though it was his first publication in five years, Kerouac used the name Jean-Louis when "Jazz of the Beat Generation" was published in April 1955. Kerouac told Cowley that he had used the name "because I have an ex-wife who is continually trying to get me in the workhouse for non-support." Kerouac also pointed out that he wasn't using a pseudonym, as his full name was "John [Jack] [Jean-Louis] Kerouac." Cowley had hoped that the publication of extracts from *On the Road* would help in getting a contract for the complete novel, and replied that "I did think it was wrong of you to change your name because John Kerouac is a good name for literary purposes, and by signing your work Jean-Louis you miss the reputation that you have already built up."

After "Jazz of the Beat Generation" was published Kerouac furiously tried to generate interest in his work and was frustrated not to hear any good news about the fate of his many manuscripts. By July 4 Kerouac was "about ready to jump off a bridge," as he wrote to Cowley after the two had met in New York.

Cowley wrote to Kerouac on July 12 with the news that Peter Matthiessen had accepted Kerouac's "The Mexican Girl" episode of *On the Road* for publication in *The Paris Review*. "The Mexican Girl" was later chosen by Martha Foley for *The Best American Short Stories* of 1956 anthology. Cowley told Kerouac that "On the Road is still being considered by Dodd, Mead. If it comes back from them Keith [Jennison, an editor at Viking] and I will take another crack at getting it accepted by Viking." Cowley also offered to write a foreword to *On the Road* so that Viking might consider it more favorably. He told Kerouac that he had written to the National Institute of Arts and Letters asking if they could send Kerouac some money through the Writers' and Artists' Revolving Fund. Meanwhile, he said, "don't get downhearted. Better times are coming."

Cowley's "warm and beautiful" letter "really made me feel good," Kerouac told Sterling Lord on July 19. "I would rather have [*On the Road*] at Viking any day, because of the integrity of such a foreword." He expressed his thanks to Cowley on the same day, telling him that "your letter made me feel good, and warm, and better than anything in years." He "hopes Dodd, Mead hurries up and gets the manuscript back to you." A foreword by Cowley would give the book "literary class and a literary kick in the ass . . . S'what I want, to be published by Viking." He wrote that he would use his own name again, but "Sterling and I agreed on JACK Kerouac rather than JOHN which I think is more natural." From Mexico in August Kerouac wrote Cowley "having just heard the good news" that he had received an award from the National Institute.

> You have been very kind, have exhibited divinely-inspired gentleness . . . have kept quiet and tranquility in yr. heart and helped helpless angels.

Kerouac wrote to Cowley on September 11 saying, "I'm glad you got the Sal Paradise ms at last. You and Keith just gotta succeed."

On September 16 Cowley replied with good news. Writing that he thought *On the Road* is "the right name for the book," Cowley told Kerouac that the book was now "being very seriously considered" by Viking and that there was "quite a good chance that we will publish it." Publication depended, wrote Cowley, on "three ifs":

> if we can figure out what the right changes will be (cuts and rearrangements); if we can be sure that the book won't be suppressed for immorality; and if it won't get us into libel suits.

In an undated in-house memo on the "libel aspects" Cowley restated his worries about the "principal difficulties" of obscenity and libel, but argued that many of the characters involved in the narrative "are not the sort who bring libel suits—in fact, many of them have read the manuscript and are rather proud to be described in it, or so I gather." What worried Cowley more were the points where "respectable" characters enter the story. Denver D. Doll would have to be "changed beyond recognition." Cowley did not believe that "Old Bull Balloon" (Burroughs) would sue: "the original of the figure comes from a fairly prominent family—courts of law are what he would like to stay at a very long distance from." Cowley wanted a second opinion before he could be sure that the book was safe for publication, and Viking called in lawyer Nathaniel Whitehorn.

If it remains unclear when, precisely, Kerouac wrote the 347-page draft, Kerouac's letter on September 11, 1955, may indicate that he had sent Cowley the new draft at this time, or that the manuscript was returned to Cowley from Dodd, Mead, and he had let Kerouac know. What is clear is that by then the 347-page draft of the novel was the one Cowley was reading. Justin W. Brierly, the Denver luminary who groomed promising young local boys for Columbia University and a figure Kerouac satirizes at length in the original version, is disguised as Beattie G. Davis in the 297-page draft. It is only in the 347-page draft that Kerouac calls him Denver D. Doll.

Agreeing with Cowley that the novel should be called *On the Road* and not *Beat Generation,* on September 20 Kerouac breezily outlined the steps he had already taken to avoid libel. These included making Denver D. Doll "an instructor at Denver Univ. instead of Denver High School." He had changed "the name of the Mexican whorehouse city from Victoria to 'Gregoria.'" He was on close terms with "'Galatea Buckle' who is only proud of being in a book." Kerouac also told Cowley:

> Any changes you want to make okay with me. Remember your idea in 1953 to dovetail trip No. 2 into Trip No. 3 making it one trip? I'm available to assist you in any re-arranging matters of course

Cowley did not think Kerouac was taking the issue of libel seriously. Writing on October 12 care of Allen Ginsberg's address in

Berkeley, where Kerouac was visiting, Cowley told him that the manuscript had been with the lawyer Viking had hired for two weeks.
Cowley explained that because the novel was primarily a record of
experiences,

> [j]ust changing the names of the characters and changing a few of
> their physical characteristics aren't enough to prevent a libel suit if
> the character can still be recognized by the details that we name. . . .
> I had better warn you again that this question of libel is serious. . . .
> The changes you mentioned in your letter aren't nearly enough. You
> had better be thinking of some further changes that would keep
> (Doll) from bringing suit.

For characters like Moriarty, Cowley wrote, "the safest course might
be to get the original of the character to sign a release." Again, Cowley repeated that these were "serious difficulties."

Two days later Kerouac fired back another optimistic letter. Report-
ing that Allen Ginsberg had "just made a sensation" reading "Howl"
at the "Six Poets at the Six Gallery" event on October 7, Kerouac said
that the problem of libel would be "easily solved." He would "speed-
ily" obtain libel releases and if this was not possible he would "make
the appropriate requisite changes . . . There is no question that you'll
have all my cooperation." Kerouac's eventual response to Viking's
concerns about the possibility of Brierly's bringing a libel suit is to
cut from the 347-page manuscript the majority of scenes in which
Denver D. Doll appears.

After seeing the publicity generated by the Six Gallery reading
Viking was keen to get Kerouac's novel into production. Tanny White-
horn sent libel release forms to Helen Taylor at Viking on October 31.
They were to be signed "by as many of John Kerouac's friends who
may have anything to do with 'On the Road' as he can possibly get."
Whitehorn delivered his report on the novel the following day.

Whitehorn's 9-page report listed page-referenced instances in the
347-page manuscript where characters who had already been dis-

guised by Kerouac might still be able to identify themselves and take exception to the way they had been portrayed. Next to the various names and page references on his copy of the report Kerouac has added handwritten notes indicating the course of action he had taken. Next to Denver D. Doll's name Kerouac has written, "Doll removed except for most casual references." "Out" is written next to many of Whitehorn's notes. Whitehorn objects to a reference to "Jane walking around in a benzedrine hallucination." Jane was Joan Vollmer Burroughs, and she had been accidentally shot dead by William Burroughs in September 1951. Next to Whitehorn's note Kerouac has written "Jane dead."

On November 2 Taylor thanked Whitehorn for the releases and for his "laborious" work on the novel. "Now it is our turn to do a lot of tedious digging and editing," she wrote, "and then we reach the next stage. I am afraid you will have to look at it again."

After receiving the "libel-clearing statement forms" Kerouac secured releases from the "two heroes," "Dean Moriarty" and "Carlo Marx." "I can get signatures from everybody," Kerouac wrote on November 14. Ginsberg signed his release "for the benefit of American literature. X. Carlo Marx, as it were."

Despite "instantly" signing and mailing the forms Kerouac was frustrated to hear nothing back from Cowley. "Did you receive those two signatures," he writes on December 23. "I sent them right back; don't tell me you didn't get em! Weeks ago." Kerouac was also frustrated when neither a contract nor the promised list of recommended changes was sent.

The spring of 1956 found Kerouac still waiting. After a series of missed connections he characterized as "malign fate," Cowley promised to send the list of recommended corrections in time for Kerouac to work on them in Washington's Skagit Valley, where Kerouac was working as a fire lookout for the summer on Desolation Peak. This delay, added to the already long wait to have the novel published, not surprisingly tested Kerouac's resolve, and he complained to Sterling Lord on April 10 that the saga was taking on "absurd-martyr-proportions I can't buy." More than once he threatened to take *On the Road* from Viking. Always he relented, convinced that Viking represented his best chance despite the collective dragging of feet on the project that continued through 1956. For the most part he released his anger in letters to Sterling Lord and unsent letters to Cowley.

Kerouac was still anxious in the fall of 1956, writing to Sterling Lord from San Francisco in September to ask "what's happening now?" "Tell me what you think about the Viking Press situation," Kerouac asked Lord, "perhaps you might suggest we change the title to WOW and publish it right away."* On October 7 Kerouac wrote from Mexico City asking Lord to retrieve "Beat Generation" from Cowley. "Tell him I respect his sincerity, but I'm not too sure about the others at Viking and tell him I don't care . . . I want that book sold on street stalls, it is a book about the streets. Do what you can . . . I've been through every conceivable disgrace now and no rejection or acceptance by publishers can alter that awful final feeling of death—of life-which-is-death."

Cowley's final acceptance report for Viking is undated but would have been written toward the end of 1956. Cowley traced the history of the book. Remembering that the novel had been rejected in 1953 "with the proviso that we'd like to see it again," Cowley wrote that Viking had subsequently worked to "remove the two great problems of libel and obscenity. . . . Moreover, Kerouac changed the story to avoid most of the libel danger . . . and Helen Taylor went over it taking out the rest of the libel, some of the obscenity, and tightening the story."

Cowley wrote that *On the Road* is not "a great or even a likable book." The "wild bohemians" of the novel were like "machines gone haywire . . . with hardly any emotions except a determination to say Yes to any new experience"

---

*From London in April 1957, and impressed by the Teddy Boy culture he found there, Kerouac wrote to Sterling Lord that "maybe it would double the sales to change the title to ROCK AND ROLL ROAD."

The book, I prophesy, will get mixed but <u>interested</u> reviews, it will have a good sale (perhaps a very good one), and I don't think there is any doubt that it will be reprinted as a paperback. Moreover it will stand for a long time as the honest record of another way of life.

On New Year's Day 1957, Kerouac reported to Sterling Lord from Florida that "the m.s. of ROAD is all ready for the printer, please tell Keith and Malcolm to have complete confidence in the libel-clearing thorough job I did on it . . . they will be pleased." Traveling to New York by Greyhound bus from Florida, Kerouac turned in the manuscript to Cowley on January 8. The signed contract between Viking and "John" Kerouac, for a novel "tentatively entitled On the Road," is dated January 10, 1957. Kerouac received $1,000 against all earnings, with $250 due on signing, $150 on acceptance, and the balance of $600 in payments of $100 for six months. The royalty agreement saw Kerouac receive 10 percent on all copies sold up to 10,000, 12.5 percent up to 12,500, and 15 percent thereafter. Kerouac reported to John Clellon Holmes on January 10 that he would be signing "contract tomorrow for sure with Viking."

On February 24 Cowley wrote to Kerouac turning down his new novel "Desolation Angels." He wrote, "Meanwhile On the Road is going through the works at a good rate—pretty soon it will all be set up in type—and then the salesmen will go out on the road with 'On the Road,' and I hope they sell a lot of copies."

With the contracts signed and the book in production Kerouac found himself isolated by Viking. Writing from Berkeley in July, and worried about how the forthcoming *Howl* obscenity trial set for August would affect *On the Road*, Kerouac complained about the "eerie silence" to Sterling Lord. "I'm real worried because you never write any more, as tho something was wrong, or is it just my imagination? I wrote a long letter to Keith Jennison, also no answer. Is ON THE ROAD going to be published? And if so, what about the final galleys I have to see, and what about the picture of me, and isn't there some kind of promotion or business going on I should know about. I tell you I am lonesome and scared not hearing from anybody."

After the small literary magazine *New Editions* published "Neal and the Three Stooges," an extract from *Visions of Cody*, in July, Kerouac sent a copy to Cowley, pointedly writing that he thought Cowley would be "amused to see my 'untouched' prose in print." Kerouac was writing to ask when he would be sent the final galleys of *On the Road*, but was interrupted in his writing by the delivery of advance copies of the novel. As described in *Desolation Angels*, Neal Cassady knocked on the door in Berkeley just as Kerouac was unpacking the books. Feeling that he had been caught "red-handed," Kerouac gave Cassady, "the hero of the poor crazy sad book," the first copy.

The cultural tensions that can be read in all of these exchanges and negotiations, the mixture of excitement and distaste shown by senior figures at Viking toward Kerouac and his work, the attempts to manage and commodify his wild book and Kerouac's enthusiastic vulnerability and complicity in that process, and the half-apprehended sense on all sides that literary and cultural history were about to be made would all be publicly played out in the reviews of *On the Road* that began to appear after the novel was finally published on September 5, 1957.

In *Minor Characters*, Joyce Johnson describes how just before midnight on September 4 she and Kerouac went to a newsstand at Sixty-sixth and Broadway to wait for copies of the *New York Times* to be delivered. When the papers came off the delivery truck, and the old man at the newsstand had cut the string that kept the newspapers in bales, Joyce and Jack bought a copy and read Gilbert Millstein's review of *On the Road* under a street lamp and then over again and again in Donnelly's bar on Columbus Avenue.

Millstein's review, in which he called the book "an authentic work of art," announced *On the Road* as "a major novel," and its publication "an historic event." Praising Kerouac's style and technical virtuosity, Millstein argued that the excesses of Sal and Dean, their "frenzied pursuit of every sensory impression," were made and intended by

Kerouac primarily "to serve a spiritual purpose." It may be that Kerouac's generation, Millstein wrote, did "not know what refuge it is seeking, but it is seeking." It was in this spiritual sense, Millstein argued, that Kerouac had taken the most challenging and difficult of the paths available to the postwar American writer identified by John Aldridge in his study, "After the Lost Generation." Kerouac, in Aldridge's words, had stated "the need for belief even though it is upon a background in which belief is impossible." This need for belief was also what John Clellon Holmes had privileged in "This Is the Beat Generation," an article commissioned by Millstein for the Sunday *New York Times* in 1951 and from which he also quoted in his review of *On the Road.* Holmes had argued that the difference between the "Lost" and "Beat" generations was in the latter's "will to believe even in the face of an inability to do so in conventional terms." "*How* to live," Holmes wrote, then became much more "crucial than *why.*"

If Millstein's identification of *On the Road* as a novel concerned most strongly with the search for affirmation in the context of a spiritually barren and fearful American society was an attempt to establish the ground on which the novel would be discussed, his view was challenged by less sympathetic reviewers who, while they could not ignore the exhuberant beauty and freshness of Kerouac's style, would not concede the seriousness of his spiritual purpose and intent. In the *New York Times* on Sunday, September 8, David Dempsey argued that "Jack Kerouac has written an enormously readable and entertaining book but one reads it in the same mood that he might visit a side-show—the freaks are fascinating although they are hardly part of our lives."

Other cultural critics were more openly hostile. Reviewing the novel for the *New York World-Telegram & Sun,* Robert C. Ruark argued that *On the Road* was not much more than a "candid admission" that Kerouac "had been on the bum for six years." Kerouac's "snivelling" characters, wrote Ruark, were "punks" who needed a kick "in the pants." In the *New Leader* on October 28, William Murray argued that the novel was certainly significant and important in the context of the "mood and meaning" of its time, but Kerouac "is most certainly not an artist, for that would imply a discipline and unity of purpose which his writing does not reflect." *On the Road* was important, Murray continued, "because it communicates directly in a non-literary way an emotional experience of our time."

What Viking publicity director Patricia McManus called the novel's "resounding, if mixed, effect" in an in-house memo dated February 6, 1958, led to *On the Road*'s quickly going through three editions. In an earlier, prepublication memo, McManus had anticipated, "judging by advance readings," that the novel would "stir-up considerable lively discussion, pro and con." By January 1958, McManus reported, "at least two colleges have adopted it for modern literature courses (how the schools are using it hasn't yet been ascertained . . . perhaps for after-curfew reading)."

The controversy over Jack Kerouac and *On the Road* became the focal contest in a larger cultural war in which Kerouac's insistence that he was on a spiritual quest, his liminal working-class, French-Canadian status, and his apparently out-of-nowhere emergence as the mythologizer and reluctant figurehead of a countercultural generation defined by opposition to cold war politics and ideology made him an open target. Kerouac's novel, written six years earlier and concerned with the "hot" and exuberant youth of the late 1940s, was mistakenly seen as direct social commentary on the "cool" youth culture of the late 1950s. Kerouac's technical success in collapsing the distinction between fiction and nonfiction also meant that the intended and conscious thematic and structural kinships *On the Road* shares with canonical American novels including, most obviously and notably, *Moby-Dick*, *The Adventures of Huckleberry Finn*, and *The Great Gatsby*, went largely unnoticed, while many readers, because it suited them to do so, simply confused Kerouac with Dean Moriarty. In his, "The Cult of Unthink," published in *Horizon*, September 15, 1958, Robert Brustein linked Kerouac with the "glowering" and inarticulate "tribal followers" of Marlon Brando and James Dean. The "Beat Generation," Brustein argued, was surly and discontented, "of much muscle and

little mind" and "prepared to offer violence with little provocation."
"It is not so long a jump," Brustein continued, "from the kick-seeking
poet to the kick-seeking adolescent who, sinking his knife into the
flesh of his victim, thanked him for the 'experience.'"

Kerouac, a lifelong pacifist who had thrown down his rifle and
walked off the field while in navy boot camp, replied to Brustein on
September 24, a week before publication of the emphatically spiritual
and pacific *The Dharma Bums* on October 2:

> None of my characters travel "in packs" or are a "juvenile gang"
> ensemble or carry knives. I conceived On the Road as a book about
> tenderness among the wild young hell-raisers like your grandfather
> in 1880 when he was a youngster. I have never exalted anyone of a
> violent nature at any time . . . Dean Moriarty and Sal Paradise were
> completely spiteless characters, unlike their critics.

Notwithstanding his attempts to engage his critics in serious
debate, Kerouac found to his cost, as Joyce Johnson writes, that what
most interviewers wanted was to get the "inside story on the Beat
Generation and its avatar." Specifically, or course, these interviewers
wanted Kerouac to explain the meaning of "Beat," the word that
began to be heard everywhere. "Beat," Johnson writes, was

> first uttered on a Times Square street corner in 1947 by the hipster-
> angel Herbert Huncke in some evanescent moment of exalted
> exhaustion, but resonating later in Jack's mind, living on to accrue
> new meaning, connecting finally with the Catholic, Latin *beatific*.
> "Beat is really saying *beatific*. See?" Jack so earnest in making his point
> so the interviewer can get it right, respecting the journalistic search
> for accuracy although he knows accuracy is not the same as truth.

Again and again, Johnson writes, Kerouac "will go through this
derivation with increasing weariness . . . the words slurring progres-
sively." So began the nightmare of what Johnson called Kerouac's
"awful success." Kerouac's drinking, always heavy, became uncon-
trolled, and the novel he had begun nearly ten years before in Ozone

Park condemned him to his fate as the mythological "King of the Beats," which is where we began.

This account is a contribution to an ongoing counternarrative intended to displace mythology and recover Kerouac as a writer, first and always. "That is how I remember Kerouac," William Burroughs wrote, "as a writer talking about writers or sitting in a quiet corner with a notebook, writing in longhand . . . You feel that he was writing all the time; that writing was the only thing he thought about. He never wanted to do anything else."

Rewriting America

Kerouac's Nation of "Underground Monsters"

Penny Vlagopoulos

Often, if you go into a bookstore in New York City, you will find Kerouac not on the shelves, but rather behind the cash register counter. As legend has it, alongside the Bible, *On the Road* is one of the most frequently stolen books. Books are not usually items deemed worthy of criminal behavior, but Kerouac continues to inspire a level of defiance that suggests his outlaw terrain spreads across generations. Although his most famous novel arose from the particular conditions of the era in which it was written, it acts as a kind of blueprint for translating the upheavals and aftershocks of its historical moment into vital, perennial concerns. At the heart of this quality is a directive to the reader to pursue the more elusive questions of our lives by excavating the places that define us as if we are discovering them for the first time—as outsiders. Kerouac dedicates *Visions of Cody,* his experimental account of traveling with Neal Cassady, to "America, whatever that is." Perhaps more than any other novelist of his generation, he approaches America's ambiguities as a venture imbued in the creative process of, as he puts it in *On the Road,* "rising from the underground." The years Kerouac spent writing about his experience on the road were, in a sense, an exploration in nation building from below.

"One night in America when the sun had gone down" begins a proto-draft of *On the Road* from 1950. This image ultimately makes its way to the last paragraph of the published version, but read as a beginning, it brings to the forefront the novel's panoramic scope, which contextualizes the "pit and prunejuice of poor beat life itself" as a "sad drama in the American night." On July 4, 1949, Kerouac writes in his journal of his plans to go from Mexico to New York and feels a "heavy melancholy, almost like pleasure" that he describes thus: "The big American night keeps closing in, redder and darker all the time. There is no home." While Kerouac could never renounce places and people in his life that constituted his sense of a home— most notably his mother, to whom he always returned, and his birthplace of Lowell, Massachusetts—he always felt the unique combination of exuberance and despair at being homeless in one's native land. The breaking-point intensity of much of Kerouac's writing, which often asks the reader to linger between intellectual assessment and emotional release, evinces just how much was at stake for Kerouac in constructing a vocabulary that could adequately account for the relationship between the individual and the nation.

"This is the story of America," Kerouac explains in *On the Road*, when describing Sal Paradise's frustrated attempt to bend the rules during a brief stint as a security guard. "Everybody's doing what they think they're supposed to do." The period after World War II that marked the start of the cold war endorsed a mythology of national unity. In NSC 68, a classified report prepared for the U.S. National Security Council in April 14, 1950, a year before Kerouac sat down to compose the *On the Road* scroll, three "realities" emerge in a section entitled "Fundamental Purpose of the United States": "Our determination to maintain the essential elements of individual freedom, as set forth in the Constitution and Bill of Rights; our determination to create conditions under which our free and democratic system can live and prosper; and our determination to fight if necessary to defend our way of life." In this section, the rhetoric used in defense of liberty is unmistakably threatening, even imperialist, in its tone. Almost a century earlier, Walt Whitman wrote, in "Democratic Vistas," of "perfect individualism" that "deepest tinges and gives character to the idea of the aggregate." In the 1950s, this paradigm seemed to reverse directions: It was the state structuring the requirements of the individual, both within national borders—a sacrifice that amounted to doing one's part for the war effort—and without.

In the year that Kerouac composed the scroll of *On the Road*, the United States expanded its bomb testing from the South Pacific to the Nevada desert, literally bringing the war home. The House Committee on Un-American Activities began its second round of hearings, in which artists and intellectuals were required to prove their innocence and loyalty to the United States and to renounce their Communist ties. Any minor offense could have been labeled deviant, and citizens suffered the curtailment of civil liberties in the name of upholding freedom from totalitarianism. This period of compulsory confession was the performance mode of a vast movement of secrecy that was so effective, as Joyce Nelson argues, because of "the purposeful fragmentation and compartment-alization of information." The less people understood about the connective tissue both within and between politics and culture, the more effective the government could be in manipulating its own population while seeking global influence and authority.

In the article that formulated the cold war policy of containment, "The Sources of Soviet Conduct," published in 1947, George Kennan stressed the connection between social harmony at home and control overseas. The United States, he argued, had to market itself as a country that was "coping successfully with the problems of its internal life and with the responsibilities of a World Power" and "holding its own among the major ideological currents of the time." Signs of weakness, according to Kennan, could have drastic consequences across the globe, as "exhibitions of indecision, disunity and internal disintegration within this country have an exhilarating effect on the whole Communist movement." In other words, dissent and contradiction were seen as malignancies threatening the very sovereignty of the nation by bolstering the enemy. The antidote, by implication, was homogeneity and consensus, no matter how compulsory.

Among Kerouac's many definitions of "Beat Generation," he

includes "a weariness with all the forms, all the conventions of the world." His sense of being alienated in his native land derived in part from his understanding that something "had gnawed in me to make me strive to be 'different' from all this." He felt a kinship with people "too *dark*, too strange, too subterranean" to fulfill the credentials of a society in which, as Stephen J. Whitfield argues, "cultural expression was thwarted and distorted" at every turn. *On the Road*, in its promotion of life lived for "the ragged and ecstatic joy of pure being," can be seen as a response to a certain level of conformity so prevalent in the nation's cultural consciousness that it had produced anxiety about what William H. Whyte, Jr., in his 1956 bestseller *The Organization Man*, warned was a society composed of middle-class workers "who have left home, spiritually as well as physically, to take the vows of organization life." This form of self-criticism that resulted from fears of an "organization man" society, however, merely produced a kind of safe space of dissent in which the most submerged levels of control could continue unchecked.

For Kerouac, it was the very systems through which bureaucratic and militaristic order were filtered that were flawed. In a July 1951 letter to Allen Ginsberg, he wrote, "I'm glad I understood exactly what it is to be a man in an office in the world. In my early days as reporter—I had a desk, a telephone—it was too easy a way to be in the world, though . . . automatic, as it were." Kerouac briefly joined the naval reserve in 1943 but once he realized that, according to the psychiatrist performing his evaluation, "individuality is subordinated to obedience and discipline" and anyone "not conforming to this regimen is of no use to the organization," he feigned madness in order to be discharged and reenlisted, instead, in the merchant marine. In his most vitriolic essay, "After Me, the Deluge," written at the end of his life in an attempt to disalign himself from both the "Hippie Flower Children" and the "top echelons of American society," he decides "I'll go back to the alienated radicals who are quite understandably alienated, nay disgusted by this scene," because, although in his view they were

hypocritical and unproductive, the people who were part of the "neu-
rological drone of money-grub" were worse.

Still, it would be wrong to read *On the Road* as the manifesto of a
generational spokesperson. After the book's overnight success, Kerouac found himself having to rescue the idea of the Beat Generation
and to rid himself of the "King of the Beats" title. At the end of his
life, constantly called upon to define his politics and his relationship
to the burgeoning counterculture, he explained that *On the Road* was
"hardly an agitational propaganda account." He did not want the
responsibility of helming an entire generation that, in fact, he barely
understood. As early as 1959, Kerouac bemoaned the "beatnik routines on TV," which implied that "it's a simple change in fashion and
manners, just a history crust" that "will only change a few dresses
and pants and make chairs useless in the livingroom and pretty soon
we'll have Beat Secretaries of State and there will be instituted new
tinsels, in fact new reasons for malice and new reasons for virtue and
new reasons for forgiveness . . ." Kerouac witnessed firsthand the
absurd trajectories of avant-garde cultural movements, which often
stray from the fundamental ideas that spawn them. He understood
how the radical potential of art becomes sanitized in shadow versions
that distill the critiques behind the original creative articulations.

Kerouac fielded the more sinister side of this misrepresentation by
challenging the absoluteness that taxonomies, with all of their attendant qualifications, require. By the end of "After Me, the Deluge," his
only solution is to "see everyone in the world as unconsolable orphans
yelling and screaming on every side to make arrangements for making a living" and ultimately "all so *lonered*." Kerouac refused the
rigidity and reductiveness of categories. *On the Road* asks that people
find the beauty in failed journeys, in the discovery of personal excess,
in feeling the sting of limits, but these are the boundaries around
which humanness is constructed. Labels, on the other hand, can
sometimes evacuate the presence of that which they attempt to contain. Kerouac criticized "those who think that the Beat Generation

means crime, delinquency, immorality, amorality," he wrote in 1959. These were the misinformed tactics of "those who attack it on the grounds that they simply don't understand history and the yearnings of human souls . . . woe unto those who don't realize that America must, will, is changing now, for the better I say." Rather than write in willful resistance to mainstream America, Kerouac mapped the human geography of a "land that never has been yet—/ And yet must be," in the words of Langston Hughes. For Dean, the character based on Neal Cassady, "Everybody's kicks, man!" But for Sal, a stand-in for Kerouac, people are "like fabulous roman candles." People amuse and serve Dean. For Sal, they are purveyors of light.

Kerouac felt too deeply the gaps between what life was supposed to be and how people actually lived it. He lamented in a journal entry from 1949, "I feel that I'm the only person in the world who doesn't know the feeling of calm irreverence—the only madman in the world therefore—the only broken fish. All the others are perfectly contented with pure life. I am not. I want a pure understanding, and then pure life." Kerouac felt a profound sense of loneliness; this stemmed partly from a spiritual understanding of human suffering that was so embedded in his Catholic upbringing, and partly from his artist's interiority, which heightened the sense of his difference even as it produced solidarity between him and people who were "mad to live, mad to talk, mad to be saved." Sal understands the compulsive need of the creative mind to collaborate: "But then they danced down the streets like dingledodies, and I shambled after as I've been doing all my life after people who interest me." At the same time, Kerouac found himself in uniquely marginal territory, searching for ways to define the particular parameters of his selfhood. On his first road trip, Sal awakes in Des Moines, in the middle of America, and doesn't know who he is: "I was just somebody else, some stranger, and my whole life was a haunted life, the life of a ghost." Here, the road momentarily eradicates Sal's identity in order to root it in a long lineage of wanderers and searchers.

On the Road radiates hope that communities might function unmediated by the sublimating forces inherent to modern society. When Sal leaves San Francisco to go to Denver at the beginning of part three, he envisions himself settling "in Middle America, a patriarch." But when he actually gets there, he finds himself "in the Denver colored section, wishing I were a Negro, feeling that the best the white world had offered was not enough ecstasy for me, not enough life, joy, kicks, darkness, music, not enough night." He explains, "I wished I were a Denver Mexican, or even a poor overworked Jap, anything but what I was so drearily, a 'white man' disillusioned." Critics have rightly pointed to the racial primitivism expressed in this passage, which can have the effect of obscuring the actual lived experience of people of color during this period. For Kerouac, however, these oppressed minorities were the most honest evocation of what an "American underground" might really mean. It is no coincidence that the "magic land at the end of the road" is in Mexico. As Sal and Dean drive to Mexico City, the "Fellahin Indians of the world" stare at the "ostensibly self-important moneybag Americans on a lark in their land" and know "who was the father and who was the son of antique life on earth," a viewpoint shared by Kerouac. His profound desire to empathize with marginalized people while also reaffirming his commitment to what he admits in *On the Road* are "white ambitions," even as he understood the near impossibility of staking equal claim to both identities socially and politically in 1949, stemmed from his own conflicted ethnic and class status.

Kerouac was born Jean-Louis Lebris de Kerouac of French-Canadian parents who immigrated to New England to find work. He grew up speaking joual, a French-Canadian working-class dialect, and throughout his career as a novelist considered himself more comfortable with joual than English, which he did not speak until he was six years old. In his introduction to *Lonesome Traveler*, he mentions that his ancestors were both Bretons and Indians. Expressing pride for both heritages, he wavered between the "Faulknerian pillar homestead" and the "steel of America covering the ground filled with the bones of old Indians and Original Americans," as he writes in *The Sub-*

terraneans. Tim Hunt argues that Kerouac's immigrant history "left him suspended between categories—neither a person of color nor a white middle-class American—and unable to resolve either the dissonance between the period's rhetorics of ethnicity and class (by which, because he was white, he was in the cultural and social mainstream) or his sense of marginality—his sense that he was finally alien and an outsider." Those who identify first and foremost as American possess a sense of entitlement that is uniquely theirs. It is something only immigrants and first-generation Americans, perhaps, can ever truly understand, because it is a sense of proprietorship they will never fully have. Writers do not dedicate a book to a nation that is unproblematically theirs, much less include a clause that admits an inability to define it ("whatever that is").

The discordant elements of Kerouac's identity turn the anthropological lens of *On the Road* to the margins of daily American life in the 1950s. Ann Douglas writes that reading the book for the first time taught her and her friends "that we were part of a continent rather than a country," and, furthermore, that "the continent had been strangely emptied out of the people usually caught on camera, yet it was filled with other people, people in motion, of various races and ethnicities, speaking many tongues, migrating from one place to another as seasonal laborers, wandering around as hobos and hitchhikers, meeting each other in brief but somehow lasting encounters." Although being a white man, no matter how compromised by other, less privileged categories of identification, still guarantees one greater advantage in *On the Road*, Kerouac also provides those considered undesirable in that era—homeless men riding the backs of trucks or penniless saxophone players, for example—some form of agency, if only because they share the stage as subjects of the road experience. Howard Zinn argues that the telling of America in terms of heroes and their victims, which entails "the quiet acceptance of conquest and murder in the name of progress," functions as "only one aspect of a certain approach to history, in which the past is told from the point of view of governments, conquerors, diplomats, leaders." If *On the*

Road is about defining America, it is also about staging an intervention into official definitions of history and nationhood.

Kerouac revisited ethnicity and class in sampling and crafting what he saw as *real* Americans, but he also challenged the confines of gender and sexuality. In the postwar period, fear of infiltration by a foreign enemy spread to include anyone who did not fit white, heteronormative standards. As Wini Breines argues in *Young, White, and Miserable: Growing Up Female in the Fifties*, "The changes that accompanied the formation of an advanced capitalist society were perceived and experienced as threats from those outside American borders and from those who had been excluded within those borders, women and blacks and homosexuals." While Kerouac's concern with race is apparent in both the scroll of *On the Road* and the published version, all blatant references to sexuality—especially homosexuality—were edited out of the 1957 edition. Sex acts are more explicit and egalitarian in the scroll. According to Ginsberg, LuAnne is "all for" divorcing Neal so that he can marry Carolyn but "says she loves his big cock—so does Carolyn—so do I." This version explores women's sexuality and freedom in an era when, as Joyce Johnson writes in her Beat memoir *Minor Characters*, people frowned at a girl from a "nice family" who left her parents' house, knowing "what she'd be up to in that room of her own." Women did not have the same degree of mobility as men and the costs of rebellion were much greater. Johnson writes, "Once we had found our male counterparts, we had too much blind faith to challenge the old male/female rules," yet "we knew we had done something brave, practically historic. We were the ones who dared to leave home."

Although the road that Kerouac depicted was only fully open to those who had the luxury of traveling it without major consequences, its liberating possibilities extended to whoever could find a way to interpret them. Marylou, Dean's lover, is on the road for a good part of the novel and seems an even stronger presence in the scroll. She never gets much of a voice in either version, but she is the witness, using the men as much as they use her, siphoning their energy and road wisdom without accountability. This, too, is a form of freedom. Although the book is about the search for the lost father, it is also about the potential for women to wrest control in the end by gaining access to experience ordinarily denied them and revising it to suit their own formulations of the road narrative. Women are catalysts for broader change as well. In the scroll, Jack remembers his mother telling him of the need for men to expiate their offenses, which instigates a train of thought ultimately left out of the exchange between Sal and his aunt in the published version: "All over the world, in the jungles of Mexico, in backstreets of Shanghai, in New York cocktail bars, husbands are getting drunk while the women stay home with the babies of the everdarkening future. If these men stop the machine and come home—and get on their knees—and ask for forgiveness—and the women bless them—peace will suddenly descend on the earth with a great silence like the inherent silence of the Apocalypse." In this passage, Kerouac anchors the relationship between America and the rest of the world on a collective redressing of wrongs, represented here through a critique of gender roles. He suggests that borders, both within and between nations, have the potential to erode if we begin to untangle our human histories of oppression, negligence, and shame through a prism of love and empathy.

On the Road asks us to consider, if not fully share, perspectives beyond those of white men, but it also endorses the creation of new versions of outsiderness. Kerouac's representation of America was a response to the disingenuousness of a "cold" war, more ominous in its implicit disavowal of the actual costs of conflict than its explicit counterpart, the "hot" war. In a parallel analogy, two years after the publication of *On the Road*, Kerouac writes that there are two styles of "hipsterism": the *cool*, represented by the "bearded laconic sage," a person "whose speech is low and unfriendly, whose girls say nothing and wear black," and the *hot*, who is "the crazy talkative shining eyed (often innocent and openhearted) nut who runs from bar to bar, pad to pad looking for everybody, shouting, restless, lushy, trying to 'make it' with the subterranean beatniks who ignore him." Most of the artists of the Beat Generation, he explains, "belong to the hot school, naturally since that hard gemlike flame needs a little heat." In the logic of war rhetoric, to be "hot" is to be unable to disguise oneself behind masks of secrecy. It is a place of vulnerability and embarrassment, an exposure to all forms of criticism. It was more important for Kerouac to be sincere than "cool." In 1949, he laments, "Resuming true serious work I find that I have grown lazy in my heart." He is frustrated with the lack of discipline he observes in his peers and wonders, "Is this the way the world is going to end—in *indifference?*" When asked by one interviewer what he was looking for, Kerouac answered that he was "waiting for God to show his face." If on a national level, "truth" was a politicized umbrella term for a particular form of ideology, for Kerouac, writing what he called his "true-story novels" was an act enmeshed in answering the "adolescent question of 'why do men go on living.'"

On the Road speaks to some urge of its readers, giving them the vocabulary with which to reimagine their daily lives in ways that are felt organically rather than fully articulated. It is something like the sensation of suddenly being shocked by the sight of a large, full moon hovering almost too low to notice, and wondering if anyone else sees it. You are a lucky participant receiving privileged information. As Douglas argues, "In the age that invented the idea of classified information, Kerouac's effort was to *de*classify the secrets of the human body and soul." Kerouac was always interested in honesty, especially to himself, at whatever cost, and often this meant offering a picture of possibility rather than providing a direct guide. In one of the most memorable parts of *On the Road*, Sal understands that Dean silently acknowledges how "I'd never committed myself before with regard to his burdensome existence," and the two men find themselves in an awkward moment of pathos and discovery: "We both felt uncertain of something." After this quiet exchange in which something "clicked in both of us" (in the scroll, Kerouac writes "both of our souls"), the two men resume their journey. It is what is not said or done that drives *On the Road*, what cannot be contained, categorized, or commodified. Sal's newfound commitment to his friend resolves itself in a question about Dean: "He was BEAT—the root, the soul of Beatific. What was he knowing?" Rather than wonder "What did he know?," a more conventional approach to the ways in which we mine each other for ideas that we convert into personal capital, Kerouac's use of the present participle indicates the open-endedness of knowledge—a creative space of contestation that begins at the edges of subjective experience.

What is so striking at first about reading the scroll manuscript, aside from seeing the original names, the sexually frank language, and certain sections that were ultimately cut, is how little the language actually differs from the published text as a whole. But the feeling of reading it is altogether new. The processes of reading and writing emerge as crucial artistic practices. Kerouac lets us toy with the option that, as he writes in a journal entry, "*It's not the words that count, but the rush of what is said.*" In a *Village Voice* review of *The Dharma Bums*, Ginsberg discusses *On the Road* and describes feeling a "sadness that this was never published in its most exciting form—its original discovery—but hacked and punctuated and broken—the rhythms and swing of it broken—by presumptuous literary critics in publishing houses." The *On the Road* scroll represents the early stage of Kerouac's increasingly innovative literary technique. In a letter to Ginsberg the following year, Kerouac wrote that while "sketching," a method suggested by his friend Ed White, he produced writing that wavered between lunatic confessionals and brilliant prose. He composed the version of *On the Road* that eventually became *Visions of Cody* in this style, much to the dismay of publishers, who repeatedly accused him of incoherency. The sense of skating on the edges of consciousness and sanity in language is felt to a much greater degree in the scroll version. Reading it is almost embarrassing, like walking in on someone's private repertoire of weaknesses. At times it seems excessively raw and uncrafted, but these reactions are exactly right. "And just like you say," Kerouac wrote to Ginsberg in 1952, "the best things we write are always the most suspected."

Kerouac's unique relationship to language was partly the result of his upbringing. As he wrote to a reviewer, "The reason I handle English words so easily is because it is not my own language. I refashion it to fit French images." This duality specific to the first-generation American—being an English-speaking citizen but not having an inherited linguistic facility to generate an incidental attitude toward language—comes through in the visceral force and unexpected tenor of Kerouac's writing. He seemed to approach words from outside of their expected meanings, as if they were found objects to be appropriated and made new. The writing style used in *On the Road*, which Kerouac eventually developed into "spontaneous prose," was heavily influenced by the jazz of the period, "in the sense of a, say, tenor man drawing a breath, and blowing a phrase on his saxophone, till he runs out of breath, and when he does, his sentence, his statement's been made . . . that's how I therefore separate my sentences, as breath separations of the mind." In 1950, he writes in his journal, "I wish to evoke that indescribable sad music of the night in America—for reasons which are never deeper than *the music*. Bop only begins to express that American music. It is the actual inner sound of a country." If reading *On the Road* is hearing this *sound* of America leaking out of a window in the distance, experiencing the scroll is like finally stumbling onto the back door of the performance.

In the scroll manuscript, Kerouac writes, "My mother was all in accord with my trip to the west, she said it would do me good, I'd been working so hard all winter and staying in too much; she even didn't say too much when I told her I'd have to hitch hike some, ordinarily it frightened her, she thought this would do me good." In the published version, this becomes, "My aunt was all in accord with my trip to the West; she said it would do me good, I'd been working so hard all winter and staying in too much; she even didn't complain when I told her I'd have to hitchhike some." "She even didn't say too much" more closely evokes spoken language than "she even didn't complain," while "ordinarily it frightened her" is the kind of afterthought one inserts while telling a story. The rhythmic immediacy in the vernacular of the first version recalls the improvisational syncopations of jazz. Jack's restlessness comes through in his repetitiveness, a technique that is prevalent throughout the scroll. Additionally, he uses only one semicolon and so the clauses lack the degree of syntactical hierarchy and causality apparent in the second version. Each sentiment is as important as the next, which parallels the search for "kicks" enacted in the novel. The subtle changes in punctuation not only alter the cadence of the section, but also dilute the effect of the meaning.

From scroll to 1957 edition, dashes and ellipses often become commas. Commas often become semicolons and colons. The flow is interrupted. Following a dash from one point to the next without stopping to construct an architecture of expected logic in a sentence more closely mimes the feeling of actually being on the road with Neal, as does sideslipping through descriptions without clear subordinate clauses. "I jumped around only in my chino pants over the thick soft rug" becomes, in the published version, "I jumped around over the thick soft rug, wearing only my chino pants." The vigorous equality of all experience in the present moment is curtailed in the second version. Reading the scroll, one understands what Kerouac means when he lists as one of the "essentials" in his "Belief & Technique for Modern Prose," "Submissive to everything, open, listening." At the same time, the scroll is a kind of jive, an insider's code, a way of changing the rules of ordinary English to critique and revise it, to contest the ways in which language enacts power. More important, it is an ultimate safeguard against co-option. Thelonious Monk once said of his jazz, "We're going to create something they can't steal because they can't play it." In an era of information control, restructuring the basic tools of communication beyond the purview of the mainstream is a subversive act.

Kerouac seemed to be grasping to know America in a way that would encode a hidden editing process, a way that would recuperate the losses and failures inherent in the very structures of our language. In early 1950, after spending an evening listening to a number of jazz greats, including Dizzy Gillespie and Miles Davis, he understood that an "art that expresses the mind of mind, and not the mind of life (the idea of mortal life on earth), is a dead art." Like the European avant-garde artists of the preceding decades, Kerouac sought to collapse the distance between life and art. In explaining the importance of 1970s punk band the Sex Pistols, Greil Marcus writes that the band's record "had to change the way a given person performed his or her commute." While reading the scroll in a local coffee shop, I recently found myself staring out the window at people going by and realizing, mid-reverie, that *On the Road* has to change the way a person drinks his or her coffee. It is simultaneously about the most minute details of one's life and the most monumental, a cartography of human desire in its extreme immensity and insignificance. In his spontaneous prose-infused biography on Kerouac entitled *Jack Kerouac: A Chicken Essay*, Victor-Lévy Beaulieu, a Québécois writer, explains that the question *"Who was I?"* was at the heart of Kerouac's project as a writer, because he knew that "the revolution is nothing if not interior."

Kerouac's questions of the self must change the way we know America. In one of my shameful memories of being embarrassed by my immigrant parents as a child, I remember criticizing my mother for exposing her foreignness in some way and her saying to me, "We do not blend easily." As I read *On the Road*, I think of what they endured—living through two brutal wars and innumerable days of poverty and death—to go to a place where the desire to blend was swiftly replaced by the need to make a space in which survival could mean something personal. *On the Road* is a kind of map for these spaces. It inspires some vestigial picture of idealism that perhaps only existed in books—something akin to Jay Gatsby's "orgastic future that year by year recedes before us." At the same time, it is a feeling of comfortable foreignness, of being perfectly outside, of edging, like the Beats, "just another step toward that last, pale generation which will not know the answers either." Kerouac lets you love to lose yourself. You become attuned to something that is ultimately outside language—some faint hum of knowingness that is only felt, all the way to the deepest core of being. The best way, I think, to experience *On the Road* is sitting alone by a window, feeling the onrush of a poem, a painting, a song about to happen, head slightly tilted toward invisible forces that ensure, no matter what, that artists will continue to, in Kerouac's words, "translate the passionate intensity of life." You are wrapped in a sense of being haunted by people and places and particular moments that drive you, like Kerouac, to "the edges of language where the babble of the subconscious begins," hoping for access to the secret PAUSE button before the thing that is revealed, so you can keep it going, whatever it is.

"Into the Heart of Things"

Neal Cassady and the Search for the Authentic

George Mouratidis

Writing of the impending release of *On the Road* at the conclusion of *Desolation Angels,* Jack Kerouac gives a markedly mythologized impression of the unexpected appearance of Neal Cassady at the very moment "Jack Duluoz" is unpacking advance copies of his novel, "all about Cody and me":

> I look up as a golden light appears in the porch door silently; and
> there stands Cody . . . Not a sound. I'm also caught red handed . . .
> with a copy of *Road* in my hands . . . I automatically hand one to Cody,
> who is after all the hero of the poor crazy sad book. It's one of the
> several occasions in my life where a meeting with Cody seems to be
> suffused with a silent golden light . . . altho I don't even know what
> it means, unless it means that Cody is some kind of angel or archan-
> gel come down to this world and I recognize it.

Spanning his *Road* novels, Kerouac's representation of his relationship with Cassady is one of contrasts, consisting of various and
distinct incarnations of Cassady between which we as readers move
in our attempt to establish a sense of his development and changing
significance. With the publication of the original scroll manuscript
of *On the Road,* the actual process of Kerouac's mutable representation of Cassady is further illuminated. We are now given a broader,
more cohesive picture of the Cassady figure's development in
Kerouac's writing; from "Neal Cassady" (the scroll) to "Dean Pomeray"
(the immediate second draft of *On the Road*) to "Cody Pomeray" (the

posthumously published *Visions of Cody*), and *then* the "Dean Moriarty" of the published *On the Road*, after which Cassady would reappear as the estranged, almost mythical "old buddy" Cody Pomeray in subsequent novels, *The Dharma Bums*, *Big Sur*, and the abovementioned *Desolation Angels*. This progression moves from the symbolic to the mythic, from *human* to *vision*, marking Kerouac's gradual separation of the *real* Cassady from his romantic vision of him. Through his mutable responses to Cassady in his *Road* novels Kerouac problematizes both the existential concern with "authentic" being particular to the postwar period, as well as the more contemporary preoccupation with authenticity in representation, showing that they are both (and respectively) ultimately unattainable as ends. Through the changing relationship between Kerouac's and Cassady's narrational counterparts and their search for "IT," along with the metamorphosis of Cassady throughout the *Road* novels, Kerouac underscores the significance of the *process* of authentication itself—the journey rather than its end—thus demonstrating that that which would be deemed most authentic is actually a *becoming* rather than being. The publication of the scroll manuscript contributes to this significance of an ongoing process of becoming by showing us as readers that there can be no authentic *On the Road*, only our perpetual movement between the different versions or "incarnations" of the narrative.

The context of Kerouac and Cassady's first meeting is quite telling in regard to the personal and symbolic significance the latter would take on in Kerouac's writing. Kerouac met Cassady in December of 1946, at the end of a yearlong period that saw his hospitalization for thrombophlebitis, the death of his father, Leo (on May 16, 1946), and the annulment of Kerouac's first marriage to Frankie Edith Parker on September 18. Four years Kerouac's junior, Cassady came to represent a reaffirmation of the life and vital youth whose inevitable ephemerality Kerouac wished to transcend, a way to challenge and rupture the bondage of Time over the individual. This haunting, suffocating sense of mortality and inevitable loss, which Kerouac would carry throughout his life, goes even further back, to the death, in 1926, of his nine-year-old brother, Gerard, when Kerouac was four. In Cassady, Kerouac also saw the brother whose death was a focal point of his devout Catholic upbringing, a connection reinforced by the fact that Cassady too was a Catholic. While referring to Cassady throughout the *Road* novels, as well as in their personal correspondence, as his "brother," Kerouac makes this connection far more explicit in the scroll manuscript: "My interest in Neal is the interest I might have had in my brother that died when I was five years old to be utterly straight about it. We have a lot of fun together and our lives are fuckt up and so there it stands." Right from the opening line of the scroll Kerouac foregrounds this sense of abandonment and loss, and also the fatherlessness he shared with Cassady, whose own father was an estranged derelict: "I first met Neal not long after my father died . . . I had just gotten over a serious illness that I won't bother to talk about except that it really had something to do with my father's death and my awful feeling that everything was dead." Cassady became a surrogate brother and father, a teacher and guide in Kerouac's search to reconnect with those he had lost—brother, father, wife, household—a way of staving off the ephemerality that brought about this sense of abandonment and ultimate elusiveness, and a way of transcending the guilt and burden of existing in their wake. "Life is not enough," Kerouac wrote in an August 1949 journal entry. What Kerouac sought was characterized by a tension between a subjective truth he found in origins—both within and without sociocultural institutions and temporal boundaries—and a sense of an objective reality which always kept such "authentic" truths at a distance, always absent, and, in that absence, romanticized and mythologized.

As both the scroll and the published version of *On the Road* attest, Cassady's absence becomes a presence through legend. This resonates with the sense of the authentic, which is established in absence, recognized more according to what it is not rather than what it is. Kerouac's close friend Hal Chase, who, like Cassady, was also originally from Denver, had shared with Kerouac the letters Cassady had sent him, telling Kerouac all he knew of the nebulous, fast-talking, car-jacking, streetwise womanizer, newly married and fresh out of the reformatory. Cassady was thus immediately established in Kerouac's mind as the consummate "outsider," an embodiment of uncompromising individuality, someone who appealed to Kerouac's own sense of sociocultural displacement. "Shit on the Russians, shit on the Americans, shit on them all. I'm going to live life my own 'lazy-no-good' way, *that's* what I'm going to do," Kerouac wrote in a journal entry of August 23, 1948, and Cassady would become a vehicle through which Kerouac could attempt to lead such an existence. In the same journal entry he first explained that his new novel, *On the Road,* would be about "two guys" who journey "in search of something they don't *really* find," the central thematic and structural motif that would remain constant throughout the novel's development, and one which would also come to characterize the relationship between Kerouac and Cassady, especially its depiction in Kerouac's prose.

Kerouac's composition of the scroll manuscript in April 1951 was coterminous with numerous works in existentialist literature. In *The Rebel* (1951), a book in which he argues that perpetual opposition is what brings about a reaffirmation of life in the midst of mass conformity, Albert Camus writes, "Every act of rebellion expresses a nostalgia for innocence and an appeal to the essence of being." Camus is best known for his novel *The Outsider* (1942). In this novel and in similar fiction the central focus for what is most often an "antihero" is the search for such an essence of being, for the authentic. In Cassady, Kerouac saw the potential for attaining such authenticity, an existence that was totally subjective and impulsive, outside the boundaries of the conservative social institutions and cultural norms— dominant at the time—above all, an existence that transcended the constrictions of objective immutable Time and its regimentation of experience and expression. "I want uninterrupted rapture," Kerouac writes in one of his *On the Road* workbooks, "Why should I compromise with anything else, or with the 'Bourgeois' calm of the backyard lawn." This fervent desire, however, provides the counterpoint to the calm he simultaneously sought in his personal relationships and in a more centered domestic existence as a household patriarch, an ideal picture splintered by that ephemerality he so wished to transcend.

In Kerouac's work, the search for the authentic is thus part of the dualism that marks his life and writing, a dualism between two distinct but nevertheless intertwined imperatives—domesticity and "kicks," tradition and progressiveness, nostalgia and possibility—an ambivalence on both a personal as well as a broader sociocultural level of significance. Kerouac's nostalgia was for an American past he romanticized and mythologized, the prewar America of the Depression, the westward expansion, and the Old West, which he imbued with "glee," "honesty," "spitelessness," and "wild selfbelieving individuality." This desire to reconnect with "old American whoopee" was at the same time intimately linked to his idyllic yet haunted youth in Lowell, Massachusetts. By locating the imperatives of individuality and innocence both in his own and America's past, the authenticity Kerouac sought pointed him outside the social and cultural mainstream, as well as indicating a displacement from his own historical time.

In the different versions of Kerouac's road narrative we see this sense of authenticity as something that is a presence only in its conspicuous absence, as something presupposed, and which only exists in its potentiality; as long as the ideal of authenticity remained intact, so too did the possibility of its realization. The quality of life which, for Kerouac, existed outside objective boundaries is incumbent in the socioculturally transgressive pursuit of authenticity, the search for the beckoning "pearl" handed to the traveler on the road, the promised "paradise" at the end of the journey: "the pearl was there, the pearl was there," as "Jack Kerouac"/Sal Paradise states, but always just out of reach. The attainability is all built on Jack/Sal's faith, and his movement driven by it, rather than any *knowledge* of its imminent realization. With the pursuit of the imponderable "IT" the only way to go is in a decentralized fashion, to go "every direction" and never be "hung up." However, we see that Jack/Sal is indeed hung up. "Neal Cassady"/Dean Moriarty's refrain of "We know time" is a call to spontaneity, to living totally subjectively in and for the moment. In so doing, he suspends the authority of Time over the individual: "*Now* is that time [emphasis added]," Neal/Dean echoes the Charlie Parker classic. This rupture of regimented time, however, is also a means through which Kerouac, via his narrational counterpart, expresses his desire to rupture the ephemerality of history—that of his own personal life and that of America's legendary past as it existed in his imagination.

Kerouac mediates the search for authenticity through his changing representations of Neal Cassady. Through him, he expresses the instability and restlessness of his own life, the ambivalences and dualism he struggled with. Neal/Dean always *moves*, oscillating between "worklife plans," marriage and family, on the one hand, and going "mad" and pursuing "IT" on the other. Jack/Sal, however, is less irreverent and uncompromising in such movements between these two dynamics, often finding this liminality a psychological and emotional impasse. His view along such an authenticating road is—like Kerouac's own view of postwar America and of Cassady himself—always Janus-like.

We see Kerouac's image of Cassady progress along an arc. Beginning in myth, legend, and ideal, Cassady becomes a reality through Kerouac's personal experience of him. However, as their relationship begins to break down, Kerouac retreats into myth and legend in his representation of Cassady. In this progression there is a simultaneous forward movement informed by a retrospective gaze, a recapping of losses and impossibilities. This dualism is exemplified in a section of the scroll manuscript where Jack is "staggering back east in search of [his] stone" in the wake of his disillusionment with his idealized West and with Neal—a section of the journey that is missing in the published novel but corresponds with Kerouac's "Rain and Rivers" journal as published in *Windblown World* (2005). Kerouac explains in the scroll the reason and purpose of such a searching journey:

All I wanted and all Neal wanted and all anybody wanted was some kind of penetration into the heart of things where, like in a womb, we could curl up and sleep the ecstatic sleep that Burroughs was experiencing with a good big mainline shot of M. and advertising executives were experiencing with twelve Scotch & Sodas in Stouffers before they made the drunkard's train to Westchester—but without hangovers. And I had many a romantic fancy then, and sighed at my star. The truth of the matter is, you die, all you do is die, and yet you live, yes you live, and that's no Harvard lie.

Here Kerouac acknowledges authenticity's unattainability and the loss of the ideal form it may take or upon which it is projected, while at the same time underscoring the inevitability, if not the necessity, of dealing with such a realization.

Kerouac first establishes Neal/Dean as the embodiment of the potentiality for authenticity when he locates him on the social and cultural margins through his criminality, as a "young jailkid shrouded in mystery." His impulsiveness and excitability, his openness and unselfconsciousness pointed to new possibilities of experience, not so much due to *who* Neal/Dean was as by what he symbolized—the yet to be known, the West yet to be reached by Jack/Sal.

The journey from New York to San Francisco in the hope of finding "IT" through the pursuit of "kicks" is the significant event in the relationship between Kerouac and Cassady's narrational counterparts. Highlighting the importance of the movement and fluidity of the search itself, aptly, they listen to Dexter Gordon's "The Hunt" before setting off: "We were all delighted, we all realized we were leaving confusion and nonsense behind and performing our one and noble function of the time, *move*." This trip, both in the scroll and published versions, is the point where Kerouac's vision of Cassady begins to unravel, when Neal/Dean—as the embodiment of and vehicle for a potential authenticity—is doubted: "I lost *faith* in Neal that year [emphasis added]," Jack/Sal states upon being immediately abandoned in San Francisco. Writing in his "Rain and Rivers" journal, Kerouac describes his disillusioning departure from San Francisco not in terms of rejection or failure but as catharsis, as having "escaped from the compulsiveness of Neal's *mystique* and *hashisch*"—a realization that the "real" Cassady and the significance Kerouac projects onto him are two distinct entities. Kerouac makes this imminent separation explicit in the scroll manuscript right at the advent of this pivotal journey: "You always expect some kind of magic at the end of the road. Strangely enough Neal and I were going to find it, *alone*, before we finished with it [emphasis added]."

Only after he is doubted does Neal/Dean become "great"—a greatness that separates him from the absolute zenith of physicality and vitality he represented as the commanding, rhapsodizing, mad mystic behind the wheel. It is when Neal/Dean is seen as *human* that Jack/Sal's ideals shift. The more he is reminded that Neal/Dean is not impervious to time, age, and mortality, the *higher*, distant, and less humanly accessible the representative image. By the third section of the narrative, Kerouac compares Neal/Dean with Rabelais' larger than life "Gargantua," burning across the land. At this juncture Neal/Dean becomes the "Holy Goof," a consequence of the romantic vision's unraveling—destitute, with bandaged thumb, never more part of the corporeal world, yet never more distinct from it in a humbled saintliness. By the end of the novel, a burned-out Neal/Dean "couldn't talk any more," fading away around the corner and slinking back across the country. It is here that Kerouac's vision of Cassady in the *Road* novels begins to take on a more complex, deeper form.

The presentation of Dean Moriarty as well as Kerouac's treatment of events in *On the Road* is a mythic, idealized retelling—the legend—but one which can only occur after the "facts" are distinguished from the romantic vision of Cassady. The scroll manuscript and the published novel frame the metamorphosis of Kerouac's response to Cassady, while in *Visions of Cody*, the events recounted and the people in them, like Cassady, are mostly separated from the mythological, visionary passages.

The Neal of the scroll is, in comparison with the Dean of the published version, less mythologized, more human. Neal's boyhood in Denver and his personal relationships—most notably those with

Allen Ginsberg, Louanne Henderson, and Justin W. Brierly—are explained in more explicit detail, providing a broader context and background for Neal. The material omitted from the published version raises the profile of other characters in the story, lessening Neal's centrality to the narrative action, especially that of Jack's journey. He is still, however, conspicuous in his absence, with Kerouac's compulsion early on in the scroll manuscript to "set the stage about Neal." The resultant demystification of the Cassady character—when read against the published version—in turn changes the nature of the Kerouac figure's relationship with the story's authentic antihero to one that is more distant, one more dependent on physical absence, giving a more realistic impression of the unraveling personal relationship depicted in the narrative.

While the role of Denver D. Doll in the published version is marginal, that of its real counterpart in the scroll, Justin W. Brierly, is major, especially given his real-life relationship with Cassady. A high-school English teacher, lawyer, Realtor, and entrepreneur, Brierly was a prominent and well-connected Denver personality during the time the scroll was written. He was also Cassady's one-time mentor and sponsor while Cassady was in the reformatory. Writing to Ed White on August 6, 1953, Kerouac refers to the scroll version of *On the Road* as "the novel in which Justin has big role, real big . . . I spose Cassady will sue." Brierly presents a stronger link to Cassady's *actual* past and private life, presenting them in greater depth. Neal's failure as Brierly's protégé, for instance, provides a context for the "war with social overtones," alienating him from his Denver friends, something never properly explained in the published novel. While Neal's status as an outsider is augmented by this displacement, it would not be until the published version that this outsider status would be fully mythologized.

The hindsight offered at various points throughout the scroll underscores a knowing acceptance of the failure of Jack's vision of Neal, and so illuminates Jack's problematic relationship with his own expectations and the ambivalent nature of his search for authenticity.

Just as Kerouac wrote *The Town and the City*, as he said, to "explain everything," in the scroll version we see the beginning of Kerouac's explanation of Cassady and his significance. After completing the scroll, Kerouac attempted to rewrite the same story, but instead composed an entirely different book, a novel he would eventually and aptly title "Visions of Neal."

In this new version of *On the Road*, which Kerouac began in May 1951, the mythologizing of Neal Cassady is increased while at the same time eventually becoming distinguished from Cassady himself. Corresponding with Cassady that October, Kerouac reassures him, "I am sending you these 3 now-typed-up-revised pages of my writing ROAD . . . to show you that 'Dean Pomeray' is *a vision* [emphasis added]." By April, 1952, Kerouac had completed yet another version of *On the Road* while staying with Cassady and his family in San Francisco. In a letter of May 18, 1952, Kerouac informs Ginsberg (also his literary agent at the time), "On the Road took its turn from conventional narrative survey of road trips etc. into a big multi-dimensional conscious and subconscious character invocation of Neal in his whirlwinds." He even tells Ginsberg, "If necessary change the title to Visions of Neal or something." Among numerous criticisms of this new version of *On the Road* in a June 11, 1952, letter to Kerouac, Ginsberg observes, "1. You still didn't cover Neal's history. 2. You covered your own reactions." Kerouac's new novel was certainly no biography but a cartography, both interior and exterior, of his *own* changing vision of Cassady and the personal significance he held for Kerouac; it was also a way for him to explore his own personal relationship with those significances. This new version of *On the Road* would eventually be published as *Visions of Cody*.

As Kerouac reconciles his complex responses to Cassady in *Visions of Cody*, we see the sense of authenticity shift from the existential to the representational. Kerouac examines Cassady as a phenomenon, in a prose style that is an exploratory multifaceted expanse. He problematizes the idea of the authentic in *Visions of Cody* by giving Cody Pomeray broader dimensions and thus a fuller representation. This offers more to the reader, more Blakean "minute particulars," than a symbolic significance would. One therefore feels that one's *experience* of this treatment is much more authentic because it is more sensorial, more evocative, even though it is the representation of Cassady furthest from the truth and closest to mythology and divinization. Cody is made to speak in various and distinct ways that deviate from Kerouac's consideration of the real-life Cassady and their unraveled personal relationship—ways which can thus be considered "inauthentic." Here, Cody becomes more a vehicle through which Kerouac could illustrate his own particular impression of the world. Now, however, rather than distinguishing Cassady from this world, Kerouac merges him into this broader vision, "the way consciousness *really* digs everything that happens" as Ginsberg would later say of Kerouac's "deep form." Kerouac now presents Cassady in the same way his polyvalent and panoramic sensorium acknowledges the world. Only after Kerouac examines in every possible detail and from every possible aspect his vision of Cassady and the romanticized landscapes and idealized projections that he symbolizes and of which he is part does Kerouac's statement that "Cody is the brother I lost" come to take on its full meaning. Kerouac understands that his romantic vision—of his own and America's past, and of authenticity—is ultimately unrealizable when focused on one particular person, place, or period. Cody is the vision and ideal whose elusiveness and loss Kerouac now accepts. He has to move through and unravel his vision of Cassady in order to relinquish it, to separate it from Cassady himself. "Cody is not dead," Kerouac writes. "He is made of the same flesh and bone as (of course) you and me." The Cassady figure is just another human being among innumerable others, extraordinary because they are *all* extraordinary, as is the world for Kerouac, now reborn and unfolding, and unfolded by him. Toward the end of *Visions of Cody* Kerouac writes, "But Cody isn't great because he is average . . . Cody can't possibly be average because I've never seen him before. I've never seen any of you before. I myself am a stranger to this world." To "accept loss forever," as Kerouac prescribes in "Belief & Technique for

Modern Prose," is to get it all down *now*, and thus immortalize the world and the people in it, before they pass with the inevitable ephemerality of time and mortality. At the conclusion of his "vertical metaphysical" examination of Cassady in *Visions of Cody*, Kerouac writes, "I not only accept loss forever, I am made of loss—I am made of Cody too."

Whether or not the Cassady in Kerouac's prose corresponds with the way Cassady *really* was is of lesser significance than the subjective truth Kerouac found in the vision of authenticity he eventually separated from Cassady, and from a sense of an imposed objective reality. In light of the textual nuances and contrasts that the scroll manuscript provides, what remains most significant is the acceptance of the loss of a romantic vision and its personal significance. Commenting on his father's death as fictionalized in *The Town and the City* Kerouac says, "George Martin is dead and gone. I don't even remember if Leo Kerouac was really completely like that. It was all in my head." Kerouac's *Road* novels mark just such a realization of the fallibility of an embodied vision of the authentic.

In the period before writing the scroll, as Kerouac was working toward a new prose style, what was key was the rejection of an objective factualism and a consequent receptiveness to a subjective impulsive truth that is immediate and, above all, true for the author himself: "People aren't interested in facts," writes Kerouac in a December 1949 journal entry, "but in ejaculations." What would, in this sense, be deemed authentic is how true Kerouac was to his own responses and experiences, both interior and exterior. Kerouac's *writing out* of his vision of the authentic was a way for him to find his own place within it—a vision now not projected only onto Cassady, but implicating him in it. This writing out illuminates a sense of authenticity in that actual process itself. What Kerouac saw in Cassady, as mutable as it was, is thus as authentic as what Kerouac saw in the world, and what he found in a more open and direct relationship with it.

Kerouac's *Road* novels form an expansive and inclusive textual terrain, and we as readers are directed across it by Kerouac's unfolding vision of Cassady. In such a movement we transgress the boundaries of what, in the modernist sense, would be considered a "true" or "classic" work of literature, one that is reductive and exclusive— self-contained, erudite, and impenetrable. This movement exemplifies what the literary critic Roland Barthes calls a "mutation" of the literary "work" into a discursive "text." The scroll manuscript, *Visions of Cody*, and *On the Road* are thus all interrelated but distinct "fragments," and it is our movement between them that, like the transgressive journey in search of an elusive authentic "IT," generates the significance of the text. The "authentic" *On the Road* is the reflected light passing between mirrors. Whether you consider the scroll manuscript an artifact or part of a discursive postmodern text, the three are dialogically bound, reflecting and illuminating one another. Like the Chicago bop musicians who, in the wake of George Shearing, keep blowing, striving to find new phrases, new explorations reflected and deflected off one another, "Something would come of it yet. There's always more, a little further—it never ends."

"The Straight Line Will Take You Only to Death"

The Scroll Manuscript and Contemporary Literary Theory

Joshua Kupetz

A tenured colleague in the history department at the small liberal-arts college where I first taught once asked, "Why do students still want to read Kerouac?" It was the fall of 2004, and the United States was at war against terror, a more nebulous adversary than either fascism or communism. I resisted the urge to reply, "You're the historian; you tell me," not simply because it was glib, which it was, but because that answer would have affirmed all the assumptions about Kerouac I had been trying to dispel in my teaching, those assumptions being that he mattered first as a personality and that what makes his texts worth reading are the ways their content intersects with cultural histories.

Read in the context of American cultural history, the scroll manuscript and *On the Road* reveal much about American social discourse of the postwar era, yet these texts must be considered literary structures before they are considered historical documents. As narratives, they are integral parts of a continuum of American prose fiction, liminal structures that in retrospect bridge the modern and the postmodern. Although any description of such a continuum should be understood as contingent and subjective—for no one objectively decides which texts matter in a tradition and which do not—the act of locating a literary text in a particular historical context can reveal its structures, processes, and ideological conventions. While the primary function of American literary criticism at the time Kerouac wrote the scroll manuscript was to locate a text's meaning, the application of contemporary theory more often attempts to understand *how*, not *what*, the text means.

The scroll manuscript and *On the Road* demonstrate Kerouac's anticipation of new developments in American narratology. A year after Kerouac composed the scroll manuscript, Carl Solomon, an editor at the publishing firm of A. A. Wyn and dedicatee of Allen Ginsberg's *Howl*, rejected Kerouac's newest draft of the novel, calling it "an incoherent mess." (The particular version that Solomon rejected would later be published as *Visions of Cody*.) In response, Kerouac wrote, "[James Joyce's] *Ulysses* which was considered difficult reading is now hailed as a classic and everyone understands it. [. . .] [Theodore Dreiser's] *Sister Carrie* sat for years in a publishing house because it was considered unprintable. By the same token, and in its time, I believe *On the Road* because its new vision roughs against the grain of established ideas is going to be considered unprintable for awhile to come." Kerouac was correct: *On the Road* was published by Viking in 1957 only after the scroll manuscript underwent a series of conventionalizing revisions, *Visions of Cody* was published posthumously in 1972, and more than fifty years would pass before the earliest complete draft of the novel, the scroll manuscript, would be published.

Many readers would quickly dismiss Kerouac's claim as hubris, yet the exchange between Solomon and Kerouac illustrates the growing schism that transformed American literary criticism in the twentieth century. In his rejection, Solomon does not contend that Kerouac's writing is inartistic, but instead he objects to the novel for its supposed lack of coherence and intelligibility. Solomon's opinion implies that a publishable novel should *cohere*, or demonstrate unity among its verbal structures, in order to communicate clearly its meaning. Kerouac rejects Solomon's judgment, thereby refuting his definition of a novel, contending that "the masses catch up to incomprehensible; incoherent finds its way to an intelligently typewritten page." Incomprehensibility, Kerouac suggests, is not a function of the text but of the reader's limited perception. Innovative narratives, he acknowledges, become comprehensible after their unfamiliar structures have been conventionalized over time.

Carl Solomon's position is consistent with New Critical discourse, the dominant school in American literary theory in the mid-twentieth century. Based upon interpretive strategies articulated in Cleanth Brooks and Robert Penn Warren's *Understanding Poetry* (1938), New Criticism locates meaning in the internal qualities of literary works, specifically the unity of their multiple verbal structures. As much as it values unity and convergence, New Criticism eschews authorial intent and historical context as bases for interpretation, although it allows that they might supplement understanding. New Critical criteria, like Solomon's argument, locate meaning inside a work that is interpreted by a reader who, like a prospector, extracts what is valuable from the unified structures and ignores the otherwise "meaningless" prose.

New Criticism was the forge within which Kerouac fashioned *The Town and the City* and the crucible from which he had to escape in order to write *On the Road*. As he struggled to clarify his ideas for *On the Road*, Kerouac understood that the post–World War II story he wanted to tell could not be fully realized through existing novelistic conventions. In response to this impediment, Kerouac writes in his *Road*-Log that he wants "a different structure as well as a different style in [*On the Road*], in contrast to T & C . . . Each chapter as a line of verse in the general epic poem, instead of each chapter as a broad-streamed prose statement in the general epic novel." By actively avoiding conventional narrative, Kerouac claims that his project would not result in a "novel," but in a new prose-narrative form that grafts two genres. To develop his poetics of prose narrative, he experimented with technique and plot, particularly in the scroll manuscript, surpassing the limitations of conventional narrative even as he helped define them.

Wolfgang Iser contends that artistic innovators always risk marginalization by readers who judge artists' works against an aesthetic standard that "art has in fact abandoned," and Kerouac's experiments are, in general, critically maligned. His willful disregard of convention, however, is not without precedent. For example, 150 years before Kerouac drafted *On the Road*, William Wordsworth acknowledged this critical anachronism in the preface to the 1800 edition of *Lyrical Ballads*. Wordsworth, who now represents the literary canon at its most conventional, admits, "an Author makes a formal engagement that he [or she] will gratify certain known habits of association." In defense of his nonconventional poetics, Wordsworth claims:

> at least [the reader] be spared any unpleasant feeling of disappointment, and that I myself may be protected from the most dishonorable accusation which can be brought against an Author, namely, that of an indolence which prevents him from endeavoring to ascertain what is his duty, and when his duty is ascertained, prevents him from performing it.

Wordsworth evokes this "duty" not to uphold it, but to excuse himself from it. While Kerouac does not include an apologetic preface with either the scroll manuscript or *On the Road* (he will write one, however, for *Visions of Cody*), his correspondence and work-journal entries establish a cogent argument for the changes he introduced into his prose narrative.

Kerouac abandoned the conventional techniques he had used when writing *The Town and the City* so that he might be "free as Joyce" when composing *On the Road*. While he continued to value form—"writing is good. Also careful about structures, and the Structure"—his concept of it was changing dramatically. Ultimately, his concept of form in the scroll manuscript loosely anticipates the tenets of structuralism, the first new theoretical school of the 1960s to decenter New Criticism. Kerouac writes that he was "not interested in The Novel" and that he wanted to be "free to wander from the laws of the 'novel' as laid down by [Jane] Austens & [Henry] Fieldings." Here, Kerouac suggests that the novel is an articulation of recognizable conventions, "laws," that will not help him tell the story that he wants to tell. By rejecting Austen, Fielding, and their imitators, Kerouac denies the

"European form" of the novel and affirms what he calls a new American prose form.

Kerouac was an avid reader of Whitman and his claims for a "modern prose [narrative] in America" echo Whitman's prophecy of an "infant genius of American poetic expression." Whitman's genius "lies sleeping far away, happily unrecognized and uninjur'd by the coteries, the art-writers, the talkers and critics of the saloons, or the lecturers in the colleges." According to Whitman, this new writer would use dialects native to the United States that originate in places Whitman describes as "Rude and course nursing-beds," although he concedes that "only from such beginnings and stocks, indigenous here, may haply arrive, be grafted, and sprout, in time, flowers of genuine American aroma, and fruits truly and fully our own." Kerouac adopts these dialects in the scroll manuscript and fully exploits them in his characterization of Dean Moriarty in On the Road, but his innovation required much more than the adoption of dialects. In his attempt to access "an area of greater spiritual pith," a metaphorical space inaccessible to him through conventional prose, Kerouac claimed he must use the "technical device" of epic poetry.

Kerouac's combination of poetic and prosaic elements invigorated his prose and made possible the most radical transformations of his narrative. In his Road-Log, Kerouac writes, "It appears I must have been learning in the past 8 months of work on . . . poetry. My prose is different, richer in texture." This textural richness, Kerouac claims, is necessary if On the Road is to be "a novel like poetry, or rather, a narrative poem, an epos in mosaic." Kerouac's use of "epos" is telling, for the term describes any unwritten narrative poem that falls outside the definition of the epic. In a journal entry from October 1949, Kerouac describes his own narrative project as a kind of epos: "I want [. . .] to bust out from the European narrative into the Mood Chapters of an American poetic 'sprawl'—if you can call careful chapters and careful prose a sprawl." While his narrative will "sprawl," Kerouac emphasizes the structural control he plans to exercise. As he explains in his letter to Solomon, his newly conceived narrative technique will engender new conventional elements, a "grammar" that will be comprehensible to future readers once it has been described.

The many false starts Kerouac made in the late 1940s and in 1950, coupled with the corresponding journal entries lamenting his difficulties, suggest that Kerouac struggled putting theory into practice when writing the early drafts of *On the Road*. Much like en plein air painters relied upon tubed paints and the French box easel to fully realize the potential of impressionism, Kerouac had to discover a new compositional technique in order to compose the structured sprawl that would become *On the Road*. The scroll allowed Kerouac to push his text beyond the parameters of conventional prose narrative by redefining the most basic limit of writing, the medium. During the earliest stages of drafting the narrative, Kerouac was an artist to whom the medium mattered. In the opening pages of his 1949 *Road*-Log, a spiral-bound financial ledger, Kerouac writes, "Something's wrong with my soul that I refuse to feel and grieve in this monetary notebook." Even seated at his writing desk with his typewriter before him, Kerouac still struggled to realize the voice for *On the Road*. Only when Kerouac had a medium that accommodated his vision could he exercise his new technique and unlock the sprawling, poetic narrative his story required.

In addition to working with technique, Kerouac experimented equally with concepts of plot. By foregrounding marginalized cultures and practices in America, Kerouac knew *On the Road* would likely be critically castigated. Kerouac's populist poetics, his belief that "an art which is not manifest to 'everybody,' is a dead art," was and remains unpopular among the literati. In this spirit he wrote, "How is a miserable hitch-hiking boy going to mean anything . . . to Howard Mumford Jones who wants everybody to be like him (middleclass, intellectual, 'responsible') before he will accept them." A writer, critic, and professor at Harvard University, Jones represented to Kerouac both the antithesis of his intended audience and the critical opinion he hoped to win. Early in the drafting process, Kerouac chose a hitchhiker as protagonist not to reflect his own experiences of the road—which at the time were few—but for aesthetic purposes. In his journal, Kerouac wonders, "Could Dostoevsky make his *lumpenproletariat* Raskolniks figure for such a guy [as Jones] today?—for such a literary class?—as anything but a bum." In this context, Kerouac's choice of subject in *On the Road* becomes a figure that signifies the "spiritual pith" he wants to evoke in the text.

In addition to his choice of subject, Kerouac reimagines the function of plot and bases his narrative on this new function. While conventional plots are episodic, unified, and suggestive of causal relationships between events, Kerouac's plot structure in the scroll manuscript is contingent and appropriates his concept of a "circle of despair." According to Kerouac, the circle of despair represents a belief that "the experience of life is a regular series of deflections" from one's goals. As one is deflected from a goal, Kerouac explains, he or she establishes a new goal from which he or she will inevitably also be deflected. To Kerouac, this series of deflections does not assume the pattern of a ship's tacking into the wind, always moving forward; instead, Kerouac illustrates these deflections as a series of right-hand turns that continue until one makes a complete circle that circumscribes an unknowable "thing" that is "central to . . . existence." Attempts to avoid the circle of despair will end in failure, Kerouac contends, for "the straight line will take you only to death."

Traces of the circle of despair appear throughout the scroll manuscript and *On the Road*. The protagonists' travels dominate much of the narrative of the scroll manuscript, and their attempt to find purpose in their perpetual movements and thwarted plans illustrates the circle of despair as a design element in the plot. Despite their frustrations, Kerouac and Cassady continue to encounter "IT," an ill-defined state of awareness that gives purpose to their divergent experiences. Before he experiences IT, Kerouac asks Cassady for a definition. Cassady replies, "'Now you're asking me im-pon-de-rables.'" Indefinable, IT exists paradoxically as a state of being inconceivable through thought or language, but knowable through experience.

The circle of despair also operates in seemingly marginal scenes in the scroll manuscript, its prevalence suggesting a pattern or "grammar" by which the contingent plot might be understood. When Kerouac plans his first trip west, he decides to hitchhike across the United States on Route 6, "one long red line . . . that led from the tip of Cape Cod clear to Ely Nevada and there dipped down to Los Angeles." Drenched below an ominous Bear Mountain, a stranded Kerouac encounters a driver who tells him "there's no traffic passes through" Route 6 and suggests an alternate route. Kerouac reflects on this, narrating, "I knew he was right. It was my dream that screwed up, the stupid hearthside idea that it would be wonderful to follow one great red line across America instead of trying various roads and routes." Kerouac's existential goal or unknown center, the eventual "pearl," remains the same, but he learns that his passage will be marked by divergences and that he will be frustrated in his efforts.

Kerouac's narratological advances in technique and plot combine to create texts that function as focal points for many of the problems that contemporary theory addresses. In addition to demonstrating Kerouac's (the author's) discontinuous, nonlinear plot, Kerouac's (the narrator's) moments of frustration at Bear Mountain can be read as a metaphor of the changes in late-twentieth century American literary theory. Just as New Criticism's clearly defined method of excavating meaning was displaced by structuralist and poststructuralist investigations into readers and reading and the disputation of "common sense" knowledge, among other questions, Kerouac's dilemma involves his shifting expectations of the road. One must remember the "stupid hearthside idea" that strands Kerouac comes from his straightforward interpretation of texts. In the scroll manuscript, Kerouac claims he has "been poring over maps of the U.S. in Ozone Park for months, even reading books about the pioneers and savouring names like Platte and Cimarron and so on," prior to choosing his route west. Kerouac is drawn to the linearity represented by Route 6 on the map and is seduced by the "wonderful" prospect of a direct passage to his destination. He expects these maps and dime-store novels to provide their meanings for him, so he bases his route on his superficial readings of them.

Kerouac's reading strategies fail him almost immediately, as do the conventional reader's. Kerouac is forced to discover a new, discursive mode of interpretation in order to move forward. As "thunderclaps . . . put the fear of God" in him below the storm-shrouded peaks, Kerouac represents the failure inherent in anticipating linearity and unity; the straight line of Route 6 threatens to "lead him only to death." Eager to proceed but deflected from his goal, Kerouac comes to understand that the method of his passage must be contingent, that progress is achievable only by "trying various roads and routes" instead of proceeding with predetermined expectations. Kerouac's readers find themselves equally stranded if they approach his mountain of unbroken text anticipating that it will offer an inherent meaning, if their expectations and interpretive strategies are based upon linearity and predetermined by novelistic conventions. However, if a reader approaches Kerouac's sprawling prose and allows the narrative to turn, to reverse, to be set back upon itself in a series of deflections, and accepts that the shifting horizon of signification is part of the experience of meaning, the reader can proceed and be "headed there at last."

As a series of deflections, Kerouac's prose narratives anticipate reader-oriented theories that establish the reader, not the text, as the site of meaning. However, contemporary theory cannot prove that meaning definitely occurs inside the reader, either, so a text's meaning is often considered an effect of the interaction between text and reader. Instead of functioning as works with meanings trapped inside hermetically sealed structures, Kerouac's narratives involve the reader in the process of discovering meaning by encountering unfamiliar structures.

Jorge Luis Borges wrote that a novel is an "axis of innumerable relationships," and the narrative developments in technique and plot in both the scroll manuscript and *On the Road* support this claim. As this new American prose narrative undermines conventions, the scroll manuscript and *On the Road* are subjects for the varied lenses of contemporary American literary analysis. A comprehensive survey of possible readings would fill volumes, if not shelves. However, a brief example of the ways deconstruction, a theoretical discourse that grew out of structuralism and that shares methods with many other poststructuralist schools (such as feminist theory and minority discourse, to name but a few), illuminates the scroll can demonstrate the range of possible readings that were marginalized by previous discourses.

At its most simple, deconstruction seeks to destabilize seemingly natural or inherent hierarchies or oppositions in a literary text. A deconstructive reading identifies oppositions within written discourse not to discredit the argument or prove logical invalidity, but to reinscribe the meaning of the opposition by disrupting what was formerly considered "given" knowledge. Deconstruction is an especially useful tool when analyzing the scroll manuscript or *On the Road* for both texts contain apparently contradictory claims that have been seen as inconsistent writing instead of opportunities for analysis.

When Sal first arrives at Old Bull Lee's home in *On the Road*, for example, his inability to perceive the fire Jane Lee sees is often read as an example of his naïveté or unreliability. By examining the passage in the scroll manuscript, which is reproduced nearly verbatim in the novel, the reader encounters a series of shifting oppositions that simultaneously undermine and support one another. When Kerouac says, "'I don't see anything,'" Joan replies, "'Same old Kerouac.'" Joan's condemnation of Kerouac for his inability to observe suggests that he is incapable of seeing empirical reality, that he does not comprehend the material world before him. However, Joan relies upon her sense of hearing to perceive the scene, saying, "I heard sirens that way," thereby undermining her critique of Kerouac's visual perception. Moreover, Joan herself is hallucinating—Kerouac continues, "She was still looking for her fire; in those days she ate three tubes of benzedrine paper a day." By using the possessive "her," Kerouac suggests that perception of the fire is possible only to Joan, that it in some way "belongs" to her. By coordinating that clause with the next which affirms her drug use, Kerouac suggests a correlation between "her fire" and her Benzedrine consumption, implying that her "fire" is a figment of her Benzedrine-fueled imagination. Therefore, in this scene, the initial critique of perception is reversed and unadulterated, rational perception is privileged over altered, irrational perception. However, this binary opposition is soon reversed, and the text argues that perception is not only rational but also intuitive.

When Kerouac attends the horse races in Graetna with Burroughs, Kerouac intuits the winner, a development that privileges nonliteral, subjective perception over literal, objective perception. Kerouac looks at the racing form, a report that encapsulates empirical data relevant to handicapping horse races, and is entranced by a name, not a statistic, that reminds him of his father: Big Pop. While Burroughs bets on Ebony Corsair, Big Pop wins and pays 50 to 1. Burroughs, who bets based upon an evaluation of racing-form data, exclaims, "You had a vision, boy, a VISION. Only damn fools pay no attention to visions," thus validating Kerouac's intuitive perception. By juxtaposing these scenes, Kerouac's reinscription of the normative, privileged opposition of the rational over the irrational is revealed: Rationality and irrationality become coequal modes, parts of the whole that is perception entire.

In the scroll manuscript, Kerouac establishes another argument dependent upon both sides of its presumptive opposition when he foregrounds the protagonists' attempt to overcome the constrictions of time. Cassady's techniques for operating outside of time, however, rely upon his strict adherence to it. In representing Cassady's timetables and ubiquitous schedules, Kerouac illustrates what Michel Foucault calls the "exhaustive use" of time, a technique that subjugates the actor to time while promising emancipation from it. The exhaustive use of time requires its meticulous subdivision, promising a "theoretically ever-growing use of time" by "extracting, from time, ever more available moments," effectively stopping it. Throughout the novel Cassady arranges appointments with precise beginning and ending times, compelling his friends and lovers to subjugate themselves to his timetable while attempting to subdivide his own time in order to make more time available, to use effectively all the time he has.

Although Allen Ginsberg frames Cassady's frantic scheduling in Denver as a device to hide his infidelity from both Louanne and Carolyn, Cassady's regimentation is a technique by which he attempts to do "everything at the same time." Kerouac's arrival in Denver adds another variable to Cassady's timetable, and in order for Cassady to make room for Kerouac in his own schedule, Cassady subdivides time further. Within minutes of seeing Kerouac, Cassady tells Carolyn:

> "It is now" (looking at his watch) "exactly one-fourteen---I shall be back at exactly THREE fourteen, for our hour of reverie together . . . so now in this exact minute I must dress, put on my pants, go back to life . . . that is to outside life, streets and whatnot, as we agreed, it is now one-FIFTEEN and time's running, running."

As his timetables suggest, Cassady's freedom from time is dependent upon his strict submission to it. Thus, by deconstructing the protagonists' flight from time and examining their techniques, time's inescapability and pervasiveness are revealed, thereby turning Neal's gift of his wristwatch to the Mexican girl on the roadside—presumably an act that signifies Cassady's defeat of time—into an act of colonization and subjugation by time.

Despite its relevance to issues raised by contemporary literary theory, the publication of the scroll manuscript reveals an immanent danger in the text. As it alters the discourse surrounding *On the Road*, ostensibly to set the record straight about the novel as a "serious" text and Kerouac as a "serious" author, the scroll manuscript's presumed closer fidelity to Kerouac's own lived experiences may reinforce many assumptions that when articulated have made *On the Road* a famous novel, not a literary one, and Kerouac an infamous author, not a serious one. The possibility of such a seemingly opposite outcome does not, however, render the publication of the scroll manuscript a critical error in judgment.

The publication of the scroll manuscript creates a necessary para-
dox that problematizes the very notion of meaning in a text and
undermines a reader's ability to confidently differentiate between fact
and fiction. As the scroll manuscript is interpreted, correctly or incor-
rectly, as a more authentic version of *On the Road*, the novel's
fictionality and Kerouac's function as author become more apparent
through comparative reading. Moreover, as the scroll manuscript
destabilizes the presumed veracity of *On the Road*—a novel long read
as a nonfictional hybrid, equal parts diary entry and autobiography—
that instability of interpretation is transferred self-reflexively to the
scroll manuscript itself. The scroll discredits its own veracity, estab-
lishing itself as a fictional prose narrative.

While Kerouac reorganizes social conventions in the text, giving
prominence to cultures and practices marginalized elsewhere in the
popular fiction of his day, he also restructures literary conventions
and allusions in a way that has not yet been entirely co-opted by contemporary narrative. Thus, *On the Road* and especially the scroll
manuscript continue to read like avant-garde texts a half century after
their composition. The publication of the scroll manuscript opens
new possibilities of interpretation for both texts. Those new possibilities foreground Kerouac's narratological advances as they highlight
the literary craft in *On the Road*, rendering finally *On the Road* as a
novel, albeit a hybrid form that bridges the "typical 'novel' arrange-
ment of experience" and the "'fibrous' . . . world, with its hint of
organic unity" of postmodernism, and the scroll manuscript as "the
first or one of the first modern prose books in America."

Fifty years after the publication of *On the Road*, readers of the scroll
manuscript might experience a disruption of the dominant hierarchy
and view the mythical Kerouac as subordinate to the writer Kerouac,
who in early 1951 developed a new form of American prose narrative
and wrote, "A lot of people say I don't know what I'm doing, but of
course, I do. Burroughs & Allen said I didn't know what I was doing
in the years of Town & City; now they know I did." Now, so do we.

SUGGESTED FURTHER READING

Beaulieu, Victor-Lévy. *Jack Kerouac: A Chicken Essay*. Stella Fischman, Toronto: The Coach House Press, 1975.

Belgrad, Daniel. *The Culture of Spontaneity: Improvisation and the Arts in Postwar America*. Chicago: University of Chicago Press, 1998.

Burroughs, William S., "Remembering Jack Kerouac," in *The Adding Machine: Collected Essays*. London: John Calder, 1985.

Cassady, Carolyn. *Off the Road: Twenty Years with Cassady, Kerouac and Ginsberg*. London: Black Spring Press, 1990.

Cassady, Neal. *Collected Letters, 1944-1967*. Dave Moore, ed. New York: Penguin, 2004.

———.*The First Third & Other Writings*. San Francisco: City Lights, 1971; 1981.

——— and Allen Ginsberg. *As Ever: The Collected Correspondence of Allen Ginsberg and Neal Cassady*. Barry Gifford, ed. Berkeley, CA: Creative Arts Book Co., 1977.

Charters, Ann. *Kerouac: A Biography*. New York: St. Martin's Press, 1973, 1987.

Clark, Tom. *Jack Kerouac: A Biography*. New York: Paragon House, 1990.

Coolidge, Clark, "Kerouac," in *Disembodied Poetics: Annals of the Jack Kerouac School*, Anne Waldman and Andrew Schelling, eds.

———. *Now It's Jazz: Writings on Kerouac & the Sounds*. Albuquerque: Living Batch Press, 1999.

Douglas, Ann, "Telepathic Shock and Meaning Excitement; Kerouac's Poetics of Intimacy," in *The Beat Generation: Critical Essays*, Kostas Myrsiades, ed.

Giamo, Ben. *Kerouac, the Word and the Way: Prose Artist as Spiritual Quester*. Carbondale, IL: Southern Illinois University Press, 2000.

Gifford, Barry, and Lawrence Lee. *Jack's Book: An Oral Biography of Jack Kerouac*. New York: Thunder's Mouth Press, 1978, 1994.

Ginsberg, Allen, "The Great Rememberer," "Kerouac's Ethic," in *Deliberate Prose: Selected Essays 1952-1995*. Bill Morgan, ed. New York: HarperCollins, 2000.

Gussow, Adam, "Bohemia Revisited: Malcolm Cowley, Jack Kerouac, and *On the Road*," *Georgia Review*, Summer, 1984, vol. XXXVIII, no. 2.

Holmes, John Clellon. *Go*. New York: Thunder's Mouth Press, 1952, 1988.

———, "The Great Rememberer," "Perpetual Visitor," "Gone in October," in *Representative Men: The Biographical Essays*. Fayetteville, AK: University of Arkansas Press, 1988.

Hunt, Tim. *Kerouac's Crooked Road: Development of a Fiction*. Berkeley, CA: University of California Press, 1981, 1996.

Johnson, Joyce. *Minor Characters: A Beat Memoir*. New York: Houghton Mifflin, 1983.

Johnson, Ronna C., "'You're Putting Me On': Jack Kerouac and the Postmodern Emergence," in *The Beat Generation: Critical Essays*, Kostas Myrsiades, ed.

Kerouac, Jack. *Atop an Underwood: Early Stories and Other Writings*. Paul Marion, ed. New York: Viking, 1999.

———. *Good Blonde & Others*. Donald Allen, ed. San Francisco: Grey Fox Press, 1993.

———. *On the Road*. New York: Viking, 1957.

———. *Pic*. New York: Grove Press, 1971.

———. *The Portable Jack Kerouac*. Ann Charters, ed. New York: Viking, 1995.

———. *Selected Letters 2 vols*. Ann Charters, ed. New York: Viking, 1995, 1999.

———. *The Town and the City*. New York: Harcourt Brace, 1950.

———. *Visions of Cody*. New York: McGraw-Hill, 1972.

———. *Windblown World: The Journals of Jack Kerouac 1947-1954*. Douglas Brinkley, ed. New York: Viking, 2004, 2006.

Lardas, John. *The Bop Apocalypse: The Religious Visions of Kerouac, Ginsberg and Burroughs*. Urbana, IL: University of Illinois Press, 2001.

Maher, Paul, ed. *Empty Phantoms: Interviews and Encounters with Jack Kerouac*. New York: Thunder's Mouth Press, 2005.

Maher, Paul. *Kerouac: The Definitive Biography*. Lanham: Taylor Trade Publishing, 2004.

Myrsiades, Kostas, ed., *The Beat Generation: Critical Essays*. New York: Peter Lang, 2002.

Skerl, Jennie, ed., *Reconstructing the Beats*. New York: Palgrave Macmillan, 2004.

Turner, Steve. *Angelheaded Hipster: A Life of Jack Kerouac*. London: Bloomsbury, 1996.

Waldman, Anne, and Andrew Schelling, eds., *Disembodied Poetics: Annals of the Jack Kerouac School*. Albuquerque, NM: University of New Mexico Press, 1994.

Weinreich, Regina. *The Spontaneous Poetics of Jack Kerouac*. Carbondale, IL: Southern Illinois University Press, 1987.

ACKNOWLEDGMENTS

First and largest thanks go to John Sampas for inviting us to undertake this project and for his steadfast faith and support. We would also like to thank Joyce Johnson, Ronna C. Johnson, Sterling Lord, David Orr, Dawn Ward, and John Shen-Sampas for their help and kindness. Special thanks go to our editor, Paul Slovak, for his enthusiasm for the project, for his clear-sighted wisdom, and for having all the answers. Many thanks also to Isaac Gewirtz, curator of the Berg Collection at the New York Public Library, for his graciousness and insight, and to his colleagues Stephen Crook, Declan Kiely, and Philip Milito. For their many kindnesses we would also like to thank David Amram and Audrey Sprenger. Thanks to Hilary Holladay, director of the Jack and Stella Kerouac School of American Studies at UMass Lowell, and to Melissa Pennell, chair of the English Department at UMass Lowell.

Howard Cunnell would like to acknowledge the assistance of the British Association for American Studies for granting me a Founders' Award to travel to New York in the spring of 2006. Thanks to Alan Stepney, Matthew Loukes, Jim MacAirt, and everyone at Karma Divers for putting the light on in my house. Thanks to Jackie and Donald and to my family: my mum Gillian, my brother Mark, still on the road after twenty years, and my inspirational and beautiful daughters Jesse, Lily, and Daisy. Special thanks go to Jeremy Cole and Frank and Rosemary Andoh for keeping me off the construction site this winter. Most important, I'd like to thank my wife, Adjoa. Like everything else, this is for her.

Penny Vlagopoulos would like to thank Ann Douglas for her expert advice and eminent Beat wisdom. Special thanks to Rachel Adams, Robert O'Meally, and Maura Spiegel for their invaluable teaching and inspiration, and to Baz Dreisinger, Mike Johnson, and Nicole Rizzuto for their assistance and encouragement. Finally, I would like to express my gratitude to my parents, Marika and Triphon, and my brother Pete for their endless support.

George Mouratidis would like to thank Kris Hemensley at Collected Works Bookshop for his expertise and passion, Gemma Blackwood for her Minervan presence throughout this project, and Garry Kinnane and Peter Otto for their illumination and encouragement. I would also like to thank my parents, Chris and Georgina, my brother John, Chris Ioannou, and Lucy Van for their constant support and understanding. Above all, a special thanks to my colleagues and friends Howard Cunnell, Joshua Kupetz, and Penny Vlagopoulos for their invaluable support, assistance, and inspiration.

Joshua Kupetz would like to thank Dan Terkla and colleagues Carol Ann Johnston, Wendy Moffat, and Robert Winston for their encouragement in teaching Kerouac in an "age of frivolous science." I would also like to thank Michele Fleming, my mother, Tabatha Griffin, my sister, and Ty Dellinger for their unending faith. Without the support of Shana Ageloff-Kupetz, my wife, I would never have known how to finish this project, in particular, or where to begin, in general.

NOTE ON THE TEXT

The scroll manuscript has been edited with the intention of presenting a text that is as close as possible to the one Kerouac produced between April 2 and April 22, 1951.

The scroll is neatly typed and there are comparatively few mistakes for a manuscript of this length, let alone one written at the speed Kerouac was working at. Kerouac added handwritten corrections and revisions to the text as notes toward a revised draft. In a letter written to Neal Cassady on May 22, 1951, Kerouac writes, "Of course since Apr. 22 I've been typing and revising. Thirty days on that." While it is not certain that Kerouac is referring here to the revisions he made *on* the scroll, and while Kerouac may have begun correcting the novel at any time, what is certain is that the corrections were added to a text he had typed first. I have stripped away these corrections and revisions and restored the lined-through typewritten text except in those places where the handwritten addition is the obvious missing word, most often a connective, in a typewritten sentence. I have not represented lines of text xxxxxx'd out by Kerouac. Dots (...) and dashes (---) are as they appear in the manuscript. Sometimes Kerouac uses four or two dots or dashes and this is shown.

I have corrected Kerouac's spelling for comprehension purposes only. Throughout the scroll, Kerouac uses many abbreviations and compound words. I have left the abbreviations intact to convey something of the pace at which Kerouac was typing. For the same reason and because these words are part of the playful music of Kerouac's prose, I have corrected only those compound words that appear accidental. Contrary to myth the scroll is for the most part conventionally punctuated. Uncorrected exceptions are Kerouac's habit of leaving questions without a question mark and his absenting punctuation marks separating speaker from dialogue in passages of recorded speech.

Nearly forty years ago Sterling Lord reported to Kerouac that the manuscript seemed "brittle," and there are a few places where the paper is torn. As might be expected these tears occur at the beginning of the text where the outside skin and first layers of the scroll are exposed and vulnerable. Most often the missing word or letter is obvious. In those very few instances where this is not the case, I have consulted Kerouac's subsequent drafts and the published text.

And because it so beautifully suggests the sound of a car misfiring before starting up for a long journey, I have left uncorrected the manuscript's opening line.

Howard Cunnell
Brixton, London, 2007

Dedicated to the memory of
Neal Cassady and Allen Ginsberg

Camerado, I give you my hand!
I give you my love more precious than money,
I give you myself before preaching or law;
Will you give me yourself? will you come travel with me?
Shall we stick to each other as long as we live?

—Walt Whitman

ON THE ROAD

The Original Scroll

I first met met Neal not long after my father died...I had just gotten over a serious illness that I won't bother to talk about except that it really had something to do with my father's death and my awful feeling that everything was dead. With the coming of Neal there really began for me that part of my life that you could call my life on the road. Prior to that I'd always dreamed of going west, seeing the country, always vaguely planning and never specifically taking off and so on. Neal is the perfect guy for the road because he actually was born on the road, when his parents were passing through Salt Lake City in 1926, in a jaloppy, on their way to Los Angeles. First reports of Neal came to me through Hal Chase, who'd shown me a few letters from him written in a Colorado reform school. I was tremendously interested in these letters because they so naively and sweetly asked for Hal to teach him all about Nietzsche and all the wonderful intellectual things that Hal was so justly famous for. At one point Allen Ginsberg and I talked about these letters and wondered if we would ever meet the strange Neal Cassady. This is all far back, when Neal was not the way he is today, when he was a young jailkid shrouded in mystery. Then news came that Neal was out of reform school and was coming to New York for the first time; also there was talk that he had just married a 16 year old girl called Louanne. One day I was hanging around the Columbia campus and Hal and Ed White told me Neal had just arrived and was living in a guy called Bob Malkin's coldwater pad in East Harlem, the Spanish Harlem. Neal had arrived the night before, the first time in NY, with his beautiful little sharp chick Louanne; they got off the Greyhound bus at 50 St. and cut around the corner looking for a place to eat and went right in Hector's, and since then Hector's cafeteria has always been a big symbol of NY for Neal. They spent money on beautiful big glazed cakes and creampuffs. All this time Neal was telling Louanne things like this, "Now darling here we are in Ny and although I haven't quite told you everything that I was thinking about when we crossed Missouri and especially at the point when we passed the Bonneville reformatory which reminded me of my jail problem it is absolutely necessary now to postpone all those leftover things concerning our personal lovethings and at once begin thinking of specific worklife plans..." and so on in the way that he had in his early days. I went to the coldwater flat with the boys and Neal came to the door in his shorts. Louanne was jumping off quickly from the bed; apparently he was fucking with her. He always was doing so. This other guy who owned the place Bob Malkin was there but Neal had apparently dispatched him to the kitchen, probably to make coffee while he proceeded with his loveproblems....for to him sex was the one and only holy and important thing in life, although he had to sweat and curse to make a living, and so on. My first impression of Neal was of a young Gene Autry---trim, thin-hipped, blue eyes, with a real Oklahoma accent. In fact he'd just been working on a ranch, Ed Uhl's in Sterling Colo. before marrying L. and coming East. Louanne was a pretty, sweet little thing, but awfully dumb and capable of doing horrible things, as she proved a while later. I only mention this first meeting of Neal because of what he did. That night we all drank beer and I got drunk and blah-blahed somewhat, slept on the other couch, and in the morning, while we sat around dumbly smoking butts from ashtrays in the gray light of a gloomy day Neal got up nervously, paced around thinking, and decided the thing to do was have Louanne making breakfast and sweeping the floor. Then I went away. That was all I knew of Neal at the outset. During the following week however he confided in Hal Chase that he absolutely had to learn how to write from him; Hal said I was a writer and he should come to me for advice. Meanwhile Neal had gotten a job in a parking lot, had a fight with Louanne in their Hoboken apartment God knows why they went there and she was so mad and so vindictive down deep that she reported him to the police, some false trumped up hysterical crazy charge, and Neal had to lam from Hoboken. So he had no place to live. Neal came right out to Ozone Park where I was living with my mother, and one night while I was working on my book or my painting or whatever you want to call it there was a knock on the door and there was Neal, bowing, shuffling obsequiously in the dark of the hall, and saying "Hel-lo, you remember me, Neal Cassady? I've come to ask you to show me how to write." "And where's Louanne?" I asked, and Neal said she'd apparently whored a few dollars together or something of that nature and gone back to Denver... "the whore!" So we went out to have a few beers because we couldn't talk like we wanted to in front of my mother, who sat in the livingroom reading her paper. She took one look at Neal and decided from the very beginning that he was a madman. She never dreamed she too'd be driving across the mad American night with him more than once. In the bar I told Neal, "For krissakes man I know very well you didn't come to me only to want to become a writer and after all what do I really know about it except you've got to stick to it with the energy of a benny addict," and he said, "Yes of course, I know exactly what you mean and in fact those problems have occurred to me but the thing that I want is the realization of those factors that should one depend on Schopenhauer's dichotomy for any inwardly realized..." and on and on in that way, things I understood not a bit and he himself didn't, and what I mean is, in those days he really didn't know what he was talking about, that is to say, he was a young jailkid all hung up on the wonderful possibilities of becoming a real intellectual and he liked to talk in the tone and using the words but in a jumbled way that he had heard "real intellectuals" talk altho mind you he wasn't so naive as that in all other things, and it took him just a few months with Leon Levinsky to become completely in there with all the terms and the jargon and the style of intellectuality. Nonetheless I loved him for his madness and we got drunk together in the Linden bar behind my house and I agreed that he could stay at my house till he found a job and we furthermore agreed to go out west sometime. That was the winter of 1947. Shortly after meeting Neal I began writing or painting my huge Town and City, and I was about four chapters on when one night, when Neal ate supper at my house, and he already had a new parkinglot job in New York, the hotel NYorker lot on 34 st., he leaned over my shoulder as I typed rapidly away and said "Come on man, those girls won't wait, make it fast," and I said "Hold on just a minute, I'll be right with you soon as I finish this chapter," and I did and it was one of the best chapters in the whole book. Then I dressed and off we flew to NY to meet some girls. As you know to go from Ozone Park to New York takes an hour by elevated and subway, and as we rode in the El over the rooftops of Brooklyn we leaned on each other with fingers waving and yelled and talked excitedly and I was beginning to get the bug like Neal. In all, what Neal was, simply, was tremendously excited with life, and though he was a con-man he was only conning because he wanted so much to live and also to get involved with people that would otherwise pay no attention to him. He was conning me, so-called, and I knew it, and he knew I knew (this has been the basis of our relation) but I didn't care and we got along fine. I began to learn from him as much as he probably learned from me. As far as my work was concerned he said, "Go ahead, every-thing you do is great." We went to New York, I forget what the situation was, two girls---there were no girls there, they were sup-posed to meet him or some such thing and they weren't there. We went to his parkinglot where he had a few things to do---change his clothes in the shack in back and spruce up a bit in front of a cracked shack mirror and so on, and then we took off. And that was the night Neal met Leon Levinsky. A tremendous thing happened when Neal met Leon Levinsky...I mean of course Allen Ginsberg. Two keen minds that they are they took to each other at the drop of a hat. Two piercing eyes glanced into two piercing eyes...the holy con-man and the great sorrowful poetic con-man that is Allen Ginsberg. From that moment on I saw very little of Neal and I was a little sorry too...Their energies met head-on. I was a lout compared; I couldn't keep up with them. The whole mad swirl of everything that was to come then began which would mix up all my friends and all I had left of my fam-ily in a big dust cloud over the American night---they talked of Burroughs, Hunkey, Vicki, ...Burroughs in Texas, Hunkey on Riker's Island, Vicki hung up with Norman Schnall at the time...and Neal told Allen of people in the west like Jim Holmes the hunchbacked poolhall rotation shark and cardplayer and queer saint...he told him

of Bill Tomson, Al Hinkle, his boyhood buddies, his street buddies...
they rushed down the street together digging everything in the early
way they had which has later now become so much sadder and per-
ceptive.. but then they danced down the street like dingledodies and
I shambled after as usual as I've been doing all my life after people
that interest me, because the only people that interest me are the mad
ones, the ones who are mad to live, mad to talk, desirous of everything at the same time, the ones that never yawn or say a commonplace
thing.. but burn, burn, burn like roman candles across the night. Allen
was queer in those days, experimenting with himself to the hilt, and
Neal saw that, and a former boyhood hustler himself in the Denver
night, and wanting dearly to learn how to write poetry like Allen, the
first thing you know he was attacking Allen with a great amorous soul
such as only a conman can have. I was in the same room, I heard them
across the darkness and I mused and said to myself "Hmm, now
something's started, but I don't want anything to do with it." So I
didn't see them for about two weeks during which time they cemented
their relationship to mad proportions. Then came the great time of
traveling, Spring, and everybody in the scattered gang was getting
ready to take one trip or another. I was busily at work on my novel
and when I came to the halfway mark, after a trip down South with
my mother to visit my sister, I got ready to travel west for the very
first time. Neal had already left. Allen and I saw him off at the 34th
street Greyhound station. Upstairs they have a place where you can
make pictures for a quarter. Allen took off his glasses and looked sinister. Neal made a profile shot and looked coyly around. I took a
straight picture that made me look, as Lucien said, like a 30 year old
Italian who'd kill anybody who said anything against his mother. This
picture Allen and Neal neatly cut down the middle with a razor and
saved a half each in their wallets. I saw those halves later on. Neal
was wearing a real western business suit for his big trip back to Denver; he'd finished his first fling in New York. I say fling but he only
worked like a dog in parkinglots, the most fantastic parkinglot attendant in the world, he can back a car forty miles an hour into a tight

squeeze and stop on a dime at the brickwall, and jump out, snake his way out of close fenders, leap into another car, circle it fifty miles an hour in a narrow space, shift, and back again into a tight spot with a few inches each side and come to a bouncing stop the same moment he's jamming in the emergency brake; then run clear to the ticket shack like a track star, hand a ticket, leap into a newly arrived car before the owner is hardly out, leap literally under him as he steps out, start the car with the door flapping and roar off to the next available parking spot: working like that without pause eight hours a night, evening rush hours and after theater rush hours, in greasy wino pants with a frayed furlined jacket and beat shoes that flap. Now he'd bought a new suit to go back home in; blue with pencil stripes, vest and all, with a watch and watch chain, and a portable typewriter with which he was going to start writing in a Denver roominghouse as soon as he got a job there. We had a farewell meal of franks and beans in a 7th avenue Riker's and then Neal got on the bus that said Chicago on it and roared off into the night. I promised myself to go the same way when Spring really bloomed and opened up the land. There went our wrangler. And this was really the way that my whole road experience began and the things that were to come are too fantastic not to tell. I've only spoken of Neal in a preliminary way because I didn't know any more than this about him then. His relation with Allen I'm not in on and as it turned out later, Neal got tired of that, specifically of queerness and reverted to his natural ways, but that's no matter. In the month of July, 1947, having finished a good half of my novel and having saved about fifty dollars from old veteran benefits I got ready to go to the West Coast. My friend Henri Cru had written me a letter from San Francisco saying I should come out there and ship out with him on an around the world liner. He swore he could get me into the engine room. I wrote back and said I'd be satisfied with any old freighter so long as I could take a few long Pacific trips and come back with enough money to support myself in my mother's house while I finished my book. He said he had a shack in Marin City and I would have all the time in the world to write there while we went through the rigmarole of getting a ship. He was living with a girl called Diane, he said she was a marvellous cook and everything would jump. Henri was an old prep school friend, a Frenchman brought up in Paris and France and a really mad guy---I never knew how mad and so mad at this time. So he expected me to arrive in ten days. I wrote and confirmed this....in innocence of how much I'd get involved on the road. My mother was all in accord with my trip to the west, she said it would do me good, I'd been working so hard all winter and staying in too much; she even didn't say too much when I told her I'd have to hitch hike some, ordinarily it frightened her, she thought this would do me good. All she wanted was for me to come back in one piece. So leaving my big half-manuscript sitting on top of my desk, and folding back my comfortable home sheets for the last time one morning, I left with my canvas bag in which a few fundamental things were packed, left a note to my mother, who was at work, and took off for the Pacific Ocean like a veritable Ishmael with fifty dollars in my pocket. What a hang up I got into at once! As I look back on it it's incredible that I could have been so damned dumb. I'd been poring over maps of the U. S. in Ozone Park for months, even reading books about the pioneers and savoring names like Platte and Cimarron and so on, and on the roadmap was one long red line called Route Six that led from the tip of Cape Cod clear to Ely Nevada and there dipped down to Los Angeles. "I'll just stay on six all the way to Ely," I said to myself and confidently started. To get to six I had to go up to Bear Mtn. New York. Filled with dreams of what I'd do in Chicago, in Denver, and then finally in San Fran, I took the 7th avenue subway to the end of the line at 242nd street, right near Horace Mann the prep school where I had actually met Henri Cru who I was going to see, and there took a trolley into Yonkers; downtown Yonkers I transferred on an outgoing trolley and went to the city limits on the east bank of the Hudson river. If you drop a rose in the Hudson river at its mysterious mouth up near Saratoga think of all the places it journeys by as it goes out to sea forever.. think of that wonderful Hudson valley. I started hitching up the thing. Five scattered shot rides took me to the desired Bear Mtn. bridge where Route 6 arched in from New England. I had visions of it, I never dreamed it would look like it did. In the first place it began to rain in torrents when I was left off there. It was mountainous. Six came from the wilderness, wound around a traffic circle (after crossing the bridge that is) and disappeared again into the wilderness. Not only was there no traffic but the rain came down in buckets and I had no shelter. I had to run under some pines to take cover; this did no good; I began crying and swearing and socking myself on the head for being such a damn fool. I was forty miles North of New York, all the way up I'd been worried about the fact that on this, my big opening day, I was only moving north instead of the desired, the so-longed for west. Now I was stuck on my northernmost hangup. I ran a quarter mile to an abandoned cute English style filling station and stood under the dripping eaves. High up over my head the great hairy Bear Mtn. sent down thunderclaps that put the fear of God in me. All I could see were smoky trees and dismal wilderness rising to the skies. "What the hell am I doing up here?" I cursed I cried for Chicago… "Even now they're all having a big time, they're doing things, I'm not there, when will I get there!" and so on….Finally a car stopped at the empty filling station, the man and the two women in it wanted to study a map. I stepped right up and gestured in the rain; they consulted; I looked like a maniac of course with my hair all wet my shoes sopping…my shoes, damn fool that I am, were Mexican huaraches that, as a fellow later said to me in Wyoming, would certainly grow something if you planted them---plantlike sieves not fit for the rainy night of America and the whole raw road night. But they let me in, and rode me <u>back</u> to Newburgh which I accepted as a better alternative than being trapped in the Bear Mtn wilderness all night. "Besides said the man there's no traffic passes through six…if you want to go to Chicago you'd do better going across the Holland tunnel in NY and head for Pittsburgh" and I knew he was right. It was my dream that screwed up, the stupid hearthside idea that it would be wonderful to follow one great red line across America instead of trying various roads and routes. That's my tragic route Six--more to come of it, too. In Newburgh it had stopped raining, I walked down to the river, and among all things I had to ride back to NY in a bus with a delegation of schoolteachers coming back from a weekend in the Mtns.- - chatter chatter blah-blah and me swearing for all the time and the money I'd wasted, and telling myself "I wanted to go west and here I've been all day and into the night going up and down, north and south, like something that can't get started." And I swore I'd be in Chicago tomorrow; and made sure of that, taking a bus to Chicago, spending most of my money, and didn't give a damn, just as long as I'd be in that damned Chicago tomorrow. The bus left at 2 o'clock in the morning from the 34 St. bus station sixteen hours after I'd more or less passed it on my way up to Route Six. Sheepishly my foolish ass was carried west. But at least I was headed there at last. I won't describe the trip to Chicago, it was an ordinary bus trip with crying babies and sometimes hot sun and countryfolk getting on at one Penn town after another, and so on, till we got on the plain of Ohio and really rolled, up by Ashtabula and straight across Indiana in the night for Chicago. I arrived in Chicago quite early in the morning, got a room in the Y and went to bed with a very few dollars in my pocket as a consequence of my foolishness. I dug Chicago after a good day's sleep. The wind from Lake Michigan, the beans, bop at the Loop, long walks around So. Halsted and No. Clark and one long walk after midnight into the jungles where a cruising car followed me as a suspicious character. At this time, 1947, bop was going like mad all over America, but it hadn't developed to what it is now. The fellows at the Loop blew, but with a tired air, because bop was somewhere between its Charley Parker Ornithology period and another period that really began with Miles Davis. And as I sat there listening to that sound of the night which it has come to represent for all of us, I thought of all my friends from one end of the country to the other and how they were really all in the same vast backyard doing something so frantic and rushing-about beneath. And for the first time in my life, the following afternoon, I went into the west. It was a warm and beautiful day for hitch-hiking. To get out of

117

the impossible complexities of Chicago traffic I took a bus to Joliet, Illinois, went by the Joliet pen, and stationed myself just outside town, after a walk through its leafy rickety streets behind, pointed my way. All the way from New York to Joliet by bus in actuality, and I had about 20 dollars left. My first ride was a dynamite truck with a red flag, about thirty miles into the great green Illinois, the truckdriver pointing out the place where Route 6 that we were on intersected Route 66 before they both shot west for incredible distances. Along about three in the afternoon after an apple pie and ice cream in a roadside stand a woman stopped for me in a little coupe. I had a twinge of hardon joy as I ran after the car. But she was a middleaged woman, actually the mother of sons my age, and wanted somebody to help her drive to Iowa. I was all for it. Iowa! not so far from Denver, and once I got to Denver I could relax. She drove the first few hours; at one point insisted on visiting an old church somewhere, like as if we were tourists, and then I took over the wheel, and though I'm not much of a driver drove clear through the rest of Illinois to Davenport, Iowa, via Rock Island. And here for the first time in my life I saw my beloved Mississippi River---dry in the summer haze, low-water, with its big rank smell that smells like the raw body of America itself because it washes it up. Rock Island----railroad tracks, shacks, small downtown section; and over the bridge to Davenport, same kind of town, all smelling of sawdust in the warm Midwest sun. Here the lady had to go on to her Iowa hometown by another route; and I got out. The sun was going down. I walked, after a few cold beers, to the edge of town, and it was a long walk. All the men were driving home from work..wearing railroad hats, baseball hats, all kinds of hats, just like afterwork in any town anywhere. One of them gave me a ride up the hill and left me at a lonely crossroads on the edge of the prairie. It was beautiful there. Across the street was a Motel, the first of the many motels I was to see in the west. The only cars that came by were farmer-cars, they gave me suspicious looks, they clanked along, the cows were coming home. Not a truck. A few cars zipped by. A hotrod kid came by with his scarf flying. The sun went all the way down and I was standing in the purple darkness. Now I was scared. There weren't even any lights in the Iowa countryside; in a minute nobody would be able to see me. Luckily a man going back to Davenport gave me a lift downtown. But I was right where I started from. I went to sit in the bus station and think this over. I ate another apple pie and ice cream, that's practically all I ate all the way across the country, I knew it was nutritious and of course it was delicious. I decided to gamble. I took a bus in downtown Davenport, after spending a half hour watching a waitress in the bus station cafe, and rode to the city limits, but this time near the gas stations. Here the big trucks roared, wham, and inside two minutes one of them cranked to a stop for me. I ran for it with my soul whoopee-ing. And what a driver...a great big tough truckdriver with popping eyes and a hoarse raspy voice who just slammed and kicked at everything and got his rig underway and paid hardly any attention to me so I could rest my tired soul a little...for one of the biggest troubles hitchhiking is having to talk to innumerable people, make them feel that they didn't make a mistake picking you up, even go so far as to entertain them almost, all of which is a great strain when you're going all the way and don't plan to sleep in hotels. The guy just yelled above the roar and all I had to do was yell back, and we relaxed. And he balled that thing clear to (Rapid City Iowa) and yelled me the funniest stories about how he got around the law in every town that had an unfair speed-limit, reiterating over and over again "Them goddamn cops can't put no flies on my ass." And he was wonderful. And he did a wonderful thing for me. Just as we rolled into Rapid City he saw another truck coming behind us, and because he had to turn off at Rapid City he blinked his tail lights at the other guy and slowed down for me to jump out, which I did with my bag, and the other truck, acknowledging this exchange, stopped for me, and once again, in the twink of nothing, I was in another big high cab all set to go hundreds of miles across the night, and was I happy! And the new truckdriver was as crazy as the other one and yelled just as much and all I had to do was lean back and relax my soul and roll on. Now I could see

Denver looming ahead of me like the Promised Land, way out there beneath the stars, across the prairie of Iowa and the plains of Nebraska, and I could see the greater vision of San Francisco beyond like jewels in the night. He balled the jack and told stories for a couple of hours, then, at Stuart, a town in Iowa where years later Neal and I were stopped for suspicion in what looked like a stolen Cadillac, he slept a few hours in the seat. I slept too; and took one little walk along the lonely brickwalls illuminated by one lamp, with the prairie brooding at the end of each little street and the smell of corn like dew in the night. He woke up with a start at dawn. Off we roared, and an hour later the smoke of Des Moines appeared ahead over the green corn-fields. He had to eat his breakfast now and wanted to take it easy, so I went right on into Des Moines the rest of the way, about four miles, hitching a ride from two boys from the U. of Iowa; and it was strange sitting in their brand new comfortable car and hear them talk of exams as we zoomed smoothly into town. Now I wanted to sleep a whole day and go on until I reached Denver. So I went to the Y to get a room, they didn't have any, and by instinct wandered down to the railroad tracks- -and there's a lot of them in Des Moines- -and wound up in a gloomy old plains inn of a hotel down by the locomotive roundhouse, and spent a wonderful long day sleeping on a big clean hard white bed with dirty remarks carved in the wall beside my pillow and the beat yellow windowshades pulled over the smoky scene of the railyards. I woke up as the sun was reddening; and that was the one distinct time in my life, the strangest moment of all, that I didn't know who I was...I was far away from home haunted and tired with travel, in a cheap hotel room I'd never seen, hearing the hiss of steam outside, and the creak of the old wood of the hotel, and footsteps upstairs and all the sad sounds, and I looked at the cracked high ceiling and really didn't know who I was for about fifteen strange seconds. I wasn't scared, I was just somebody else, some stranger, and my whole life was a haunted life, the life of a ghost...I was halfway across America, at the dividing line between the East of my youth and the West of my future, and maybe that's why it happened right there and then that strange red afternoon. But I had to get going and stop moaning, so I picked up my bag, said so long to the old hotelkeeper sitting by his spittoon, and went to eat. I ate apple pie and ice cream---it was getting better as I got deeper into Iowa, the pie bigger, the ice cream richer. There were the most beautiful bevies of girls everywhere I looked in Des Moines that afternoon---they were coming home from hi school, but I had no time now for thoughts like that and promised myself a ball in Denver. Allen Ginsberg was already in Denver; Neal was there; Hal Chase and Ed White were there, it was their hometown; Louanne was there; and there was mention of a mighty gang including Bob Burford, his beautiful blonde sister Beverly; two nurses that Neal knew, the Gullion sisters; and even Allen Temko my old college writing buddy was there. I looked forward to all of them with joy and anticipation. So I rushed past the pretty girls, and the prettiest girls in the world live in Des Moines, Iowa. A crazy guy with a kind of toolshack on wheels, a truck full of tools, that he drove standing up like a modern milkman, gave me a ride up the long hill; where I immediately got a ride from a farmer and his son heading out for Adel in Iowa. In this town, under a big elm tree near a gas station, I made the acquaintance of another hitch-hiker who was going to be with me a considerable part of the rest of the way. He was of all things a typical New Yorker, an Irishman who'd been driving a truck for the Post Office most of his worklife and was now headed for a girl in Denver and a new life. I think he was running away from something in NY, the law most likely. He was a real rednose young drunk of 30 and would have bored me ordinarily except my senses were sharp for any kind of human friendship. He wore a beat sweater and baggy pants and had nothing with him in the way of a bag---just a toothbrush and handkerchiefs. He said we ought to hitch together. I should have said no, because he looked pretty awful on the road. But we stuck together and got a ride from a taciturn man to Stuart Iowa, a town in which I was destined to be really stranded. We stood in front of the railroad ticketshack in Stuart waiting for the westbound traffic till the sun went down, a good five hours...dawdling away the time at first telling about ourselves, then he told dirty stories, then we just ended up kicking pebbles and making goofy noises of one kind and another. We got bored; I decided to spend a buck on beer; we went to a riotous old buck's saloon in Stuart and had a few. There he got as drunk as he ever did in his Ninth Avenue night back home and yelled joyously in my ear all the sordid dreams of his life. I sort of liked him; not that he was a good sort, as he later proved, but he was enthusiastic about things. We got back on the road in the darkness and of course nobody stopped and nobody came by much. This went on until three o'clock in the morning; we spent some time trying to sleep on the bench at the railroad ticket office, but the telegraph clicked all night and we couldn't sleep and big freights were slamming around outside. We didn't know how to hop a proper hiball, we'd never done it before, whether they were going east or west and how to find out and what boxcars to pick and so on.. So when the Omaha bus came through just before dawn we hopped on it and joined the sleeping passengers---for this I spent most of the last of my few bucks, his fare as well as mine. His name was Eddie. He reminded me of my cousin-in-law from Brooklyn. That was why I stuck with him. It was like having an old friend along...a dumb smiling goodnatured sort to goof along with. We arrived at Council Bluffs at dawn; I looked out; all winter I'd been reading of the great wagon parties that held council there before hitting the Oregon and Santa Fe trails; and of course now it was only cute suburban cottages of one damn dumb kind and another, all laid out in the dismal gray dawn. Then Omaha, and by God the first cowboy I saw, walking along the bleak walls of the wholesale meat warehouses with a great big ten gallon hat on and Texas boots, looking like any beat character of the brickwall dawns of the east except for the getup. We got off the bus and walked clear up the hill, the long hill formed by the mighty Missouri over the millenniums, alongside of which Omaha is built, and got out to the country and stuck our thumbs out. We got a brief ride to a further crossroads from a wealthy rancher with a ten-gallon hat, who said the Valley of Nebraska (platte) was as great as the Nile Valley of Egypt, and as he said so I saw the great trees in the distance that snaked with the riverbed and the great verdant fields around it, and almost agreed with him. Then as we were standing there and it was starting to get cloudy another cowboy, this one six foot tall with a modest half-gallon hat, called us over and wanted to know if either one of us could drive. Of course Eddie could drive, and he had a licence and I didn't. He had two cars with him that he was driving back to Montana. His wife was sleeping at Grand Island in a motel and he wanted us to drive one of the cars there, where she'd take over. At that point he was going north and that was the limit of our ride with him. But it was a good 100 miles into Nebraska and of course we jumped for it. Eddie drove alone, the cowboy and myself following, and no sooner were we out of town that he started to ball that jack ninety miles an hour out of sheer exuberance. "Damn me, what's that boy doing!" the cowboy shouted, and took off after him. It began to be like a race. For a minute I thought Eddie was trying to get away with the car---and for all I know that's what he meant to do. But Old Cowboy stuck to him and caught up with him and tooted the horn. Eddie slowed down. The cowboy tooted to stop. "Damn, boy, you're liable to get a flat going that speed. Can't you drive a little slower." "Well I'll be damned, was I really going ninety?" said Eddie. "I didn't realize it on this smooth road." "Just take it a little easy and we'll all get to Grand Island in one piece." "Sure thing." And we resumed our journey. Eddie had calmed down and probably even got sleepy. So we drove 100 miles across Nebraska, following the winding So Platte with its verdant fields. "During the depression," said the cowboy to me, "I used to hop freights at least once a month. In those days you'd see hundreds of men riding a flat car or in a box car, and they weren't just bums, they were all kinds of men out of work and going from one place to another and some of them just wandering. It was like that all over the west. Brakemen never bothered you in those days. I don't know about today. Nebraska I ain't got no use for. Why in the middle 1930's this place wasn't nothing but a big dustcloud as far as the eye could see. You couldn't breathe. The ground was black. I was here in those days.

They can give Nebraska back to the Indians far as I'm concerned. I hate this damn place more than any place in the world. Montana's my home now, Missoula. You come up there sometime and see God's country." Later in the afternoon I slept and got some rest when he got tired talking---he was an interesting talker. We stopped along the road for a rest and a bite to eat. The cowboy went off to have a spare tire patched and Eddie and I sat down in a kind of homemade diner. I heard a great laugh, the greatest laugh in the world, and here came this rawhide oldtimer Nebraska farmer with a bunch of other boys into the diner; you could hear his raspy cries clear across the plains, across the whole gray world of them that day. Everybody else laughed with him. He didn't have a care in the world and had the hugest regard for everybody nevertheless. I said to myself, "Wham listen to that man laugh. That's the west, here I am in the West." He came booming into the diner calling Maw's name from a distance, and she made the sweetest cherrypie in Nebraska and I had some with a mountainous scoop of ice cream on top. "Maw, rustle me up some grub afore I have to start eatin myself raw or some damn silly idee like that" and he threw himself on a stool and went "Hyaw hyaw hyaw hyaw! and thow some beans in it." It was just the spirit of the west sitting right next to me. I wished I knew his whole raw life and what the hell he'd been doing all these years besides laughing and yelling like that. "Whooee," I told my soul, and the cowboy came back and off we went to Grand Island. We got there in no time flat. He went to fetch his sleeping wife and off to whatever fate awaited him in the intervening years since, and Eddie and I resumed on the road. We got a ride from a couple of young fellows, wranglers, teenagers, countryboys in a put-together jaloppy and were left off somewhere up the line in a thin drizzle of rain. Then an old man who said nothing and God knows why he picked us up took us to (Preston) Nebraska. Here Eddie stood forlornly in the road in front of a staring bunch of short squat Omaha Indians who had nowhere to go and nothing to do. Across the road was the railroad track and the water-tank saying "Preston." "Damn me," said Eddie with amazement, "I've been in this town before. It was years ago, during the fucking war, at night, late at night when everybody was sleeping, I went out on the platform to smoke, and there we was in the middle of nowhere and black as hell and I look up and see that name Preston written on the watertank..bound for the Pacific, everybody snoring, every damn dumb sucker, and we only stayed a few minutes stoking up or something and off we went. Damn me, this Preston! -- I hated this place ever since!" And we were stuck in Preston. As in Davenport Iowa somehow all the cars were farmer-cars; and once in a while a tourist car, which is worse, with old men driving and their wives pointing out the sights or poring over maps, and sitting back like they do in their livingrooms all over America looking at everything with suspicious faces. The drizzle increased and Eddie got cold; he had very little clothes. I fished a wool plaid shirt from my canvas bag and he put it on. He felt a little better. I had a cold. I bought cough drops in a rickety Indian store of some kind. I went to the little two-by-four post office and wrote my mother a penny postcard. We went back to the gray road. There she was in front of us, Preston, written on the watertank. The Rock Island balled by. We saw the faces of Pullman passengers go by in a blur. The train howled off across the plains in the direction of our desires. It started to rain harder. But I knew I'd get there. A tall, lanky fellow in a gallon hat stopped his car on the wrong side of the road and came over to us; he looked like a sheriff. We prepared our stories secretly. He took his time coming over. "You boys going to get somewhere, or just going?" We didn't understand his question and it was a damned good question. "Why?" we said. "Well I own a little carnival that's pitched a few mile down the road and I'm looking for some old boys willing to work and make a buck for themselves. I've got a roulette concession and a wooden ring concession, you know, the kind you throw around dolls and take your luck. You boys want to work for me you can get 30% of the take." "Room and board?" "You can get a bed but no food. You'll have to eat in town for that. We travel some." We thought it over. "It's a good opportunity," he said and waited patiently for us to make up our minds. We felt silly and didn't know what to say and I for one didn't want to get hung up with a carnival I was in such a bloody hurry to get to the gang in Denver. I said "I don't know, I'm going as fast as I can and I don't think I have the time." Eddie said the same thing, and the old man waved his hand and casually sauntered back to his car and drove off. And that was that. We laughed about it awhile and speculated what it would have been like. I for one had visions of a dark and dusty night on the plains, and the faces of Nebraska families wandering by, Okies mostly, with their rosy children looking at everything with awe, and I know I would have felt like the Devil himself rooking them with all those cheap carnival tricks that they make you do…and the ferris wheel revolving in the flatlands darkness, and Godalmighty the sad music of the merry-go-round and me wanting to get on to my goal…and sleeping in some gilt wagon on a bed of burlap. Eddie turned out to be a pretty absentminded pal of the road. A funny old contraption rolled by, driven by an old man, it was made of some kind of aluminum, square as a box, a trailer no doubt, but a weird crazy Nebraska homemade trailer, and he was going very slow and stopped. We rushed up; he said he could only take one; without a word, after a look from me, Eddie jumped in and slowly rattled from my sight, and wearing my wool plaid shirt, the very shirt I'd worn to write the first half of my book. Well, lackaday, I kissed the shirt goodbye, it only had sentimental value in any case, besides of which, though I didn't know it, I was destined to retrieve it some ways up the road. I waited in our personal godawful Preston for a long, long time, several hours; I kept thinking it was getting night but actually it was only early afternoon, but dark. Denver, Denver, how would I ever get to Denver. I was just about giving up and planning to sit over coffee in a stew when a fairly new car stopped, driven by a young guy. I ran like mad. "Where you going?" "Denver." "Well I can take you a hundred miles up the line. "Grand, grand, you saved my life." "I used to hitch hike myself, that's why I always pickup a fellow." "I would too if I had a car." And so we talked, and he told me about his life, which wasn't very interesting and I started to sleep some and woke up right outside the town of North Platte, where he left me off. And I wasn't thinking about much but the greatest ride in my life was about to come up, a truck, with a flatboard at the back, with about already five boys sprawled out on it and the drivers, two young blonde farmers from Minnesota were picking up every single soul they found on that road---the most smiling cheerful couple of handsome bumkins you could ever wish to see, both wearing cotton shirts and overalls, nothing else, both thick-wristed and earnest, with broad howareyou smiles for anybody and anything that came across their path. I ran up, said "Is there room?" They said "Sure, hop on, 's'room for everybody." So I did. I was amazed by the simplicity of the whole ride; I wasn't on the flatboard before the truck roared off, I lurched, a rider grabbed me, and I sat down some. Somebody passed a bottle of rotgut, the bottom of it. I took a big swig in the wild lyrical drizzling air of Nebraska. "Whooee, here we go!" yelled a kid with a baseball cap, and they gunned up the truck to seventy and passed everybody on the road. "We been riding this sonofabitch since Omaha. These guys never stop. Every now and then you have to yell for pisscall otherwise you have to piss off the air and hang on, brother, hang on." I looked at the company. There were two young farmer boys from North Dakota in red baseball caps, which is the standard NoDakota farmer boy hat, and they were headed for the harvests: their old men had given them leave to hit the road for a summer. Then there were two young city boys, from Columbus Ohio, high school footballplayers, chewing gum, winking, singing in the breeze, and they said they were hitch hiking around the US for the summer. "We're going to LA!" they yelled. "What you going to do there?" "Hell, we don't know. Who cares?" Then there was a tall slim fellow whose name was Slim and he came from Montana, he said, and he had a sneaky look. "Where you from?" I asked; I was lying next to him on the platform, you couldn't sit without bouncing off; it had no rails. And he turned slowly to me, opened his mouth and said, "Mon-ta-na." And finally there was Mississippi Gene and his charge. Mississippi Gene was a little dark guy who rode freight trains around the country, a 30 year old hobo but with a youthful look so you couldn't tell exactly what age he was. And he sat on the boards crosslegged, looking out over the fields without saying anything for hundreds of miles, and finally at one point turned to me and said "Where you headed?" I said Denver. "I got a sister there but I ain't seed her for several couple years." His language was melodious and slow. His charge was a sixteen year old tall blond kid, also in hobo rags, and that is to say they wore old clothes that had been turned black by the soot of railroads and the dirt of boxcars and sleeping on the ground. The blond kid was also quiet and he seemed to be running away from something, and it figured to be the law the way he looked straight ahead and wet his lips in worried thought. They sat side by side, silent buddies, and said nothing to anyone else. The farmboys and the high school boys bored them; Montana Slim however spoke to them occasionally with a sardonic and insinuating smile. They paid no attention to him. Slim was all insinuation. I was afraid of his long goofy grin that he opened up straight in your face and held there half-moronically. "You got any money?" he said to me. "Hell no, maybe enough for a pint of whisky till I get to Denver. What about you?" "I know where I can get some." "Where?" "Anywhere. You can always folly a man down an alley can't you?" "Yeah, I guess you can." "I ain't beyond doing it when I really need some dough. Headed up to Montana to see my father. I'll have to get off this rig at Cheyenne and move up some other way, these crazy boys are going to Los Angeles." "Straight?" "All the way---if you want to go to L.A. you got a ride." I mulled this over, the thought of zoomingallnight across Nebraska, Wyoming and the Utah desert in the morning and then the Nevada desert most likely in the afternoon, and actually arriving in Los Angeles California within a foreseeable space of time almost made me change my plans. But I had to go to Denver. I'd have to get off at Cheyenne too, and hitch south 90 miles to Denver. I was glad when the two Minnesota farmboys in the cab decided to stop in No. Platte and eat; I wanted to have a look at them. They came out of the cab and smiled at all of us. "Pisscall!" said one. "Time to eat!" said the other. But they were the only ones in the party who had money to buy food. We all shambled after them to a restaurant run by a whole bunch of women and sat around over hamburgers while they wrapped away enormous meals just like they were back in their mother's kitchen. They were brothers: they were transporting farm machinery from Los Angeles to Minnesota and making good money at it. So on their trip to the Coast empty they picked up everybody on the road. They'd done this about five times now; they were having a hell of a time. They liked everything. They never stopped smiling. I tried to talk to them---actually it was a kind of dumb attempt on my part to befriend the captains of our ship and there was no reason to, because they treated the crew with equal respect---and the only response I got were two sunny smiles and large white corn-fed teeth. Everybody had joined them in the restaurant except the two hobo kids, Gene and his boy. When we all got back they were still sitting in the truck forlorn and disconsolate. Now the darkness was falling. The drivers had a smoke; I jumped at the chance to go buy a bottle of whisky to keep warm in the rushing cold air of night. They smiled when I told them. "Go ahead, hurry up." "You can have a couple shots!" I reassured them. "Oh no, we never drink, go ahead." Montana Slim and the two high school boys wandered the streets of North Platte with me till I found a whisky store. They chipped in some, and Slim some, and I bought a fifth. Tall sullen men watched us go by from false-front buildings; the main street was lined with square box-houses. There were immense vistas of the plains beyond every sad street. I felt something different in the air in North Platte, I didn't know what it was. In five minutes I did. We got back on the truck and roared off, same speed. It got dark quickly. We all had a shot, and suddenly I looked, and the verdant farmfields of the So. Platte began to disappear and in their stead, so far you couldn't see to the end of it, appeared long flat wastelands of sand and sagebrush. I was astounded. "What in the hell is this?" I cried out to Slim. "This is the beginning of the rangelands, boy. Hand me another drink." "Whoopee!" yelled the high school boys. "Columbus so long! What would Sparkie and the boys say if they was here. Yow!" The drivers had switched up front; the fresh brother was gunning the truck to the limit. The road changed too; humpy in the middle, with soft shoulders and a ditch on both sides about four feet deep, so that the truck bounced and teetered from one side of the road to the other, miraculously only when there no cars coming the opposite way, and I thought we'd all take a somersault. But they were tremendous drivers. They swapped at the wheel all the way from Minnesota to palmy L.A. without stopping more than 10 minutes to eat. How that truck disposed of the Nebraska nub!---the nub that sticks out over Colorado. And soon I realized I was actually at last over Colorado, though not officially in it, but actually looking southwest towards Denver itself a few hundred miles away. I yelled for joy. We passed the bottle. The great blazing stars came out, the far receding sand hills got dim. I felt like an arrow that could shoot out all the way. And suddenly Mississippi Gene turned to me from his crosslegged patient reverie, and opened his mouth, and leaned close, and said "These plains put me in the mind of Texas." "Are you from Texas?" "No sir, I'm from Green-vell Muzz-sippy" and that was the way he said it. "Where's that kid from?" "He got into some kind of trouble back in Mississippi so I offered to help him out. Boy's never been out on his own so I offered to help some. I take care of him best as I can, he's only a child." Although Gene was white there was something of the wise and tired old Negro in him, and something very much like Hunkey the NY dope addict in him, but a railroad Hunkey, a traveling epic Hunkey, crossing and recrossing the country every year, south in the winter and north in the summer and only because he has no place he can stay in without getting tired of it and because there's nowhere to go but everywhere, and keep rolling under the stars, generally the western stars. "I been to Og-den a couple times. If you want to ride on to Og-den I got some friends there we could hole up with." "I'm going to Denver from Cheyenne." "Hell, go right straight thu, you don't get a ride like this everyday." This too was a tempting offer. What was in Ogden. "What's Ogden?" I said. "It's the place where most of the boys pass thu and always meet there, you're liable to see anybody there." In my earlier days I'd been to sea with a tall rawboned fellow from Ruston La. called Big Slim Hubbard, William Holmes Hubbard, who was hobo by choice; as a little boy he'd seen a hobo come up to ask his mother for a piece of pie, and she had given it to him, and when the hobo went off down the road the little boy had said, "Ma what is that fellow?" "Why that's a ho-bo." "Ma, I want to be a ho-bo someday." "Shet your mouth, that's not for the like of the Hubbards." But he never forgot that day, and grew up, after a short spell playing football at LSU, and did become a hobo. Slim and I spent many nights telling stories and spitting tobacco juice in paper containers. There was something so indubitably reminiscent of Big Slim Hubbard in Mississippi Gene's demeanor that I came out and said "Do you happen to have met a fellow called Big Slim Hubbard somewhere?" And he said "You mean the tall fellow with the big laugh?" "Well, that sounds like him. He came from Ruston Louisiana." "That's right, Louisiana Slim he's sometimes called. Yessir, I shore have met Big Slim." "And he used to work in the East Texas oil fields?" "East Texas is right. And now he's punching cows." And that was exactly right; and still I couldn't believe Gene could have really known Slim, whom I'd been looking for more or less for years. "And he used to work in tugboats in NY?" "Well now, I don't know about that." "I guess you only know him in the West." "I reckon, I ain't never been to NY." "Well, damn me, I'm amazed you know him. This is a big country. Yet I knew you must have known him." "Yessir, I know Big Slim pretty well. Always generous with his money when he's got some. Mean tough fellow, too; I seen him flatten a police-man in the yards at Cheyenne, one punch." That sounded like Big Slim; he was always practising that one punch in the air; he looked like Jack Dempsey, but a young Jack Dempsey who drank. "Damn!" I yelled into the wind, and I had another shot, and by now I was feeling pretty good. Every shot was wiped away by the rushing wind of the open truck, wiped away of its bad effects and the good effect sank in my stomach. "Cheyenne, here I come!" I sang. "Denver, look out for your boy." Montana Slim turned to me, pointed at my shoes, and commented "You reckon if you put them things in the ground something'll grow up?" Without cracking a smile, of course, and the other boys heard him and laughed. And they were the silliest shoes in America; I brought them along specifically because I didn't want my feet to sweat in the hot road for fear I'd develop another case of phlebitis, and except for the rain in Bear Mtn. they proved to be the best possible shoes for my journey. So I laughed with them. And they'd become pretty ragged by now, the bits of colored leather stuck up like pieces of a fresh pineapple, with my toes showing through. Well, we had another shot and laughed. As in a dream we zoomed through small crossroad towns smack out of the darkness and passed long lines of lounging harvest hands and cowboys in the night and were back out there. They watched us pass in one motion of the head and we saw them slap their thighs from the continuing dark the other side of town---we were a funny looking crew. A lot of men were in this country at that time of year, it was harvest time. The Dakota boys were fidgeting. "I think we'll get off at the next pisscall, seems like there's a lot of work around here." "All you got to do is move north when it's over here," counseled Montana Slim, "and jess follow the harvest till you get to Canada." The boys nodded vaguely; they didn't take much stock in his advice. Meanwhile the blond young fugitive sat the same way; every now and then Gene leaned over from his Buddhistic trance over the rushing dark plains and said something tenderly in the boy's ear. The boy nodded. Gene was taking care of him, even his moods and his fears. I wondered where the hell they would go and what they could do. They had no cigarettes. I squandered my pack on them I loved them so. They were grateful and gracious. They never asked; I kept offering. Montana Slim had his own but never passed the pack. We zoomed through another crossroads town, passed another line of tall lanky men in jeans, clustered in the dim light like moths on the desert, and returned to the tremendous darkness...and the stars overhead were as pure and bright, because of the increasingly thin air as we mounted the high hill of the western plateau about a foot a mile, so they say, and a mile a minute, pure clean air, and no trees obstructing any low-levelled stars anywhere. And once I saw a moody whitefaced cow in the sage by the road as we flitted by. It was like riding a railroad train, just as steady and just as straight. By and by we came to a town, slowed down, Montana Slim said "Ah, pisscall" but the Minnesotans didn't stop and went right on through. "Damn, I gotta piss," said Slim. "Go over the side" said somebody. "Well, I <u>will</u>" he said, and slowly, as we all watched he inched to the back of the platform on his ass, holding on as best he could till his legs dangled over. Somebody knocked on the window of the cab to bring this to the attention of the brothers. Their great smiles broke as they turned. As just as Slim was ready to proceed, precarious as it was already, they began zig-zagging the truck at 70 miles an hour. He fell back a moment; we saw a whale's spout in the air; he struggled back to a sitting position. They swung the truck. Wham, over he went on his side, pissing all over himself. In the roar we could hear him faintly cursing with the whine of a man far across the hills. "Damn...damn.." He never knew we were doing this deliberately, he just struggled with his lot, and just as grim as Job. When he was finished, as such, he was wringing wet, and now he had to edge and shimmy his way back, and with a most woebegone look, and everybody laughing, except the sad blond boy, and the Minnesotans roaring in the cab. I handed him the bottle to make up for it. "What the hail," he said, "was they doing that on purpose?" "They sure were." "Well damn me, I didn't know that. I know I tried it back in Nebraska and didn't have half so much trouble." We came suddenly into the town of Ogallala, and here the fellows in the cab called out "Pisscall!" and with great good delight. Slim stood sullenly by the truck rueing a lost opportunity. The two Dakota boys said goodbye to everybody and figured they'd start harvesting here. We watched them disappear in the night towards the shacks at the end of town where lights were burning, where a watcher of the night in jeans said the employment men would be. I had to buy more cigarettes. Gene and the blond boy followed me to stretch their legs. We walked into the least likely place in the world, a kind of lonely plains sodafountain for the local teenage girls and boys. They were dancing, a few of them, to the music on the jukebox. There was a lull when we came in. Gene and Blondey just stood there looking at nobody; all they wanted were cigarettes. There were some pretty girls, too. And one of them made eyes at Blondey and he never saw it and if he had, he wouldn't have cared he was so sad and gone. I bought a pack each for them; they thanked me. The truck was ready to go. It was getting on midnight now and cold. Gene who'd been around the country more times than he could count on his fingers and toes said the best thing to do now was for all of us to bundle up under the big tarpaulin or we'd freeze. In this manner, and with the rest of the bottle, we kept warm as the air grew ice cold and pinged our ears. The stars seemed to get brighter the more we climbed the High Plains. We were in Wyoming now. Flat on my back I stared straight up at the magnificent firmament, glorying in the time I was making, in how far I had come from sad Bear Mtn. after all, how everything worked out in the end, and tingling with kicks at the thought of what lay ahead of me in Denver---whatever, whatever it would be and good enough for me. And Mississippi Gene began to sing a song. He sang it in a melodious quiet voice, with a river accent, and it was simple, just "I got a purty little girl, she's sweet six-teen, she's the purti-est thing you ever seen," repeating it with other lines thrown in, all concerning his life in general and how far he'd been and how he wished he could go back to her but he done lost her. I said "Gene that's the prettiest song." "It's the sweetest I know," he said with a smile. "I hope you get where you're going and be happy when you do." "I always make out and move along one way or the other." Montana Slim was asleep. He woke up and said to me "Hey Blackie, how about you and me making Cheyenne together tonight before you go to Denver." "Sure thing." I was drunk enough to go for anything. And the truck reached the outskirts of Cheyenne, we saw the high red lights of the local radio station, and suddenly we were bucking through a great strange crowd of people that poured on both sidewalks. "Hell's bells, it's Wild West Week" said Slim. Great crowds of businessmen, fat businessmen in boots and tengallon hats, with their hefty wives in cowgirl attire bustled and whoopeed on the wooden sidewalks of old Cheyenne; further down were the long stringy boulevard lights of new downtown Cheyenne. The celebration was focusing on oldtown. Blank guns went off. The saloons were crowded to the sidewalk. I was amazed and at the same time I had never seen anything so really ridiculous: in my first shot at the west I was seeing to what absurd devices it had fallen to keep its proud tradition. Man I rubbed my eyes. We had to jump off the truck and say goodbye, the Minnesotans weren't interested in hanging around. I was sad to see them go and realized that I would never see any of them again, but that's the way it was. "You'll freeze your ass tonight," I warned, "then you'll burn 'em in the desert tomorrow afternoon." "That's allright with me long's as we get out of this cold night" said Gene. And the truck left, threading its way through the crowds and nobody paying any attention to the strangeness of it and of the kids inside the tarpaulin watching the town like babes from a coverlet. I watched it disappear into the night. Mississippi Gene was gone; bound for Og-den and then God knows what. I was with Montana Slim and we started in hitting the bars. I had about ten dollars, eight of which I foolishly squandered that night on drinking. First we milled with all the cowboydudded tourists and oilmen and ranchers, at bars, in doorways, on the sidewalk, then I shook Slim for awhile who by now was wandering a little slaphappy in the street from all the whisky and beer: he was that kind of drinker, his eyes got glazed, in a minute he'd be telling an absolute stranger about things. I went into a chili joint and the waitress was Spanish and beautiful. I ate, and then I wrote her a little love note on the back of the bill. The chili joint was deserted; everybody was drinking. I told her to turn the bill over. She read it and laughed. It was a little poem about how I wanted her to come and see the night with me. "I'd love to Chiquito but I have a date with my boyfriend." "Can't you shake him?" "No, no, I don't" she said sadly; and I loved the way she said it. "Some other time I'll come by here," I said, and she said "Any time, kid." Still I hung around just to look at her and had another cup of coffee. Her boyfriend came in sullenly and wanted to know when she was off. She bustled around to close the place quick. I had to get out. I gave her a smile when I left. Things were going on as wild as ever outside, except that the fat burpers were getting drunker and whooping up louder. It was funny. There were Indian chiefs wandering around in big headdresses and really solemn among the flushed drunken faces. I saw Slim tottering along and joined him. He said "I just wrote a postcard to my Paw in Montana. You reckon you can find a mailbox and put it in." It was a strange request; he gave me the postcard and tottered through the swinging doors of a saloon. I took the card, went to the box and took a quick look at it. "Dear Paw, I'll be home Wednesday. Everything's all right with me and I hope the same's with you. Richard." It gave me a different idea of him; how tenderly polite he was with his father. I went in the bar and joined him. Sometime in the distant dawn I planned to get on the road for Denver, the last 100 miles but instead of that we picked up two girls who were wandering in the crowds, a pretty young blonde and a fat brunette sister of some kind. They were dumb and sullen but we wanted to make them. We took them to a rickety nightclub that was already closing and there I spent all but two dollars on Scotches for them and beer for us. I was getting drunk and didn't care; everything was fine. My whole being and purpose was pointed at the little blonde's middle; I wanted to go in there with all my strength. I hugged her and wanted to tell her. The nightclub closed and we all wandered out in the rickety dusty streets. I looked up at the sky; the pure wonderful stars were still there, burning. The girls wanted to go to the bus station so we all went, but they apparently wanted to go there to meet some sailor who was there waiting for them, a cousin of the fat girl's, and the sailor had friends with him. I said to the blonde "What's up." She said she wanted to go home, in Colorado just over the line south of Cheyenne. "I'll take you in a bus," I said. "No, the bus stops on the hiway and I have to walk across that damned prairie all by myself. I spend all afternoon looking at the damn thing and I don't aim to walk over it tonight." "Ah listen, we'll take a nice walk in the prairie flowers." "There ain't no flowers there," she said. "I want to go to New York, I'm sick and tired of this. Ain't no place to go but Cheyenne and ain't nothing in Cheyenne." "Ain't nothing in New York." "Hell there ain't" she said with a curl of her lips. The bus station was crowded to the doors. All kinds of people were waiting for buses or just standing around; there were a lot of Indians, who watched everything with their stony eyes. The girl disengaged herself from my talk and joined the sailor and the others. Slim was dozing on a bench. I sat down. The floors of bus stations are the same all over the country, they're always covered with butts and spit and a sadness that only bus stations have. For a moment it was no different than being in Newark except that I knew the great hugeness outside that I loved so much. I rued the way I had broken up the purity of my entire trip, saving every dime and not drinking and not dawdling and really making time, by fooling around with this sullen girl and spending all my money. It made me sick. I hadn't slept in so long I got too tired to curse and fuss and went off to sleep; eventually I curled up on the entire seat with my canvas bag for a pillow, and in that way slept till eight o'clock in the morning among the dreamy murmurs and noises of the station and of hundreds of people passing. I woke up with a big headache. Slim was gone...to Montana I guess. I went outside. And there in the blue air I saw for the first time, in hints and mighty visitation, far off, the great snowy-tops of the Rocky Mountains. I took a deep breath. I had to get to Denver, at once. First I ate a breakfast, a modest one of toast and coffee and one egg, and then I cut out of town to the hiway. The Wild West festival was still going on, I left it behind me: they were having rodeos and the whooping and jumping was about to start all over again. I wanted to see my gangs in Denver. I went over a railroad overpass and reached a crossroads of shacks where two highways forked off, both for Denver. I took the one nearest the mountains so I could look at them, and pointed myself that way. I got a ride right off from a young fellow from Connecticut who was driving around the country in his jaloppy painting; he was the son of an editor in the East. He talked and talked; I was sick from drinking and from the altitude. At one point I almost had to stick my head out the window. But I made it, and by the time he let me off at Longmont Colo. I was feeling normal again and had even started telling him about the state of my own travels. He wished me luck. It was beautiful in Longmont. Under a tremendous old tree was a bed of green lawngrass belonging to a gas station. I asked the attendant if I could sleep there and he said sure; so I stretched out a wool shirt, lay my face flat on it, with an elbow out, and with one eye cocked at the snowy Rockies in the hot sun for just a moment, I fell asleep for two delicious hours, the only discomfiture being an occasional Colorado ant. "And here I am in Colorado!" I kept thinking gleefully. "Damn! damn! damn! I'm making it!" And after a refreshing sleep filled with cobwebby dreams of my past life in the East I got up, washed in the station men's room, and strode off fit and slick as a fiddle to get me a rich thick milkshake at the roadhouse to put some freeze in my hot tormented stomach. Incidentally a very beautiful Colorado gal shook me that cream, she was all smiles too; I was grateful, it made up for last night. I said to myself, "Wow! What'll <u>Denver</u> be like!" I got on that hot road and off I went to Denver in a brand new car driven by a Denver businessman of about thirty five. He went seventy. I tingled all over; I counted minutes and subtracted miles. In a minute just over the rolling wheatfields all golden beneath the distant snows of Estes I'd be seeing old Denver at last. I pictured myself in a Denver bar that night, with all the gang, and in their eyes I would be strange and ragged and like the Prophet that has walked across the land to bring the dark Word, and the only Word I had was Wow. The man and I had a long warm conversation about our respective schemes in life and before I knew it we were going over the Denargo fruitmarkets outside Denver, there was smoke, smokestacks, railyards, redbrick buildings and the distant downtown graystone buildings and here I was in Denver. He let me off at Larimer street. I stumbled along with the most wicked grin of joy in the world among the old bums and beat cowboys of Larimer street. It was also the biggest city I'd seen since Chicago and the bigcity buzz made me jump. As I say, in those days I didn't know Neal as well as I do now, and the first thing I wanted to do was look up Hal Chase immediately, which I did. I called up his house, talked to his mother---she said, "Why Jack what are you doing in Denver? Did you know Ginger was here?"---and of course I knew Ginger was there but that was not my reason for coming. Ginger was Hal's girl; I played around with her a bit in New York when he wasn't looking. For this I was really and genuinely sorry and I hoped Hal still felt the same about me. I don't think he did but he never showed it, the thing about Hal being, he was always as clever as a woman. Hal is a slim blond boy with a strange witchdoctor face that goes with his interest in anthropology and pre-history Indians. His nose beaks softly and almost creamily under a golden flair of hair; he has the grace of a western hotshot who's danced in roadhouses and played a little football. A quavering twang comes out when he speaks---"The thing I always like, Jack, about the plains indians was the way they always got s'danged embarrassed after they boasted the number of scalps they got...in Ruxton's Life in the Far West there's an Indian who gets red all over blushing because he got so many scalps and runs like hell into the plains to glory over his deeds in hiding. Damn, that tickled me!" Hal's mother located him, in the drowsy Denver afternoon, working over his Indian basketmaking in the local museum. I called him there; he came and picked me up in his old Ford coupe that he used to take trips in the mountains to "dig" for Indian objects. He came into the bus station wearing jeans and a big smile. I was sitting on my bag on the floor talking to the very same sailor who'd been in the Cheyenne bus station with me, asking him what happened to the blonde. He was so bored he didn't answer. Hal and I got into his little coupe and the first thing he had to do was get maps at the State building. Then the next thing he had to see an old schoolteacher, and so on, and all I wanted to do was drink beer. And in the back of my mind was the wild, wild thought - - "Where is Neal and what is he doing right now?" Hal had decided not to be Neal's friend anymore, for some odd reason, since the winter, and he didn't even know where he lived. "Is Allen Ginsberg in town?" "Yes---" but he wasn't talking to him any more either. This was the beginning of Hal Chase's withdrawal from our general gang---and he was going to stop talking to me too in a short while. But I didn't know this, and the plans were for me to take a nap in his house that afternoon at least. The word was that Ed White had an apartment waiting for me up Colfax avenue, that Allan Temko was already living in it and was waiting for me to join him. I sensed some kind of conspiracy in the air and this conspiracy lined up two groups in the gang: it was Hal Chase and Ed White and Allan Temko, together with the Burfords, generally agreeing to ignore Neal Cassady and Allen Ginsberg. I was smack in the middle of this interesting war. There were social overtones too that I'll explain. First I must set the stage about Neal: he was the son of a wino, one of the most tottering bums of Larimer street and had in fact been brought up generally on Larimer street and thereabouts. Neal used to plead in court at the age of six to have his father let free. He used to beg in front of Larimer alleys and sneak the money back to his father who waited among the broken bottles with an old bum buddy. Then when Neal grew up he began hanging around the Welton poolhalls and set a Denver record for stealing cars and went to the reformatory. From the age of eleven to seventeen he was usually in reform school. His specialty was stealing cars, gunning for girls coming out of high school in the afternoon, driving them out to the mountains, screwing them, and coming back to sleep in any available hotel bath tub in town. Meanwhile his father, once a very respectable and hardworking barber, had become a complete wino---a wine alcoholic which is worse than whisky alcoholic---and was reduced to riding freights to the South in the winter, to Texas, and back to Denver in the summer. Neal had brothers on his dead mother's side---she died when he was small---but they also disliked him. Neal's only buddies were the poolhall boys- -a bunch I came to meet a few days later. Then Justin W. Brierly, a tremendous local character who all his life had specialized in developing the potentialities of young people, had in fact been tutor to Shirley Temple for MGM in the thirties, and was now a lawyer, a realtor, director of the Central City Opera Festival and also an English teacher in a Denver high school, discovered Neal. Brierly came to knock on a client's door; this client was always drunk and having wild parties. When Brierly knocked on the door the client was drunk upstairs. There was a drunken Indian in the parlor, and Neal---ragged and dirty from recent work in a Nebraska manure field---was screwing the maid in the bedroom. Neal ran down to answer the door with a hardon. Brierly said "Well, well, what is this?" Neal ushered him in. "What is your name? Neal Cassady? Neal you'd better learn to wash your ears a little better than that or you'll never get on in this world." "Yes sir," said Neal smiling. "Who is your Indian friend? What's going on around here? These are strange goingson I must say." Justin W. Brierly was short bespectacled ordinary-looking middlewest businessman; you couldn't distinguish him from any other lawyer, realtor, director on 17th and Arapahoe near the financial district; except that he had a streak of imagination which would have appalled his confreres had they but known. Brierly was purely and simply interested in young people, especially boys. He discovered them in his English class; taught them the best he knew in Literature; groomed them; made them study till they had astounding marks; then he got them scholarships to Columbia University and they returned to Denver years later the product of his imagination - - always with one shortcoming, which was the abandonment of their old mentor for new interests. They went further afield and left him behind; all he knew about anything was gleaned from what he'd made them learn; he had developed scientists and writers and youthful city politicians, lawyers and poets, and talked to them; then he dipped back into his reserve of boys in the high school class and groomed them to dubious greatness. He saw in Neal the great energy that would someday make him not a lawyer or a politician, but an American saint. He taught him how to wash his teeth, his ears; how to dress; helped him get odd jobs; and put him in high school. But Neal immediately stole the principal's car and wrecked it. He went to reform school. Justin W. stuck by him. He wrote him long encouraging letters; chatted with the warden; brought him books; and when Neal came out Justin gave him one more chance. But Neal fouled up again. Whenever any of his poolhall buddies developed a hatred for a local prowlcar cop they went to Neal to do their revenge; he stole the prowlcar and wrecked it, or otherwise damaged it. Soon he was back in reform school and Brierly washed his hands of him. They became in fact tremendous ironical enemies. In the past winter in N.Y. Neal had tried one last crack for Brierly's influence; Allen Ginsberg wrote several poems, Neal signed his name to them and they were mailed to Brierly. Taking his annual trip to N.Y. Brierly faced all of us one evening in Livingston lobby on the Columbia campus. There was Neal, Allen, myself and Ed White and Hal Chase. Said Brierly "These are very interesting poems you've sent me, Neal. May I say that I was surprised." "Ah well," said Neal, "I've been studying you know." "And who is this young gentleman here in the glasses?" inquired Brierly. Allen Ginsberg stepped up and announced himself. "Ah," said Brierly, "this is most interesting. I understand that you are an excellent poet." "Why, have you read any of my things?" "Oh," said Brierly, "probably, probably"---and Ed White, whose love of subtlety later drove him mad over Boswell's Old Sam Johnson, twinkle eyed all over. He gripped me in the arm and whispered "You think he doesn't know?" I guessed he did. That was Neal's and Brierly's last stand together. Now Neal was back in Denver with his demon poet. Brierly raised an ironical eyebrow and avoided them. Hal Chase avoided them on secret principles of his own. Ed White believed they were out for no good. They were the underground monsters of that season in Denver, together with the poolhall gang, and symbolizing this most beautifully Allen had a basement apartment on Grant street and we all met there many a night that went to dawn---Allen, Neal, myself, Jim Holmes, Al Hinkle and Bill Tomson. More of these others later. My first afternoon in Denver I slept in Hal Chase's room while his mother went on with her housework downstairs and Hal worked at the museum. It was a hot high-plains afternoon in July. I would not have slept if it hadn't been for Hal Chase's father's invention. Hal Chase's father was a mad self-styled inventor. He was old, in his seventies, and seemingly feeble, thin and drawn-out and telling stories with a slow, slow relish; good stories too, about his boyhood on the Kansas Plains in the eighties when for diversion he rode ponies bareback and chased after coyotes with a club and later became a country schoolteacher in West Kansas and finally a businessman of many devices in Denver. He still had his old office over the garage in a barn down the street---the rolltop desk was still there, together with countless dusty papers of past excitement and moneymaking. He invented a special air conditioner of his own. He put an ordinary fan in a window frame but somehow conducted cool water through coils in front of the whirring blades. The result was perfect---within four feet of the fan, and then the water apparently turned into hot steam in the hot day and the downstairs part of the house was just as hot as usual. But I was sleeping right under the fan on Hal's bed with its big bust of Goethe staring at me, and I comfortably went to sleep, only to wake up in five minutes freezing to death; I put a blanket on and still I was cold. Finally it was so cold I couldn't sleep and I went downstairs. The old man asked me how his invention worked. I said it worked damned good and I meant it within bounds. I liked the man. He was lean with memories. "I once made a spot remover that has since been copied by big firms in the East. I've been trying to collect on that for some years now. If I only had enough money to raise a decent lawyer...." But it was too late to raise a decent lawyer; and he sat in his house dejectedly. This was the home of Hal Chase. In the evening we had a wonderful dinner his mother cooked, venison steak, that Hal's brother had shot in the mountains. Ginger was staying at Hal's. She looked fetching but there were other things troubling me as the sun went down. Where was Neal? As darkness came Hal drove me into the mysterious night of Denver. And then it all started. The following ten days were as W.C. Fields says "Fraught with eminent peril..." and mad. I moved in with Allan Temko in the really swank apartment that belonged to EdW's folks. We each had a bedroom, food in the icebox, kitchenette and a huge livingroom where Temko sat in his silk dressinggown idly composing his latest Hemingwayan short story---a colic, red-faced, pudgy hater of everything who could turn on the warmest and most charming smile in the world when real life confronted him sweetly in the night. He sat like that at his desk, and I jumped around only in my chino pants over the thick soft rug. He'd just written a story about a guy who comes to Denver for the first time. His name is Phil. His traveling companion is a mysterious and quiet fellow named Sam. Phil goes out to dig Denver and gets all hungup with arty types. He comes back to the hotel room. Lugubriously he says "Sam, they're here too." And Sam is just looking out the window sadly. "Yes," says Sam, "I know." And the point was that Sam didn't have to go and look to know this. The arty types were all over America sucking up its blood. Temko and I were great pals; he thought I was the farthest thing from an arty type. Temko liked good wines, just like Hemingway. He reminisced about his recent trip to France. "Ah Jack, if you could sit with me high in the Basque country with a cool bottle of Poignon dix-neuf, then you'd know there are other things besides boxcars." "I know that, it's just that I love boxcars and I love to read the names on them like Missouri Pacific, Great Northern, Rock Island Line..By Gad, Temko, if I could tell you everything that happened to me hitching here." The Burfords lived a few blocks away. This was a delightful family---a youngish mother, part owner of a useless goldmine, with two sons and four daughters. The wild son was Bob Burford, Ed White's boyhood buddy. Bob came roaring in to get me and we took to each other right away. We went off and drank in the Colfax bars. Bob's chief sister was a beautiful blonde called Beverly---a tennis playing, surf riding doll of the West. She was Ed White's girl. And Temko, who was only passing through Denver and doing so in real style in the apartment, was going out with Ed White's sister Jeanne for the summer. I was the only guy without a girl. I asked everybody "Where's Neal?" They made smiling negative answers. Then finally it happened. The phone rang, and who should be on the phone, but Allen Ginsberg. He gave me the address of his basement apartment. I said "What are you doing in Denver? I mean what are you <u>doing</u>? What's going on?" "Oh wait till I tell you." And I rushed over to meet him. He was working in May's department store nights; crazy Bob Burford called him up from a bar getting janitors to run after Allen with a story that somebody had died. Allen immediately thought it was me that had died. And Burford said over the phone "Jack's in Denver" and gave him my address and phone. "After you, I thought Burroughs had died" said Allen when we met and clasped hands. "And where is Neal?" "Neal is in Denver. Let me tell you." And he told me that Neal was making love to two separate girls at the same time, they being Louanne his first wife, who waited for him in a hotel room, and Carolyn a new girl who waited for him in a hotel room. "Between the two of them he rushes to me for our own unfinished business." "And what business is that?" I asked all ears. "Neal and I are embarked on a tremendous season together. We're trying to communicate with absolute honesty and absolute completeness everything on our minds. Sometimes we stay up two days getting down to the bottom of our minds. We've had to take benny. We sit on the bed, crosslegged, facing each other. I have finally taught Neal that he can do anything he wants, become mayor of Denver, marry a millionairess or become the greatest poet since Rimbaud. But he keeps rushing out to see the midget auto races. I go with him. He jumps and yells excitedly. You know Jack, Neal is really hung up on things like that.." Ginsberg said "Hmm" in his soul and thought about this. We got silent as we always do after talking everything over. "What's the schedule?" I said. There was always a schedule in Neal's life and it was growing more complicated every year. "The schedule is this: I came off work half an hour ago. In that time Neal is screwing Louanne at the hotel and gives me time to change and dress. At one sharp he rushes from Louanne to Carolyn---of course neither one of them knows what's going on---and screws her once, giving me time to arrive at one-thirty. Then he comes out with me---first he has to beg with Carolyn who's already started hating me---and we come here to talk till six in the morning. We usually spend more time than that but it's getting awfully complicated and he's pressed for time. Then at six he goes back to Louanne---and he's going to spend all day tomorrow running around to get the necessary papers for their divorce. Louanne's all for it but she insists on screwing in the interim. She says she loves his big cock---so does Carolyn---so do I." I nodded as I always do. Then he told me how Neal had met Carolyn. Bill Tomson the poolhall boy had found her in a bar and took her to a hotel; pride taking over his sense he invited the whole gang to come up and see her. Everybody sat around talking with Carolyn. Neal did nothing but look out the window. Then when everybody left Neal merely looked at Carolyn, pointed at his wrist, made the sign "four" (meaning he'd be back at four) and went out. At three the door was locked to Bill Tomson. At four it was opened to Neal. I wanted to rush out and see what the madman was doing about all this. Also he had promised to fix me up; he knew all the girls in Denver. "If you want girls just come to me, that Neal is just a pool-hall pimp" said Bob Burford. "Yes but he's a terrific guy." "Terrific? He's just smalltime. I can show you some real wild guys. Did you ever hear of Cavanaugh? He can lick any guy in Denver..." But that wasn't the point. I rushed out with Allen to find the point. We went through the rickety streets round by Welton & 17th in the odorous Denver night. The air was soft, the stars so fine, the promise of every cobbled alley so great, that I thought I was in a dream. We came to the room-inghouse where Neal haggled with Carolyn. It was an old redbrick building surrounded by wooden garages and old trees that stuck up from behind fences. We went up carpeted stairs. Allen knocked; then he darted to the back to hide, he didn't want Carolyn to see that it was him who'd knocked. I stood in the door. Neal opened it stark naked. I saw Carolyn on the bed, one beautiful creamy thigh covered with black lace, a blonde, look up with mild wonder. "Why Ja-a-ack" said Neal. "Well now....ah...hem..yes, of course...you've arrived..you old sonofabitch you finally got on that old road...well now look here....we must....yes, yes at once....we must, we really must! Now Carolyn," and he swirled on her, "Jack is here, this is my old buddy from New Yor-r-k, this is his first night in Denver and it's absolutely necessary for me to take him out and fix him up with a girl.." "But what time will you be back." "It is now" (looking at his watch) "exactly one-fourteen----I shall be back at exactly THREE fourteen, for our hour of revery together, real sweet revery darling, and then as you know, as I told you and as we agreed, I have to go and see Brierly about those papers---in the middle of the night strange as it seems and as I too roughly explained"--(this was a coverup for his rendez-vous with Allen who was still hiding)---"so now in this exact minute I must dress, put on my pants, go back to life, that is to outside life, streets and whatnot, as we agreed, it is now one-FIFTEEN and time's running, running.." "Well allright Neal, but please be sure and be back at three." "Just as I said, darling, and remember not three but three-fourteen---are we straight in the deepest and most wonderful depths of our souls dear darling?" and he went over and kissed her several times. On the wall was a nude drawing of Neal, enormous dangle and all, done by Carolyn. I was amazed. Everything was so crazy, and I still had San Francisco to make. Off we rushed into the night; Allen joined us in an alley. And we proceeded down the nar-rowest strangest and most crooked little city street I've ever seen deep in the heart of Denver Mexican-town. We talked in loud voices in the sleeping stillness. "Jack," said Neal, "I have just the girl waiting for you at this very minute---if she's off duty" (looking at his watch) "a nurse Helen Gullion, fine chick, slightly hung up on a few sexual dif-ficulties which I've tried to straighten up and I think you can manage you fine gone daddy you..So we'll go there at once, throw a pebble, no we'll ring the bell, I know how to get in...we must bring beer, no they have some themselves, and Damn!" he said socking his palm "I've just got to get into her sister Ruth tonight." "What?" said Allen, "I thought we were going to talk." "Yes yes after." "Oh these Denver doldrums!" yelled Allen to the sky. "Isn't he the finest sweetest fel-low in the world." said Neal punching me in the ribs. "Look at him, LOOK at him!" And Allen began his monkeydance in the streets of life as I'd seen him do so many times everywhere in New York. And all I could say was "Well what the hell are we doing in Denver?" "Tomorrow Jack I know where I can find you a job" said Neal revert-ing to businesslike tones "so I'll call on you, soon as I have an hour off from Louanne and cut right into that apartment of yours, say hello

147

to Temko, and take you on a trolley (damn, I've no car!) to the Denargo markets where you can begin working at once and collect a paycheck come Friday. We're really all of us bottomly broke. I haven't time to work in weeks. Friday night beyond all doubt the three of us...the old threesome of Allen Neal and Jack must go to the midget auto races and for that I can get us a ride from a guy downtown I know..." And on and on into the night. We got to the hospital dormitory where the nurse sisters lived. The one for me was still on duty, the sister that Neal wanted was in. We sat down on her couch. I was scheduled at this time to call Bob Burford: I did: he came rushing over at once. Coming in the door he took off his shirt and undershirt and began hugging the absolute stranger Ruth Gullion. Bottles rolled on the floor. Three o'clock came. Neal rushed off for his hour of reverie with Carolyn. He was back on time. The other sister showed up. We all needed a car now, we were making too much noise. Bob Burford called up a buddy with a car. He came. We all piled in; Allen was trying to conduct his scheduled talk with Neal in the backseat but there was too much confusion. "Let's all go to my apartment!" I shouted. We did; the moment the car stopped there I jumped out and stood on my head in the grass. All my keys fell out, I haven't found them since. We rushed shouting into the apartment. Allan Temko stood barring our way in his silk dressinggown. "I'll have no goingon like this in Ed White's apartment!" "What?" we all shouted. There was confusion. Burford was rolling in the grass with one of the nurses. Temko wouldn't let us in. We swore to call Ed White and confirm the party and also invite him. Instead we all rushed back to the Denver downtown bars and nothing came of it. I suddenly found myself alone in the street with no money. My last dollar was gone. I walked five miles up Colfax to my comfortable bed in the apartment. Temko had to let me in. I wondered if Neal and Allen were having their heart-to-heart. I would find out later. The nights in Denver are cool and I slept like a log. Then everybody began planning a tremendous trek to the mountains en masse. This news came in the morning together with a phonecall that complicated matters---my old roadfriend Eddie, who took a blind chance and called. Now I had the opportunity to get my shirt back. Eddie was with his girl in a house off Colfax. He wanted to know if I knew where to find work and I told him to come over, figuring Neal would know. Neal arrived hurrying. Temko and I were having a hasty breakfast that I always cooked. Neal wouldn't even sit down. "I have a thousand things to do, in fact hardly any time to take you down Denargo but let's go man." "Wait for my roadbuddy Eddie." Temko found our hurrying troubles amusing. He'd come to Denver to write leisurely. He treated Neal with extreme deference. Neal paid no attention. Temko never dreamed Neal in a few years would become such a great writer or even that anyone would ever write his story as I am. He talked to Neal like this--"Cassady what's this I hear about you screwing three girls at the same time." And Neal shuffled on the rug and said "Oh yes, oh yes, that's the way it goes" and looked at his watch, and Temko snuffed down his nose. I felt sheepish rushing off with Neal---Temko insisted he was a moron and a fool. Of course he wasn't and I wanted to prove it to everybody somehow. We met Eddie. Neal paid no attention to him either and off we went in a trolley across the hot Denver noon to find the jobs. I hated the thought of it. Eddie talked and talked like he always did. We found a man in the markets who agreed to hire both of us; work started at four o'clock in the morning and went till six. The man said "I like boys who like to work." "You've got your man" said Eddie, but I wasn't so sure about myself. "I just won't sleep" I decided. There were so many other interesting things to do. Eddie showed up the next morning, I didn't. I had a bed and Temko bought food for the icebox and in exchange for that I cooked and washed the dishes. Meantime I got all involved in everything. A big party took place at the Burford's one night. The Burford mother was gone on a trip. Bob Burford simply called everybody he knew and told them to bring whiskey; then he went through his address book for girls. He made me do most of the talking. A whole bunch of girls showed up. I used the phone to call Allen and find what Neal was doing now. Neal was coming at three in the morning. I went there after the party. Allen's basement apartment was on

Grant street in an old redbrick roominghouse near a church. You went down an alley, down some stone steps, opened a old raw door and went through a kind of cellar till you came to his board door. It was like the room of a Russian saint. One bed, a candle burning, stonewalls that oozed moisture, and a crazy makeshift ikon of some kind that he made for the occasion. He read me his poetry. It was called "Denver Doldrums." Allen woke up in the morning and heard the "vulgar pigeons" yakking in the streets outside his cell; he saw the "sad nightingales" which reminded him of his mother nodding on the branches. A grey shroud fell over the city. The mountains---the magnificent Rockies that you could see to the West from any part of town---were "papier mache." The whole universe was crazy and cockeyed and extremely strange. He wrote of Neal as a "child of the rainbow" who bore his torment in his agonised cock. He referred to him as "Oedipus Eddie" who had to "scrape bubblegum off windowpanes." He referred to Brierly as "dancingmaster death." He brooded in his basement over a huge journal in which he was keeping track of everything that happened everyday---everything Neal did and said. Allen told me of his trip in a bus. "Coming through Missouri there occurred a miraculous lightning storm that transformed the firmaments into a great electrical evil frenzy. Everybody in the bus was frightened. I said 'Don't be frightened, it's only a Sign.' Imagine Missouri---where Burroughs and Lucien are from." "That's also where some of Neal's folks came from." "I don't know," said Allen growing sad, "What shall I do?" "Why don't you go down to Texas and see Burroughs and Joan?" "I want Neal to come with me." "How can he do that with all his women?" "Oh, I don't know." Neal came in at three in the morning. "Everything's straight," he announced. "I'm going to divorce Louanne and marry Carolyn and go live with her in San Francisco. But this is only after you and I, dear Allen, go to Texas, dig Bill, that gone cat I've never met and both of you've told me so much about, and then I'll go to San Fran." Then they got down to business. They sat on the bed crosslegged and looked straight at each other. I slouched in a nearby chair and saw all of it. They began with an abstract thought, discussed it; reminded each other of another abstract point forgotten in the rush of events; Neal apologized but promised he could get back to it and manage it fine; bringing up illustrations. "And just as we were crossing Wazee I wanted to tell you about how I felt of your frenzy with the midgets and it was just then, remember, you pointed out that old bum with the hardon in his baggy pants and said he looked just like your father?" "Yes, yes, of course I remember; and not only that, but it started a train of my own, something real wild that I had to tell you. I'd forgotten it, now you just reminded me of it---" and two new points were born. They hashed these over. Then Allen asked Neal if he was honest and specifically if he was being honest with <u>him</u> in the bottom of his soul. "Why do you bring that up again?" "There's one last thing I want to know…" "But, dear Jack, you're listening, you're sitting there, we'll ask Jack, what would he say." And I said, "That last thing is what you can't get, Allen. Nobody can get to that last thing. We keep on living in hopes of catching it once for all…" "No no no, you're talking absolute bullshit and Wolfean romantic posh!" said Allen, and Neal joined in: "I didn't mean that at all, but we'll let Jack have his own mind, and in fact, don't you think Allen there's a kind of a dignity in the way he's sitting there and digging us, crazy cat came all the way across the country..old Jack won't tell, old Jack won't tell." "It isn't that I won't tell," I protested, "I just don't know what you're both driving at or trying to get at…I know it's too much for anybody." "Everything you say is negative." "Then what is it you're trying to do?" "Tell him." "No, you tell him." "There's nothing to tell," I laughed. I had on Allen's hat, I pulled it down over my eyes. "I want to sleep" I said. "Poor Jack always wants to sleep." I kept quiet. They started in again. "When you borrowed that nickel to make up the check for the chick-enfried steaks.." "No, man, the chili! Remember, the Texas Star?" "I was mixing it with Tuesday. When you borrowed that nickel you said, now listen, YOU said 'Allen this is the last time I'll impose on you,' as if, and really, you meant that I had agreed with you about no more imposing." "No, no, no, I didn't mean that---you harken back now if you will my dear fellow to the night Louanne was crying in the room, and when, turning to you and indicating by my extra added sincerity of tone which we both knew was contrived but had its intention, that is, by my playacting I showed that...but wait, that isn't it..." "Of course that isn't it! Because you forget that...but I'll stop accusing you. Yes is what I said..." And on, on into the night they talked like this. At dawn I looked up. They were tying up the last of the morning's matters. "When I said to you that I had to sleep because of Louanne, that is, seeing her this morning at ten I didn't bring my peremptory tone to bear in regards to what you'd just said about the unnecessariness of sleep but only, ONLY mind you because of the fact that I absolutely, simply, purely and without any whatevers have to sleep now, I mean, man, my eyes are closing, they're redhot, sore, tired, beat..." "Ah child," said Allen. "We'll just have to sleep now. Let's stop the machine." "You can't stop the machine!" yelled Allen at the top of his voice. The first birds sang. "Now, when I raise my hand" said Neal, "we'll stop talking, we'll both understand purely and without any hassel that we are simply stopping talking, and we'll just sleep." "You can't stop the machine like that." "Stop the machine" I said. They looked at me. "He's been awake all this time listening. What were you thinking Jack?" I told them that I was thinking they were very amazing maniacs and that I had spent the whole night listening to them like a man watching the mechanism of a watch that reached clear to the top of Berthoud pass and yet was made with the smallest works of the most delicate watch in the world. They smiled. I pointed my finger at them and said "If you keep this up you'll both go crazy but let me know what happens as you go along." We also talked about the possibility of their coming to Frisco with me. I walked out and took a trolley to my apartment and Allen Ginsberg's papier-mache mtns. grew red as the great sun rose from the eastward plains. In the afternoon I was involved in that trek to the mountains and didn't get to see Neal or Allen for five days. Beverly Burford had use of her employer's car for the weekend. We brought suits and hung them on the windows and took off for Central City, Bob Burford driving, Ed White lounging in the back, and Beverly up front. It was my first view of the interior of the Rockies. Central City is an old mining town that was once called the Richest Square Mile in the World, where a veritable shelf of silver had been found by the old buzzards who roamed the hills. They grew wealthy overnight and had a beautiful little opera house built in the midst of their steep shacks on the slope. Lillian Russell had come there; opera stars from Europe. Then Central City became a ghost town, till the energetic Chamber of Commerce types of the new West decided to revive the place. They polished up the opera house and every summer stars from the Metropolitan Opera came out and performed. It was a big vacation for everybody. Tourists came, from everywhere, even Hollywood stars. We drove up the mountain and found the narrow streets chockfull of chichi tourists. I thought of Temko's Sam and Temko was right. Temko himself was there turning on his big social smile to everybody and oohing and aahin most sincerely over everything. "Jack" he cried clutching my arm "just look at this old town. Think how it was a hundred, what the hell, only eighty, sixty years ago; they had opera!" "Yeah," I said imitating one of his characters, "but they're here." "The bastards" he cursed. But he rushed off to enjoy himself, Jean White on his arm. Beverly Burford was an enterprising blonde. She knew of an old miner's house at the edge of town that we boys could sleep in for the weekend; all we had to do was clean it out. We could also throw vast parties in there. It was an old shack of a thing covered with an inch of dust inside; it even had a porch and a well in back. Ed White and Bob Burford rolled up their sleeves and started in cleaning it, a major job that took them all afternoon and part of the night. But they had a bucket of beerbuttles and everything was fine. As for me, I was scheduled to be a guest at the opera, Justin W. Brierly had arranged it, and escorted Bev on my arm. I wore a suit of Ed's. Only a few days ago I'd come in to Denver like a bum; this afternoon I was all racked up sharp in a suit, with a beautiful well-dressed blonde on my arm, bowing to dignitaries and chatting in the lobby under chandeliers. I wondered what Mississippi Gene would say if he could see.

The opera was Fidelio, Beethoven's mighty work. "What gloom!" cried the baritone rising out of the dungeon under a groaning stone.... I cried for it. That's how I see life too. I was so interested in the opera that for awhile I forgot the circumstances of my crazy life and got lost in the great mournful sounds of Beethoven and the rich Rembrandt tones of his story. "Well Jack, how did you like our production for this year?" asked Brierly proudly in the street outside. "What gloom, what gloom," I said, "it's absolutely great." "The next thing you'll have to do is meet the members of the cast" he went on in his official tones but luckily he forgot this in the rush of other things and vanished. It was a matinee performance I'd seen; there was another one in the evening scheduled. I'll tell you how I came at least, if not to the pleasure of meeting the members of the cast, to using their bathtub and best towels. Incidentally I must explain here why Brierly thought enough of me to make arrangements of all sorts for my benefit. Hal Chase and Ed White were his most highly regarded charges; they'd been to college with me; we'd roamed New York together and talked. Brierly's first impression of me was none too favorable...I was sleeping on the floor, drunk, when he came to visit Hal one Sunday morning in New York. "Who's this?" "That's Jack." "So that's the famous Jack. What is he doing sleeping on the floor?" "He does that all the time." "I thought you said he was a genius of some kind." "Oh sure he is, can't you see it?" "I must say it requires some difficulty. I thought he was married, where's his wife?" I was married at the time. "Oh she just went on going; Jack gave up, she's in the West End bar with an undertaker who's got a couple hundred dollars and buys everybody drinks." After which I rose from the floor and shook Mr. Brierly's hand. He wondered what Hal saw in me; and still did in Denver that summer and never really thought I'd amount to anything. It was precisely what I wanted him and the whole world to think; then I could sneak in, if that's what they wanted, and sneak out again, which I did. Bev and I went back to the miner's shack, I took off my duds and joined the boys in the cleaning. It was an enormous job. Allan Temko sat in the middle of the front room that had already been

cleaned and refused to help. On a little table in front of him he had
his bottle of beer and his glass. As we rushed around with buckets of
water and brooms he reminisced, "Ah if you could just come with me
sometime and drink Cinzano and hear the musicians of Bandol then
you'd be living." Temko was an officer in the Navy; he got drunk and
began giving orders. Burford had a habit concerning Temko's irritat-
ing overweeningness; he pointed at him with a limp finger, turned to
you with awe and said "Cherry? You think he's cherry?" Temko paid
no attention. "Ah," he said, "then there's Normandy in the summers,
the sabots, the fine Rhine wine. Come on Sam," he said to his invisible pal "take the wine out of the water and let's see if it got cold
enough while we fished."- - straight out of Hemingway, it was. We
called the girls that went by in the street. "Come on help us clean up
the joint. Everybody's invited to our party tonight." They joined in.
We had a huge crew working for us. Finally the singers in the opera
chorus, mostly young kids, came over and pitched in. The sun went
down. Our day's work over Ed, Burford and I decided to sharp up for
the big night. We went across town to the roominghouse where the
opera stars were living, also Brierly. From across the night we heard
the beginning of the evening performance. "Just right, said Burford.
"Latch on to some of these toothbrushes and towels and we'll spruce
up a bit." We also took hairbrushes, colognes, shaving lotions and
went laden into the bathroom. We all took baths and sang like opera
stars. Burford wanted to wear the first tenor's tie but Ed White pre-
vailed with his casual good sense. "Isn't this great?" Ed White kept
saying. "Using the opera stars' bathroom and towels and shaving
lotion." And razors. It was a wonderful night. Central City is two
miles high; at first you get drunk on the altitude, then you get tired,
and there's a fever in your soul. We approached the lights around the
opera house down the narrow dark street; then we took a sharp right
and hit some old saloons with swinging doors. Most of the tourists
were in the opera. We started off with a few extra size Jumbo beers.
There was a player piano. Beyond the backdoor was a view of the
mountainsides in the moonlight. I let out a Yahoo. The night was on.

We rushed back to our miner's shack. Everything was in preparation for the big party. The girls Bev and Jean cooked up a snack of beans and franks and then we danced to our own music, and started on the beer for fair. The opera over, great crowds of young girls came piling into our place. Burford and Ed and I licked our lips. We grabbed them and danced. There was no music, just dancing. The place filled up. People began to bring bottles. We rushed out to hit bars and rushed back. The night was getting more and more frantic. I wished Neal and Allen were there- -then I realized they'd be out of place and unhappy. They were like the man with the dungeon stone and the gloom, rising from the underground, the sordid hipsters of America, a new beat generation that I was slowly joining. The boys from the chorus showed up. They began singing "Sweet Adeline." They also sang phrases such as "Pass me the beer" and "What are you doing with your face hanging out" and great long baritone howls of "Fi-de-lio!" "Ah me, what gloom!" I sang. The girls were terrific. They went out in the backyard and necked. There were beds in the other rooms, the uncleaned dusty ones, and I had a girl sitting on it and was talking with her when suddenly there was a great inrush of young ushers from the opera, half of them hired by Brierly, who just grabbed girls and kissed them without proper come-ons. Teenagers, drunk, dishevelled, excited…they ruined our party. Inside of five minutes every single girl was gone and a great big fraternity type party got underway with banging of beer bottles and roars. Bob and Ed and I decided to hit the bars. Temko was gone, Bev and Jean were gone. We tottered into the night. The opera crowd was out, jamming the bars from bar to wall. Temko was shouting above heads. Justin W. Brierly was shaking hands with everybody and saying "Good afternoon, how are you?" and when midnight came he was saying "Good afternoon, how are you?" At one point I saw him rushing the Mayor of Denver off somewhere. Then he came back with a middleaged woman; next minute he was talking to a couple of young ushers in the street. The next minute he was shaking my hand without recognizing me and saying "Happy New Year, m'boy." He wasn't drunk on liquor, just drunk on what he liked---thousands of people milling, and he the director of it. Dancingmaster Death indeed. But I liked him, I always liked J. W. Brierly. He was sad. I saw him threading through the crowd in loneliness. Everybody knew him. "Happy New Year," he called, and sometimes "Merry Christmas." He said this all the time. At Christmas he said Happy Halloween. There was an artist in the bar who was highly respected by everyone; Justin had insisted that I meet him and I was trying to avoid it; his name was Bellaconda or some such thing. His wife was with him. They sat sourly at a table. There was also some kind of Argentinian tourist at the bar. Burford gave him a shove to make room; he turned and snarled. Burford handed me his glass and knocked him down on the brass rail with one punch. The man was momentarily out. There were screams; Ed and I scooted Burford out. There was so much confusion the sheriff couldn't even thread his way through the crowd to find the victim. Nobody could identify Burford. We went to other bars. Temko staggered up a dark street. "What the hell's the matter? Any fights? Just call on me." Great laughter rang from all sides. I wondered what the Spirit of the Mountain was thinking; and looked up, and saw jackpines in the moon, and saw ghosts of old miners, and wondered about it. In the whole eastern dark wall of the Divide this night there was silence and the whisper of the wind, except in the ravine where we roared; and on the other side of the Divide was the great western slope, and the big plateau that went to Steamboat Springs, and dropped, and led you to the Eastern Colorado desert and the Utah desert; all in darkness now as we fumed and screamed in our mountain nook, mad drunken Americans in the mighty land. And beyond, beyond, over the Sierras the other side of Carson sink was bejewelled bay-encircled nightlike old Frisco of my dreams. We were situated on the roof of America and all we could do was yell, I guess---across the night, eastward over the plains where somewhere an old man with white hair was probably walking towards us with the Word and would arrive any minute and make us silent. Burford exceeded all bounds; he insisted on going back to the bar where he'd fought. Ed and I didn't like what he did but stuck to him.

He went up to Bellaconda the artist and threw a hiball in his face; his sister Bev screamed "No Bob, not that!" We dragged him out. He was beyond himself. A baritone singer from the chorus joined us and we went to a regular Central City bar. Here he called the waitress a whore. A group of sullen men were ranged along the bar; they hated tourists. One of them said "You boys better be out of here by the count of ten." We were. We staggered back to the shack and went to sleep. In the morning I woke up and turned over; a big cloud of dust rose from the mattress. I yanked at the window; it was nailed. Ed White was in the bed too. We coughed and sneezed. Our breakfast consisted of stale beer. Beverly came back from her hotel and we got our things together to leave. But we had to go and watch Bellaconda the artist, at Brierly's orders, mixing things in his kiln; it would constitute Burford's apology. We all stood around the kiln as the artist lectured. Burford smiled and nodded and tried to look interested and looked sheepish as hell. Brierly stood by proudly. Beverly leaned on me wearily. I cut out and went to the ushers' dormitories and found a toilet; as I sat there I saw an eye in the keyhole. "Who's that in there?" said the voice. "Jack" I said. It was Brierly; he was wandering around and had got bored with the kiln. Everything seemed to be collapsing. As we were going down the steps of the miner's house Beverly slipped and fell flat on her face. Poor girl was overwrought. Her brother and Ed and I helped her up. We got back in the car; Temko and Jean joined us. The sad ride back to Denver began. Suddenly we came down from the mountain and overlooked the great sea-plain of Denver; heat rose as from an oven. We began to sing songs. I was itching to get on to San Francisco. That night I found Allen and to my amazement he told me he'd been in Central City with Neal. "What did you do?" "Oh we ran around the bars and then Neal stole a car and we drove back down the mountain curves ninety miles an hour." "I didn't see you." "We didn't know you were there." "Well man, I'm going to San Francisco." "Neal has Ruth lined up for you tonight." "Well then I'll put it off." "I had no money; I sent my mother an airmail letter asking her for fifty dollars and said it would be the last money I'd ask; after that she would be getting money back from me, as soon as I got that ship. Then I went to meet Ruth Gullion and took her back to the apartment. I got her in my bedroom after a long talk in the dark of the front room. She was a nice little girl, simple and true, and tremendously frightened of sex; she said it was because she saw such awful things in the hospital. I told her it was beautiful. I wanted to prove this to her. She let me prove it, but I was too impatient and proved nothing. She sighed in the dark. "What do you want out of life?" I asked and I used to ask that all the time of girls. "I don't know" she said. "Just work and try to get along." She yawned. I put my hand over her mouth and told her not to yawn. I tried to tell her how excited I was about life and the things we could do together; saying that, and planning to leave Denver in two days. She turned away wearily. We lay on our backs looking at the ceiling and wondering what God had wrought when he made life so sad and disinclined. We made vague plans to meet in Frisco. My moments in Denver were coming to an end. I could feel it when I walked her home in the holy Denver night and on the way back stretched out on the grass of an old church with a bunch of hoboes and their talk made me want to get back on that road. Every now and then one would get up and hit a passerby for a dime. They talked of harvests moving North. It was warm and soft. I wanted to go and get Ruth again and tell her a lot more things, and really make love to her this time, and calm her fears about men. Boys and girls in America have such a sad time together; sophistication demands that they submit to sex immediately without proper preliminary talk. Not courting talk---real straight talk about souls, for life is holy and every moment is precious. I heard the Denver & Rio Grande locomotive howling off to the mountains. I wanted to pursue my star further. Temko and I sat sadly talking in the midnight hours. "Have you ever read The Green Hills of Africa? It's Hemingway's best." We wished each other luck. We would meet in Frisco. I saw Burford under a dark tree in the street. "Goodbye Bob, when do we meet again?" I went to look for Allen and Neal- -nowhere to be found. Ed White shot his hand up in the air and said "So you're leaving Yo." We called each other Yo. "Yep," I said. I wandered around Denver. It seemed to me every bum on Larimer St. maybe was Neal Cassady's father, Old Neal Cassady they called him, the Barber. I went in the Windsor hotel where father and son had lived and where one night Neal was frightfully waked up by the legless man on the rollerboard who shared the room with them who came thundering across the floor on his terrible wheels to touch the boy. I saw the little midget newspaperselling woman with the short legs, on the corner of Curtis and Fifteenth. "Man," Neal told me, "think of lifting her in the air and fucking her!" I walked around the sad honkytonks of Curtis street: young kids in jeans and red shirts, peanut shells, movie marquees, shooting parlors. Beyond the glittering street was darkness, and beyond the darkness, the West. I had to go. At dawn I found Allen. I read some of his enormous journal, slept there, and in the morning, drizzly and gray, tall sixfoot Al Hinkle came in with Bill Tomson- -a handsome kid---and Jim Holmes the hunchback poolshark. Jim Holmes had saintly big blue eyes but he was a mumbling bore. He wore a beard; he lived with his grandmother. Big Al was the son and brother of a cop family. Bill Tomson claimed he could run faster than Neal. They sat around and listened with abashed smiles as Allen Ginsberg read them his apocalyptic mad poetry. I slumped in my chair, finished. "Oh ye Denver birds!" cried Allen. We all filed out and went up a typical cobbled Denver alley between incinerators smoking slowly. "I used to roll my hoop up this alley" Hal Chase had told me. I wanted to see him do it; I wanted to see Denver ten years ago when they were all children and in the sunny cherryblossom morning of Springtime in the Rockies they rolled their hoops up the joyous alleys full of promise...the whole gang. And Neal, ragged and dirty, prowling by himself with a preoccupied frenzy. Bill Tomson and I walked in the drizzle; I went to Eddie's girl's house and got my wool plaid shirt back---the shirt of Preston Nebraska. It was all there, all tied up, the whole enormous sadness of a shirt. Bill Tomson said he'd meet me in Frisco. Everybody was going to Frisco. I went and found my money had arrived. The sun came out, and Ed White rode a trolley with me to the bus station. I bought my ticket to San Fran, spending half of the fifty, and got on at two o'clock in the afternoon. Ed White waved goodbye. The bus rolled out of the storied eager Denver streets. "By God I gotta come back and see what else will happen!" I promised. In a last minute phone call Neal said he and Allen might join me on the Coast; I pondered this, and realized also I hadn't talked to Neal for more than five minutes in the whole time. Anyway I was gone, and this is what Neal and Allen did. Neal concluded his business with his girls and the two boys, giggling happily, took off for Texas on the road. Someone in Denver saw them going down South Broadway; Neal was running and jumping to catch high leaves, Allen, according to the informant, "was making notes about it." This was the story told by Dan Burmeister, of whom more later. They journeyed days and nights to Texas; in all that time they didn't sleep and talked continually. Nothing was left undecided and undiscussed. On the highway, by Raton rocks, by windy panhandle grasses at Amarillo, in the bushy heart of Texas, they talked and talked, till arriving near Waverly Texas down near Houston where Bill Burroughs lived so much had been decided that they kneeled in the dark of the road, facing each other, and made vows of eternal friendship & love. Allen blessed him; Neal acknowledged. They kneeled and chanted till their knees were sore. And as they wandered around the woods looking for Bill's house they suddenly saw Bill Burroughs himself loping along a fence with a fishing pole. He'd been fishing in the bayou. "Well," he said, "I see you boys finally made it. Joan and Hunkey been wondering where you've been." "Is Hunkey here?" they cried joyously. "He's been here most conspicuously..." "Wow! Damn! Whoopee!" cried Neal. "Now I get to dig Hunkey too! Less go, less go!" There began a series of events there that ended up in New York at just the time I got back there myself. But meanwhile I was rolling along in San Francisco and I'll get to them later. I was two weeks late meeting Henri Cru. The bus trip from Denver to Frisco was uneventful except that my whole soul leaped to it the nearer we got to Frisco. Cheyenne again...in the afternoon this time...and then went over the rangelands; crossing the

Divide at midnight at Creston, arriving Salt Late City at dawn, a city of sprinklers, the least likely place for Neal to have been born; then out to Nevada in the hot sun, Reno by nightfall, its twinkling Chinese streets; then up the Sierra Nevada, pines, stars, mountain lodges signifying Frisco romances---a little boy in the back seat crying to his mother "Mama when do we get home to Truckee?" And Truckee itself, homey Truckee and then down the hill to the flats of Sacramento. I suddenly realized I was in California. Warm palmy air---air you can kiss---and palms. Along the storied Sacramento river on a superhighway; into the hills again; up, down; and suddenly the vast expanse of bay---it was just before dawn---with the sleepy lights of Frisco festooned across. Crossing the Oakland Bay Bridge I slept for the first time since Denver soundly; so that I was rudely jolted in the bus station at Market and Third into the memory of the fact that I was in San Francisco three thousand two hundred miles from my mother's house in Ozone Park, Long Island. I wandered out like a haggard ghost, and there she was, Frisco, long bleak streets with trolley wires all shrouded in fog and whiteness. I stumbled about a few blocks. Weird bums (it was Mission st.) asked me for dimes in the dawn. I heard music somewhere. "Boy am I going to dig all this later! But now I've got to find Henri Cru." And following his instructions I took a bus and rode out over the Golden Gate bridge to Marin City. The sun was making a terrific haze over the Pacific as we crossed Golden Gate, a haze I couldn't look into, and so this was the shining shield of the China-going world ocean and it wore a terrible aspect especially as I was scheduled to sail out on it. Marin City where Henri Cru lived was a collection of shacks in a valley, housing project shacks built for Navy yard workers during the war; it was really a canyon, and a deep one, treed profusedly on all slopes. There were special stores and barbershops and tailorshops for the people of the Project. It was, so they say, the only community in America where whites and Negroes lived together voluntarily; and that was so, and a wild joyous place I've never seen since. On the door of Henri's shack was the note he had pinned up there three weeks ago. "Jack Claptrap!" (in huge letters, printed) "If nobody's home climb in through the window." And it said "Signed Henri Cru." The note was weather beaten and gray by now---but Henri hadn't given up. I climbed in and there he was sleeping with his girl Diane- -on a bed he stole from a merchant ship as he told me later; imagine the electrician of a merchant ship sneaking over the side in the middle of the night with a bed, and weaving and straining at the oars to shore. This barely explains Henri Cru. The reason I'm going into everything that happened in Sanfran is because it ties up with everything else all the way down the line. Henri Cru and I met at prep school years ago; but the thing that really tied us together was my former wife. Henri found her first. He came into my dorm room one night and said "Kerouac get up, the old maestro has come to see you." I got up, and dropped some pennies on the floor when I put my pants on. It was four in the afternoon; I used to sleep all the time in college. "All right, all right, don't drop your gold all over the place. I have found the gonest little girl in the world and I am going straight to the Lion's Den with her tonight." And he dragged me to meet her. A week later she was going with me. She said she despised Henri. Henri was a tall dark handsome Frenchman- -he looked a kind of Marseilles blackmarketeer of twenty---because he was French he had to talk in jazz American---his English was perfect, his French was perfect---he liked to dress sharp, slightly on the collegiate side, and go out with fancy blondes and spend a lot of money. It's not that he never forgave me for screwing off with his Edie---only it was always a point that tied us together, and from the very first day that guy was loyal to me and had real affection for me, and God knows why. When I found him in Marin City that morning he had fallen on the beat and evil days that come to all young guys in their middle twenties. He was reduced to hanging around waiting for a ship, and to earn his living he had a job as a special guard in the barracks across the canyon. His girl Diane had a bad tongue and gave him a calling down every day. They spent all week saving pennies and went out Saturdays to spend fifty bucks in three hours. Henri wore shorts around the shack, with a crazy Army cap on his head; Diane went around with her hair up.

Thus attired they yelled at each other all week. I never saw so many snarls in all my born days. But on Saturday night, smiling graciously at one another, they took off like a pair of successful Hollywood characters and went on the town. Henri wanted to get Diane into the movies; he wanted to make a Hollywood writer out of me; he was nothing but plans. He woke up and saw me come in the window. His great laugh, one of the greatest laughs in the world, dinned in my ear. "Aaaaah Kerouac, he comes in through the window, he follows instructions to a T. Where have you been, you're two weeks late!" He slapped me on the back, he punched Diane in the ribs, he leaned on the wall and laughed and cried, he pounded the table so you could hear it everywhere in Marin city and that great long "Aaaaah" laugh resounding around Marin city. "Kerouac!" he screamed. "The one and only indispensable Kerouac." I had just come through the little fishing village of Sausalito and the first thing I said was "There must be a lot of Italians in Sausalito." "There must be a lot of Italians in Sausalito!" he shouted at the top of his lungs.. "Aaaaah!" he pounded himself, he fell on the bed, he almost rolled on the floor. "Did you hear what Kerouac said? There must be a lot of Italians in Sausalito? Aaaaah-haaa! Hoo! Wow! Whee!" He got red like a beet laughing. "Oh you slay me, Kerouac, you're the funniest man in the world, and here you are, you finally got here, he came in through the window, you saw him Diane, he followed instructions and came in through the window...Aaah! Hooo!" The strange thing was that next door to Henri lived a Negro man called Mr. Snow whose laugh, I swear here on the Bible, was positively and finally the one greatest laugh in all this world. I can't describe it now...I will in a moment when the time comes. But this Mr. Snow began his laugh from the supper table when his old wife said something casual; he apparently got up choking, leaned on the wall, looked up to heaven, and started; he ended staggering thru the door, leaning on neighbors' walls, he was drunk with it, he staggered thruout marin city in the shadows raising his whooping triumphant call to the demon god that must have prodded his ass to do it... I don't know if he ever finished supper. There's a possibility that Henri

164

without knowing it was picking up from this amazing man Mr. Snow..
And I say tho Henri was having worklife problems and bad lovelife
with a sharp-tongued woman he at least had learned to laugh almost
better than anyone in the world and I saw all the fun we were going
to have in Frisco. The pitch was this: Henri slept with Diane in the
bed across the room, and I slept in the cot by the window. I was not
to touch Diane. Henri at once made a speech concerning this. "I don't
want to find you two playing around when you think I'm not looking.
You can't teach the old maestro a new tune. This is an original saying
of mine." I looked at Diane. She was a fetching hunk- - a honey-
colored creature, but there was hate in her eyes for both of us. Her
ambition was to marry a rich man. She came from a smalltown in
Kansas. She rued the day she ever took up with Henri. On one of his
big show off weekends he spent a hundred dollars on her and she
thought she'd found an heir. Instead she was all hung up in this shack
and for lack of anything else she had to stay there. She had a job in
Frisco, she had to take the Greyhound bus at the crossroads and go
in everyday. She never forgave Henri for it. He made the best of things.
I was to stay in the shack and write a shining original story for a Hollywood studio. Henri was going to fly down in a Stratosphere liner
with his harp under his arm and make us all rich; Diane was to go
with him; he was going to introduce her to his buddy's father who
was a famous director and an intimate of WC Fields. So the first week
I stayed in the shack in Marin City writing furiously at some gloomy
tale about New York that I thought would satisfy a Hollywood director, and the trouble with it was that it was too sad. Henri couldn't
barely read and so he never even saw it, he just carried it down to
Hollywood a few weeks later. Diane was too bored and hated us too
much to bother reading it. I spent countless rainy hours drinking coffee and scribbling. Finally I told Henri it wouldn't do; I wanted a job;
I had to depend on them for cigarettes. A shadow of disappointment
crossed Henri's brow---he was always being disappointed about the
funniest things. He had a heart of gold. He arranged to get me the
same kind of job he had, as a guard in the barracks. I went through

the necessary routine and to my surprise the bastards hired me. I was sworn in by the local police Chief, given a badge, a club, and now I was a special policeman. I wondered what Neal and Allen and Burroughs would say about this. I had to have Navy blue trousers to go with my black jacket and cop cap; for the first two weeks I had to wear Henri's trousers; since he was so tall, and had a potbelly from eating voracious meals out of boredom, I went flapping around like Charley Chaplin to my first night of work. Henri gave me a flashlight and his .32 automatic. "Where'd you get this gun?" "On my way to the Coast last summer I jumped off the train at North Platte Nebraska to stretch my legs and what did I see in the window but this wonderful little gun which I promptly bought and barely made the train." And I tried to tell him what North Platte Nebraska meant to me---buying the whiskey with the boys---and he slapped me on the back and said I was the funniest man in the world. With the flashlight to illuminate my way I climbed the steep walls of the south canyon, got up on a highway streaming with cars in the night Frisco-bound, scrambled down the other side almost falling, and came to the bottom of a ravine where a little farmhouse stood near a creek and where every blessed night the same dog barked at me for months. Then it was a fast walk along a silvery dusty road beneath inky trees of California---a road like in the Mark of Zorro and a road like all the roads you see in Western B movies---I used to take out my gun and play cowboys in the dark. Then I climbed another hill and there were the barracks. These barracks were for the temporary quartering of overseas construction workers. The men who came through stayed there waiting for their ship. Most of them were bound for Okinawa. Most of them were running away from something---usually the law. There were tough groups of brothers from Alabama, shifty men from New York, all kinds from all over. And knowing full well how horrible it would be to work a full year in Okinawa they drank. The job of the special guards was to see that they didn't tear the barracks down. We had our headquarters in the main building, just a wooden contraption with panelwalled offices. Here at a rolltop desk we sat around shifting our guns off our asses and yawning, and the old cops told stories. It was a horrible crew of men, men with copsouls, all except Henri and I. Henri was only trying to make a living, so was I, but these men wanted to make arrests and get compliments from the Chief in town. They even went so far as to say that if you didn't make at least one arrest a month you'd be fired. I gulped at the prospect of making an arrest. What actually happened was that I was as drunk as anybody in the barracks the night all hell broke loose. This was the night when the schedule was so arranged that I was all alone for six hours...the only cop on the grounds; and not that anybody knew it, but everybody in the barracks seemed to have gotten drunk that night. It was because their ship was leaving in the morning. They drank like seamen do the night before the anchor goes up. I sat in the office, in a rolltop chair, with my feet on the desk, reading Blue Book adventures about Oregon and the north country, when I suddenly realized there was a great hum of activity in the usually quiet night. I went out. Lights were burning in practically every damned shack on the grounds. Men were shouting, bottles were breaking. It was do or die for me. I took my flashlight and went to the noisiest door and knocked. Someone opened it about six inches. "What do you want?" I said "I'm guarding these barracks tonight and you boys are supposed to keep quiet as much as you can" or some such silly remark. They slamd the door in my face. I stood looking at the wood of it against my nose. It was like a western movie; the time had come for me to assert myself. I knocked again. They opened up wide this time. "Listen" I said "I don't want to come around bothering you fellows but I'll lose my job if you make too much noise." "Who are you?" "I'm a guard here." "Never seen you before." "Well, here's my badge." "What are you doing with that pistolcracker on your ass?" "It isn't mine" I apologized "I borrowed it." "Have a drink, for krissakes." I didn't mind if I would. I took two. I said "Okay boys? You'll keep quiet boys? I'll get hell you know." "It's allright kid," they said, "go make your rounds, come back for another drink if you want one." And I went to all the doors in this manner and pretty soon I was as drunk as anybody else. Come dawn, it was my duty to put up the American flag on a sixty foot pole, and this morning I put it up upsidedown and went home to bed. When I came back in the evening the regular corp of cops were sitting around grimly in the office. "Say bo, what was all the noise around here last night. We've had complaints from people who live in those houses across the canyon." "I don't know" I said "it sounds pretty quiet right now." "The whole contingent's gone. You was supposed to keep order around here last night---the Chief is yelling at you---and another thing---do you know you can go to jail for putting the American flag upsidedown on a government pole." "Upsidedown?" I was horrified; of course I hadn't realized it; I did it every morning mechanically. I shook out its dust in dew and hauled her up. "Yessir," said a fat cop who'd spent thirty years as a guard in the horrible prison known as San Quentin, "you could go to jail for doing something like that." The others nodded grimly. They were always sitting around on their asses; they were proud of their jobs. They took their guns out and talked about them, but they never pointed them. They were itching to shoot somebody. Henri and me. Let me tell you about the two worst cops. The fat one who had been a San Quentin guard was potbellied and about sixty, retired and couldn't keep away from the atmospheres that had nourished his dry soul all his life. Every night he drove to work in his 37 Buick, punched the clock exactly on time, and sat down at the rolltop desk. They said he had a wife. Then he laboured painfully over the simple form we all had to fill out every night--- rounds, time, what happened and so on. Then he leaned back and told stories. "You should have been here about two months ago when me and Tex" (that was the other horrible cop, a youngster who wanted to be a Texas ranger and had to be satisfied with his present lot) "me and Tex arrested a drunk in Barrack G. Boy you should have seen the blood fly. I'll take you over there tonight and show you the stains on the wall. We had him bouncing from one wall to another, first Tex hit him with his club, then I did, then Tex took out his revolver and snapped him one, and I was just about to try it myself when he sub- sided and went quietly. That fellow swore to kill us when he got out of jail---got thirty days---here it is SIXTY days and he ain't showed up." And this was the big point of the story. They'd put such a fear in him that he was too yellow to come back and try to kill them. I began to worry he might try it and mistake me for Tex in a dark barrack alley. The old cop went on, sweetly reminiscing about the horrors of San Quentin. "We used to march 'em like an Army platoon to breakfast. Wasn't one man out of step. Everything went like clockwork. You should have seen it. I was a guard there for thirty years. Never had any trouble. Those boys knew we meant business. Now a lot of fellows get soft guarding prisoners and they're the ones that usually get in trouble. Now you take you- - from what I've been observing about you, you seem to me a little bit too LEENENT with the men." He raised his pipe and looked at me sharp. "They take advantage of that, you know." I knew that. I told him I wasn't cut out to be a cop. "Yes, but that's the job that you APPLIED FOR. Now you got to make up your mind one way or the other, or you'll never get anywhere. It's your duty. You're sworn in. You can't compromise with things like this. Law & order's got to be kept." I didn't know what to say: he was right: but all I wanted to do was sneak out into the night and disappear somewhere, and go and find out what everybody was doing all over the country. The other cop, Tex, was short, squat, muscular, with a blond crewcut, and a nervous twitch in his neck like a boxer always punching one fist into another. He rigged himself out like a Texas ranger of old. He wore a revolver down low, with ammunition belt, and carried a small quirt of some kind and pieces of leather hanging everywhere like if he was a walking torture chamber: shiny shoes, low-hanging jacket, cocky hat, everything but boots. He was always showing me holds: reaching down under my crotch and lifting me up nimbly. In point of strength I could have thrown him clear to the ceiling with the same hold and I knew it well; but I never let him know for fear he'd want a wrestling match. A wrestling match with a guy like that could end up in shooting. I'm sure he was a better shot; I'd never had a gun in my life. It scared me to even load one. He desperately wanted to make arrests. One night we were alone on duty and he came back pissing mad. "I told some boys in there to keep quiet and they're still making noise. I told them twice. I always give a man two chances. Not three. You come with me, and I'm going back there and arrest them." "Well let me give them a third chance," I said, "I'll talk to them." "No sir, I never gave a man more than two chances." I sighed. Here we go. We went to the offending room and Tex opened the door and told everybody to file out. It was embarrassing. Every single one of us was blushing. This is the story of America. Everybody's doing what they think they're supposed to do. So what if a bunch of men talk in loud voices and drink in the night. But Tex wanted to prove something. He made sure to bring me along in case they jumped him. They might have. They were all brothers, all from Alabama. We all strolled back to the station. Tex in front and me in back. One of the boys said to me "Tell that crotch-eared meanass to take it easy on us, we might get fired for this and never get to Okinawa." "I'll talk to him." In the station I told Tex to forget it. He said, for everybody to hear, and blushing, "I don't give anybody no more than two chances." "What the hail," said the Alabaman, "what different does it make. We might lose our jobs." Tex said nothing and filled out the arrest forms. He arrested only one of them; he called the prowl car in town. They came and took him away. The other brothers walked off sullenly. "What's Ma going to say?" they said. One of them came back to me. "You tell that Texas sonofabitch if my brother ain't out of jail tomorrow night he's going to get his ass fixed." I told Tex, in a neutral way, and he said nothing. The brother was let off easy and nothing happened. The contingent shipped out; a new wild bunch came in. If it hadn't been for Henri Cru I wouldn't have stayed at this job two hours. But Henri Cru and I were on duty alone many a night and that's when everything jumped. We made our first round of the evening in a leisurely way, Henri trying all the doors to see if they were locked and hoping to find one unlocked. He'd say "For years I've an idea to develop a dog into a superthief who'd go in to these guys rooms and take dollars out of their pockets. I'd train him to take nothing but green money; I'd make him smell it all day long. If there was any humanly possible way I'd train him to take only twenties." Henri was full of such mad schemes; he talked about that dog for weeks. Only once an unlocked door. I didn't like the idea so I sauntered on down the hall. Henri stealthily opened it up. He came face to face with the very thing he despised and loathed in life. This was the face of the barracks supervisor. Henri hated that man's face so much that he told me "What's the name of that Russian author you're always talking about- -the one who put the newspapers in his shoe and walked around in a stovepipe hat he found in a garbage pail." This was an exaggeration of what I'd told Henri of Dostoevsky the holy Russian novelist saint. "Ah, that's it...that's IT...DOSTIOFFSKI...A man with a face like that supervisor can only have one name...it's Dostioffski." He was face to face with Dostioffski the supervisor, the manager, the boss man of the place. The only unlocked door he ever found belonged to Dostioffski. Not only that, but D. was asleep when he heard someone fiddling with his doorknob. He got up in his paja-mas. He came to the door looking twice as ugly as usual. When Henri opened it he saw a haggard face suppurated with hatred and dull fury. "What is the meaning of this?" "I was only trying this door...I thought this was the...ah..moproom. I was looking for a mop." "What do you MEAN you were looking for a mop." "Well..ah." And I stepped back and said "One of the men puked in the hall upstairs. We have to mop it up." "This is NOT the moproom. This is MY room. Another inci-dent like this and I'll have you fellows investigated and thrown out! Do you understand me clearly?" "A fellow puked upstairs," I said again. "The moproom is down the hall. Down there"- - and he pointed, and waited for us to go and get a mop, which we did, and foolishly carried it upstairs. I said "Goddamn it Henri you're always getting us into trouble. Why don't you lay off. Why do you have to steal all the time." "The world owes me a few things, that's all. You can't teach the old maestro a new tune. You go on talking like that and I'm going to start calling you Dostioffsky." "Okay Hank. Go put the mop back." "You go put the mop back. I've not given up on these doors." He claimed he once found a man sleeping with a dollar sticking out of his pocket. "Did you take it?" "I'm not in California, which is a land of fruit and nuts, either you go nuts or you go fruit, for the benefit of what my mother used to call my health. You stick with the old maestro and we'll make beautiful music on their evil skulls. Kerouac I'm absolutely convinced beyond the shadow of a doubt that this Dostioffsky, this man, this worm, is nothing but a thief because of the shape of his evil skull." Henri was a compulsive thief. He was just like a little boy. Somewhere in his past, in his lonely schooldays in France, they'd taken everything from him; his parents just stuck him in schools and left him there; he was browbeaten and thrown out of one school after another; he walked the French roads at night devising curses out of his innocent stock of words. He was out to get back everything he'd lost; there was no end to his loss; this thing would drag on forever. The barracks cafeteria was our meet. We looked around to make sure nobody was looking and especially to see if any of our copfriends were lurking about to check on us, then I squatted down and Henri put a foot on each shoulder and up we went. He opened the window, which was never locked, as he saw to it in the evenings, scrambled through and came down on the flour table. I was a little more agile and just jumped and crawled in. Then we went to the soda fountain. Here, realizing a dream of mine from infancy, I took the cover off the chocolate ice cream and stuck my hand in wrist-deep and hauled me up a skewer of ice cream and licked at it. Then we got ice cream boxes and stuffed them---poured chocolate syrup over and sometimes strawberries too---took wooden spoons---then walked around in the dispensary, the kitchens, opened iceboxes to see what we could take home in our pockets. I often tore off a piece of roastbeef and wrapped it in a napkin. "You know what President Truman said," Henri would say, "we must cut down on the cost of living." One night I waited a long time as he filled a huge box full of groceries. Then we couldn't get it through the window. Henri had to unpack everything and put it back. But he was racking his brain. Later in the night, when he went off duty and I was all alone on the base, a strange thing happened. I was taking a walk along the old canyon trail just to chance meeting a deer---Henri had seen deers around, the Marin country being wild even in 1947---when I heard a frightening noise in the dark. It was a huffing and a puffing. I thought it was a rhinoceros coming for me in the dark. I grabbed my gun, I grabbed my balls. A tall figure appeared in the canyon gloom; it had an enormous head. Suddenly I realized it was Henri with a huge box of groceries on his shoulder. He was moaning and groaning from the enormous weight of it. He'd found the key to the cafeteria somewhere and just got his groceries out the front door. I said "Henri I thought you were home. What the hell are you doing?" And he said "You know what President Truman said, we must cut down on the cost of living." And I heard him huff and puff into the darkness. I've already described that awful trail back to our shack up hill and dale; he hid the groceries in the tall grass and came back to me. "Jack I just can't make it alone. I'm going to divide it into two boxes and you're going to help me." "But I'm on duty." "I'll watch the place while you're gone. Things are getting rough all around. We've just got to make it the best way we can and that's all there is to it." He wiped himself. "Whoo! I've told you time and time again Jack that we're buddies, and we're in this thing together. There's just no two ways about it. The Dostioffskis, the Chief Davies, the Texes, the Dianes, all the evil skulls of this world are out for our skin. It's up to us to see that nobody pulls any schemes on us. They've got a lot more up their sleeves besides a dirty arm. Remember that. You can't teach the old maestro a new tune." "Whatever are we going to do about shipping out?" I finally asked. We'd been doing these things for ten weeks. I was making fifty-five dollars a week and sending my mother an average of forty. I'd spent only one evening in San Francisco in all that time. My life was wrapped in the shack, in Henri's battles with Diane, and in the middle of the night at the barracks. Henri was gone off in the dark to get another box. I struggled with him on that old Zorro road. We piled up the groceries a mile high on Diane's kitchen table. She woke up and rubbed her eyes. "You know what President Truman said? He said for us to cut down on the cost of living." She was delighted. I suddenly began to realize that everybody in America is a natural born thief. I was getting the bug myself. I even began to try to see if doors were locked. The other cops were getting suspicious of us; they saw it in our eyes; they understood with unfailing instinct what was on our minds. Years of experience had taught them the likes of Henri and Me. In the daytime Henri and I went out with the gun and tried to shoot quail in the hills. Henri sneaked up to within three feet of the clucking birds and let go a blast of the .32. He missed. His tremendous laugh roared over the California woods and over America. "The time has come for you and me to go and see the Banana King." It was Saturday; we got all spruced up and went down to the bus station at the crossroads. Here we spent an hour playing the pinball machine. We knew how to tip on it and left a hundred games there for anybody who wanted some fun. Henri's huge laugh resounded everywhere we went. He took me to see the Banana King. "You must write a story about the Banana King" he warned me. "Don't pull any tricks on the old maestro and write about something else. The Banana King is your meat. There stands the Banana King." The Banana King was an old man selling bananas on the corner. I was completely bored. But Henri kept punching me in the ribs and even dragging me along by the collar. "When you write about the Banana King you write about the human interest things of life." We strolled through the streets of San Francisco. Henri had no use for Chinatown. He took me back to see the Banana King. I told him I didn't give a damn about the Banana King. "Until you learn to realize the importance of the Banana King you will know absolutely nothing about the human interest things of the world," said Henri emphatically. On the highway in back of our shack, up the hill, Henri planted birdseed in the ditch in the hope of raising a crop of marijuana. The only time we went to look at the progress of the thing a cruising car pulled up beside us. "What are you boys doing?" "Oh, we're members of the Sausalito police force, we work down there at the barracks. Just spending an afternoon off." The cops went away. Down by the Sausalito waterfront Henri suddenly whipped out his gun and shot at the gulls. Nobody noticed, except an old woman with a bag of groceries who turned around. "AAAAh*hoo!" howled Henri. There was an old rusty freighter out in the bay that was used as a buoy. Henri was all for rowing out to it, so one afternoon Diane packed a lunch and we hired a boat and rowed out to it. Henri brought some tools. Diane took all her clothes off and lay down to sun herself on the flying bridge. I watched her from the poop. Henri went clear down to the boilerrooms below, where rats scurried around, and began hammering and banging away for copper lining that wasn't there. I sat in the dilapidated officer's mess. It was an old, old ship, it had been beautifully appointed at one time. There was scrollwork in the wood, and old built in seachests. This was the ghost of the San Francisco of Jack London. I dreamed at the sunny messboard. Rats ran in the pantry. Once upon a time there'd been a blue-eyed sea captain dining in here. Now his bones were wove with immemorial pearls. I joined Henri in the bowels below. He yanked at everything loose. "Not a thing. I thought there'd be copper, I thought there'd be at least an old wrench or two. This ship's been stripped by a bunch of thieves." It had been standing in the bay for years. The copper had been thieved by a hand a hand no more. I said to Henri "I'd love to sleep in this old ship some night when the fog comes in and the thing creaks and you hear the big B*O of the buoys." Henri was astounded; his admiration for me doubled. "Jack I'll pay you five dollars if you have the nerve to do that. Don't you realize this thing may be haunted by the ghosts of old seacaptains. I'll not only pay you five I'll row you out and pack you a lunch and lend you blankets and candle." "Agreed!" I said. Henri ran to tell Diane. He was amazed at my courage. I wanted to jump down from a mast and land right in her cunt, but I was true to Henri's promise. I averted my eyes from her. Meanwhile I began going to Frisco more often; I tried everything in the books to make a girl. I even spent a whole night with a girl on a parkbench, till dawn, without success. She was a blonde from Minnesota. There were plenty of queers however. Several times I went to Sanfran with my gun and when a queer approached me in a barjohn I took out the gun and said

"Eh? Eh? What's that you say?" They bolted. I've never understood why I did that, I knew queers all over the country. It was just the loneliness of San Francisco and the fact that I had a gun. I had to show it to someone. I walked by a jewelry store and had the sudden impulse to shoot up the window, take out the finest rings and bracelets and run to give them to Diane. Then we could flee to Nevada together. These were mad dreams. The time was coming for me to leave Frisco or I'd go crazy. I wrote long letters to Neal and Allen at Bill's shack in the Texas bayou. They said they were ready to come join me in Sanfran as soon as this and that was ready. The fantastic story of what they were doing down in Texas came to me later. Meanwhile everything began to collapse with Henri and Diane and me. The September rains came, and with it harangues. Henri had flown down to Hollywood with her, bringing my sad silly movie original, and nothing had happened; the famous director Gregory LaCava was drunk and paid no attention to them; they hung around his Malibu beach cottage; they started fighting in front of other guests; there were recriminations behind the wire fence that barred them from the swimmingpool, and they flew back. The final topper was the racetrack. Henri saved all his money, about a hundred dollars, spruced me up in some of his clothes, put Diane on his arm and off we went to Golden Gate racetrack near Richmond across the Bay. To show you what a heart that guy had: he put half of our stolen groceries in a tremendous brown-paper bag and took them to a poor widow he knew in Richmond. We went with him. There were sad ragged children, a housing project much like our own, wash flapping in the California sun. The woman thanked Henri. She was the sister of some seaman he vaguely knew. "Think nothing of it Mrs. Carter," said Henri in his most elegant and polite tones, "there's plenty more where that came from." We proceeded to the racetrack. He made incredible twenty-dollar bets to win and before the seventh race he was broke. With our last two food dollars he placed still another bet and lost. We had to hitch hike back to San Francisco. I was on the road again. A gentleman gave us a ride in his snazzy car. I sat up front with him. Henri was trying to put a story down that he'd lost his wallet in back of the grandstand at the track. "The truth is," I said, "we lost all our money on the races, and to forestall any more hitching from racetracks from now on we go to a bookie, hey Henri?" Henri blushed all over. The man finally admitted he was an official of the Golden Gate track. He let us off at the elegant Palace Hotel; we watched him disappear among the chandeliers, his pockets full of money, his head held high. "Wagh! Whoo!" howled Henri in the evening streets of Frisco. "Kerouac rides with the man who runs the racetrack and SWEARS he's switching to bookies, Diane! Diane!" he punched and mauled her- -"Positively the funniest man in the world! There must be lots of Italians in Sausalito. Aaaah-how!" He wrapped himself around a pole to laugh. But it started raining that night as Diane gave dirty looks to both of us. Not a cent left in the house. The rain drummed on the roof. "It's going to last for a week" said Henri. He had taken off his beautiful suit, he was back in his miserable shorts and Army cap and T-shirt. His great brown sad eyes stared at the planks of the floor. The gun lay on the table. We could hear Mr. Snow laughing his head off across the rainy night somewhere. "I get so sick and tired of that sonofabitch," snapped Diane. She was on the go to start trouble. She began needling Henri. He was busy going thru his little black book in which were names of people, mostly seamen, who owed him money. Beside their names he wrote curses in red ink. I dreaded the day I'd ever find my way in that book. Lately I'd been sending so much money to my mother that I only bought four five dollars worth of groceries a week. In keeping with what President Truman said I added a few more dollars worth. But Henri felt it wasn't my proper share; so he'd taken to hanging his grocery slips, the long ribbon slips with itemised prices, on the wall of the kitchen for me to see and understand. Diane was convinced Henri was hiding money from her, and me too for that matter. She threatened to leave him. Henri curled his lip "Where do you think you'll go?" "Charlie." "CHARLIE? A groom at the racetrack? Do you hear that Jack, Diane is going to go and put the latch on a groom at the racetrack. Be sure and bring your broom dear, the horses are going to eat a lot of oats this week with my hundred dollar bill." Things grew to worse proportions; the rain roared. Diane originally lived in the place first, so she told Henri to pack up and get out. He started packing. I pictured myself all alone in this rainy shack with that shrew. I tried to intervene. Henri pushed Diane. She made a jump for the gun. Henri gave me the gun and told me to hide it; there was a clip of eight shells in it. Diane began screaming, and finally she put on her raincoat and went out in the mud to get a cop, and what a cop!---if it wasn't our old friend San Quentin. Luckily he wasn't home. She came back all wet. I hid in my corner with my head between my knees. Gad what was I doing three thousand miles from home? Why had I come here? Where was my slowboat to China? "And another thing you dirty cuntlapper" yelled Diane "tonight was the last time I'll ever make your filthy brains and eggs, and your filthy lamb curry, so you can fill your filthy belly and get fat and sassy right before my eyes." "It's allright," Henri just said quietly, "it's perfectly all right. When I took up with you I didn't expect roses and moonshine and I'm not surprised this night and this day. I tried to do a few things for you---I tried my best for both of you---you've both let me down. I'm terribly, terribly disappointed in both of you" he continued in absolute sincerity "I thought something would come of us together, something fine and lasting, I tried, I flew to Hollywood, I got Jack a job, I bought you beautiful dresses, I tried to introduce you to the finest people in San Francisco. You refused, you both refused to follow the slightest wish I had. I asked for nothing in return. Now I ask for one last favor and then I'll never ask a favor again. My father is coming to San Francisco next Saturday night. All I ask is that you come with me and try to look as though everything is the way I've written him...in other words, you, Diane, you are my woman; and you Jack, you are my friend. I've arranged to borrow a hundred dollars for Saturday night. I'm going to see that my father has a good time and can go away without any reason in the world to worry about me." This surprised me. Henri's father was a distinguished French professor in Columbia University and a member of the Legion of Honor in France.

I said "You mean to tell me you're going to spend a hundred dollars on your father---he's got more money than you'll ever have!---you'll be in debt man!" "That's all right," said Henri quietly and with defeat in his voice "I ask only one last thing of you---that you, TRY at least to make things look all right. I love my father and I respect him. He's coming with his young wife, straight from a summer of teaching at Banff in Canada. We must show him every courtesy." There were times when Henri was really the most gentlemanly person in the world. Diane was impressed and looked forward to meeting his father; she thought he might be a catch if his son wasn't. Saturday night rolled around. I had already quit my job with the cops, just before being fired for not making enough arrests, and this was going to be my last Saturday night. Henri and Diane went to meet his father at the hotel room first; I had traveling money and got crocked in the bar downstairs. Then I went up to join them all, late as hell. His father opened the door, a distinguished little man in pince nez glasses. "Ah" I said on seeing him, "Monsieur Cru, how are you? Je suis haut!" I cried, which was intended to mean, in French "I am high, I have been drinking," but means absolutely nothing in French. The man was perplexed. I had already screwed up Henri. He blushed at me. We all went to a swank restaurant to eat, Alfred's on the North Beach, where poor Henri spent a good fifty dollars for the five of us drinks and all. And now there transpired the worst thing ever. Who should be sitting at the bar in Alfred's but my old friend Allan Temko!---he had just arrived from Denver and got a job on the Sanfran Chronicle. He was crocked. He wasn't even shaved. He rushed over and slapped me on the back as I lifted a hiball to my lips. He threw himself down on the booth beside Mr. Cru and leaned over the man's soup to talk to me. Henri was all red as a beet. "Won't you introduce your friend Jack?" he said with a weak smile. "Allan Temko of the San Francisco Chronicle" I tried to say with a straight face. Diane was furious at me. Temko began chatting in the Monsieur's ear. "How do you like teaching High School French?" he yelled. "Pardon me, but I don't teach High School French." "Oh, I thought you taught High School French."

He was being deliberately rude. I remembered the night he wouldn't let us have our party in Denver; but I forgave him. I forgave everybody, I gave up, I got drunk. I began talking moonshine and roses to the Monsieur's young wife. She was a real Parisian woman, about thirty five, sexy and aloof but warm and womanly. I piled indignities to the ceiling. I drank so much I had to rush out of the booth for a leak every two minutes, and to do so I had to hop over the Monsieur's lap. Everything was falling apart. My stay in San Francisco was coming to an end. Henri would never talk to me again. It was horrible because I really loved Henri and I was one of the very few people in the world who knew what a genuine and grand fellow he was. It would take years for him to get over with. How disastrous all this was compared to the nights I wrote him in Ozone Park and planned my red line Route Six across America. Here I was at the end of America...no more land...and now there was nowhere to go but back. I determined at least to make my trip a circular one: I decided then and there to go to Hollywood and back through Texas to see my bayou gang, then the rest be damned. Temko was thrown out of Alfred's. Dinner was over anyway so I joined him, that is to say, Henri suggested it, and I went off with Temko to drink. We sat at a table in the Iron Pot and Temko said "Sam, I don't like that fairy at the bar" in a loud voice. "Yeah Jake?" I said. "Sam," he said, "I think I'll get up and conk him." "No Jake," I said, carrying on with the Hemingway imitation, "just aim from here and see what happens." We ended up swaying on a street-corner. I never dreamed I'd be back on that same streetcorner two years later---and then again three years later. I said goodbye to Temko. In the morning, as Henri and Diane slept, and as I looked with some sadness at the big pile of wash Henri and I were scheduled to do in the Bendix machine in the shack in the back (which had always been such a joyous sunny operation among the colored women and with Mr. Snow laughing his head off) I decided to leave. I went out on the porch. "No dammit" I said to myself. "I promised I wouldn't leave till I climbed that mountain." That was the big side of the canyon that led mysteriously to the Pacific ocean. So I stayed another day. It was

Sunday. A great heat wave descended; it was a beautiful day, the sun turned red at three. I started up the mountain at three and got to the top at four. All those lovely California cottonwoods brooded on all sides. I felt like playing cowboys. Near the peak there were no more trees, just rocks and grass. Cattle were grazing on top of the Coast. There was the Pacific, a few more foothills away, blue and vast and with a great wall of white advancing from the legendary Potato Patch where Frisco fogs are born. Another hour and it would come streaming through Golden Gate to shroud the romantic city in white, and a young man would hold his girl by the hand and climb slowly up a long white sidewalk with a bottle of Tokay in his pocket. That was Frisco; and beautiful women standing in white doorways, waiting for their man; and Coit Tower, and the Embarcadero, and Market street, and the eleven teeming hills. Lonely Frisco for me then---which would buzz a few years later when my soul got stranger. Now I was only a youth on a mountain. I stooped, looked between my legs, and watched the world upside down. The brown hills led off towards Nevada; to the South was my legendary Hollywood; to the North the mysterious Shasta country. Down below was everything: the barracks where we stole our tiny box of condiments, where Dostioffski's tiny face had glared at us, where Henri had me hide the toy-gun and where our squeaking yells had transpired. I spun around till I was dizzy; I thought I'd fall down as in a dream, clear off the precipice. "Oh where is the girl I love?" I thought, and looked everywhere, as I had looked everywhere in the little world below. And before me was the great raw bulge and bulk of my American continent; somewhere far across gloomy crazy New York was throwing up its cloud of dust and brown steam. There is something brown and holy about the East; and California is white like washlines and empty-souled---at least that's what I thought then. I'd learn better later. Now it was time to pursue my moon along. In the morning Henri and Diane were asleep as I quietly packed and slipped out the window the same way I'd come in, and left Marin City with my canvas bag. And I never spent that night on the old ghostship, the Admiral Freebee it was called, and Henri and

I were lost. In Oakland I had a beer among the bums of a saloon with a wagon wheel in front of it, and I was on the road again. I walked clear across Oakland to get on the Fresno road. I was on the verge of entering that great buzzing valley of the world, the San Joaquin, where I was destined to meet and love a wonderful woman and go through the craziest adventures of all before I got back home. Two rides took me to Bakersfield four hundred miles south. The first one was the mad one: a burly blond kid in a souped-up rod. "See that toe?" he said as he gunned the heap to eighty and passed everybody on the road. "Look at it." It was swathed in bandages. "I just had it amputated this morning. The bastards wanted me to stay in the hospital. I packed my bag and left. What's a toe." Yes indeed, I said to myself, look out now, and I hung on. You never saw a driving fool like that. He made Tracy in no time. Tracy is a railroad town; brakemen eat surly meals in diners by the tracks. Trains howl away across the valley. The sun goes down long and red. All the magic names of the Valley unrolled---Manteca, Madera, all the rest. Soon it got dusk, a grapey dusk, a purple dusk over tangerine groves and long melon fields; the sun the color of pressed grapes, slashed with burgundy red, the fields the color of love and Spanish mysteries. I stuck my head out the window and took deep breaths of the fragrant air. It was the most beautiful of all moments. The madman was a brakeman with the SP and he lived in Fresno; his father was also a brakeman. He lost his toe in the Frisco yards switching. I didn't quite understand how. He drove me into buzzing Fresno and let me off the south side of town. I went for a quick coke in a little grocery store by the tracks and here came a melancholy Armenian youth along the red boxcars, and just at that moment a locomotive howled, and I said to myself, "Yes, yes, Saroyan's town." Whither went that Mourad?---to what glooms? What Fresno dreams? I had to go South; I got on the road. A man in a brandnew pickup truck picked me up. He was from Lubbock Texas and was in the trailer business. "You want to buy a trailer?" he asked me. "Any time, look me up." He told stories about his father in Lubbock. "One night my old man left the day's receipts sittin' on top of the safe, plumb forgot. What happened...a thief came in the night, acetylene torch and all, broke open the safe, riffled up the papers, kicked over a few chairs and left. And that thousand dollars was sitting there right on top of the safe, what do you know about that?" It was an amazing story. What time I was making too, four hundred miles in seven hours! Ahead of me burned the vision of Golden Hollywood. Nothing behind me, everything ahead of me, as is ever so on the road. He left me off the south side of Bakersfield and then my adventure began. It grew cold. I put on the flimsy Army raincoat I'd bought in Oakland for $3 and shuddered in the road. I was standing in front of an ornate Spanish style motel that was lit like a jewel. The cars rushed by, L.A.-bound. I gestured frantically. It was too cold. I stood there till midnight, two hours straight, and cursed and cursed. It was just like Stuart Iowa again. There was nothing to do but spend a little over two dollars for a bus the remaining miles to Los Angeles. I walked back along the highway to Bakersfield and into the station, and sat down on a bench. In the madness of the night you never can dream what will happen---and I never dreamed I'd sit on that bench again a week later, going North, and under the wildest and dearest circumstances. I had bought my ticket and was waiting for the L.A. bus when all of a sudden I saw the cutest little Mexican girl in slacks come cutting across my sight. She was in one of the buses that had just pulled in. Her breasts stuck out straight and true; her little flanks looked delicious; her hair was long and black; and her eyes were great big blue things with a soul in it. I wished I was on the same bus with her. A pain stabbed my heart, as it did every time I saw a girl I loved who was going the opposite direction in this too-big world of ours. The announcer called the L.A. bus. I picked up my bag and got on it; and who should be sitting alone in it, but the Mexican girl. I sat right opposite her and began scheming right off. I was so lonely, so sad, so tired, so quivering, so broken, so beat---all of it had been too much for me---that I got up my courage, the courage necessary to approach a strange girl, and acted. Even then I spent five minutes beating my thighs in the dark as the bus rolled. "You gotta, you gotta or you'll die! Damn fool talk to her! What's wrong with you? Aren't you tired of yourself by now?" And before I knew what I was doing I leaned across the aisle to her---she was trying to sleep on the seat---and said, "Miss, would you like to use my raincoat for a pillow?" She looked up with a smile and said "No, thank you very much." I sat back trembling; I lit a butt. I waited till she looked at me, with a sad little sidelook of love, and I got right up and leaned over her. "May I sit with you, Miss?" "If you wish." And this I did. "Where going?" "L.A." I loved the way she said L.A.; I love the way everybody says L.A. on the Coast, it's their one and only golden town when all is said and done. "That's where I'm going too!" I cried. "I'm very glad you let me sit with you, I was very lonely and I've been traveling a hell of a lot." And we settled down to telling our stories. Her story was this: she had a husband and child. The husband beat her so she left him, back at Selma south of Fresno, and was going to L.A. to live with her sister awhile. She left her little son with her family, who were grape-pickers and lived in a shack in the vineyards. She had nothing to do but brood. I felt like putting my arms around her right away. We talked and talked. She said she loved to talk with me. Pretty soon she was saying she wished she could go to New York too. "Maybe we could!" I laughed. The bus groaned up Grapevine Pass and then we were coming down into the great sprawls of light. Without coming to any particular agreement we began holding hands, and in the same way it was mutely and beautifully and purely decided that when I got my hotel room in L.A. she would be beside me. I ached all over for her; I leaned my head in her beautiful hair. Her little shoulders drove me mad, I hugged her and hugged her. And she loved it. "I love love" she said closing her eyes. I promised her beautiful love. I gloated over her. Our stories were told, we subsided into silence and sweet anticipatory thoughts. It was as simple as that. You could have all your Gingers and Beverlies and Ruth Gullions and Louannes and Carolyns and Dianes in this world, this was my girl and my kind of girlsoul, and I told her that. She confessed she saw me watching her in the bus station. "I thought you was a nice college boy." "Oh I'm a college boy!" I said. The bus arrived in Hollywood. In the gray dirty dawn, like the dawn Joel McRea met Veronica Lake in the picture Sullivan's Travels in a diner, she slept in my lap. I looked greedily out the window: stucco houses and palms and drive ins, the whole mad thing, the ragged promised land, the fantastic end of America. We got off the bus at Main street which was no different than where you get off a bus in Kansas City or Chicago or Boston, redbrick, dirty, characters drifting by, trolleys grating in the dawn, the whorey smell of a big city. And here my mind went haywire, I don't know why. I began getting the foolish paranoiac idea that Beatrice---her name---was a common little hustler who worked the buses for a guy's bucks, and that she had regular appointments like ours in L.A. where she brought the sucker first to a breakfast place, where her pimp waited, and then to a certain hotel to which he had access with his gun or his whatever. I never confessed this to her. We ate breakfast and a pimp kept watching us; I fancied Bea was making secret eyes at him. I was tired. Goofy terror took over my soul and made me petty and cheap. "Do you know that guy?" I said. "What guy?" I let it drop. She was slow and hungup about everything she did; it took her a long time to eat, and smoke a cigarette, and she talked too much; I kept thinking she was stalling for time. But this was all utter nonsense. The first hotel we hit had a room and before I knew it I was locking the door behind me and she was sitting on the bed taking off her shoes. I kissed her meekly. Better she'd never know. To relax our nerves I knew we needed whisky, especially me. I ran out and fiddled all over twelve blocks of town till I found a pint of whiskey for sale at of all places, a newsstand. I ran back all energy. Bea was in the bathroom fixing her face. I poured one big drink in a waterglass and we had slugs. Oh it was sweet and delicious and worth my whole lugubrious voyage. I stood behind her at the mirror and we danced in the bathroom that way. I began talking about my friends back east. I said "You ought to meet a great girl I know called Vicki. She's a sixfoot redhead. If you came to New York she'd show you where to get work." "Who is this sixfoot redhead?" she demanded suspiciously. "Why do you tell me about her?" In her simple soul she couldn't fathom my kind of glad nervous talk. I let it drop. She began to get drunk in the bathroom. "Come on to bed!" I kept saying. "Sixfoot redhead, hey? And I thought you was a nice college boy, I saw you in your lovely sweater and I said to myself 'Hmm ain't he nice.' No! And no! And no! You have to be a goddam pimp like all of them!" "What on earth are you talking about?" "Don't stand there and tell me that sixfoot redhead ain't a madame, cause I know a madame when I hear about one, and you, you're just a pimp like all the rest I meet, everybody's a pimp." "Listen Bea, I am not a pimp. I swear to you on the Bible I am not a pimp. Why should I be a pimp. My only interest is you." "All the time I thought I met a nice boy. I was so glad, I hugged myself and said 'Hmm a real nice boy instead of a pimp.'" "Bea," I pleaded with all my soul, "please listen to me and understand. I'm not a pimp." An hour ago I thought <u>she</u> was a hustler. How sad it was. Our minds, with their store of madness, had diverged. O gruesome life how I moaned and pleaded, and then I got mad and realized I was pleading with a dumb little Mexican wench and I told her so; and before I knew it I picked up her red pumps and hurled them at the bathroom door and told her to get out. "Go on, beat it!" I'd sleep and forget it; I had my own life; my own sad and ragged life forever. There was a dead silence in the bathroom. I took all my clothes off and went to bed. Bea came out with tears of sorriness in her eyes. In her simple and funny little mind had been decided the fact that a pimp does not throw a woman's shoes against the door and does not tell her to get out. In reverent and sweet little silence she took all her clothes off and slipped her tiny body into the sheets with me. It was brown as grapes. I bit her poor belly where a Caesarian scar reached clear to her button. Her hips were so narrow she couldn't bear a child without getting gashed open. Her legs were like little sticks. She was only four foot ten. She spread her little legs and I made love to her in the sweetness of the weary morning. Then, two tired angels of some kind, hungup forlornly in an L.A. shelf, having found the closest and most delicious thing in life together, we fell asleep and slept till late afternoon. For the next fifteen days we were together for better or for worse. When we woke up we decided to hitch hike to New York together; she was going to be my girl in town. I envisioned wild complexities with Neal and Louanne and everybody, a season, a new season. First we had to work to earn enough money for the trip. Bea was all for starting at once with the twenty dollars I had left. I didn't like it. And like a damnfool I considered the problem for two days, as we read the wantads of wild new L.A. papers I'd never seen before in my life, in cafeterias and bars, until my twenty dwindled to just over ten. The situation was growing. We were very happy in our little hotel room. In the middle of the night I got up because I couldn't sleep, pulled the cover over baby's brown shoulder, and examined the L.A. night. What brutal, hot, siren-whining nights they are! Right across the street there was trouble. An old rickety rundown roominghouse was the scene of some kind of tragedy. The cruiser was pulled up below and the cops were questioning an old man with gray hair. Sobbings came from within. I could hear everything, together with the hum of my hotel neon. I never felt sadder in my life. L.A. is the loneliest and most brutal of American cities; New York gets godawful cold in the winter but there's a feeling of whacky comradeship somewhere in some streets. L.A. is a jungle. South Main street, where Bea and I took strolls with hotdogs, was a fantastic carnival of lights and wildness. Booted cops frisked people on practically every corner. The beatest characters in the country swarmed on the sidewalks---all of it under those soft southern California stars that are lost in the brown halo of the huge desert encampment L.A. really is. You could smell tea, weed, I mean marijuana floating in the air, together with the chili beans and beer. That grand wild sound of bop floated from beerparlors; it mixed medleys with everykind of cowboy and boogiewoogie in the American night. Everybody looked like Hunkey. Wild negroes with bop caps and goatees came laughing by; then longhaired brokendown hipsters straight off route 66 from New York, then old desert rats carrying packs and heading for a parkbench at the Plaza, then Methodist ministers with ravelled sleeves, and an occasional Nature Boy saint in beard and sandals. I wanted to meet them all, talk to everybody, but Bea and I were too busy trying to get a buck together. We went to Hollywood to try to work in the drugstore at Sunset and Vine. Now there was a corner! Great families off jaloppies from the hinterlands stood around the sidewalk gaping for sight of some movie star and the movie star never showed up. When a limousine passed they rushed eagerly to the curb and ducked to look: some character in dark glasses sat inside with a bejewelled blonde. "Don Ameche! Don Ameche!" "No George Murphy! George Murphy!" They milled around looking at one another. Handsome queer boys who had come to Hollywood to be cowboys walked around wetting their eyebrows with hincty fingertips. The most beautiful little gone gals in the world cut by in slacks; they came to be starlets; they ended up in Drive Ins. Bea and I tried to find work at the Drive Ins. It was no soap anywhere. Hollywood Boulevard was a great screaming frenzy of cars; there were minor accidents at least once a minute; everybody was rushing off towards the furthest palm...and beyond that was the desert and nothingness. Hollywood Sams stood in front of swank restaurants arguing exactly the same way Broadway Sams argue at Jacob's Beach New York, only they wore Palm Beach suits and their talk was cornier. Tall cadaverous preachers shuddered by. Fat women ran across the Boulevard to get in line for the quiz shows. I saw Jerry Colonna buying a car at Buick Motors: he was inside the vast plateglass window fingering his mustachio. Bea and I ate in a cafeteria downtown which was decorated to look like a grotto. All the cops in L.A. looked like handsome gigolos; obviously, they'd come to L.A. to make the movies. Everybody had come to make the movies, even me. Bea and I were finally reduced to trying to get jobs on South Main street among the beat characters who made no bones about their beatness and even there it was no go. We still had eight dollars. "Man I'm going to get my clothes from Sis and we'll hitch-hike to New York" said Bea. "Come on man. Let's do it. If you can't boogie I know I'll show you how." That last part was a song of hers. We hurried to her sister's house in the rickety Mexican shacks somewhere beyond Alameda Avenue. I waited in a dark alley behind Mexican kitchens because her sister wasn't supposed to see me and like it. Dogs ran by. There were little lamps illuminating the little rat alleys. I could hear Bea and her sister arguing in the soft warm night. I was ready for anything. Bea came out and led me by the hand to Central Avenue, which is the colored main drag of L.A. And what a wild place it is, with chickenshacks barely big enough to house a jukebox and the jukebox blowing nothing but blues, bop and jump. We went up dirty tenement stairs and came to the room of Bea's friend, Margarina, a colored girl, who owed Bea a skirt and a pair of shoes. Margarina was a lovely mulatoo; her husband was black as spades and kindly. He went right out and bought a pint of whisky to host me proper. I tried to pay part of it but he said no. They had two little children. The kids bounced on the bed, it was their play-place. They put their arms around me and looked at me with wonder. The wild hummingnight of Central Avenue---the nights of Hamp's Central Avenue Breakdown---howled and boomed along outside. I thought it was wonderful, every bit of it. They were singing in the halls, singing from their windows, just hell be damned and lookout. Bea got her clothes and we said goodbye. We went down to a chickenshack and played records on the jukebox. A couple of negro characters whispered in my ear about tea. One buck. I said okay. The connection came in and motioned me to the cellar pisshouse, where I stood around dumbly as he said "Pick up, man, pick up." "Pick up what?" I said. He had my dollar already. He was afraid to point at the floor. I looked everywhere; he motioned with his head at the floor. It was no floor, just basement. There lay something that looked like a little brown turd. He was absurdly cautious. "Got to look out for myself, things ain't cool this past week." I picked up the turd, which was a brownpaper cigarette, and went back to Bea and off we went to the hotel room to get high. Nothing happened. It was Bull Durham tobacco. I wished I was wiser with my money. Bea and I had to decide absolutely and once and for all what to do: we decided to hitch to New York with our remaining monies. She picked up five dollars from her sister that night. We had about thirteen or less. So before the daily room rent was due again we packed up and took off on a red car to Arcadia, California, where Santa Anita is located under snowcapped mountains. It was night. We were pointed towards that enormity which is the American continent. Holding hands we walked several miles down the road to get out of the populated district. It was Saturday night. A thing that made me madder than I'd been ever since I left Ozone Park happened: we were standing under a roadlamp thumbing when suddenly cars full of young kids roared by with streamers flying. "Yaah! yaah! we won! we won!" they all shouted. Then they yoo-hooed us and got great glee out of seeing a guy and a girl on the road. Dozens of such cars passed full of young faces and "throaty young voices" as the saying goes. I hated every single one of them. Who did they think they were yaahing at somebody on the road just because they were little highschool punks and their parents carved the roast beef on Sunday afternoons. Who did they think they were making fun of a girl reduced to poor circumstances with a man she wanted to stick with. We were minding our own business. And we didn't get a blessed ride. We had to walk back to town and worst of all we needed coffee and had the misfortune of going into the only place open, which was a highschool sodafountain, and all the kids were there and remembered us. Now they saw the added fact that Bea was Mexican. I refused to go on another minute. Bea and I wandered in the dark. I finally decided to hide from the world one more night with her and the morning be damned. We went into a motel court and bought a comfortable suite for about four dollars--- shower, bath towels, wall radio and all. We held each other tight and talked. I loved this girl in that season we had together, and it was far from finished. In the morning we boldly struck out on our new plan. We were going to take a bus to Bakersfield and work picking grapes. After a few weeks of that we were headed for New York in the proper way, by bus. It was a wonderful afternoon riding up to Bakersfield with Bea: we sat back, relaxed, talked, saw the countryside roll by and didn't worry about a thing. We arrived in Bakersfield in late afternoon. The plan was to hit every fruit wholesaler in town. Bea said we could live in tents on the job. The thought of living in a tent and picking grapes in the cool California mornings hit me right. But there were no jobs to be had and much confusion with everybody giving us innumerable tips and places to go that didn't materialize a job. Nevertheless we ate a Chinese dinner and set out with reinforced bodies. We went across the SP tracks to Mexican town. Bea jabbered with her brethren asking for jobs. It was night now, and the little Mextown street was one blazing bulb of lights: movie marquees, fruit stands, penny arcades, Five and Tens. Hundreds of rickety trucks and mudspattered jalopies were parked. Whole Mexican fruitpicking families wandered around eating popcorn. Bea talked to innumerable Mexicans and got all kinds of confused information. I was beginning to despair. What I needed, what Bea needed too was a drink, so we bought a quart of California port for 35c and went to the boxcars in back to drink. We found a place where hobos had drawn up crates to sit over fires. We sat there and drank the wine. On our left were the boxcars, sad and sooty red beneath the moon; straight ahead the lights and airport pokers of Bakersfield proper; to our right a tremendous aluminum Quonset warehouse. I mention this because exactly a year and a half later I came right by there again with Neal and I pointed it out to him. Ah it was a fine night, a warm night, a wine-drinking night, a moony night, and a night to hug your girl and talk and spit and be heavengoing. This we did. She was a drinking little fool and kept up with me and passed me and went right on talking till midnight. We never budged from those crates. Occasionally bums passed, Mexican mothers passed with children, and the prowlcar came by and the cop got out to piss but most of the time we were alone and mixing up our souls ever more and ever more till it would be terribly hard to say goodbye. At midnight we got up and goofed towards the highway. Bea had a new idea. We would hitch hike to Selma her hometown and live in her brother's garage. Anything was all right with me. On the road, not far from that damned and fated Spanish style motel- -that great good motel that hung me up and made me meet Bea---I made Bea sit down on my bag to make her look like a woman in distress. Right off a truck stopped and we ran for it all glee-giggles. The man was a good man, his truck was poor. He roared her up and crawled on up the Valley. We got to Selma in the wee hours before dawn. I had finished the wine while Bea slept and I was proper stoned. We got out and roamed the quiet leafy square of the little California town---a whistle stop on the S.P. We went to find her brother's buddy who would tell us where he was; nobody was home. It all went on in rickety alleys of little Mextown. As dawn began to break I lay flat on my back in the lawn of the town square and kept saying over and over again, "You won't tell what he done up in Weed will you? What'd he do up in Weed? You won't tell will you? What'd he do up in Weed?" This was from the picture Of Mice and Men with Burgess Meredith talking to (Geo. Bancroft.) Bea giggled. Anything I did was allright with her. I could lay there and go on doing that till the ladies came out for church and she wouldn't care. But finally I decided because her brother was in these parts we'd be all set soon and I took her to an old hotel by the tracks and we went to bed comfortably. Five dollars left. In the morning Bea got up early and left to find her brother. I slept till noon; when I looked out the window I suddenly saw an S.P. freight going by with hundreds and hundreds of hoboes reclining on the flatcars and rolling merrily along with packs for pillows and funny papers before their noses and some munching on good California grapes picked up by the watertank. "Damn!" I yelled. "Hooee! It _is_ the promised land." They were all coming from Frisco; in a week they'd all be going back in the same grand style. Bea arrived with her brother, her brother's buddy and her child. Her brother was a wildbuck Mexican hotcat with a hunger for booze, a great good kid. His buddy was a big flabby Mexican who spoke English without much accent and was loud and overanxious to please. I could see he had eyes for Bea. Her little boy was Raymond, seven years old, darkeyed and sweet. Well there we were, and another wild day began. Her brother's name was Freddy. He had a 38 Chevvy . We piled into that and took off for parts unknown. "Where we going?" I asked. The buddy did the explaining---his name was Ponzo, that's what everybody called him. He stank. I found out why. His business was selling manure to farmers, he had a truck. Freddy always had three or four dollars in his pocket and was happygolucky about things. He always said "That's right man, there you go---dah you go, dah you go!" And he went. He drove seventy miles an hour in the old heap and we went to Madera beyond Fresno to see some farmers. Freddy had a bottle "Today we drink, tomorrow we work. Dah you go man---take a shot." Bea sat in back with her baby; I looked back at her and saw the flush of joy in her face. The beautiful green countryside of October in California reeled by madly. I was guts and juice again and ready to go. "Where do we go now man?" "We go find a farmer with some manure laying around- -tomorrow we drive back in the truck and pick it up. Man we'll make a lot of money. Don't worry about nothing." "We're all in this together!" yelled Ponzo. I saw that was so- -everywhere I went everybody was in it together. We raced through the crazy streets of Fresno and on up the Valley to some farmers in backroads. Ponzo got out of the car and conducted confused conversations with old Mexican farmers; nothing of course came of it. "What we need is a drink!" yelled Freddy and off we went to a crossroads saloon. Americans are always drinking in crossroads saloons on Sunday afternoons; they bring their kids; there are piles of manure outside the screendoor; they gabble and brawl over brews; everything's fine. Come nightfall the kids start crying and the parents are drunk. They go weaving back to the house. Everywhere in America I've been in crossroads saloons drinking with whole families. The kids eat popcorn and chips and play in back. This we did. Freddy and I and Ponzo and Bea sat drinking and shouting with the music; little baby Raymond goofed around with other children around the jukebox. The sun began to get red. Nothing had been accomplished. What was there to accomplish? "Manana," said Freddy, "manana man we make it; have another beer, man, dah you go, DAH YOU GO!" We staggered out and got in the car; off we went to a highway bar. Ponzo was a big loud vociferous type who knew everybody in San Joaquin valley apparently. From the highway bar I went with him alone in the car to find a farmer; instead we wound up in Madera Mextown digging the girls and trying to pick up a few for him and Freddy; and then, as purple dusk descended over the grape country, I found myself sitting dumbly in the car as he argued with some old Mexican at the kitchen door about the price of a watermelon the old man grew in the backyard. We had a watermelon; we ate it on the spot and threw the rinds on the old man's dirt sidewalk. All kinds of pretty little girls were cutting down the darkening street. I said "Where in the hell are we?" "Don't worry man" said big Ponzo "tomorrow we make a lot of money, tonight we don't worry." We went back and picked up Bea and her brother and the kid and drove to Fresno. We were all raving hungry. We bounced over the railroad tracks in Fresno and hit the wild streets of Fresno Mextown. Strange Chinamen hung out of windows digging the Sunday night streets; groups of Mex chicks swaggered around in slacks; mambo blasted from jukeboxes; the lights were festooned around like Halloween. We went into a Mexican restaurant and had tacos and mashed pinto beans rolled in tortillas; it was delicious. I whipped out my last shining five dollar bill which stood between me and the Long Island shore and paid for the lot. Now I had two bucks. Bea and I looked at each other. "Where we going to sleep tonight baby?" "I don't know." Freddy was drunk; now all he was saying was "Dah you go man---dah you go man" in a tender and tired voice. It had been a big day. None of us knew what was going on, or what the Good Lord appointed. Poor little Raymond fell asleep on my arm. We drove back to Selma. On the way we pulled up sharp at a roadhouse on the highway---highway 99. Freddy wanted one last beer. In back of the roadhouse were trailers and tents and a few rickety motel-style rooms. I inquired about the price and it was two bucks. I asked Bea how about it and she said fine, because we had the kid on our hands now and had to make him comfortable. So after a few beers in the saloon, where sullen Okies reeled to the music of a cowboy band. Bea and I and Raymond went into a motel room and got ready to hit the sack. Ponzo kept hanging around; he had no place to sleep. Freddy slept at his father's house in the vineyard shack. "Where do you live Ponzo?" I asked. "Nowhere man. I'm supposed to live with Big Rosey but she threw me out last night. I'm gonna get my truck and sleep in it to-night." Guitars tinkled. Bea and I gazed at the stars together and kissed. "Manana," she said, "everything'll be allright tomorrow, don't you think Jackie-honey man?" "Sure baby, manana." It was always manana. For the next week that was all I heard, Manana, a lovely word and one that probably means heaven. Little Raymond jumped in bed clothes and all and went to sleep; sand spilled out of his shoes, Madera sand. Bea and I got up in the middle of the night and brushed the sand off the sheets. In the morning I got up, washed and took a walk around the place. We were five miles out of Selma in the cotton fields and grape vineyards. I asked the big fat woman who owned the camp if any of the tents were vacant. The cheapest one, a dollar a day, was vacant. Bea and I scraped up a dollar and moved into it. There was a bed, a stove and a cracked mirror hanging from a pole; it was delightful. I had to stoop to get in, and when I did there was my baby and my baby-boy. We waited for Freddy and Ponzo to arrive with the truck. They arrived with beer bottles and started to get drunk in the tent. "How about the manure?" "Too late today----tomorrow man we make a lot of money, today we have a few beers. What do you say, beer?" I didn't have to be prodded. "Dah you go---DAH YOU GO!" yelled Freddy. I began to see that our plans for making money with the manure truck would never materialize. The truck was parked outside the tent. It smelled like Ponzo. That night Bea and I went to sleep in the sweet night air beneath our dewy tent and made sweet old love. I was just getting ready to go to sleep when she said "You want to love me now?" I said "What about Raymond." "He don't mind. He's asleep." But Raymond wasn't asleep and he said nothing. The boys came back the next day with the manure truck and drove off to find whiskey; they came back and had a big time in the tent. That night Ponzo said it was too cold and slept on the ground in our tent wrapped in a big tarpaulin smelling of cowflaps. Bea hated him; she said he hung around her brother in order to get close to her. Nothing was going to happen except starvation for Bea and me, so in the morning I walked around the countryside asking for cottonpicking work. Everybody told me to go to the farm across the highway from the camp. I went, and the farmer was in the kitchen with his women. He came out, listened to my story, and warned me he was only paying so much per hundred pound of picked cotton, three dollars. I pictured myself picking at least three hundred pounds a day and took the job. He fished out some long canvas bags from the barn and told me the picking started at dawn. I rushed back to Bea all glee. On the way a grapetruck went over a bump in the road and threw off great bunches of grape on the hot tar. I picked it up and took it home. Bea was glad. "Raymond and me'll come with you and help." "Pshaw!" I said. "No such thing!" "You see, you see, it's very hard picking cotton. I show you how." We ate the grapes and in the evening Freddy showed up with a loaf of bread and a pound of hamburg and we had a picnic. In a larger tent next to ours lived a whole family of Okie cottonpickers; the grandfather sat in a chair all day long, he was too old to work; the son and daughter, and their children, filed every dawn across the highway to my farmer's field and went to work. At dawn the next day I went with them. They said the cotton was heavier at dawn because of the dew and you could make more money than in the afternoon. Nevertheless they worked all day from dawn to sundown. The grandfather had come from Nebraska during the great plague of the Thirties---that selfsame dustcloud my Montana cowboy had told me about---with the entire family in a jaloppy truck. They had been in California ever since. They loved to work. In the ten years the old man's son had increased his children to the number of four, some of whom were old enough now to pick cotton. And in that time they had progressed from ragged poverty in Simon Legree fields to a kind of smiling respectability in better tents, and that was all. They were extremely proud of their tent. "Ever going back to Nebraska?" "Pshaw, there's nothing back there. What we want to do is buy a trailer." We bent down and began picking cotton. It was beautiful. Across the field were the tents, and beyond them the sere brown cottonfields that stretched out of sight, and over that the snowcapped Sierras in the blue morning air. This was so much better than washing dishes on South Main street. But I knew nothing about picking cotton. I spent too much time disengaging the white ball from its crackly bed; the others did it in one flick. Moreover my fingertips began to bleed; I needed gloves, or more experience. There was an old Negro couple in the field with us. They picked cotton with the same Godblessed patience their grandfathers had practised in prewar Alabama: they moved right along their rows, bent and blue, and their bags increased. My back began to ache. But it was beautiful kneeling and hiding in that earth: if I felt like resting I did, with my face on the pillow of brown moist earth. Birds sang an accompaniment. I thought I had found my life's work. Bea and Raymond came waving at me across the field in the hot lullal noon and pitched in with me. Be damned if little Raymond wasn't faster than I was!---and of course Bea was twice as fast. They worked a-head of me and left me piles of clean cotton to add to my bag, Bea workmanlike piles, Raymond little childly piles. I stuck them in with sorrow. What kind of an old man was I that I couldn't support his own ass let alone theirs. They spent all afternoon with me. When the sun got red we trudged back together. At the end of the field I unloaded my burden on a scale, it weighed a pound and a half, and I got a buck fifty. Then I borrowed one of the Okie boys' bicycle and rode down 99 to a crossroads grocer store where I bought cans of cooked spaghetti and meatballs, bread, butter, coffee and cake, and came back with the bag on the handlebars. LA-bound traffic zoomed by; Frisco-bound harassed my tail. I swore and swore. I looked up at the dark sky and prayed to God for a better break in life and a better chance to do something for the little people I loved. Nobody was paying any attention to me up there. I should have known better. It was Bea who brought my soul back: on the tent stove she warmed up the food and it was one of the greatest meals of my life. Sighing like an old Negro cottonpicker, I reclined on the bed and smoked a cigarette. Dogs barked in the cool night. Freddy and Ponzo had given up calling in the evenings. I was satisfied with that. Bea curled up beside me, Raymond sat on my chest, and they drew pictures of animals in my notebook. The light of our tent burned on the frightful plain. The cowboy music twanged in the roadhouse and carried across the fields all sadness. It was allright with me. I kissed my baby and we put out the lights. In the morning the dew made the tent sag; I got up with my towel and toothbrush and went to the general motel toilet to wash; then I came back, put on my pants which were all torn from kneeling in the earth and had been sewed by Bea in the evening; put on my ragged strawhat which had originally been Raymond's toy hat; and went across the highway with my canvas cottonbag. Every day I earned approximately a dollar and a half. It was just enough to buy groceries in the evening on the bicycle. The days rolled by. I forgot all about the East and all about Neal and Allen and the bloody road. Raymond and I played all the time: he liked me to throw him up in the air and down on the bed. Bea sat mending clothes. I was a man of the earth precisely as I had dreamed I would be in Ozone Park. There was talk that Bea's husband was back in Selma and out for me; I was ready for him. One night the Okies went mad in the roadhouse and tied a man to a tree and beat him to a pulp with sticks. I was asleep at the time and only heard about it. From then on I carried a big stick with me in the tent in case they got the idea we Mexicans were fouling up their trailer camp. They thought I was a Mexican, of course; and I am. But now it was getting on in October and getting much colder in the nights. The Okie family had a woodstove and planned to stay for the winter. We had nothing, and besides the rent for the tent was due. Bea and I bitterly decided we'd have to leave. "Go back to your family" I gnashed "For God's sake you can't be batting around tents with a baby like Raymond; the poor little tyke is cold." Bea cried because I was criticizing her motherly instincts; I meant no such thing. When Ponzo came in the truck one gray afternoon we decided to see her family about the situation. But I mustn't be seen and would have to hide in the vineyard. We started for Selma; the truck broke down and simultaneously it started to rain wildly. We sat in the old truck cursing. Ponzo got out and toiled in the rain. He was a good old guy after all. We promised each other one more big bat. Off we went to a rickety bar in Selma Mextown and spent an hour sopping up the brew. I was through with my chores in the cottonfield. I could feel the pull of my own life calling me back. I shot my mother a penny postcard and asked for another fifty across the land. We drove to Bea's family's shack. It was situated on an old road that ran between the vineyards. It was dark when we got there. They left me off a quarter-mile up and drove to the door. Light poured out of the door; Bea's six other brothers were playing their guitars and singing. The old man was drinking wine. I heard shouts and arguments. They called her a whore because she'd left her no good husband and gone to L.A. and left Raymond with them. But the sad fat brown mother prevailed, as she always does among the great Fellaheen peoples of the world, and Bea was allowed to come back home. The brothers began to sing gay songs. I huddled in the cold rainy wind and watched everything across the sad vineyards of October in the Valley. My mind was filled with that great song "Lover Man" as Billy Holliday sings it. "Someday we'll meet, and you'll dry all my tears, and whisper sweet, little words in my ear, hugging and a-kissing, Oh what we've been missing, Lover Gal Oh where can you be..." It's not the words so much as the great harmonic tune and the way Billy sings it, like a woman stroking her man's hair in soft lamplight. The winds howled. I got cold. Bea and Ponzo came back and we rattled off in the old truck to meet Freddy. Freddy was now living with Ponzo's woman Big Rosey; we tooted the horn for him in rickety alleys. Big Rosey threw him out. Everything was collapsing. That night Bea held me tight, of course, and told me not to leave. She said she'd work picking grapes and make enough money for both of us; meanwhile I could live in Farmer Heffelfinger's barn down the road from her family. I'd have nothing to do but sit in the grass all day and eat grapes. In the morning her cousins came to get us in another truck. I suddenly realized thousands of Mexicans all over the countryside knew about Bea and I and that it must have been a juicy, romantic topic for them. The cousins were very polite and in fact charming.. I stood on the truck platform with them as we rattled into town, hanging on to the rail and smiling pleasantries, talking about where we were in the war and what the pitch was. There were five cousins in all and every one of them was nice. They seemed to belong to the side of Bea's family that didn't fuss off like her brother. But I loved her brother. I loved that wild Freddy. He swore he was coming to New York and join me. I pictured him in New York putting off everything till manana. He was drunk in a field someplace that day. I got off the truck at the cross-roads and the cousins drove Bea home. They gave me the high-sign from the front of the house: the father and mother weren't home, they were off picking grapes. So I had the run of the house for the after-noon. It was a four-room shack; I couldn't imagine how the whole family managed to live in there. Flies flew over the sink. There were no screens, just like in the song. "The window she is broken and the rain she is coming in." Bea was at home now and puttering around pots. Her two sisters giggled at me. The little children screamed in the road. When the sun came out red through the clouds of my last Valley afternoon Bea led me to Farmer Heffelfinger's barn. Farmer Heffelfinger had a prosperous farm up the road. We put crates together, she brought blankets from the house and I was all set except for a great hairy tarantula that lurked at the pinpoint top of the barn-roof. Bea said it wouldn't harm me if I didn't bother it. I lay on my back and stared at it. I went out to the cemetery and climbed a tree. In the tree I sang "Blue Skies." Bea and Raymond sat in the grass; we had grapes. In California you chew the juice out of grapes and spit the skin away, a real luxury. Nightfall came. Bea went home for supper and came to the barn at nine o'clock with delicious tortillas and mashed beans. I lit a woodfire on the cement floor of the barn to make light. We screwed on the crates. Bea got up and cut right back to the shack. Her father was yelling at her, I could hear him from the barn. She'd left me a cape to keep warm; I threw it over my shoulder and skulked through the moonlit vineyard to see what was going on. I crept to the end of a row and kneeled in the warm dirt. Her five brothers were singing melodious songs in Spanish. The stars bent over the little roof; smoke poked from the stovepipe chimney. I smelled mashed beans and chili. The old man growled. The brothers kept right on yodelling. The mother was silent. Raymond and the kids were giggling in the bedroom. A California home! I hid in the grapevines digging it all. I felt like a million dollars; I was adventuring in the crazy American night. Bea came out slamming the door behind her. I accosted her on the dark road. "What's the matter?" "Oh we fight all the time. He wants me to go to work tomorrow. He says he don't want me fooling around. Jackie I want to go to New York with you." "But how?" "I don't know honey. I'll miss you I love you." "But I have to leave." "Yes, yes. We screw one more time then you leave." We went back to the barn; I made love to her under the tarantula. What was the tarantula doing? We slept awhile on the crates. She went back at midnight; her father was drunk; I could hear him roaring; then there was silence as he fell asleep. The stars folded over the sleeping countryside. In the morning Farmer Heffelfinger stuck his head through the horse gate and said "How you doing young fella?" "Fine. I hope it's all right my staying here." "Sure thing. You going with that little Mexican floozie?" "She's a very nice girl." "Very pretty too. I think the bull jumped the fence. She's got blue eyes." We talked about his farm. Bea brought my breakfast. I had my canvas bag all packed and ready to go to New York, as soon as I picked up my money in Selma. I knew it was waiting there for me by now. I told Bea I was leaving. She had been thinking about it all night and was resigned to it. Emotionlessly she kissed me in the vineyards and walked off down the row. We turned at a dozen paces, for love is a duel, and looked at each other for the last time. "See you in New York Bea" I said. She was supposed to drive to New York in a month with her brother. But we both knew she wouldn't make it somehow. At a hundred feet I turned to look at her. She just walked on back to the shack, carrying my breakfast plate in one hand. I bowed my head and watched her. Well lackadaddy, I was on the road again. I walked down the highway to Selma eating black walnuts from the walnut tree, I went on the SP tracks and balanced along the rail, I passed a watertower and a factory. This was the end of something. I went to the telegraph office of the railroad for my money order from New York. It was closed. I swore and sat on the steps to wait. The ticketmaster got back and invited me in. The money was in, my mother had saved my lazy ass again. "Who's going to win the World Series next year?" said the gaunt old ticketmaster. I suddenly realized it was Fall and that I was going back to New York. A great joy piled up to the top of me. I told him it would be Braves and Red Sox; it turned out to be Braves and Indians, World Series 1948. But now it was 1947, year of grace. In the great sere October I was leaving the San Joaquin valley; and in that moment things were happening in Texas that I must tell about now, to give richness to the circumstances that made Neal and I crisscross and miss each other in the land that Fall. Neal and Allen lived in Bill Burroughs' bayou shack for a month. They slept on a cot, so did Hunkey; Bill and Joan had a bedroom with the baby girl Julie. The days were all the same: Bill got up first, went puttering in the yard where he was growing a marijuana garden and where he was constructing a Reichian orgone accumulator. This is an ordinary box big enough for a man to sit inside on a chair: a layer of wood a layer of metal and another layer of wood gathers in orgones from the atmosphere and holds them captive long enough for the human body to absorb more than a usual share. According to Reich orgones are atmospheric vibratory atoms of the life-principle. People get cancer because they run out of orgones. Bill thought his orgone accumulator would be improved if the wood he used was as organic as possible: so he tied bushy bayou leaves and twigs to his mystical outhouse. It stood there in the hot flat yard, an exfoliate machine clustered and bedecked with maniacal contrivances. Bill slipped off his clothes and went in to sit and moon over his navel. He came out roaring for breakfast and sex. His long gaunt body struggled back to the shack, his shriveled and vulturous neck barely supporting the bony skull in which was stored all the accumulated knowledge of thirty-five years of crazy life. More of him later. "Joan" he said "you got breakfast ready? If you haven't I'll go catch me a catfish. Neal! Allen! You're sleeping your lives away---young men like you. Get up, we got to drive to McAllen and get some groceries." For about fifteen minutes he glowed and bustled around the house rubbing his hands together eagerly. When everybody got up and dressed Bill's day was finished, all his energy had run out, the orgones had slipped out of the million orifices in his weazeled flanks and withered arms where he plied the morphine needle. Joan tried to find him. He was hiding in his room taking the first fix of the morning. He came out glassy-eyed and calm. Neal did all the driving; from the moment he met Bill he was his chauffeur. They had a jeep. They drove to crossroads stores and bought groceries and Benzedrine inhalers. Hunkey came along with them hoping they'd go as far as Houston so he could slip into the streets and mingle with the characters. He was tired of wearing a straw hat and carrying buckets of water for Joan. There's a photo of him raking the marijuana garden with his immense strawhat; he looks like a coolie; the shack is in the background with washbuckets on the porch and little Julie shading her eyes to watch. There's another photo of Joan simpering over a cookpot; her hair is long and unkempt; she's high on benny and God knows what she's saying as the camera is snapped... "Don't point that nasty old thing at me." Neal wrote me long letters on a crate telling me everything. He sat at Bill's feet in the front room. Bill snuffed down his nose and told long stories. When the sun turned red Bill always whipped out a stick of homegrown tea for the general appetite. Everybody blasted as they ran hither and yon in the shack at various chores. Then Joan cooked a lovely supper. They sat over the remains ---beady-eyed Allen brooding and saying "Hmm" in the big Texas night; eager Neal yelling "Yes! Yes!" to everything everybody said, sulky Hunkey in his purple pants fishing around old drawers for a roach, weary Joan turning her face away, and Bill---Uncle Bill they called him ---sitting with his long legs crossed and fingering his shotgun. He suddenly leaped up and let go a doublebarrel blast out the open window. A spavined old runaway horse ran across his line of fire. The buckshot ripped through a rotted Bayou trunk. "My Gawd!" cried Bill "I've shot a horse!" They all ran out; the horse was galloping into the swamps. "You mean that wormy old nasty old thing" scoffed Joan. "That's not a horse." "What is it if it ain't a horse." "Alistair says it's a witch." Alistair was a gloomy farmer neighbor who sat on his fence all day. "The trouble with the world is," he said, "there's just too many Je-e-e-e-e-ews" with his long beaked nose sniffing the air. He had a divining rod and walked around with it. When it tipped from his palm he claimed there was water below. "How does that divining rod work?" asked Bill. "It ain't IT so much as me" said Alistair. He came over one day; just as he arrived it started to thunder. "Well I guess I brought the rain with me" he said gloomily. The gang sat around playing Billy Holliday records in the Texas bayou night. Hunkey predicted the end of the world would start in Texas. "There's just too many chemical plants and chain gangs around here, I can feel it in the air, it's all sinister." Joan agreed. "The chain reaction will start here." They talked about the Texas City explosion which they'd all heard one afternoon. All their heads nodded in confirmation of this apocalyptic event. "It won't be long" said Joan. Bill snuffed down his nose and kept his secrets to himself. Hunkey---little dark Hunkey with the Oriental face---went out at night and picked rotten sticks in the bayou. There were fascinating varieties of disintegration to be found. He discovered new kinds of worms. Finally he said he began to find them in his skin. He spent hours at the mirror picking them out. Then the time came for all of them to move to New York. Bill suddenly got bored with the bayou. He had an income of fifty dollars a week from his family, he always had a big roll in his pocket. He sent Joan and the baby girl by train and he and Hunkey and Neal would drive up by jeep. Allen entered into a gloomy period which he called the "Bayou Doldrums." Neal was tired of the terrible strain of talking and talking with Allen all the time; they began to wrangle. Allen went down to the Houston waterfront and suddenly found himself in the union hall signing on a ship for Dakar, West Africa. Two days later he shipped out. He returned to New York two months later wearing a bushy beard and the "Dakar Doldrums" under his arm. Neal drove Bill and Hunkey and a few household things in the jeep to New York. He didn't stop once---Texas, Louisiana, Alabama, So. Carolina, No. Carolina, Virginia and on up. They arrived in Manhattan at dawn and went straight to Vicki with an ounce of tea that she bought at once. They were broke. Neal drove Bill all around metropolitan New York in search of an apartment. Hunkey disappeared on Times Square and was finally arrested for carrying weed and given a stretch on Riker's Island. The evening that Bill Burroughs finally found an apartment was the California afternoon that I left Selma. I was eager to find them and join them. I walked along the tracks in the long sad October light of the valley hoping for an SP freight to come along so I could join the grape-eating hoboes and read the funnies with them. It didn't come. I got out on the highway and hitched a ride at once. It was the fastest whoopingest ride of my life. The driver was a fiddler for a famous California cowboy band. He had a brand new car and drove eighty mile an hour. "I don't drink when I drive" he said and handed me a pint. I took a drink and offered him one. "What the hail" he said and drank. We made Selma to LA in the amazing time of four hours flat ---about 250 miles. The valley unreeled before my eyes again. I had vibrated up and down the Hudson Valley and now I was vibrating up and down the San Joaquin Valley on the other side of the world. It was strange. "Whoopee!" yelled the fiddler. "Say now lookee here, my bandleader had to fly to Oklahoma for his father's funeral this morning and I got to lead the band tonight and we're on the air for a half hour. Do you reckon I can get some benzedrine someplace. I ain't never said a word over the air." I told him to buy an inhalor in any drugstore. He got drunk. "You reckon you could do the announcing for me. I'll lend you a suit. You seem to talk a mite good English. What you say?" I was all for it---all the way from rickety Mexican trucks to announcing a radio show in 24 hours. Why else should I live? But he forgot about it and that was all right with me too. I asked him if he ever heard Dizzy Gillespie play trumpet. He slapped his thigh. "That cat is PLUMB frantic!" We dropped off Grapevine Pass. "Sunset Boulevard, ha-haaa!" he howled. He dropped me off right in front of Columbia Pictures studio in Hollywood; I was just in time to run in and pick up my rejected original. Then I bought my bus ticket to New York. The bus leaving at ten I had four hours to dig

Hollywood alone. First I bought a loaf of bread and salami and made myself ten sandwiches to cross the country with. I had a dollar left. I sat on the low cement wall in back of a Hollywood parking lot and made the sandwiches using a piece of flat wood I found on the ground and cleaned to spread the mustard. As I laboured at this absurd task great Kleig lights of a Hollywood premiere stabbed in the sky, that humming West Coast sky. All around me were the noises of the crazy gold coast city. And this was my Hollywood career- -this was my last night in Hollywood and I was spreading mustard on my lap in back of a parkinglot john. I forgot to mention that I didn't have enough money for a bus ticket all the way to New York, only Pittsburgh. I figured to worry about that when I got to Pittsburgh. My sandwiches under one arm and canvas bag in the other I strolled around Hollywood a few hours. Whole families that had driven from the country in old jaloppies went put-put-put across Sunset and Vine with their eager faces searching everywhere for movie stars. All they saw was other families in other jaloppies doing the same thing. They came from Okie flats outside Bakersfield, San Diego, Fresno and San Berdoo; they read movie magazines; the little boys wanted to see Hopalong Cassidy conducting his great white horse across the traffic; the little girls wanted to see Lana Turner in a deep embrace with Robt. Taylor in front of Whelan's; the mothers wanted to see Walter Pidgeon in tophat and tails bowing at them from the curb; the fathers---gaunt crazy jaloppy Americans---scented money in the air. They were ready to sell their daughters to the highest bidder. On the sidewalk characters swarmed. Everybody was looking at everybody else. It was the end of the continent, no more land. Somebody had tipped the American continent like a pinball machine and all the goofballs had come rolling to LA in the southwest corner. I cried for all of us. There was no end to the American sadness and the American madness. Someday we'll all start laughing and roll on the ground when we realize how funny it's been. Until then there is a lugubrious seriousness I love in all this. At dawn my bus was zooming across the Arizona desert----Indio, Blythe, Salome (where she danced); the great

206

dry stretches leading to Mexican mountains in the south. Then we swung north to the Arizona mountains, Flagstaff, Clifftown. I had a book with me I stole from a Hollywood stall, "Le Grand Meulnes" of Alain-Fournier, but I preferred reading the American landscape as we went along. Every bump, rise and stretch in it mystified my longing. In inky night we crossed New Mexico immersed; at gray dawn it was Dalhart Texas; in the bleak Sunday afternoon we rode through one Oklahoma flat-town after another; at nightfall it was Kansas. The bus roared on. I was going home in October. Everybody goes home in October. In Wichita I got off the bus to hit the head. There was a young man in a loud Kansas herringbone suit saying so long to his Minister father. A minute later I saw an eye watching me from a hole in the johnbooth as I sat. A note was slipped through. "I offer you anything on this side if you will put it through." I caught a glimpse of a loud Kansas herringbone suit through the hole. "No thanks" I said through the hole. What a sad Sunday night for the Kansas minister's son; what Wichita doldrums. In a small Kansas town a clerk said to me "There's nothing to do around here." I looked down the end of the street at the infinite spaces beyond the last tumbleshack. We arrived in St. Louis at noon. I took a walk down by the Mississippi River and watched the logs that came floating from Montana in the North---grand odyssiac logs of our continental dream. Old steamboats with their scrollwork more so scrolled and withered by weathers sat in the mud inhabited by rats. Great clouds of afternoon overtopped the Mississippi Valley. The bus roared through Indiana cornfields that night; the moon illuminated the ghostly gathered husks; it was almost Halloween. I made the acquaintance of a girl and we necked all the way to Indianapolis. She was near sighted. When we got off to eat I had to lead her by the hand to the lunch counter. She bought my meals, my sandwiches were all gone; in exchange I told her long stories. She was coming from Washington State where she spent the summer picking apples. Her home was in an upstate New York farm. She invited me to come there. We made a date to meet at a New York hotel anyway. She got off at Columbus Ohio and I slept all the way to

Pittsburgh. I was wearier than I'd been for years and years. I had three hundred and sixty five miles yet to hitch hike to New York and a dime in my pocket. I walked five miles to get out of Pittsburgh and two rides, an apple truck and a big trailer truck, took me to Harrisburg in the soft Indian Summer rainy night. I cut right along. I wanted to get home. It was the night of the Ghost of the Susquehanna. I never dreamed I'd get so hung up. In the first place I didn't know it but I was walking back to Pittsburgh on an older highway. Neither did the Ghost. The Ghost was a shriveled, little old man with a paper satchel who claimed he was headed for "Canady." He walked very fast, commanding me to follow, and said there was a bridge up ahead we could cross. He was about sixty years old; talked incessantly of the meals he had, how much butter they gave him for pancakes, how many extra slices of bread, how the old men had called him from a porch of a charity home in Maryland and invited him to stay for the weekend, how he took a nice warm bath before he left; how he found a brand new hat by the side of the road in Virginia and that was it on his head; how he hit every Red Cross in town and showed them his veteran World War 1 credentials; how they treated him; how the Harrisburg Red Cross was not worthy of the name; how he managed in this hard world and sometimes sold neckties. But as far as I could see he was just a semi-respectable walking hobo of some kind who covered the entire Eastern Wilderness on foot hitting Red Cross offices and sometimes bumming on Main Street corners for a dime. We were bums together. We walked seven miles along the mournful Susquehanna. It is a terrifying river. It has bushy cliffs on both sides that lean like hairy ghosts over the unknown waters. Inky night covers all. Sometimes from the railyards across the river rises a great red locomotive flare that illuminates the horrid cliffs. It was drizzling too. The little man said he had a fine belt in his satchel and we stopped for him to fish it out. "I got me a fine belt here somewheres---got it in Frederick Maryland. Damn, now did I leave that thing on the counter at Fredericksburg?" "You mean Frederick." "No, no, Fredericksburg Virginia!" He was always talking about Frederick Maryland and Fredericksburg Virginia. He walked right in the road in the teeth of advancing traffic and almost got hit several times. I plodded along in the ditch. Any minute I expected the poor little madman to go flying in the night dead. We never found that bridge. I left him at a railroad underpass and in the dark because I was so sweaty from the hike I changed shirts and put on two sweaters; a roadhouse illuminated my sad endeavors. A whole family came walking down the dark road and wondered what I was doing. Strangest thing of all a tenorman was blowing very fine blues in this Pennsylvania hick house; I listened and moaned. It began to rain harder. A man gave me a ride back to Harrisburg and told me I was on the wrong road. I suddenly saw the little man standing under a street lamp with his thumb stuck out---poor forlorn man, poor lost sometimes-boy now broken ghost of the penniless wilds. I told my driver the story and he stopped to tell the old man. "Look here fella, you're on your way West not East." "Heh?" said the little ghost. "Can't tell me I don't know my way around here. Been walking this country for years. I'm headed for Canady." "But this ain't the road to Canada, this is the road to Pittsburgh and Chicago." The little man got disgusted with us and walked off. The last I saw of him was his bobbing little white bag dissolving in the darkness of the mournful Alleghenies. "Hey" I yelled. He was muttering to himself. He had no use for quitters like me. "I'm going right... straight...into..her!" he said about Canada; he said he knew a place on the border where he could slip in unnoticed, said he was going to ride a freight up there. "Lehigh Valley, Lackawanna, Erie, I ride 'em all." I thought all the wilderness of America was in the West till the Ghost of the Susquehanna showed me different. No, there is a wilderness in the East, it's the same Wilderness Ben Franklin plodded in the oxcart days when he was postmaster, when George Washington was a wildbuck Indian fighter, when Daniel Boone told stories by Pennsylvania lamps and promised to find the Gap; when Bradford built his road and men whooped her up in log cabins. There were no great Arizona spaces for the little man, just the bushy wilderness of Eastern Pennsylvania, Maryland and Virginia, the backrounds, the

blacktar roads that curve among the mournful rivers like Susquehanna, Monongahela, old Potomac and Monocacy. This experience
thoroughly shattered me; that night in Harrisburg bore me the punishment of the damned, and ever since. I had to sleep in the railroad
station on a bench; at dawn the ticketmasters threw me out. Isn't it
true that you start your life a sweet child believing in everything under
his father's roof, then comes the day of the Laodiceans, when you
know you are wretched, and miserable, and poor, and blind, and
naked, and with the visage of a gruesome grieving ghost you go shuddering through nightmare life. I stumbled haggardly out of the station;
I had no more control. All I could see of the morning was a whiteness
like the whiteness of the tomb. I was starving to death. All I had left
in the form of calories were the last of the coughdrops I'd bought in
Preston Nebraska months ago; these I sucked for their sugar. I didn't
know how to panhandle. I stumbled out of town with barely enough
strength to reach the city limits. I knew I'd be arrested if I spent
another night in Harrisburg. Cursed city! Bad morning! Where were
the mornings of my boyhood vision? What's a man going to do? Life
is one irony after another, because the ride I then proceeded to get
was the ride of a skinny haggard man who believed in controlled starvation for the sake of health. When I told him I was starving to death
as we rolled east he said "Fine, fine, there's nothing better for you. I
myself haven't eaten for three days. I'm going to live to be a hundred
and fifty years old." He was a ghost---a bag of bones---a floppy doll---
a broken stick---a maniac. I could have gotten a ride with an affluent
fat man who'd say "Let's stop at this restaurant and have some pork-
chops and beans." No, I had to get a ride that morning with a maniac
who believed in controlled starvation for the sake of health. Somewhere in New Jersey he grew lenient and took out bread and butter
sandwiches from the back of the car. They were hidden among his
salesman samples. He was selling plumbing fixtures around Pennsylvania. I devoured the bread and butter. Suddenly I began to laugh. I
was all alone in the car waiting for him as he made business calls in
Allentown, N.J., and I laughed and laughed. Gad, I was sick and tired

of life. But the madman drove me home to New York. Suddenly I found myself on Times Square. I had traveled eight thousand miles around the American continent and I was back on Times Square; and right in the middle of a rush hour too, making me see with my innocent road eyes the absolute madness and fantastic hoorair of New York with its millions and millions hustling forever for a buck among themselves...grabbing, taking, giving, sighing, dying, just so they could be buried in those awful cemetery cities beyond Long Island City. The high towers of the land...the other end of the land....the place where Paper America is born. I stood in a subway doorway trying to get up enough nerve to pick up a beautiful long butt and everytime I stooped great crowds rushed by and obliterated it from my sight and finally it was crushed. I had no money to go home in the subway. Ozone Park is fifteen miles from Times Square. Can you picture me walking those last fifteen miles through Manhattan and Brooklyn? It was dusk. Where was Hunkey? I dug the Square for Hunkey; he wasn't there, he was in Riker's Island behind bars. Where Neal?- -where Bill? where everybody? Where life? I had my home to go to, my place to lay my head down and recoup the losses I had suffered, and figure the gain that I knew was in there somewhere too. I had to panhandle a dime for the subway. I finally hit a Greek minister who was standing around the corner. He gave me the dime with a nervous lookaway. I rushed immediately to the subway. When I got home I ate everything in the ice box. My mother got up and looked at me. "Poor little John" she said in French "you're thin, you're thin. Where have you been all this time?" I had on two shirts and two sweaters; my canvas bag had torn cottonfield pants and the tattered remnants of my huarache shoes in it. My mother and I decided to buy a new refrigerator with the money I had sent her from California; it was to be the first one in the family. She went to bed and late at night I couldn't sleep and just smoked in bed. My half-finished manuscript was on the desk. It was October, home, and work again. The first cold winds rattled the windowpane and I had made it just in time. Neal had come to my house, slept several nights there waiting for me;

spent afternoons talking to my mother as she worked on a great ragrug wove of all the clothes in my family for years, which was now finished and spread on my bedroom floor as complex and as rich as the passage of time itself; and then left, two days before I arrived, crossing my path probably somewhere in Pennsylvania or Ohio, to go to San Francisco---of all places in this world---and hunt my missing footsteps there. He had his own life there; Carolyn had just gotten an apartment. It had never occurred to me to look her up while I was in Marin City. Now it was too late and I had also missed Neal. I never dreamed that first night at home I would see Neal again and that it would start all over again, the road, the whirlwind road, more than I ever in my wildest imaginings foresaw. BOOK TWO: It was a year and a half before I saw Neal again. I stayed home all that time, finished my book and began going to school on the G.I. Bill of Rights. At Christmas 1948 my mother and I went down to visit my sister in the South laden with presents. I had been writing to Neal and he said he was coming East again; and I told him if so he would find me in Rocky Mount, North Carolina, between Xmas and New Year. One day when all our Southern relatives were sitting around the parlor in Rocky Mount, gaunt men and women with the old southern soil in their eyes talking in low whining voices about the weather, the crops and the general weary recapitulation of who had a baby, who got a new house and so on, a mud-spattered '49 Hudson drew up in front of the house on the dirt road. I had no idea who it was. A weary young fellow, muscular and ragged in a T-shirt, unshaven, red-eyed came to the porch and rang the bell. I opened the door and suddenly realized it was Neal. He had come all the way from San Francisco to my sister's door in North Carolina, and in an amazingly short time because I had just written my last letter telling where I was. In the car I could see two figures sleeping. "I'll be Gawd-damned! Neal! Who's in the car?" "Hel-lo, hel-lo man, it's Louanne. And Al Hinkle. We gotta have a place to wash up immediately, we're dogtired." "But how did you get here so fast." "Ah man, that Hudson goes!" "Where did you get it?" "I bought it with my savings. I've been working as a brakeman on the Southern Pacific railroad making four hundred dollars a month." There was utter confusion in the following hour. In the first place, my Southern relatives had no idea what was going on, or who, or what Neal, Louanne and Al Hinkle were; they dumbly stared. My mother and my sister went in the kitchen to consult. There were, in all, eleven people in the little southern house. Not only that but my sister had just decided to move from that house and half her furniture was gone; she and her husband and baby were coming to Ozone Park to live with us in the little apartment. When Neal heard this he at once offered his services with the Hudson. He and I would carry furniture to New York in two fast trips and bring my mother back the tail end of the second trip. This was going to save us a lot of money. It was agreed upon. My sister made a spread and the three battered travelers sat down to eat. Louanne had not slept since Denver; I thought she looked older and more beautiful now. Let me describe everything that had happened and why Louanne was with Neal. He had lived happily with Carolyn in San Francisco ever since that Fall in 1947; he got a job on the railroad and made a lot of money. He became the father of a cute little girl, Cathy Jo Ann Cassady. Then suddenly he blew his top and while walking down the street one day he saw a '49 Hudson for sale and rushed to the bank for his entire roll. He bought the car on the spot. Al Hinkle was with him. Now they were broke. Neal calmed Carolyn's fears and told her he'd be back in a month. "I'm going to New York and bring Jack back." She wasn't too pleased at this prospect. "But what is the purpose of all this? Why are you doing this to me?" "It's nothing, it's nothing darling---ah---hem---Jack has pleaded and begged with me to come and get him, it is absolutely necessary for me to---but we won't go into all these explanations---and I'll tell you why...no listen, I'll tell you why." And he told her why, and of course it made no sense. Big tall Al Hinkle also worked on the railroad with Neal. They had just been laid off during a strike. Al had just met a girl called Helen who was living in San Francisco on her savings. These two mindless cads decided to bring the girl along to the East and have her foot the bill.

Al cajoled and pleaded; she wouldn't go unless he married her. In a whirlwind few days Al Hinkle married Helen, with Neal rushing around to get the necessary papers, and a few days before Christmas they rolled out of San Francisco at seventy miles per, headed for LA and the snowless southern road. In LA they picked up a sailor in a Travel Bureau and took him along for fifteen dollars worth of gas. He was bound for Indiana. They also picked up a woman with her idiot daughter, for four dollars gas fare to Arizona, and zoomed off. Neal sat the idiot girl with him up front and dug her, as he said "All the way man! such a gone sweet little soul. Oh we talked, we talked, we talked of fires and the desert turning to a paradise and her parrot that swore in Spanish." Dropping off these passengers they proceeded to Tucson. All along the way Helen Hinkle, Al's new wife, kept complaining that she was tired and wanted to sleep in a motel. If this kept up they'd spend all her money long before North Carolina. Two nights she forced a stop and blew tens on motels! By the time they got to Tucson she was broke. Neal and Al gave her the slip in a hotel lobby and resumed the voyage alone, with the sailor, and without a qualm. Al Hinkle was a tall calm unthinking fellow who was completely ready to do anything Neal asked him; and at this time Neal was too busy for scruples. He was roaring through Las Cruces New Mexico when he suddenly had an explosive yen to see his sweet firstwife Louanne again. She was up in Denver. He swung the car North, against the feeble protests of the sailor, and zoomed into Denver in the evening. He ran and found Louanne in a hotel. They had ten hours of wild lovemaking. Everything was decided again; they were going to stick. Louanne was the only girl Neal ever really loved. He was nauseous with regret when he saw her face again, and when, as of yore, he pleaded and begged at her knees for the joy of her being. She understood Neal; she stroked his hair; she knew he was mad. To soothe the sailor Neal fixed him up with a girl in a hotel room over the bar where the old poolhall gang always drank, at Glenarm and 14th. But the sailor refused the girl and in fact walked off in the night and they never saw him again; he evidently took a bus to Indiana. Neal,

Louanne and Al Hinkle roared east along Colfax and out to the Kansas plains. Great snowstorms overtook them. In Missouri, at night, Neal had to drive with his scarf-wrapped head stuck out the window with snowglasses that made him look like a monk peering into the manuscripts of the snow because the windshield was covered with an inch of ice. He drove by the birth county of his forbears without a thought. In the morning the car skidded on an icy hill and flapped into a ditch. A farmer offered to help them out. They got all hung up when they picked up a hitch hiker who promised them a dollar if they let him ride to Memphis. In Memphis he went into his house, puttered around looking for the dollar, got drunk, and said he couldn't find it. They resumed across Tennessee: the rods were busted from the accident. Neal had been driving ninety, now he had to stick to a steady seventy or the whole motor would go whirring down the mountainside. They crossed the Smoky Mountains in midwinter. When they arrived at my sister's door they had not eaten for thirty hours---just candy and cheese Crax. They ate voraciously as Neal, sandwich in hand, stood bowed and jumping before the big phonograph listening to a wild bop record I just bought called "The Hunt," with Dexter Gordon and Wardell Gray blowing their tops before a screaming audience that gave the record fantastic frenzied volume. The Southern folk looked at one another and shook their heads in awe. "What kind of friends does Jack have anyway?" they said to my sister. She was stumped for an answer. Southerners don't like madness the least bit, not Neal's kind. He paid absolutely no attention to them. The madness of Neal had bloomed into a weird flower. I didn't realize this till he and I and Louanne and Hinkle left the house for a brief spin in the Hudson, when for the first time we were alone and could talk about anything we wanted. Neal grabbed the wheel, shifted to second, mused a minute rolling, suddenly seemed to decide something and shot the car full-jet down the road in a fury of decision. "Allright now Children," he said rubbing his nose and bending down to feel the emergency and pulling cigarettes out of the compartment and swaying back and forth as he did these things and drove "the time has come for us to decide what we're going to do for the next week. Crucial, crucial. Ahem!" He dodged a mule wagon; in it sat an old Negro plodding along. "Yes!" yelled Neal. "Yes! Dig him! Now consider his soul---stop awhile and consider," and he slowed down the car for all of us to turn and look at the old jazzbo moaning along. "Oh yes, dig him sweet, now there's thoughts in that mind that I would give my last arm to know; go climb in there and find out just what he's poorass pondering about this year's turnip greens and ham. Jack you don't know it but I once lived with a farmer in Arkansas for a whole year, when I was eleven, I had awful chores, I had to skin a dead horse once, I haven't been to Arkansas since Xmas 1943, exactly 6 years ago, when Ben Gowen and I were chased by a man with a gun who owned the gun we were trying to steal; I say all this to show you that of the South I can speak...I have known...I mean man I dig the south, I know it in and out----I've dug your letters to me about it. Oh yes, oh yes," he said trailing off and stopping altogether, and suddenly jumping back to seventy and hunching over the wheel to go. He stared doggedly ahead. Louanne was smiling serenely. This was the new and complete Neal, grown to maturity. I could see that Louanne and Hinkle had been digging up these past several days with amazed love. I said to myself "My God he's changed." Fury spat out of his eyes when he told of things he hated; great glows of joy replaced this when he suddenly got happy; every muscle twitched to live and go. "Oh man the things I could tell you" he said poking me "Oh man we must absolutely find the time.. What has happened to Allen. We all get to see Allen darlings, first thing tomorrow. Now Louanne we're getting some bread and meat to make a lunch for New York. How much money do you have Jack? We'll put everything in the back seat, Mrs. K's furniture, and all of us will sit up front cuddly and close and tell stories as we zoom to New York. Louanne honeycunt you sit next to me, Jack next, then Al at the window, big Al to cut off drafts whereby he comes into using the robe this time...And then we'll go off to sweet life cause now is the time and WE ALL KNOW TIME!" He rubbed his jaw furiously, he swung the car and passed three trucks, he roared into downtown Rocky Mountain looking in every direction and seeing everything in an arc of 180 degrees around his eyeballs without moving his head. Bang, he found a parkingspace in no time and we were parked. He leaped out of the car. Furiously he hustled into the railroad station; we followed sheepishly. He bought cigarettes. He had become absolutely mad in his movements: he seemed to be doing everything at the same time. It was all a shaking of the head, up and down, sideways, jerky vigorous hands, quick walking, sitting, crossing of the legs, uncrossing, getting up, rubbing of the hands, rubbing his balls, hitching his pants, looking up and saying "Am" and sudden slitting of the eyes to see everywhere; and all the time he was poking me in the ribs and talking, talking. It was very cold in Rocky Mt.; they'd had an unseasonal snow. He stood in the long bleak Main Street that runs along the Seaboard Railroad clad in nothing but a T-shirt and low-hanging pants with the belt unbuckled, as though he was about to take them off. He came sticking his hand in to talk to Louanne; he backed away fluttering his hands before her. "Oh yes I know! I know YOU, I know YOU Darling!" His laugh was maniacal; it started low and ended high, exactly like the laugh of a radio maniac, only faster and more like a titter. A tittering maniac. Then he kept reverting to businesslike tones. There was no purpose in our coming downtown but he found purposes. He made us all hustle, Louanne for the lunch groceries, me for a paper to dig the weather report, Al for cigars. Neal loved to smoke cigars. He smoked one over the paper and talked. "Ah, our holy American slopjaws in Washington are planning fur-ther inconveniences---ah---hem!---aw---hup! hup!" and he leaped off and rushed to see a colored girl that just then passed outside the station. "Dig her" he said standing with limp finger pointed, fingering his genitalia with a goofy smile "that little gone black lovely. Ah! Hmm!" We got in the car and roared back to my sister's house. I had been spending a quiet Christmas in the country, as I realized when we got back into the house and I saw the Christmas tree, the presents and smelled the roasting turkey, and listened to the talk of the relatives, but now the bug was on me again and the bug's name was Neal Cassady and I was off on another spurt around the road. We packed my sister's boxes of clothes and dishes and a few chairs in back of the car and took off at dark, promising to be back in thirty hours. Thirty hours for a thousand miles North and South. But that's the way Neal wanted it. It was a tough trip and none of us noticed it; the heater was not working and consequently the windshield developed fog and ice. Neal kept reaching out while driving seventy to wipe it with a rag and make a hole to see the road. In the spacious Hudson we had plenty room all four of us to sit up front. A blanket covered our laps. The radio was not working. It was a brand new car bought five days ago and already it was broken. There was only one instalment paid on it too. Off we went, north to Virginia, on 101, a straight two-lane highway without much traffic. And Neal talked, no one else talked. He gestured furiously, he leaned as far as me sometimes to make a point, sometimes he had no hands on the wheel and yet the car went as straight as an arrow, not for once deviating the slightest bit from the white line in the middle of the road that unwound kissing our left front tire. I didn't realize this was going to be the case all the way to California before this new season was over. It was a completely meaningless set of circumstances that made Neal come and similarly I went off with him for no reason. In New York I had been attending school and romancing around with a girl called Pauline, a beautiful Italian honey-haired darling that I actually wanted to marry. All these years I was looking for the woman I wanted to marry. I couldn't meet a girl without saying to myself, "What kind of wife would she make?" I told Neal and Louanne about Pauline. Louanne suddenly leaped to the situation. She wanted to know all about Pauline, she wanted to meet her. We zoomed through Richmond, Washington, Baltimore and up to Philadelphia on a winding country road and talked. "I want to marry a girl" I told them "so I can rest my soul with her till we both get old. This can't go on all the time...all this franticness and jumping around. We've got to go someplace, find something." "Ah now man" said Neal "I've been digging you for years about the HOME and marriage and all those fine wonderful things about your soul." On my right sat Al Hinkle who had married a girl for gas fare. I felt I was defending my position. It was a sad night; it was also a merry night. In Philadelphia we went into a lunchcart and ate hamburgers with our last food dollar. The counter-man- -it was three A.M.- -heard us talk about money and offered to give us the hamburgers free, plus more coffee, if we all pitched in and washed dishes in the back because the regular man hadn't shown up. We jumped to it. Al Hinkle said he was an old pearldiver from way back and pitched his long arms into the dishes. Neal stood googing around with a towel, so did Louanne; finally they started necking among the pots and pans; they withdrew to a dark corner in the pantry. The counterman was satisfied as long as Al and I did the dishes. We finished them in fifteen minutes. When daybreak came we were zooming through New Jersey with the great cloud of Metropolitan NY rising before us in the snowy distance. Neal had a sweater wrapped around his ears to keep warm. He said we were a band of Arabs coming in to blow up New York. We swished through the Lincoln tunnel and came out on Times Square. "Oh damn I wish I could find Hunkey. Everybody look sharp, see if they can find him." We all scoured the sidewalks. "Good old gone Hunkey...Oh you should have SEEN him in Texas." So now Neal had come about four thousand miles from Frisco, via Arizona and up to Denver, inside four days with innumerable adventures sandwiched in and it was only the beginning. We went to my house in Ozone Park and slept. I was the first to wake up, late in the afternoon. Neal and Louanne were sleeping on my bed, Al and I on my mother's bed. Neal's battered unhinged trunk lay sprawled on the floor with socks sticking out. A phone call came for me from the drugstore downstairs. I ran down; it was from New Orleans. Bill Burroughs in his high whining voice was making a complaint. It seemed a girl called Helen Hinkle had just arrived at his house for a guy Al Hinkle. Bill had no idea who these people were. Helen Hinkle was a tenacious loser. I told Bill to reassure her that Hinkle was with Neal and I and that most likely we'd be picking her up in New Orleans on the way to the Coast. Then the girl herself talked on the phone. She wanted to know how Al was. She was all concerned about his happiness. "How did you get from Tucson to New Orleans?" I asked. She said she wired home for money and took a bus. She was determined to catch up with Al because she loved him. I went upstairs and told Big Al. He sat in the chair with a worried look. "Alright now," said Neal suddenly waking up and leaping out of bed "what we must do is eat, at once, Louanne rustle around the kitchen see what there is, Jack you and I go downstairs and call Allen, Al you see what you can do straightening out the house." I followed Neal bustling downstairs. The guy who ran the drugstore said "You just got another call...this one from San Francisco...for a guy called Neal Cassady. I said there wasn't anybody by that name." It was Carolyn calling Neal. The drugstore man, Sam, a tall calm friend of mine, looked at me and scratched his head. "Geez, what are you running, an international whorehouse?" Neal tittered maniacally. "I dig you man!" He leaped into the phonebooth and called Frisco collect. Then we called Allen at his home in New Jersey and told him to come in. Allen arrived two hours later. Meanwhile Neal and I got ready for our return trip alone to North Carolina to pick up the rest of the furniture and bring my mother back. Allen Ginsberg came, poetry under his arm, and sat in an easy chair watching us with beady eyes. For the first half hour he refused to say anything, or that is, he refused to commit himself. He had quieted down since the Denver Doldrum days; the Dakar Doldrums had done it. In Dakar, wearing a beard, he had wandered the backstreets with little children who led him to a witchdoctor who told him his fortune. He had snapshots of crazy streets with grass huts, the hip back-end of Dakar. He said he almost jumped off the ship like Hart Crane on the way back. It was the first time he was seeing Neal since they parted in Houston. Neal sat on the floor with a music box and listened with tremendous amazement at the little song it played... "A Fine Romance" - - "Little tinkling whirling doodlebells. Ah! Listen! We'll all bend down together and look into the center of the music box till we learn about the secrets... tinklydoodlebell, whee." Al Hinkle was also sitting on the floor; he had my drumsticks; he suddenly began beating a tiny beat to go with the music box that we barely could hear. Everybody held their breath to listen. "Tick....tack...tick-tick....tack-tack." Neal cupped a hand over his ear, his mouth hanged open, he said "Ah! Whee!" Allen watched this silly madness with slitted eyes. Finally he slapped his knee and said "I have an announcement to make." "Yes? Yes?" "What is the meaning of this voyage to New York? What kind of sordid business are you on now? I mean, man, whither goest thou?" "Whither goest thou?" echoed Neal with his mouth open. We sat and didn't know what to say; there was nothing to talk about any more. The only thing to do was go. Neal leaped up and said we were ready to go back to North Carolina. He took a shower, I cooked up a big platter of rice with all that was left in the house, Louanne sewed his socks and we were ready to go. Neal and Allen and I zoomed into New York. We promised to see him in thirty hours, in time for New Year's Eve. It was night. We left Allen at Times Square and went back across the tunnel and into New Jersey. Taking turns at the wheel, Neal and I made North Carolina in ten hours. "Now this is the first time we've been alone and in a position to talk for years" said Neal. And he talked all night. As in a dream we were zooming back through sleeping Washington and back in the Virginia wilds, crossing the North Carolina line at daybreak, pulling up at my sister's door at nine A.M. And all this time Neal was tremendously excited about everything he saw, everything he talked about, every detail of every moment that transpired. He was out of his mind with real belief. "And of course now no one can tell us that there is no God. We've passed through all forms. You remember Jack when I first came to New York and I wanted Hal Chase to teach me about Nietzsche. You see how long ago? Everything is fine, God exists, we know time. Everything since the Greeks has been predicated wrong. You can't make it with geometry and geometrical systems of thinking. It's all THIS!" He wrapped his finger in his fist; the car hugged the line straight and true. "And not only that but we both understand that I couldn't have time to explain why I know and you know God exists." At one point I moaned about life's troubles, how poor my family was, how much I wanted to help Pauline who was also poor and had a daughter. "Troubles, you see, is the generalization-word for what God exists in. The thing is not to get hung up. My head rings!" he cried clasping his head. He rushed out of the car like Groucho Marx to get cigarettes---that furious ground-hugging walk with the coat tails flying, except he had no coat tails. "Since Denver, Jack, a lot of things...Oh, the things...I've thought and thought. I used to be in reform school all the time, I was a young punk, asserting myself---stealing cars a psychological expression of my position, hincty to show. All my jail-problems are pretty straight now. As far as I know I shall never be in jail again. The rest is not my fault." We passed a little kid who was throwing stones at the cars in the road. "Think of it" said Neal. "One day he'll put a stone through a man's windshield and the man will crash and die...all on account of that little kid. You see what I mean? God exists without qualms. As we roll along this way I am positive beyond no doubt that everything will be taken care of for us...that even you, as you drive, fearful of the wheel" (I hated to drive and drove carefully) "the thing will go along of itself and you won't go off the road and I can sleep. Furthermore we know America, we're at home; I can go anywhere in America and get what I want because it's the same in every corner, I know the people, I know what they do. We give and take and go in the incredibly complicated sweetness zig-zagging every side." There was nothing clear about the things he said, but what he meant to say was somehow made pure and clear. He used the word "pure" a great deal. I had never dreamed Neal would become a mystic. These were the first days of his mysticism which would lead to the strange ragged W.C. Fields saintliness of his later days. Even my mother listened to him with a curious half-ear as we roared back north to New York that same night with the furniture in the back. Now that my mother was in the car Neal settled down to talking about his worklife in San Francisco. He went over every single detail of what a brakeman has to do, demonstrating every time we passed railyards and even at one point jumping out of the car to show me how a brakeman makes the high-sign for a through-train. My mother retired to the back seat and went to sleep. In Washington at four A.M. Neal called Carolyn collect again in Frisco. Shortly after this as we pulled out of Washington a cruising car overtook us with siren going and we had a speeding ticket in spite of the fact that we were only going about thirty. It was the California license plate that did it. "You guys think you can rush through here as fast as you want just because you come from California?" said the cop. I went with Neal to the sergeant's desk and we tried to explain to the police that we had no money. They said Neal would have to spend the night in jail if we didn't round up the money. Of course my mother had it, fifteen dollars, she had twenty in all and it was going to be just fine. And in fact while we were arguing with the cops one of them went out to peek at my mother who sat wrapped in the back of the car. She saw him. "Don't worry, I'm not a gunmoll... if you want to come in and search the car go right ahead....I'm going home with my son and this furniture isn't stolen, it's my daughter's, she just had a baby and she's coming to live with me." This flabbergasted Sherlock and he went back in the station house. My mother had to pay the fine for Neal or we'd be stuck in Washington; I had no license. He promised to pay it back; and he actually did, exactly a year and a half later and to my mother's pleased surprise. My mother---a respectable woman hung up in this sad world, and well she knew the world. She told us about the cop. "He was hiding behind the tree trying to see what I looked like. I told him...I told him to search the car if he wanted. I've nothing to be ashamed of." She knew Neal had something to be ashamed of, and me too, by virtue of my being with Neal, and Neal and I accepted this sadly. My mother once said the world would never find peace until men fell at their women's feet and asked for forgiveness. This is true. All over the world, in the jungles of Mexico, in backstreets of Shanghai, in New York cocktail bars, husbands are getting drunk while the women stay home with the babies of the everdarkening future. If these men stop the machine and come home---and get on their knees---and ask for forgiveness---and the women bless them---peace will suddenly descend on the earth with a great silence like the inherent silence of the Apocalypse. But Neal knew this, he'd mentioned it many times. "I've pleaded and pleaded with Louanne for a peaceful sweet understanding of pure love between us forever with all hassels thrown out---she understands---her mind is bent on something else---she's after me---she won't understand how much I love her---she's knitting my doom." "The truth of the matter is we don't understand our women, we blame on them and it's all our fault" I said. "But it isn't as simple as that" warned Neal. "Peace will come suddenly, we won't understand when it does, see man?" Doggedly, bleakly, he pushed the car through New Jersey; at dawn I drove across the Pulaski Skyway as he slept in the back. We arrived at Ozone Park at nine in the morning to find Louanne and Al Hinkle sitting around smoking butts from the ashtrays; they hadn't eaten since Neal and I left. My mother paid for the groceries and cooked up a tremendous breakfast. Now it was time for the western threesome to find new living quarters in Manhattan proper. Allen had a pad on York Avenue; they were moving in in the evening. We slept all day, Neal and I, and woke up as a great snowstorm ushered in New Year's Eve 1948. Al Hinkle was sitting in my easy chair telling about the previous New Year's. "I was in Chicago. I was broke. I was sitting at the window of my hotel room on North Clark street and the most delicious smell rose to my nostrils from the bakery downstairs. I didn't have a dime but I went down and talked to the girl. She gave me bread and coffee cakes free. I went back to my room and ate them. I stayed in my room all night. In Farmington Utah once, where I went to work with Ed Uhl, you know Ed Uhl the rancher's son in Denver, I was in my bed and all of a sudden I saw my dead mother standing in the corner with light all around her. I said 'Mother!' She disappeared. I have visions all the time," said Al Hinkle nodding his head. "What are you going to do about Helen?" "Oh we'll see. When we get to New Orleans. Don't you think so, huh?" He was starting to turn to me as well for advice; one Neal wasn't enough for him. "What are you going to do with yourself Al?" I asked. "I don't know" he said. "I just go along. I dig life." He repeated it, following Neal's line. He had no direction. He sat reminiscing that night in Chicago and the hot coffee cakes in the lonely room. The snow whirled outside. A big party was on hand in New York, we were all going. Neal packed his broken trunk, put it in the car, and we all took off for the big night. My mother was happy with the thought that my sister was moving in the following week; she sat with her paper and waited for the midnight New Year's Eve broadcast from Time's Square. We roared into New York swerving on ice. I was never scared when Neal drove; he could handle a car under any circumstances. The radio had been fixed and now he had wild bop to urge us along the night. I didn't know where all this was leading, I didn't care. Just about that time a strange thing began to haunt me. It was this: I had forgotten something. There was a decision that I was about to make before Neal showed up and now it was driven clear out of my mind but still hung on the tip of my mind's tongue. I kept snapping my finger trying to remember it. I even mentioned it. And I couldn't even tell if it was a real decision or just a thought I had decided to make and forgot to do... haunted, flabbergasted, made sad. It had to do somewhat with the Shrouded Stranger. Allen Ginsberg and I once sat down together, knee to knee in two chairs, facing, and I told him a dream I had about a strange Arabic figure that was pursuing me across the desert; that I tried to avoid; that finally overtook me just before I reached the Protective City. "Who is this?" said Allen. We pondered it. I proposed it was myself wearing a shroud. That wasn't it. Something, someone, some spirit was pursuing all of us across the desert of life and was bound to catch us before we reached heaven. Naturally, now that I look back on it, this is only death: death will overtake us before heaven. The one thing that we yearn for in our living days, that makes us sigh and groan and undergo sweet nauseas of all kinds, is the remembrance of some lost bliss that was probably experienced in the womb and can only be reproduced- -tho we hate to admit it- -in death. But who wants to die? But more of this later. In the rush of events that took place I kept thinking about this in the back of my mind. I told Neal and he instantly recognized it as the mere simple longing for pure death; and because we're all of us never in life again, he, rightly, would have nothing to do with it, and I agree with him now. We went looking for my New York gang of friends. I have a tremendous and interesting gang of friends in New York. New York is such a crazy town, the crazy flowers bloom there too. We went to Ed Stringham's first…Ed Stringham is a sad handsome fellow, sweet, generous and amenable; only once in a while he suddenly has fits of depression and rushes off without saying a word to anyone. This night he was overjoyed. "Jack where did you find these absolutely wonderful people? I've never seen anyone like them." "I found them in the West." Neal was having his kicks: he put on a jazz record, grabbed Louanne, held her tight, and bounced against her with the beat of the music. She bounced right back. It was simple as that, a real love dance. John Holmes came in with a huge gang. The New Year's weekend began and lasted three days and three nights. Great gangs got in the Hudson and swerved in the snowy New York streets from party to party. I brought Pauline and her sister to the biggest party. When Pauline saw me with Neal and Louanne her face darkened…she sensed the madness they put in me. "I don't like you when you're with them." "Ah it's allright, it's just kicks. We only live once. We're having a good time." "No, it's sad and I don't like it." Then Louanne began making love to me; she said Neal was going to stay with Carolyn and she wanted me to go with her. "Come back to San Francisco with us. We'll live together. I'll be a good girl for you." But I knew Neal loved Louanne, and I also knew Louanne was doing this to make Pauline jealous, and I wanted nothing of it. Still and all I licked my lips for the luscious blonde. Louanne and Pauline were a couple of firstclass beauties. When Pauline saw Louanne pushing me into the corners and giving me the word and forcing kisses on me she accepted Neal's invitation to go out in the car; but they just talked and drank some of the Southern moonshine I left in the compartment. Everything was being mixed up and all was falling. I knew my affair with Pauline wouldn't last much longer. She wanted me to be <u>her way</u>. She was married to a mechanic who treated her badly. I was willing to marry her and bring her baby daughter and all if she divorced the mechanic; but there wasn't even enough money to get a divorce and the whole thing was hopeless, besides of which Pauline would never understand me because I like too many things and get all confused and hungup running from one thing to another till I drop. This is the night, what it does to you. I had nothing to offer anybody except my own confusion. The parties were enormous; there were at least a hundred people at Herb Benjamin's basement apartment in the west nineties. People overflowed into the cellar compartments near the furnace. Something was going on in every corner, on every bed and couch, not an orgy, but just a New Year's party with frantic screaming and wild radio music. There was even a Chinese girl. Neal ran like Groucho Marx from group to group digging everybody. Periodically we rushed out to the car to pick up more people. Lucien came. Lucien is the hero of my New York gang, as Neal is the chief hero of the Western. They immediately took a dislike for each other. Lucien's girl suddenly socked Lucien on the jaw with a roundhouse right. He stood reeling. She carried him home. Some of our mad newspaper friends rushed in from the office with bottles. There was a tremendous and wonderful snowstorm going on outside. Al Hinkle made Pauline's sister and disappeared with her; I forgot to say that Al Hinkle is a very smooth man with the women. He's six foot four, mild, affable, agreeable, dumb and delightful. He helps women on with their coats. That's the way to do things. At five o'clock in the morning we were all rushing through a backyard of a tenement and climbing in through a window of an apartment where a huge party was going on. At dawn we were back at Ed Stringham's. People were drawing pictures and drinking stale beer. I slept with a girl called Rhoda---poor Rhoda--- with all our clothes on, for no reason, just slept on the same couch. Great groups filed in from the old Columbia campus bar. Everything in life, all the faces of life, were piling into the same dank room. At John Holmes' the party went on. John Holmes is a wonderful sweet fellow who wears glasses and peers out of them with delight. He began to learn "Yes!" to everything just like Neal at this time, and hasn't stopped since. To the wild sounds of Dexter Gordon and Wardell Gray blowing "The Hunt" Neal and I played catch with Louanne over the couch; she was no small doll either. Neal went around with no undershirt, just his pants, barefoot, till it was time to hit the car and fetch more people. Everything happened. We found the wild ecstatic Allen Anson and spent a night at his house in Long Island. Allen Anson lives in a nice house with his aunt; when she dies the house is all his. Meanwhile she refuses to comply to any of his wishes and hates his friends. He brought this ragged gang of Neal, Louanne, Al and I and began a roaring party. The woman prowled upstairs; she threatened to call the police. "Oh shut up you old bag!" yelled Anson. I wondered how he could live with her like this. He had more books than I've ever seen in all my life...two libraries, two rooms loaded from floor to ceiling around all four walls, and such books as "The Explanation of the Apocalypse" in ten volumes. He played Verdi operas and pantomimed them in his pajamas with the great rip down the back. He didn't give a damn about anything. He is a great scholar who goes reeling down the NY waterfront with original 14th century musical manuscripts under his arm, shouting. He crawls like a great spider through the streets. His excitement blew out of his eyes in great stabs of fiendish light. He rolled his neck in spastic ecstasy. He lisped, he writhed, he flopped, he moaned, he howled, he fell back in despair. He could hardly get a word out he was so excited with life. Neal stood before him with head bowed repeating over and over again "Yes...yes...yes." He took me into a corner. "That Allen Anson is the greatest most wonderful of all. That's what I was trying to tell you...that's what I want to be...I want to be like him. He's never hung up, he goes every direction, he lets it all out, he knows time, he has nothing to do but rock back and forth, Man he's the end! You see, if you go like him all the time you'll finally get it." "Get what?" "IT! IT! I'll tell you---now no time, we have no time now." Neal rushed back to watch Allen Anson some more. George Shearing the great jazz pianist, Neal said, was exactly like Allen Anson. Neal and I went to see Shearing at Birdland in the midst of the long mad weekend. The place was deserted, we were the first customers, ten o'clock. Shearing came out, blind, led by the hand to his keyboard. He was a distinguished looking Englishman with a stiff white collar, slightly beefy, blond, with a delicate English summer's night air about him that came out in the first rippling sweet number he played as the bass player leaned to him reverently and thrummed the beat. The drummer, Denzel Best, sat motionlessly except for his wrists snapping the brushes. And Shearing began to rock; a smile broke over his ecstatic face; he began to rock in the piano seat, back and forth, slowly at first, then the beat went up, he began rocking fast, his left foot jumped up with every beat, his neck began to rock crookedly, he brought his face down to the keys, he pushed his hair back, his combed hair dissolved, he began to sweat. The music picked up. The bassplayer hunched over and socked it in, faster and faster. It seemed faster and faster, that's all. Shearing began to play his chords; they rolled out of the piano in great rich showers, you'd think the man wouldn't have time to line them up. It rolled and rolled like the sea. Folks yelled for him to "Go!" Neal was sweating; the sweat poured down his collar. "There he is! That's him! Old God! Old God Shearing! Yes! Yes! Yes!" And Shearing was conscious of the madman behind him, he could hear every one of Neal's gasps and imprecations, he could sense it tho he couldn't see. "That's right!" Neal said. "Yes!" Shearing smiled; he rocked. Shearing rose from the piano dripping with sweat; these were his great days before he became cool and commercial. When he was gone Neal pointed to the empty piano seat. "God's empty chair" he said. On the piano a horn sat; its golden shadow made a strange reflection along the desert caravan painted on the wall behind the drums. God was gone; it was the silence of his departure. It was a rainy night. It was the myth of the rainy night. Neal was popeyed with awe. This madness would lead nowhere. I didn't know what was happening to me, and I suddenly realized it was only the T that we were smoking, Neal had bought some in New York. It made me think that everything was about to arrive---the moment when you know all and everything is decided forever. I left everybody and went home to rest. My mother said I was wasting my time hanging around with Neal and his gang. I knew that was bull too. Life is life, and kind is kind. What I wanted was to take one more magnificent trip to the west coast and get back in time for the spring semester in school. And what a trip it turned out to be! I only went along for the ride, and to see what else Neal was going to do, and finally, also, knowing Neal would go back to Carolyn in Frisco, I wanted to have an affair with Louanne, and I did. We got ready to cross the groaning continent again. I drew my G.I. check and gave Neal $18 to mail to his wife; she was waiting for him to come home and she was broke. What was on Louanne's mind I don't know. Al Hinkle as ever just followed. There were long funny days spent in Allen's apartment before we left. He went around in his bathrobe and made semi-ironical speeches as follows: "Now I'm not trying to take your hincty sweets from you but it seems to me the time has come to decide what you are and what you're going to do." Allen was working as copyboy for AP. "I want to know what all this sitting around the house all day is intended to mean. What all this talk is and what you propose to do. Neal, why did you leave Carolyn and pick up Louanne." No answer---giggles. "Louanne, why are you travelling around the country like this and what are your womanly intentions concerning the shroud?" Same answer. "Al Hinkle, why did you abandon your new wife in Tucson and what are you doing here sitting on your big fat ass. Where's your home? what's your job?" Al Hinkle bowed his head in genuine befuddlement. "Jack---how comes it you've fallen on such sloppy days and what have you done with Pauline?" He adjusted his bathrobe and sat facing us all. "The days of wrath are yet to come. The baloon won't sustain you much longer. And not only that but it's an abstract baloon. You'll all go flying to the west coast and come staggering back in search of your stone." In these days Allen had developed a tone of voice which he hoped sounded like what he called The Voice of Rock; the whole idea was to stun people into the realization of the rock. "You pin a dragon to your hats," he warned us, "you're up in the attic with the bats." His mad eyes glittered at us. Since the Dakar Doldrums he had finally gone through a terrible period which he called the Holy Doldrums, or Harlem Doldrums, when he lived in Harlem in midsummer and at night woke up in his lonely room and heard "the great machine" descending from the sky; and when he walked on 125th street "under water" with all the other fish. It was a riot of crazy ideas that had come to occupy his brain. He made Louanne sit on his lap and commanded her to subside. He told Neal "Why don't you just sit down and relax. Why do you jump around so much?" Neal ran around putting sugar in his coffee and saying "Yes! yes! yes!" At night Al Hinkle slept on the floor on cushions, Neal and Louanne pushed Allen out of bed and went to it, and Allen sat up in the kitchen over his kidney stew mumbling the predictions of the rock. I came in days and watched everything. Al Hinkle said to me "Last night I walked clear down to Times Square and just as I arrived I suddenly realized I was a ghost---it was my ghost walking on the sidewalk." He said these things to me without comment, nodding his head emphatically. Ten hours later in the midst of someone else's conversation Al would suddenly say "Yep, it was my ghost walking on the sidewalk." Suddenly Neal leaned to me earnestly and said "Jack I have something to ask of you---very important to me---I wonder how you'll take it---we're buddies aren't we?" "Sure are, Neal." He almost blushed. Finally he came out with it: he wanted me to lay Louanne. I didn't ask him why because I knew. He wanted to test something in himself and he wanted to see what Louanne was like with another man. We were sitting in Ross Bar on Eighth Avenue when he proposed the idea; we'd spent an hour walking Times Square looking for Hunkey. Ross Bar is the hoodlum bar of Times Square; it changes names every year. You walk in there and you don't see a single girl, even in the booths, just a great mob of young men dressed in all varieties of hoodlum cloth---from red shirts to zoot suits: it is also the hustler's bar, the boys who make a living among the sad old homos of the Eighth Avenue night. Neal walked in there with his eyes slitted to see every single face. There were wild Negro queers, sullen guys with guns, shiv-packing seamen, thin

non-committal junkies, and an occasional well-dressed middleaged
detective posing as a bookie and hanging around half for interest and
half for duty. It was the typical place for Neal to put down his request.
All kinds of evil plans are hatched in Ross Bar---you can sense it in
the air---and all kinds of mad sexual routines are initiated to go with
it. The safecracker not only proposes a certain loft on Fourteenth
Street to the hoodlum but that they sleep together. Kinsey spent a lot
of time in Ross Bar interviewing some of the boys; I was there the
night his assistant came, in 1945. Hunkey and Allen were interviewed.
Neal and I drove back to York Avenue and found Louanne in bed.
Hinkle was roaming his ghost around New York. Neal told her what
we had decided. She said she was pleased. I wasn't so sure myself. I
had to prove that I'd go through with it. The bed was the bed my
father had died in---I had given it to Allen a week before, Neal and I
had driven it in from the Island. My father had been a big man and
the bed sagged in the middle. Louanne lay there, with Neal and I on
both sides of her poised on the upjutting mattress-ends, not knowing
what to say. I said "Ah hell I can't do this." "Go on man, you promised!" said Neal. "What about Louanne?" I said. "Come on Louanne,
what do you think?" "Go ahead" she said. She grabbed me and I tried
to forget Neal was there. Every time I realized he was lying there, stiff
as a board and listening for every sound in the dark I couldn't make
it. I kept rolling off. It was horrible. "We must all relax" said Neal.
"I'm afraid I can't make it. Why don't you go in the kitchen a minute?"
Neal did so. Still my heart wasn't in it. Louanne was a lovely woman
to have wrapped around you; she was warm and she was ready; and
extremely languid. I whispered we would try it again in San Francisco
when things were right. It was 3 children of the earth trying to decide
something in the night and having all the weight of past centuries
balooning in the dark before them. There was a strange quiet in the
apartment. I went and tapped Neal and told him to go to Louanne;
and I retired on the couch. I heard them frantically rocking the bed
back and forth: to my amazement I realized Neal was, shall we say,
devouring her, and this was the usual routine with them. Only a guy

who's spent five years in jail can go to such maniacal helpless extremes; beseeching at the very portals of the womb with a completely physical realization of the sources of life-bliss; trying to get back in there once and for all, while living, and adding to it the living sexual frenzy and rhythm. This is the result of years looking at dirty pictures behind bars; looking at the legs of women in magazines; evaluating the hardness of the steel halls and the softness of the woman who is not there. Jail is where you promise yourself the right to live. Neal had never seen his mother's face. Every new girl, every new wife, every new child was an addition to his bleak impoverishment. Where was his father---old bum Neal Cassady the Barber, riding freights, working as a scullion in railroad cookshacks, stumbling, down-crashing in wino alley nights, expiring on coal piles, dropping his yellowed teeth one by one in the gutters of the West. Neal had every right to die the sweet deaths of complete love of his Louanne. Her own father was a cop in L.A. who had made many an incestuous hint. She showed me a picture; a little mustache, slick hair, cruel eyes, polished belt and gun. I didn't want to interfere, I just wanted to follow. Allen came back at dawn and put on his bathrobe. He wasn't sleeping any more these days. "Ech!" he screamed. He was going out of his mind from the confusion of jam on the floor, pants, dresses thrown hither, cigarette butts, dirty dishes, open books---it was a great forum we were having. Every day the world groaned to turn and we were making our appalling studies of the night. Louanne was black and blue from a fight with Neal about something: his face was scratched. It was time to go. We drove to my house, a whole gang of ten, to get my bag and call Bill Burroughs in New Orleans from the phone in the bar where Neal and I had our first talk years ago when he came to my door to learn to write. We heard Bill's whining voice eighteen hundred miles away. "Say what do you boys expect me to do with this Helen Hinkle? She's been here two weeks now hiding in her room and refusing to talk to either Joan or me. Have you got this character Al Hinkle with you? For krissakes bring him down and get rid of her. She's sleeping in our best bedroom and's run clear out of money. This ain't a hotel."

We assured Bill with whoops and cries over the phone---there was Neal, Louanne, Allen, Hinkle, me, John Holmes, his wife Marian, Ed Stringham, God knows who else, all yelling and drinking beer over the phone at befuddled Burroughs who above all things hated confusion. "Well" he said "maybe you'll make better sense when you get down here." I said goodbye to my mother and promised to be back in two weeks and took off for California again. You always expect some kind of magic at the end of the road. Strangely enough Neal and I were going to find it, alone, before we finished with it. The New York kids stood around the car on York Avenue and waved goodbye. Rhoda was there; also Geo. Wickstrom and Les Connors and someone else, the remnants of the big New Year's weekend that was never to be surpassed. "That's right, that's right" Neal kept saying and all the time he was only concerned with locking the trunk and putting the proper things in the compartment and sweeping the floor and getting all ready for the purity of the road again...the purity of moving and getting somewhere, no matter where, and as fast as possible and with as much excitement and digging of all things as possible. We roared off---at the last minute Rhoda decided to ride down to Washington with us and come back by bus. She was in love with Big Al by now and they sat in the backseat necking as once again Neal pushed the Hudson thru the Lincoln Tunnel and we were in New Jersey. It was drizzling and mysterious at the beginning of our voyage. I could see that it was all going to be one big saga of the mist. "Whooee!" yelled Neal. "Here we go!" And he hunched over the wheel and gunned her; he was back in his element, everybody could see that. We were all delighted, we all realized we were leaving confusion and nonsense behind and performing our one and noble function of the time, <u>move</u>. And we moved! We flashed past the mysterious white signs in the night somewhere in New Jersey that say SOUTH (with an arrow) and WEST (with an arrow) and took the south one. New Orleans! It burned in our brains. From the dirty snows of "frosty fagtown New York" as Neal called it, all the way to the greeneries and river smells of old New Orleans at the washed-out bottom of America; then west,

<u>then</u> some. Louanne and Neal and I sat in front and had the warmest talk about the goodness and joy of life. Neal suddenly became tender. "Now dammit, look here all of you, we all must admit that everything is fine and there's no need in the world to worry, and in fact we should realize what it would mean to us to UNDERSTAND that we're not REALLy worried about ANYTHING. Am I right?" We all agreed. "Here we go, we're all together...what did we do in New York...let's forgive." We all had our spats back there. "That's behind us, merely by miles and inclinations. Now we're heading down to New Orleans to dig old Bill Burroughs and ain't that going to be kicks and listen will you to this old tenorman blow his top"----he shot up the radio volume till the car shuddered---"and listen to him tell the story and put down true relaxation and knowledge." We all jumped to the music and agreed. The purity of the road. The white line in the middle of the hiway unrolled and hugged our left front tire as if glued to our groove. Neal hunched his muscular neck, T-shirted in the winter night, and blasted the car along. In no time we were at the approaches of Philadelphia. Ironically we were going over the same road to North Carolina for the third time; it was our route. I kept wondering what it was that I had forgotten to do back in New York; it unrolled behind me more and more and I forgot more and more what it was. I brought it up. Everybody tried to guess what I had forgotten. It was no use. We had forty dollars to go all the way. All we had to do was pick up hitch hikers and bum quarters off them for gas, as soon as we got rid of Rhoda. Rhoda began saying she wanted to come to New Orleans; with Al Hinkle's wife already waiting there for him that was a fine idea. Neal said nothing; he knew in his own mind he was going to throw her out in Washington. In Philadelphia we lost route One and suddenly found ourselves groping down a narrow little tar road in the woods. "We've suddenly come into fairytale route-one in the mother hubbard woods. Dig it....gingerbread houses ahead..." We had no idea where we were. Neal was pleased to go on with the fairytale awhile; finally the road came to a dead end in a swamp. "The end of the road?" I said, kidding. He wheeled the car around and we roared

back to Philly and got on route one and arrived in Baltimore in an hour and a half. Neal insisted I drive thru Baltimore for traffic practice; that was allright except he and Louanne insisted on steering while they kissed and fooled around. It was crazy; the radio was on fullblast. Neal beat drums on the dashboard till a great sag developed in it. The poor Hudson---the slowboat to China---was receiving her beating. "Oh man what kicks!" yelled Neal. "Now Louanne, listen really honey, you know that I'm capable of doing everything at the same time and I have unlimited energy...now in San Francisco we must go on living together...I know just the place for you....at the end of the SP day run, San Luis Obispo, I'll be home every night....I'll be back at Carolyn's every morning....We can work it, we've done it before." It was alright with Louanne, she was really out for Carolyn's scalp. The understanding had been that Louanne would switch to me in Frisco but I now began to see they were going to stick and I was going to be left alone on my ass at the other end of the continent. But why think about that when all the golden land's ahead of you and all kinds of unforeseen events wait lurking to surprise you and make you glad you're alive to see. We arrived in Washington at dawn. It was the day of Harry Truman's inauguration for his second term in the presidency. Great displays of war might were lined along Pennsylvania Avenue as we rolled by in our battered boat. There were B-29s, PT boats, artillery, all kinds of war materiel laid out in the snowy grass; the last thing was a regular small ordinary lifeboat that looked pitiful and foolish. Neal slowed down to look at it. He kept shaking his head in awe. "What are these people up to? Our holy American slopjaws... Harry's sleeping somewhere in this town...Good old Harry...Man from Missouri, as I am...That must be his own boat." We suddenly found ourselves trapped in a circular drive from which there was no exit. We had to go to the end of it. We huzzahed; there was a restaurant and we were hungry. But the restaurant was closed. We had to run back over the same no-exit circular drive till we found the human hiway again. I've never seen that strange thing since; it's in Virginia just off a Washington bridge; there's no way out but to patronize the restaurant and if the restaurant is closed that's your tough shit. That was all right; we found a lunchcart. Hinkle immediately jammed coffee cakes in his jacket; he was a compulsive thief. I could see it was going to be some trip. We ate and paid half of what we ate. In the scraggly Virginia dawn poor Rhoda, head bowed, huddled in her coat, not wanted for Cal, made her way back to a crossroads bus stop on foot. That was the last of Rhoda. Neal went to sleep in the backseat and Hinkle drove. We gave him specific instructions to take it easy. No sooner were we snoring that he gunned the car up to eighty, bad rods and all, and not only that but he made a triple pass at a spot where a cop was arguing with a motorist---he was in the fourth lane of a four-lane hiway, going the wrong way. Naturally the cop took after us with his siren whining. We were stopped. He told us to follow him to the station house. There was a mean cop in there who took an immediate dislike for Neal; he could smell jail all over him. He sent his cohort outdoors to question Louanne and I privately. They wanted to know how old Louanne was, they were trying to whip up a Mann Act idea. But she had her marriage license. Then they took me aside alone and wanted to know who was sleeping with Louanne. "Her husband" I said quite simply. They were curious. Something was fishy. They tried some amateur Sherlocking by asking the same questions twice expecting us to make a slip. I said "Those two fellows are going back to work on the railroad in California, this is the short one's wife, and I'm a friend on a two week vacation from college." The cop smiled and said "Yeah? Is this really your own wallet?" Finally the mean one inside fined Neal twenty five dollars. We told them we only had forty to go all the way to the Coast; they said that made no difference to them. When Neal protested the mean cop threatened to take him back to Pennsylvania and slap a special charge on him. "What charge." "Never mind what charge? Don't worry bout that wise guy." We had to give them forty. Then Al Hinkle, who was the culprit, offered to go to jail so we could resume our journey. Neal considered it. The cop was infuriated; he said "If you let your buddy go to jail I'm taking you back to Pennsylvania right now. You hear that?" It was all confused. We had to give them the money; most of it was in my pocket. When they saw where it came from they gave me dirty looks. All we wanted to do was go. "Another speeding ticket in Virginia and you lose your car" said the mean cop as a parting volley. Neal was red in the face. We drove off silently. It was just like an invitation to steal to take all our trip-money away. They knew we were broke and had no relatives on the road or relatives to wire for money or anything. The American police are involved in psychological warfare against those Americans who don't frighten them with imposing papers and threats. There's no defense. Poor people have to expect to have their lives interfered with ad infinitum by these neurotic busybodies. It's a Victorian police force; it peers out of musty windows and wants to inquire about everything, and can make crimes if the crimes don't exist to their satisfaction. Neal was so mad he wanted to come back to Virginia and shoot the cop as soon as he had a gun. "Pennsylvania!" he scoffed. "I wish I knew what that charge was! Vag, probably; take all my money and charge me vag. Those guys have it so damned easy. They'll out and shoot you if you complain, too." There was nothing to do but get happy with ourselves again and forget about it. When we got through Richmond we began forgetting about it and soon everything was OK. In the Virginia wilderness suddenly we saw a man walking on the road. Neal zoomed to a stop. I looked back and said he was only a bum and probably didn't have a cent. "We'll just pick him up for kicks!" laughed Neal. The man was a ragged bespectacled mad type walking along reading a paperbacked muddy book he'd found in a culvert by the road. He got in the car and went right on reading; he was incredibly filthy and covered with scabs. He said his name was Herbert Diamond and that he walked all over the USA knocking and sometimes kicking at Jewish doors and demanding money. "Give me money to eat. I am Jew." He said it worked very well and that it was coming to him. We asked him what he was reading. He didn't know. He didn't bother to look at the title page. He was only looking at the words, as tho he had found the real Torah where it belonged, in the Wilderness. "See? see? see?" cackled Neal poking my ribs. "I told you it was kicks. Everybody's kicks, man!" We carried Diamond all the way to Rocky Mt North Carolina. My sister was no longer there, she had just moved to Ozone Park with my mother before I left. Here we were back on the long bleak street with the railroad track running down the middle and the sad sullen Southerners loping in front of hardware stores and Five and Tens. Diamond said "I see you people need a little money to continue your journey. You wait for me and I'll go hustle up a few dollars at a Jewish home and I'll go along with you as far as Alabama." Neal was all for it. Suddenly I remembered that Alan Temko had relatives in Rocky Mt., Jewish relatives, jewellers in the town. I told Diamond to find and hit the Temko jewelery store. His eyes lit up. He rushed off. Neal was all beside himself with happiness; he and I rushed off to buy bread and cheese spread for a lunch in the car. Louanne and Al waited in the car. We spent two hours in Rocky Mt. waiting for Herbert Diamond to show up; he was hustling for his bread somewhere in town but we couldn't see him. The sun began to grow red and late. It occurred to us Diamond would never show up. "What happened to him? Maybe Temko's relatives took him in; maybe he's sitting right in front of the fireplace right now telling about his adventures with crazy people in Hudsons." We remembered the time Temko had thrown us out of the party in Denver, the night of the nurses and the night I'd lost my key. We rolled all over the car laughing. Diamond never showed up so we roared out of Rocky Mt---"Now you see Jack, God does exist, because we keep getting hungup with this town, no matter what we try to do, and you'll notice the strange biblical name of it, and that strange biblical character who made us stop here once more, and all things tied together all over like rain connecting everybody the world over by chain touch..." Neal rattled on like this; he was overjoyed and exuberant. He and I suddenly saw the whole country like an oyster for us to open; and the pearl was there, the pearl was there. Off we roared South. We picked up another hitch hiker. This was a sad young kid who said he had an aunt who owned a grocery store in Dunn, No. Carolina, right outside Fayetteville. "When we get there I can bum a buck off her." "Right! Fine! Let's go!" We were in Dunn in an hour, at dusk. We drove to where the kid said his aunt had the grocery store. It was a sad little street that dead-ended at a factory wall. There was a grocery store but there was no aunt. We wondered what the kid was talking about. We asked him how far he was going; he didn't know. It was a big hoax; once upon a time, in some lost backalley adventure, he had seen the grocery store in Dunn, N.C., and it was the first story that popped into his disordered feverish mind. We bought him a hotdog but Neal said we couldn't bring him along because we needed room to sleep and room for hitch hikers who could buy a little gas. This was sad but true. We left him in Dunn at nightfall. This wasn't the only young kid with an aunt owning a grocery store that we were going to find this trip; there was another haunting our track two thousand miles along the road. I drove through South Carolina and all the way beyond Macon Georgia as Neal, Louanne and Al slept. All alone in the night I had my own thoughts and held the car to the white line in the holy road. What was I doing? where was I going? I'd soon find out. I got dogtired beyond Macon and woke up Neal to resume. We got out of the car for air and suddenly both of us were stoned with joy to realize that in the darkness all around us was fragrant green grass and the smell of fresh manure and warm waters. "We're in the South! We've left the winter!" Faint daybreak illuminated green shoots by the side of the road. I took a deep breath; a locomotive howled across the darkness, Mobile bound. So were we. I took off my shirt and exulted. Ten miles down the road Neal drove into a filling station with the motor off, noticed that the attendant was asleep at the desk, jumped out, quietly filled the gastank, saw to it the bell didn't ring, and rolled off like an Arab with a five-dollar tankful of gas for our pilgrimage. Otherwise we would never have made it to New Orleans and Bill Burroughs' rickety old house in the Algiers swamps. I slept and woke up to the crazy exultant sounds of music and Neal and Louanne talking and the great green land rolling by. "Where are we?" "Just pas't the tip of Florida, man, Flomaton it's called." Florida! We were rolling down to the coastal plain and Mobile; up ahead were great soaring clouds of the Gulf of Mexico. It was only fifteen hours since we'd said goodbye to everybody in the dirty snows of the North. We stopped at a filling station and there Neal and Louanne played piggyback around the tanks and Hinkle went inside and stole three packs of cigarettes without trying. We were fresh out. Rolling into Mobile over the long tidal highway we all took our winter clothes off and enjoyed the southern temperature. This was when Neal started telling his life story and when, beyond Mobile, he came upon an obstruction of wrangling cars at a crossroads and instead of slipping around them just balled right through the driveway of the gas station and went right on without relaxing his steady continental seventy. We left gaping faces behind us. He went right on with his tale. "I tell you it's true, I started at nine, with a girl called Milly Mayfair in back of Rod's Garage on Grant street- -same street Allen lived on in Denver. That's when my father was still barbering a bit. I remember my aunt yelling out the window 'What are you doing down there in back of the garage?' Oh honey Louanne if I'd only known you then! Wow! How sweet you must have been at nine." He tittered maniacally; he stuck his finger in her mouth and licked it; he took her hand and rubbed it over himself. She just sat there smiling serenely. Big long Al Hinkle just sat looking out the window talking to himself. "Yes sir, I thought I was a ghost that night on Times Square." He was also wondering what Helen Hinkle would say to him in New Orleans. Neal went on: "One time I rode a freight from New Mexico clear to LA---I was eleven years old, I'd lost my father in a freight, we were all in a hobo jungle, I was with a man called Big Red, my father was out drunk in a boxcar---it started to roll - - Big Red and I missed it----I didn't see my father for months. I rode the wrong freight to California. All the way, thirty five hours, I hung on with one hand from the rail and under my other arm I clutched a loaf of bread. This is no story---this is true. When I got to LA I was so starved for milk and cream that I got a job in a dairy and the first thing I did I drank two quarts of heavy cream and puked." "Poor Neal" said Louanne and she kissed him. He stared ahead proudly. He loved her. We were suddenly driving along the blue waters of the Gulf for fair and at the same time a momentous mad thing began on the radio: it was the Chicken Jazz n' Gumbo disc jockey show from New Orleans, all mad jazz records, colored records, with the disc jockey saying "Don't worry 'bout NOTHING!" We saw New Orleans in the night ahead of us with joy. Neal rubbed his hands over the wheel. "Now we're going to get our kicks!" At dusk we were coming into the humming streets of New Orleans. "Oh smell the people!" yelled Neal with his face out the window sniffing. "Ah! God! Life!" He swung around a trolley. "Yes!" He darted the car into the traffic of Canal Street. "Wheee!" He staggered the car and looked in every direction for girls. "Look at _her_!" The air was so sweet in New Orleans it seemed to come in soft bandanas; and you could smell the river, and really smell the people, and muds, and molasses and every kind of tropical exfoliation with your nose suddenly removed from the dry-ices of a northern winter. We bounced in our seats. "And dig her!" yelled Neal pointing at another woman. "Oh I love, love, love women! I think women are wonderful! I live women!" He spat out the window; he groaned; he clutched his head. Great beads of sweat fell from his forehead from pure excitement and exhaustion. We bounced the car up on the Algiers ferry and found ourselves crossing the Mississippi river by boat. "Now we must all get out and dig the river and the people and smell the world" said Neal bustling with his sunglasses and cigarettes and leaping out of the car like a jackinthebox. We followed. On rails we leaned and looked at the great brown father of waters rolling down from mid-America like the torrent of broken souls---bearing Montana logs and Dakota muds and Iowa-vales and every cundrum clear to Three Forks where the secret began in ice. Smoky New Orleans receded on one side; old sleepy Algiers with its warped woodsides bumped us on the other. Negroes were working in the hot afternoon stoking the ferry furnaces that burned red and made our tires smell. Neal dug them hopping up and down in the heat. He rushed around the deck and upstairs with his baggy pants hanging halfway down his belly. Suddenly I saw him eagering on the flying bridge. I expected

him to take off on wings. I heard his mad laugh all over the boat---
"Hee hee hee hee he!" Louanne was with him. He covered everything
in a jiffy, came back with the full story, jumped in the car just as
everybody was tooting to go and we slipped off passing two or three
cars in a narrow space and found ourselves darting through Algiers.
"Where? where?" Neal was yelling. We decided first to clean up at a
gas station and inquire for Bill's whereabouts. Little children were
playing in the drowsy river afternoon; girls were going by with bandanas and cotton blouses and bare legs. Neal ran up the street to see
everything. He looked around; he nodded; he rubbed his belly. Big Al
sat back in the car with his hat over his eyes, smiling at Neal. Then
we went to Bill Burroughs house outside town near the river levee. It
was a road that ran across a swampy field. The house was a dilapidated old heap with sagging porches running around and weeping
willows in the yard; the grass was a yard high, old fences leaned, old
barns collapsed. There was no one in sight. We pulled right into the
yard and saw washtubs on the back porch. I got out and went to the
screendoor. Joan Adams was standing in it with her eyes cupped
towards the sun. "Joan" I said. "It's me. It's us." She knew that. "Yes
I know. Bill isn't here now. Isn't that a fire or something over there."
We both looked towards the sun. "You mean the sun?" "Of course I
don't mean the sun----I heard sirens that way. Don't you see a pecu-
liar glow." It was towards New Orleans; the clouds were strange. "I
don't see anything" I said. Joan snuffed down her nose. "Same old
Kerouac." That was the way we greeted each other after four years;
Joan used to live with my wife and I in New York. "And is Helen Hinkle here?" I asked. She was still looking for her fire; in those days she
ate three tubes of benzedrine paper a day. Her face, once plump and
Germanic and pretty, had become stony and red and gaunt. She had
caught polio in New Orleans and limped a little. Sheepishly Neal and
the gang came out and more or less made themselves at home. Helen
Hinkle came out of her stately retirement in the back of the house to
meet her tormentor. Helen was a Greek girl from Fresno. She was
pale and looked like tears all over. Big Al pas't his hand through his

hair and said hello. She looked at him steadily. "Where have you been? Why did you do this to me?" And she gave Neal a dirty look; she knew the score. Neal paid absolutely no attention; what he wanted now was food; he asked Joan if there was anything. The confusion began right there. Poor Bill came home in his Texas Chevvy and found his house invaded by maniacs; but he greeted me with a nice warmth I hadn't seen in him for a long time. He had bought this house in New Orleans with some money he made growing cotton in the Rio Grande valley with an old Harvard schoolmate whose father, a mad paretic, had died and left a fortune. Bill himself only got $50 a week from his own family, which wasn't too bad except that he spent almost that much per week on a drug habit...morphine; and his wife was also expensive, gobbling up about ten dollars worth a week of benny tubes. Their foodbill was the lowest in the country; they never ate; the children never ate either. They had two wonderful children, Julie, eight years old, and little Willie one year. Willie ran around stark naked in the yard, a little blond child of the rainbow who would someday jabber in the streets of Mexico City with Indian ragamuffins and hold his own. Bill called him "the Little Beast," after W.C. Fields. He came driving into the yard and unrolled himself from the car bone by bone, and came over wearily, wearing glasses, felt hat, shabby suit, long, lean, strange and laconic, saying "Why Jack, you finally got here; let's go in the house and have a drink." It would take all night to tell about Bill Burroughs; let's just say now, he was a teacher, and had every right to teach because he learned all the time; and the things he learned were the facts of life, not out of necessity but because he wanted to. He dragged his long thin body around the entire US and most of Europe and No. Africa in his time only to see what was going on; he married a German countess in Yugoslavia to get her away from the Nazis in the Thirties; there are pictures of him with big cocaine Berlin gangs with wild hair leaning on one another; there are other pictures of him in a Panama hat surveying the streets of Algiers in Morocco. He never saw the German countess again. He was an exterminator in Chicago, a bartender in New York, a summons server in

Newark. In Paris he sat at cafe tables watching the sullen French faces go by. In Athens he looked out of his hotel window at what he called the ugliest people in the world. In Istanbul he threaded his way through crowds of opium addicts and rug sellers, looking for the facts. In English hotels he read Spengler and the Marquis de Sade. In Chicago he planned to hold up a Turkish bath, hesitated just two minutes too long for a drink, and wound up with two dollars and had to make a run for it. He did all these things merely for the experience. He was a dawdler of the oldfashioned European school somewhat along the lines of Stefan Sweig, the young Thomas Mann, and Ivan Karamazov. Now the final study was the drug habit. He was now in New Orleans slipping along the streets with shady characters and haunting connection bars. There is a strange story about his Harvard days that illustrates something else about him: he had friends for cocktails in his well-appointed rooms one afternoon when suddenly his pet ferret rushed out and bit someone on the ankle; and as everybody hightailed out the door, probably screaming, as he knew many fags in those days, and still does, Bill leaped up and grabbed his shotgun, said "He smells that old rat again" and shot a hole in the wall big enough to shove fifty rats through. On the wall hung a picture of an ugly old Cape Cod house. His friends said "Why do you have that ugly thing hanging there?" and Bill said "I like it because it's ugly." All his life was in that line. Once I knocked on his door in the 60th slums in New York and he opened it wearing a derby hat, a vest with nothing else under, and long striped sharpster pants; in his hands he had a cookpot, birdseed in the pot, and was trying to mash the seed to roll a cigarette with. He also experimented boiling codeine cough syrup down to a black mash---that didn't work too well. He spent long hours with Shakespeare, the "Immortal Bard" he called him, on his lap. In New Orleans he had begun to spend long hours with the Mayan Codices on his lap and although he went on talking the book lay open all the time. I was young and I said once "What's going to happen to us when we die?" and he said "When you die you're just dead, that's all." He had a set of chains in his room that he said he used with his psychoanalyst;

they were experimenting with narco-analysis and found that Bill had seven separate personalities each growing worse and worse on the way down till finally he was a raving idiot and had to be restrained with chains. The top personality was an English Lord, the bottom the idiot. Halfway he was an old Negro who stood in line waiting with everyone else and said "Some's bastards, some's ain't, that's the score." Bill had a sentimental streak about the old days in America, especially 1910 when you could get morphine in a drugstore without prescription and Chinamen smoked opium in their evening windows and the country was wild and brawling and free with abundance and any kind of freedom for everyone. His chief hate was Washington bureaucracy; second to that, Liberals; also cops. He spent all his time talking and teaching others. Joan sat at his feet, so did I, so did Neal; and so had Allen Ginsberg. We'd all learned from him. He was a gray, nondescript looking fellow you wouldn't notice on the street, unless you looked closer and saw his mad bony skull with its strange youthfulness and fire---a Kansas minister with exotic phenomenal fires and mysteries. He had studied medicine in Vienna, known Freud too; had studied anthropology, read everything; and now he was settling to his life's work, which was the study of things themselves in the streets of life and the night. He sat in his chair; Joan brought drinks, martinis. The shades by his chair were always drawn, day and night; it was his corner of the house. On his lap were the Mayan codices and an air gun which he occasionally raised to pop benzedrine tubes across the room. I kept rushing around putting up new ones. We all took shots. Meanwhile we talked. Bill was curious to know the reason for this trip. He peered at us and snuffed down his nose. "Now Neal, I want you to sit quiet a minute and tell me what you're doing crossing the country like this." Neal could only blush and say "Ah well, you know how it is." "Jack, what are you going to the Coast for?" "Only for a few days, I'm coming back to school." "What's the score with this Al Hinkle, what kind of character is he?" At that moment Al was making up to Helen in the bedroom; it didn't take him long. We didn't know what to tell Bill about Al Hinkle. Seeing that we didn't know anything about ourselves he whipped out three sticks of tea and said to go ahead, supper'd be ready soon. "Ain't nothing better in the world to give you an appetite. I once ate a horrible lunchcart hamburg on tea and it seemed like the most delicious thing in the world. I just got back from Houston last week, went to see Kells about our cotton. I was sleeping in a motel one morning when all of a sudden I was blasted out of bed. This damned guy had just shot his wife in the room next to mine. Everybody stood around confused and the guy just got in his car and drove off, left the shotgun on the floor for the sheriff. They finally caught him in Houma drunk as a Lord. Man ain't safe going around this country any more without a gun." He pulled back his coat and showed us his revolver. Then he opened the drawer and showed us the rest of his arsenal. In New York he once had a machinegun under his bed. "I got something better than that now...a german sheintoth gas gun, look at this beauty, only got one shell. I could knock out a hundred men with this gun and have plenty of time to make a getaway. Only thing wrong I only got one shell." "I hope I'm not around when you try it" said Joan from the kitchen. "How do YOU know it's a gas shell." Bill snuffed; he never paid any attention to her sallies but he heard them. His relation with his wife was one of the strangest: they talked till late at night: Bill liked to hold the floor, he went right on in his dreary monotonous voice, she tried to break in, and never could; at dawn he got tired and then Joan talked and he listened snuffing down his nose. She loved that man madly, but in a mental delirious way of some kind; there was never any mooching and mincing around, just talk and after all a very deep companionship that none of us would ever be able to fathom. Something curiously unsympathetic and cold between them was really a form of humour by which they communicated their own set of subtle vibrations. Love is all; Joan was never more than ten feet away from Bill and never missed a word he said, and he spoke in a very low voice too. Neal and I were yelling about a big night in New Orleans and wanted Bill to show us around. He threw a damper on this. "New Orleans is a very dull town. It's against the law to go to the colored section. The bars are insufferably dull." I said "There must be some ideal bars in town." "The ideal bar doesn't exist in America. An ideal bar is something that's gone beyond our ken. In 1910 a bar was a place where men went to meet during or after work and all there was was a long counter, brass rails, spittoon, player piano for music, a few mirrors and barrels of whiskey at ten cents a shot together with barrels of beer at five cents a mug. Now all you get is chromium, drunken women, fags, hostile bartenders, anxious owners who hover around the door worried about their leather seats and the law; just a lot of screaming at the wrong time and deadly silence when a stranger walks in." We argued about bars. "All right," he said, "I'll take you to New Orleans tonight and show you what I mean." And he deliberately took us to the dullest bars. We left Joan with the children; supper was over; she was reading the want ads of the New Orleans Times Picayune. I asked her if she was looking for a job; she only said it was the most interesting part of the paper. You could see her point---a strange woman. Bill rode into town with us and went right on talking. "Take it easy Neal, we'll get there, I hope; hup, there's the ferry, you don't have to drive us clear into the river." He held on. Neal had gotten worse since Texas, he confided in me. "He seems to me to be headed for his ideal fate, which is compulsive psychosis dashed with a jigger of psychopathic irresponsibility and violence." He looked at Neal out of the corner of his eye. "If you go to California with this madman you'll never make it. Why don't you stay in New Orleans with me. We'll play the horses over to Graetna and relax in my yard. I've got a nice set of knives and I'm building a target. Some pretty juicy dolls downtown too, if that's in your line these days." He snuffed. We were on the ferry and Neal had leaped out to lean over the rail. I followed, but Bill sat on in the car snuffing. There was a mystic wraith of fog over the brown waters that night, together with dark driftwoods; and across the way New Orleans glowed orange bright, with a few dark ships at her hem, ghostly fogbound Cereno ships with Spanish balconies and ornamental poops, till you got up close and saw they were just old freighters from Sweden and Panama. The ferry-fires glowed

248

in the night; the same Negroes plied the shovel and sang. Old Big Slim Hubbard had once worked on the Algiers as a ferry deckhand; this made me think of Mississippi Gene too; and as the river poured down from mid-America by starlight I knew, I knew like mad that everything I had ever known and would ever know was One. Strange to say, too, that night we crossed the ferry with Bill Burroughs a girl committed suicide off the deck; either just before or just after us; we saw it in the paper the next day. The girl was from Ohio; she might as well have come floating down to New Orleans on a log, and saved her soul. We hit all the dull bars in the Latin Quarter with Bill and went back home at midnight. That night Louanne took everything in the books: she took tea, goofballs, benny, liquor and even asked Bill for a shot of M, which of course he didn't give her. She was so saturated with elements of all kinds that she came to a standstill and stood goofy on the porch with me. It was a wonderful porch Bill had. It ran clear around the house. By moonlight, with the willows, it looked like an old Southern mansion that had seen better days. In the house Joan sat reading the wantads in the kitchen; Bill was in the bathroom taking a fix, clutching his old black necktie in his teeth for a tourniquette and jabbing with the needle into his scrawny arm with the thousand holes; Al Hinkle was sprawled out with Helen in the massive master bed that Bill and Joan never used; Neal was rolling tea; and Louanne and I imitated Southern aristocracy. "Why Miss Lou, you look lovely and most fetching tonight." "Why thank you, Crawford, I sure do appreciate the nice things you say." Doors kept opening around the crooked porch and members of our sad drama in the American night kept popping out to find out where everybody was. Finally I took a walk alone to the Levee. I wanted to sit on the muddy bank and dig the Mississippi River; instead of that I had to look at it with my nose against a wire fence. When you start separating the people from their rivers what have you got? "Bureaucracy!" says Bill; he sits with Kafka on his lap, the lamp burns above him, he snuffs. His old house creaks. And the Montana log rolls by in the big black river of the night. "T'ain't nothing but bureaucracy. And Unions!

Especially Unions!" But dark laughter would come again. It was there in the morning when I got up bright and early and found Bill and Neal in the backyard. Neal was wearing his gas station coveralls and helping Bill. Bill had found a great big piece of thick rotten wood and was desperately yanking at little nails imbedded in it with a hammerhook. We stared at the nails, there were millions of them, they were like worms. "When I get all these nails out of this I'm going to build me a shelf that'll last a THOUSAND YEARS!" said Bill, every bone shuddering with senile excitement. "Why Jack, do you realize the shelves they build these days crack under the weight of a clock after six months or generally collapse, same with houses, same with clothes. These bastards have invented plastics by which they could make houses that last FOREVER. And tires. Americans are killing themselves by the millions every year with defective rubber tires that get on the road and blow up. They could make tires that never blow up. Same with tooth powder. There's a certain gum they've invented and they won't show it to anybody that if you chew it as a kid you'll never get a cavity for the rest of your born days. Same with clothes. They can make clothes that last forever. They prefer making cheap goods so everybody'll have to go on working and punching timeclocks and organizing themselves in sullen unions and floundering around while the big grab goes on in Washington and Moscow." He raised his big piece of rotten wood. "Don't you think this'll make a splendid shelf." It was early in the morning, his energy was at its peak. The poor fellow took so much junk in his system he could only weather the vast proportion of his day in that chair with the lamp burning at noon. But in the morning he was magnificent. We began throwing knives at the target. He said he'd seen an Arab in Tunis who could stick a man's eye from forty feet. This got him going on his Aunt who went to the Casbah in the Thirties. "She was with a party of tourists led by a guide. She had a diamond ring on her little finger. She leaned on a wall to rest a minute and an Arab rushed up and sliced off her little finger ring and all before she could let out a cry. She suddenly realized she had no little finger. Hi-hi-hi-hi-hi!" When he laughed he compressed his lips together and made it come out from his belly, from way faraway, and doubled up to lean on his knees. He laughed a long time. "Hey Joan!" he yelled gleefully. "I was just telling Neal and Jack about my aunt in the Casbah!" "I heard you" she said across the lovely warm Gulf morning from the kitchen door. Great beautiful clouds floated overhead, valley clouds that made you feel the vastness of old tumbledown holy America from mouth to mouth and tip to tip. Go on. Bill was all pep and juices. "Say, did I ever tell you about Kell's father. He was the funniest old man you ever saw in your life. He had paresis which eats away the forepart of your brain and you get so's you're not responsible for anything that comes into your mind. He had a house in Texas and had carpenters working 24 hours a day putting on new wings. He'd leap up in the middle of the night and say 'I don't want that goddamn wing; put it over there.' The carpenters had to take everything down and start all over again. Come dawn you'd see them hammering away at the new wing. Then the old man'd get bored with that and say 'Goddamn it I wanta go to Maine!' and he'd get into his car and drive off a hundred miles an hour---great showers of chicken feathers followed his track for hundreds of miles. He'd stop his car in the middle of a Texan town just to get out and buy some whiskey. Traffic would honk all around him and he'd come rushing out of the store yelling 'Shet your goddamn noith you bunth of bathats!' He lisped; when you have paresis you lips, I mean you lisps. One night he came to my house in St. Louis and tooted the horn and said 'come on out and let's go to Texas to see Kells.' He was going back from Maine. He claimed he bought a house in Long Island overlooking a jewish cemetery 'cause he liked to see s'many dead Jews. Oh, he was horrible. I could tell you stories about him all day. Say, ain't this a nice day?" And it sure was. The softest breezes blew in from the levees; it was worth the whole trip. We rushed into the house after Bill to go and measure the wall for a shelf. He showed us the dining table he built. It was made of wood six inches thick. "This is a table that'll last a thousand years!" said Bill leaning his long thin face at us maniacally. He banged on it. In the evenings he sat at this table picking at his food and throwing the bones to the cats. He had seven cats. "I love cats. I especially like the ones that squeal when I hold 'em over the bath tub." He insisted on demonstrating but someone was in the bathroom. "Well," he said, "we can't do that now. Say, I been having a fight with the neighbors next door." He told us about the neighbors; they were a vast crew with sassy children who threw stones over the rickety fence at Julie and Willie and sometimes at Bill. He told them to cut it out; the old man rushed out and yelled something in Portuguese. Bill went in the house and came back with his shotgun. We scoured the yard for things to do. There was a tremendous fence Bill had been working on to separate him from the obnoxious neighbors; it would never be finished, the task was too much. He rocked it back and forth to show us how solid it was. Suddenly he grew tired and quiet and went in the house and disappeared in the bathroom for his morning fix, or mid-morning, pre-lunch. He came out glassy-eyed and calm, and sat down under his burning lamp. The sunlight poked feebly behind the drawn shade. "Say, why don't you fellows try my accumulator in the front room. Put some juice in your bones. I always rush up and take off ninety miles an hour for the nearest whore house, hor hor hor!" This was his "laugh" laugh---when he wasn't really laughing. "Say Jack, after lunch let's you and me go play the horses over to the bookie joint in Graetna." He was magnificent. He took a nap after lunch in his chair, the air gun on his lap, and little Willie curled around his neck sleeping. It was a pretty sight, father and son, a father that would certainly never bore his son when it came to finding things to do and talk about. He woke up with a start and stared at me. It took him a minute to recognize who I was. "What are you going to the Coast for Jack?" he asked, and went back to sleep a moment. In the afternoon we went to Graetna, just Bill and me. We drove in his old Chevvy. Neal's Hudson was low and sleek; Bill's Chevvy was high and rattly. It was just like 1910. The bookie joint was located near the waterfront in a big chromium-leather bar that opened up in the back to a tremendous hall where entries and numbers were posted on the wall. Louisiana characters lounged around with Racing Forms. Bill and I had a beer, and casually Bill went over to the slot machine and threw a half-dollar piece in. The counter clicked "Jackpot"--"Jackpot"---"Jackpot"---and the last Jackpot hung for just a moment and slipped off to "Cherry." He had lost a hundred dollars or more just by a cunthair. "Damn!" yelled Bill. "They got these things adjusted. You could see it right then. I had the jackpot and the mechanism clicked it back. Well, what you gonna do." We examined the Racing Form. I hadn't played the horses in years and was bemused with all the new names. There was one horse called "Big Pop" that sent me into a temporary trance thinking of my father, who used to play the horses with me. I was just about to mention it to Bill when he said "Well I think I'll try this Ebony Corsair here." Then I finally said it: "Big Pop reminds me of my father." He mused for just a second, his clear blue eyes fixed on mine hypnotically so that I couldn't tell what he was thinking or where he was. Then he went over and bet on Ebony Corsair. Big Pop won and paid 50 to 1. "Damn!" said Bill. "I should have known better, I've had experience with this before. Oh when will we ever learn?" "What do you mean?" "Big Pop is what I mean. You had a vision, boy, a VISION. Only damn fools pay no attention to visions. How do you know your father, who was an old horseplayer, just didn't momentarily communicate to you that Big Pop was going to win the race. The name brought the feeling up in you. That's what I was thinking about when you mentioned it. My cousin in Missouri once bet on a horse that had a name that reminded him of his mother and it won and paid a big price. The same thing happened this afternoon." He shook his head. "Ah, let's go. This is the last time I'll ever play the horses with you around, all these visions drive me to distraction." In the car as we drove back to his old house he said "Mankind will someday realize that we are actually in contact with the dead and with the other world whatever it is; right now we could predict, if we only exerted enough mental will, what is going to happen within the next hundred years and be able to take steps to avoid all kinds of catastrophes. When a man dies he undergoes a mutation in his brain that we know nothing about now but which will be very clear someday if scientists get on the ball. The bastards right now are only interested in seeing if they can blow up the world." We told Joan about it. She snuffed. "It sounds silly to me." She plied the broom around the kitchen. Bill went in the bathroom for his afternoon fix. Out on the road Neal and Al Hinkle were playing basketball with Julie's ball and a bucket nailed on the lamppost. I joined in. Then we turned to feats of athletic prowess. Neal completely amazed me. He had Al and I hold a bar of iron up to our waists, and just standing there he popped right over it holding his heels. "Go ahead, raise it." We kept raising it till it was chest-high. Still he jumped over it with ease. Then he tried the running broadjump and did at least 20 feet. Then I raced him down the road. I can do the hundred in 10:3. He passed me like the wind. As we ran I had a mad vision of Neal running through all of life just like that...his bony face outthrust to life, his arms pumping, his brow sweating, his legs twinkling like Groucho Marx, yelling "Yes! Yes man, you sure can go!" But nobody could go as fast as him, and that's the truth. Then Bill came out with a couple of knives and started showing us how to disarm a would-be shivver in a dark alley. I for my part showed him a very good trick, which is, falling on the ground in front of your adversary and gripping him with your ankles and flipping him over on his hands and grabbing his wrists in full nelson. He said it was pretty good. He demonstrated some jiu jitsu. Little Julie called her mother to the porch and said "Look at the silly men." She was eight years old. She was such a cute sassy little thing Neal couldn't take his eyes off her. "Wow. Wait till she grows up! Can you see her cuttin' down Canal street with a hincty eye. Ah! Oh!" He hissed through his teeth. We spent a mad day in downtown New Orleans walking around with the Hinkles. Neal was out of his mind that day. When he saw the T&NO freight trains in the yard he wanted to show me everything at once. "You'll be a brakeman 'fore I'm thru with you!" He and I and Al Hinkle ran across the tracks and hopped a freight; Louanne and Helen were waiting in the car. We rode the freight a halfmile into the piers waving at brakemen and firemen. They showed me the proper way to jump off

a moving boxcar: the backfoot first to leave the other foot for jumping off the ground when you hit. They showed me the refrigerator
boxes, "reefers," good for a ride on any winter night. "Remember
what I told you about New Mexico to LA?" cried Neal. "This was the
way I hung on." We got back to the girls later and of course they were
mad. Al and Helen had decided to get a room in New Orleans and
stay there and work. This was okay with Bill who was getting sick and
tired of the whole mob. The invitation, originally, was for me to come
alone. In the front room where Neal and Louanne slept there was jam
and coffee stains and empty benny tubes all over the floor; what's
more it was Bill's workroom and he couldn't get on with his shelves.
Poor Joan was driven to distraction by the continual jumping and run-
ningaround on the part of Neal. We were waiting for my next GI
check to come through, my mother was forwarding it. Then we were
off, the three of us, Neal, Louanne, me. When the check came I realized I hated to leave Bull's wonderful house so suddenly but Neal was
all energies and ready to go. In a sad red dusk we were finally seated
in the car and Joan, Julie, Willie, Bill, Al and Helen stood around in
the high grass smiling. It was goodbye. At the last moment Neal and
Bill had a misunderstanding over money: Neal had wanted to borrow:
Bill said it was out of the question. The feeling reached back to Texas
days. Con-man Neal was antagonizing people away from him by
degrees. He giggled maniacally and didn't care; he rubbed his balls,
stuck his finger in Louanne's dress, slurped up her knee, frothed at
the mouth and said "Darling you know and I know that everything is
straight between us at last beyond the furthest abstract definition in
metaphysical terms or any terms you want to specify or sweetly
impose or harken back"---and so on, and zoom went the car and we
were off again for California. What is that feeling when you're driving away from people and they recede on the plain till you see their
specks dispersing?---it's the too-huge world vaulting us in, and it's
goodbye. But we lean forward to the next crazy venture beneath the
skies. We had all kinds of trouble getting to Frisco, and once there I
got stuck and had to "stagger back East" as Allen predicted, but who

cares and I didn't. We wheeled through the sultry old light of Algiers, back on the ferry, back towards the muddy-splashed crabb'd old ships across the river, back on Canal, and out; on a two-lane hiway to Baton Rouge in purple darkness; swung west there, cross't the Mississippi at a place called Port Allen and tore across the state of Louisiana in a matter of three hours. Port Allen---Poor Allen---where the river's all rain and roses in a misty pinpoint darkness and where we swung around a circular drive in yellow foglight and suddenly saw the great black body below a bridge and crossed eternity again. What is the Mississippi River?---a washed clod in the rainy night, a soft plopping from drooping Missouri banks, a dissolving, a riding of the tide down the eternal waterbed, a contribution to brown foams, a voyaging past endless vales and trees and levees, down along, down along, by Memphis, Greenville, Eudora, Vicksburg, Natchez, Port Allen, and Port Orleans and Point of the Deltas, by Potash, Venice and the Night's Great Gulf, and out. So the stars shine warm in the Gulf of Mexico at night. From the soft and thunderous Carib comes electricity, and from the Continental Divide where rain and rivers are decided come swirls, and the little raindrop that in Dakota fell and gathered mud and roses rises resurrected from the sea and flies on back to go and bloom again in waving mells of the Mississippi's bed, and lives again. So we Americans together tend as rain to the All-River of Togetherness to the sea, and out, and we don't know where. With the radio on to a mystery program, and as I looked out the window and saw a sign that said USE COOPER'S PAINT and I said "Okay I will" we rolled across the hoodwink night of the great Louisiana plains---Lawtell, Eunice, Kinder and DeQuincey, western rickety towns becoming more bayou-like as we reached the Sabine. In old Opelousas I went into a grocery store to buy bread and cheese while Neal saw to gas and oil. It was just a shack; I could hear the family eating supper in the back. I waited a minute; they went on talking. I took bread and cheese and slipped out the door. We had barely enough money to make Frisco. Meanwhile Neal took a carton of cigarettes from the gas station and we were stocked for the voyage---gas, oil, cigarettes and food. He pointed the car straight down the road. Somewhere near Starks we saw a great red glow in the sky ahead; we wondered what it was; in a moment we were passing it. It was a fire beyond the trees, there were many cars parked on the highway. It must have been some kind of fishfry and on the other hand it might have been anything. The country turned strange and dark near Deweyville. Suddenly we were in the swamps. "Man do you imagine what it would be like if we found a jazzjoint in these swamps, with great big black fellas moanin' guitar blues and drinking snakejuice and makin' signs at us?" "Yes!" There were mysteries around here. The car was going over a dirt road elevated off the swamps that dropped on both sides and drooped with vines. We passed an apparition; it was a colored man in a white shirt walking along with his arms upspread to the inky firmament. He must have been praying or calling down a curse. We zoomed right by; I looked out the back window to see his white eyes. "Whoo" said Neal. "Lookout. We better not stop in this here country." At one point we got stuck at a crossroads and stopped the car anyway. Neal turned off the headlamps. We were surrounded by a great forest of viney trees in which we could almost hear the slither of a million copperheads. The only thing we could see was the red ampere button on the Hudson dashboard. Louanne squealed with fright. We began laughing maniac laughs to scare her. We were scared too. We wanted to get out of this mansion of the snake, this mireful drooping dark and zoom on back to familiar American ground and cowtowns. There was a smell of oil and dead water in the air. This was a manuscript of the night we couldn't read. An owl hooted. We took a chance on one of the dirt roads and pretty soon we were crossing the evil old Sabine river that is responsible for all these swamps. With amazement we saw great structures of light ahead of us. "Texas! It's Texas! Beaumont oiltown!" Huge oil tanks and refineries loomed like cities in the oily fragrant air. "I'm glad we got out of there" said Louanne. "Let's play some more mystery programs now." We zoomed through Beaumont, over the Trinity River at Liberty and straight for Houston. Now Neal got talking about his Houston days in 1947. "Hunkey! that mad

Hunkey! I look for him everywhere I go and I never find him. He used to get us so hungup in Texas here. We'd drive in with Bill for groceries and Hunkey'd disappear. We'd have to go looking for him in every shooting gallery in town." We were entering Houston. "We had to look for him in this niggertown most of the time. Man, he'd be blasting with every mad cat he could find. One night we lost him and took a hotel room. We were supposed to bring ice back to Joan because her food was rotting. It took us two days to find Hunkey. I got hungup myself---I gunned shopping women in the afternoon, right here, downtown, supermarkets"---we flashed by in the empty night---"and found a real gone dumb girl who was out of her mind and just wandering trying to steal an orange. She was from Wyoming. I took her back to the room. Bill was drunk. Allen was writing poetry. Hunkey didn't show up till midnight, at the jeep. We found him sleeping in the backseat; he said he took about five sleeping pills. Man if my memory could only work the way my mind works I could tell you every detail of the things we did---Ah! but we know time. Everything takes care of itself. I could close my eyes and this car would take care of itself." In the empty Houston streets of four o'clock in the morning a motorcycle kid suddenly roared through all bespangled and bedecked with glittering buttons, visor, slick black jacket, a Texas poet of the night, girl gripped on his back like a papoose, hair flying, onward-going, singing "Houston, Austin, Fort Worth, Dallas- -and sometimes Kansas City---and sometimes old Antone, ah-haaa!" They pinpointed out of sight. "Wow! Dig that gone gal on his belt! Yes!" Neal tried to catch up with them. "Now wouldn't it be fine if we could all get together and have a real going goofbang together with everybody sweet and fine and agreeable no hassels...Ah! But we know time." He bent to it and pushed the car. Beyond Houston his energies great as they were gave out and I drove. Rain began to fall just as I took the wheel. Now we were on the great Texas plain and as Neal said "You drive and drive and you're still in Texas tomorrow night." The rain lashed down. I drove through a rickety little cow-town with a muddy mainstreet and found myself in a dead end. "Hey, what do

I do?" They were both asleep. I turned and crawled back through town. There wasn't a soul in sight and not a single light. Suddenly a horseman in a raincoat appeared in my headlamps. It was the sheriff. He had a ten-gallon hat drooping in the torrent. "Which way to Austin?" He told me politely and I started off. Outside town I suddenly saw two headlamps flaring directly at me in the lashing rain. Woops, I thought I was on the wrong side of the road; I eased right and found myself rolling in the mud; I rolled back to the road. Still the headlamps came straight for me. At the last minute I realized the other driver was on the wrong side of the road and didn't know it. I swerved at thirty into the mud; it was flat, no ditch, thank God. The offending car backed up in the downpour. Four sullen fieldworkers snuck from their chores to brawl in drinking shacks, all white shirts and dirty brown arms, sat looking at me dumbly in the night. The driver was as drunk as the lot. He said "Which way t'Houston." I pointed my thumb back. I was thunderstruck in the middle of the thought that they had done this on purpose just to ask directions, as a panhandler advances on you straight up the sidewalk to bar your way. They gazed ruefully at the floor of their car where empty bottles rolled and clanked away. I started the car; it was stuck in the mud a foot deep. I sighed in the Texas rainy wilderness. "Neal" I said "wake up." "What?" "We're stuck in the mud." "What happened?" I told him. He swore up and down. We put on old shoes and sweaters and barged out of the car into the driving rain. I put my back on the rear fender and lifted and heaved; Neal stuck chains under the swishing wheels. In a minute we were bespotted with mud. We woke up Louanne to these horrors and made her gun the car while we pushed. The tormented Hudson heaved and heaved. We were in the middle of nowhere. Suddenly it jolted out and went skidding across the road. There weren't any cars for miles. Louanne pulled it up just in time and we ran in. That was that---and the work had taken thirty minutes and we were soaked and miserable. I fell asleep all caked with mud; and in the morning when I woke up the mud was solidified and outside there was snow. We were near Fredericksburg Texas in the high plains. It was the worst winter in Texas and Western history, January 1949, when cattle perished like flies in great blizzards and snow fell on San Francisco and LA. We were all miserable. We wished we were back in New Orleans with Al Hinkle who at that very moment was sitting on Mississippi levees talking to old men with white hair instead of looking for an apartment and a job, typical of him. Louanne was driving, Neal was sleeping. She drove with one hand on the wheel, and the other reaching back to me in the backseat. She cooed promises about San Francisco. I slavered miserably over it. At ten I took the wheel---Neal was out for hours---and drove several hundred dreary miles across the bushy snows and ragged sage hills. Cowboys went by in baseball caps and earmuffs, looking for cows. Comfortable little homes with chimneys smoking appeared along the road at intervals. I wished we could go in for buttermilk and beans in front of the fireplace. At Sonora I again helped myself to free bread and cheese while the proprietor chatted with a big rancher on the other side of the store. Neal huzzahed when he heard it; he was hungry. We couldn't spend a cent on food. "Yass, yass," said Neal watching the ranchers loping up and down Sonora mainstreet, "everyone of them is a bloody millionaire, thousand head of cattle, workhands, buildings, money in the bank. If I lived around here I'd go be an idiot in the sagebrush, I'd jack off, I'd lick up the branches, I'd look for pretty cowgirls---hee hee hee hee! Damn! Bam!" He socked himself. "Yes! Right! Oh me!" We didn't know what he was talking about any more. He took the wheel and drove the rest of the way across the state of Texas, about five hundred miles, clear to El Paso, arriving at dusk and not stopping except once when he took all his clothes off, near Ozona, and ran like a jackal through the sage yipping and leaping. Cars zoomed by and didn't see him. He scurried back to the car and drove on. "Now Jack, now Louanne, I want both of you to take all your clothes off---now what's the sense of clothes---and sun your bellies with me. Come on!" We were driving west into the sun; it fell in through the windshield. "Open your belly as we drive into it." Louanne took her clothes off: I decided not to be a fuddy and did likewise. We sat in the front seat.

Louanne took out coldcream and applied to us for kicks. Every now and then a big truck zoomed by: the driver in high cab caught a glimpse of a golden beauty sitting naked with two naked men: you could see them swerve a moment as they vanished out the rear window. Great sage plains, snowless now, rolled on. Soon we were in the orange-rocked Pecos canyon country. Blue distances opened up in the sky. We got out of the car to examine an old Indian ruin. Neal did so stark naked. Louanne and I put on our overcoats. We wandered among the old stones hooting and howling. Certain tourists caught sight of Neal naked in the plain but they could not believe their eyes and wobbled on. In the middle of the Pecos country we all began talking about what we would be if we were Old West characters. "Neal, you'd be an outlaw for sure" I said "but one of those crazy-kick-outlaws galloping across the plains and shooting up saloons." "Louanne would be the dancing hall beauty. Bill Burroughs would live at the end of town, a retired Confederate colonel, in a big house with all the shutters drawn and come out only once a year with his shotgun to meet his connection in a Chinese Alley. Al Hinkle would play cards all day and tell stories in a chair. Hunkey would live with the Chinamen; you'd see him cut under a streetlamp with an opium pipe and a queue." "What about me?" I said. "You'd be the son of the local newspaper publisher. Every now and then you'd go mad and ride with the wildbuck gang for kicks. Allen Ginsberg---he'd be a scissors sharpener coming down from the mountain once a year with his wagon and he'd be predicting fires and fellows in from the border would make him dance with hotfoot bullets. Joan Adams...she'd live in the shuttered house, she'd be the only real lady in town but nobody'd ever see her." We went on and on, scouring our rogues' gallery. In later years Allen would come down from the mountain bearded and wouldn't have scissors any more, just songs of catastrophe; and Burroughs would no longer come out of his house once a year; and Louanne would shoot old Neal as he staggered drunk from his shack; and Al Hinkle would outlive us all telling stories to youngsters in front of the Silver Dollar. Hunkey would be found dead one cold winter morning in an alley. Louanne would inherit the dance hall and become a madame and a power in the town. I would disappear to Montana never to be heard from again. At the last minute we threw in Lucien Carr---he would disappear from Pecos City and come back years later darkened by African suns with an African Queen for a wife and ten black children and a fortune in gold. Bill Burroughs would go mad one day and start shooting at the whole town from his window; they'd set the torch to his old house and everything would burn and Pecos City would be a charred ruins and ghost town in the orange rocks. We looked around for a likely site. The sun was going down. I fell asleep dreaming the legend. Neal and Louanne parked the car near Van Horn and made love while I slept. I woke up just as we were rolling down the tremendous Rio Grande Valley through Clint and Ysleta to El Paso. Louanne jumped to the back seat, I jumped to the front seat, and we rolled along. To our left across the vast Rio Grande spaces were the moorish reddish mounts of the Mexican border; soft dusk played on the peaks; beyond lay adobe houses, blue nights, shawls and guitar music---and mysteries, and the future of Neal and myself. Straight ahead lay the distant lights of El Paso sown in a tremendous valley so big that you could see several railroads puffing at the same time in every direction, as though it was the valley of the world. We descended into it. "Clint Texas!" said Neal. He had the radio on to the Clint station. Every fifteen minutes they played a record; the rest of the time it was all commercials about a correspondence high school course. "This program is beamed all over the West" cried Neal excitedly. "Man I used to listen to it day and night in reform school and prison. All of us used to write in. You get a high school diploma by mail, facsimile thereof, if you pass the test. All the young wranglers in the West I don't care who at one time or another write in for this; it's all they hear, you tune the radio in Sterling Colorado, Lusk Wyoming, I don't care where, you get Clint Texas, Clint Texas. And the music is always cowboy hillbilly and Mexican, absolutely the worst program in the entire country and nobody can do anything about it. They have a tremendous beam, they've got the land hogtied." We saw the high antenna beyond the shacks of Clint. "Oh man the things I could tell you!" cried Neal almost weeping. Eyes bent on Frisco and the Coast we came into El Paso Texas as it got dark, broke. We absolutely had to get some money for further gas or we'd never make it. We tried everything. We buzzed the Travel Bureau but no one was going west that night. The Travel Bureau is where you go for share-the-gas rides, legal in the West. Shifty characters wait with battered suitcases. We went to the Greyhound bus station to try to persuade anybody from taking a bus for the coast and giving us the money instead. We were too bashful to approach anyone. We wandered around sadly. It was cold outside. A college boy was sweating at the sight of luscious Louanne and trying to look unconcerned. Neal and I consulted the matter but decided we weren't pimps. Suddenly a crazy dumb young kid fresh out of reform school attached himself to us, and he and Neal rushed out for a beer. "Come on man, let's go mash somebody on the head and get his money." "I dig you man!" yelled Neal. They rushed off. For a moment I was worried; but Neal only wanted to dig the streets of El Paso with the kid and get his kicks. They straggled off. Louanne and I waited in the car. She put her arms around me and made love. I said "Dammit Louanne wait till we get to Frisco." "I don't care. Neal's going to leave me anyway." "When are you going back to Denver?" "I don't know. I don't care what I'm doing. Can I go back East with you?" "We'll have to get some money in Frisco." "I know where you can get a job in a lunchcart behind the counter and I'll be a waitress. I know a hotel where we can stay on credit. We'll stick together. Gee, I'm sad." "What are you sad about kid?" "I'm sad about everything. Oh damn, I wish Neal wasn't so crazy now." Neal came twinkling back giggling in the streets and jumped in the car. "What a crazy cat that was, whoo! Did I dig him! I used to know thousands of guys like that, they're all the same, their minds work in uniform clockwork, no time, no time---" And he shot up the car, hunched over the wheel, and roared out of El Paso. "We'll just have to pick up hitch hikers. I'm positive we'll find some. Hup! hup! here we go. Lookout!" he yelled at a motorist, and swung around him, and dodged a truck and bounced over the city limits. Across the river were the jewel lights of Juarez. Louanne was watching Neal as she had watched him clear across the country and back. Out of the corner of her eye---with a sullen sad air, as though she wanted to cut off his head and hide it in her closet, an envious and rueful love that she knew would never bear fruit because he was too mad. Neal was convinced Louanne was a whore; he confided in me that she was a pathological liar. But when she watched him like this it was love, too; and when Neal noticed he always turned with his false flirtatious smile where a moment ago he was only dreaming in his eternity. Then Louanne and I both laughed---and Neal gave no sign of discomfiture, just a goofy glad grin that said to us "Ain't we getting our kicks ANYWAY?" And that was it. Outside El Paso, in the darkness, we saw a small huddled figure with thumb stuck out. It was our promised hitchhiker. We pulled up and backed to his side. "How much money you got kid?" The kid had no money; he was about seventeen, pale, strange, with one undeveloped crippled hand and no suitcase. "Ain't he sweet" said Neal turning to me with a serious awe. "Come on in fella, we'll take you out---" The kid saw his advantage. He said he had an aunt in Tulare California who owned a grocery store and as soon as we got there he'd have some money for us. Neal rolled on the floor laughing, it was so much like the kid in Carolina. "Yes! yes!" he yelled. "We've all got aunts, well let's go, let's see the aunts and the uncles and the grocery stores all the way along the road and get our kicks." And we had a new passenger, and a fine little guy he turned out to be, too. He didn't say a word, he listened to us. After a minute of Neal's talk he was probably convinced he had joined a car of madmen. He said he was hitch hiking from Alabama to Oregon, where his home was. We asked him what he was doing in Alabama. "I went to visit my uncle, he said he'd have a job for me in a lumber mill. The job fell through so I'm coming back home." "Goin' home," said Neal, "goin' home, yes I know, we'll take you home, far as Frisco anyhow." But we didn't have any money. Then it occurred to me I could borrow five dollars from my old friend Alan Harrington in Tucson Arizona. Immediately Neal said it was all settled and we were going to Tucson. And we did. Passing Las Cruces New Mexico in the night, the same Las Cruces that had been Neal's pivot on the way east, we arrived in Arizona at dawn and I woke up from a deep sleep to find everybody sleeping like lambs and the car parked God knows where because I couldn't see out the steamy windows. I got out of the car. We were parked in the mountains: There was a heaven of sunrise, cool purple airs, red mountainsides, emerald pastures in valleys, dew, and transmuting clouds of gold; on the ground gopher holes, cactus, mesquite. It was time for me to drive on. I pushed Neal and the kid over and went down the mountain with the clutch in and the motor off to save gas. In this manner I rolled into Benson Arizona. It occurred to me that I had a pocket watch someone had just given me in New York for a birthday present. At the filling station I asked the man if he knew a pawnshop in Benson. It was right next door to the station. I knocked, someone got up out of bed, and in a minute I had a dollar for the watch. It went into the tank. Now we had enough gas for Tucson. But suddenly a big pistolpacking trooper appeared just as I was ready to pull out and asked to see my driver's license. "The fellow in the backseat has the license," I said. Neal and Louanne were sleeping together under the blanket. The cop told Neal to come out. Suddenly he whipped out his gun and yelled "Keep your hands up!" "Officer," I heard Neal say in the most unctuous and ridiculous tones, "officah, I was only buttoning my flah." Even the cop almost smiled. Neal came out, muddy, ragged, T-shirted, rubbing his belly, cursing, looking everywhere for his license and his car papers. The cop rummaged thru our back trunk. All the papers were square. "Only checking up" he said with a broad smile. "You can go on now. Benson ain't a bad town actually, you might enjoy it if you had breakfast here." "Yes yes yes" said Neal paying absolutely no attention to him and drove off. We all sighed with relief. The police are suspicious when gangs of youngsters come by in new cars without a cent in their pockets and have to pawn watches. "Oh they're always interfering" said Neal "but he was a much better cop than that rat in Virginia.

They try to make headline arrests, they think every car going by is some big Chicago gang. They ain't got nothing else to do." We drove on to Tucson. Tucson is situated in beautiful mesquite riverbed country overlooked by the snowy Catalina range. The city is one big construction job; the people transient, wild, ambitious, busy, gay; washlines, trailers; bustling downtown streets with banners; altogether very Californian. Fort Lowell Road, out where H. lived, wound along lovely riverbed trees in the flat desert. We passed innumerable Mexican shacks in the shady sand till a few adobe houses appeared and the rural PO box with Alan Harrington's name shining like the promised land on it. We saw Harrington himself brooding in the yard. The poor fellow never dreamed what was bowling down on him. He was a writer, he had come to Arizona to work on his book in peace. He was a tall gangly shy satirist who mumbled to you with his head turned away and always said funny things. His wife and baby were with him in the adobe house, a small one that his Indian stepfather had built. His mother lived across the yard in her own house. She was an excited American woman who loved pottery, beads and books. Harrington had heard of Neal through letters from New York. We came down on him like a cloud, everyone of us hungry, even Alfred the crippled hitchhiker. Harrington was wearing an old Harvard sweater and smoking a pipe in the keen desert air. His mother came out and invited us into her kitchen to eat. We cooked noodles in a great pot. I wanted to meet Harrington's wild Indian stepfather; he was nowhere around, he got drunk for days on end and howled in the desert like a coyote till the cops threw him in jail. Harrington's six Indian cousins were also in jail at the time. Neal kept saying "Oh do I dig her!" about H.'s mother. She showed us her favorite rugs and chattered with us like a child. The Harringtons were from Boston. "Who is that fellow with the embryonic hand?" asked H. looking away. "Is that Al Dinkle?" "No, no, we left him in New Orleans." "Why are you all going to the Coast?" "I don't know." To add to the confusion John Holmes' mother suddenly appeared in the yard: she was driving East with friends and had stopped by to see Mrs. H. Neal shuffled and bowed in the sand and talked to her. Now there were seven visitors going both ways roaming around the yard. H.'s little boy Steve darted among us on his bicycle. We all drove to a crossroads liquor store where Harrington cashed a check for five dollars and handed me the money. Then he said we might as well visit his friend who had a ranch in the canyon, John by name. We drove up and piled into the guy's house. John was a big gigolo with a beard married to the girl who owned the ranch. They had an immense picture window in the living-room that looked out over the mesquite valley. They had bop records, everything to drink, a maid, two children who came home from school on horseback and every conceivable comfort. An immense party took place. It started in the afternoon and ended at midnight. Once I looked out the picture window and saw Alan Harrington galloping by on a horse with a shot of whisky in his hand. Neal did tremendous fever-ish things with big handsome bearded John: he took him out for a ride in the Hudson and apparently demonstrated his soul by driving a hundred miles an hour, then by weaving languidly in the traffic, then by barely missing posts and cactus, so when they came back John gripped my arm and said: "Are you going all the way to the Coast with that crazy cat? If I were you I wouldn't try it. That cat is <u>really</u> crazy." He and Neal were both sweating with excitement. There were new dents on the car. The maid was preparing a big ranch dinner for us in the kitchen. Neal tried to make her, then he tried to make John's wife. John tried to make Louanne. Poor little Alfred fell asleep exhausted on the livingroom rug; he was a long ways from Alabama and a long ways from Oregon and suddenly thrown into a frantic ranch party in the mountains of the night. When Neal vanished with the pretty wife and John went upstairs with Louanne I was beginning to get scared things would explode before we had time to eat, so I ladeled out some chili with the maid's permission and ate standing up. I began to hear arguments and crashing glass upstairs. John's wife was throwing things at him. I went out and rode the old horse a half-mile down the valley and back. Harrington came running and leaping over the mesquite with a shotglass in his hand for me. It was almost empty when he reached me. We heard roaring bop music and cries from the house. "What are we doing here?" I thought, looking up at the beautiful Arizona stars. John came running out of the house and leaped on the horse, dug his heels in, whacked with his hand and galloped licketysplit into the darkness. He was blowing off steam. The horse had to stand all the punishment of our madness. It was just an old horse and could hardly run. Finally John passed out and we woke up Alfred and got in the car and drove back to Harrington's house. There was a brief goodbye. "It certainly was pleasant" said Harrington looking away. Beyond some trees across the sand a great neon sign of a roadhouse glowed red. Harrington always went there for a beer when he was tired of writing. He was very lonely, he wanted to get back to New York. It was sad to see his tall figure receding in the dark as we drove away, just as the other figures in New York and New Orleans: they stand uncertainly underneath immense skies and everything about them is drowned. Where go? what do? what for? - - sleep. But this foolish gang was bending onwards. Outside Tucson we saw another hitch hiker in the dark road. This was an Okie from Bakersfield California who put down his story: "Hot damn, I left Bakersfield with the Travel Bureau car and left my gui-tar in the trunk of another one and they never showed up..gui-tar and cowboy duds, you see I'm a moo-sician, I was headed for Arizona to play with Johnny Mackaw's Sagebrush Boys. Well hell, here I am in Arizona broke and m'gui-tar's been stoled. You boys drive me back to Bakersfield and I'll get the money from my brother. How much you want?" We wanted just enough gas to make Frisco from Bakersfield, about three dollars. Now we were five in the car. Off we went. I began recognizing towns in Arizona I'd passed in 1947---Wickenburg, Salome, Quartzsite. In the Mojave desert I drove the car for an hour in a tremendous crosswind that threw shrouds of sand across the headlamps and bucked the car from side to side. Then we started climbing. Our plan was to avoid LA traffic and just make it to San Bernardino and Tehatchapi Pass. In the middle of the night we overtopped the lights of Palm Springs from a mountain road. At dawn, in snowy passes, we labored towards the town of Mojave which was the entry way to the great Tehatchapi pass. Mojave is in the valley formed by the desert plateau descending to the west with the high Sierras straight ahead north; the whole place a bewildering view of the ends of the world, with railroads toiling in all directions in the vastness and sending up smoke-signals like nation to nation. The Okie woke up and told funny stories; sweet little Alfred sat smiling. Okie told us he knew a man who forgave his wife for shooting him and got her out of her jail, only to be shot for a second time. We were passing a woman's prison when he told it. Up ahead we saw the Tehatchapi Pass starting up. Neal took the wheel and carried us clear to the top of the world. We passed a great shroudy cement factory in the canyon. Then we started down. Neal cut off the gas, threw in the clutch and negotiated every hairpin turn and passed cars and did everything in the books without the benefit of acceleration. I held on tight. Sometimes the road went up again briefly: he merely passed cars without a sound. He knew every rhythm and every kick of a first class pass. When it was time to U-turn left around a low stonewall that overlooked the bottom of the world he just leaned far over to his left, hands on the wheel, and carried it that way; and when the turn snaked to the right again, this time with a cliff on our left, he leaned far to the right making Louanne and me lean with him and negotiated thus. In this way we floated down to the San Joaquin valley. It lay spread a mile below, virtually the floor of California, green and wondrous from our aerial shelf. We made thirty miles without using gas. It was very cold in the Valley that winter. Suddenly we were all excited. Neal wanted to tell me everything he knew about Bakersfield as we reached the city limits. He showed me rooming-houses where he stayed, watertanks where he jumped off the train for grapes, Chinese restaurants where he ate, parkbenches where he met girls and certain places where he'd done nothing but just sit and wait around. "Man I spent hours on that very chair in front of that drug-store!" He remembered all....every pinochle game, every woman, every sad night. And suddenly we were passing the place in the rail-yards where Bea and I had sat under the moon drinking wine, on those bum crates, in October 1947 and I tried to tell him. But he was too excited. "This is where Hinkle and I spent a whole morning drinking beer trying to make a real gone little waitress from Watsonville, no it was Tracy, yes Tracy and her name was Esmeralda O man something like that." Louanne was planning what to do the moment she arrived in Frisco. Alfred said his aunt would give him plenty of money up in Tulare. The Okie directed us to his brother in the flats outside town. We pulled up at noon in front of a little rose-covered shack and the Okie went in and talked with some women. We waited fifteen minutes. "I'm beginning to think this guy has no more money than I have" said Neal. "We get more hung up! There's probably nobody in the family that'll give him a cent." The Okie came out sheepishly and directed us to town. "Hotdamn, I wisht I could find my brother." He made inquiries. He probably felt he was our prisoner. Finally we went to a big bread bakery and the Okie came out with his brother who was wearing coveralls and was apparently the truck mechanic inside. He talked with his brother a few minutes. We waited in the car. Okie was telling all his relatives his adventures and the loss of his guitar. But he got the money, and he gave it to us, and we were all set for Frisco. We thanked him and took off. Next stop was Tulare. Up the valley we roared. I lay in the back seat, exhausted, giving up completely, and sometime in the afternoon while I dozed the muddy Hudson zoomed by the tents outside Selma where I had lived and loved and worked in the spectral past. Neal was bent rigidly over the wheel pounding the rods up to his hometown: only a month ago he had come down this same road with Al and Helen Hinkle bound for North Carolina. There I was in the backseat, accomplished. I was sleeping when we finally arrived in Tulare; I woke up to hear the insane details. "Jack wake up! Alfred found his aunt's grocery store but do you know what happened, his aunt shot her husband and went to jail. The store's closed down. We didn't get a cent. Think of it! The things that happen, the trou-bles on all sides, the wonderful events... wheee!" Alfred was biting his fingernails. We were turning off the Oregon-road at Madera and there we made our farewell with little

Alfred. We wished him luck and godspeed to Oregon. He said it was the best ride he ever had. It was: he ate royally, he was at a party in a ranch, he rode horseback, he heard stories, he felt pretty good about it; but looked awful forlorn when we put him down where we'd found him, on the side of the road with his thumb stuck out, and darkness coming. We had to make Frisco. The golden goal loomed ahead. Neal Louanne and I leaned forward in the front, all alone again, and zoomed. It seemed like a matter of minutes when we began rolling in the foothills before Oakland and suddenly reached a height and saw stretched out ahead of us the fabulous white city of San Francisco on her eleven mystic hills with the blue Pacific and its advancing wall of potato patch fog beyond, and smoke and goldenness in the late afternoon of time. "There she blows!" yelled Neal. "Wow! Made it! Just enough gas! Give me water! No more land! We can't go any further cause there ain't no more land! Now Louanne darling you and Jack go immediately to a hotel and wait for me to contact you in the morning as soon as I have definite arrangements made with Carolyn and call up Funderbuck about my railroad watch and you and Jack buy the first thing hit town a paper for the wantads and…and…and.." and he drove into the Oakland Bay-Bridge and it carried us in. The downtown office buildings were just sparkling on their lights; it made you think of Sam Spade. The fog rolled in, the buoys went B-O in the bay. Market Street was a riot of crowds and sailors and girls; smells of hotdogs and food; noisy bars; screeching traffic; cable-cars---and all of it in soft delightful air that made us drunk when we staggered out of the car on O'Farrell street and sniffed and stretched. It was like getting onshore after a long voyage at sea; the slopy street reeled under our feet; secret chop sueys from Frisco Chinatown floated in the air. We took all our things out of the car and piled them on the sidewalk. Suddenly Neal was saying goodbye. He was bursting to see Carolyn and find out what happened. Louanne and I stood dumbly in the street and watched him drive away. "You see what a bastard he is?" said Louanne. "Neal will leave you out in the cold any time it's in his interest." "I know" I said, and I looked back East and sighed. We had no money. Neal hadn't mentioned money. "Where are we going to stay?" We wandered around carrying our bundles of rags in the narrow romantic streets. Everybody looked like a broken-down movie extra, a withered starlet; -disenchanted stunt-men, midget auto racers, poignant California characters with their end-of-the-continent sadness, handsome decadent Casanovish men, puffy-eyed motel blondes, hustlers, pimps, whores, masseurs, bellhops, a lemon lot and how's a man going to make a living with a gang like that. Nevertheless Louanne had been around these people- - this is O'Farrell and Powell and thereabouts---and a grayfaced hotel clerk let us have a room on credit. That was the first step. Then we had to eat, and didn't do so till midnight when we found a niteclub singer in her hotel room who turned an iron upside down on a coathanger in the wastebasket and warmed up a can of pork & beans. I looked out the window at the winking neons; and said to myself "Where is Neal and why isn't he concerned about our welfare?" I lost faith in him that year. It was our last meet, no more. I stayed in San Francisco a week and had the beatest time of my life. Louanne and I walked around for miles looking for food-money, we even visited some drunken seamen in a flophouse on Mission street that she knew; they offered us whiskey. In the hotel we lived together two days. I realized that now Neal was out of sight Louanne had no real interest in me; she was trying to reach Neal through me, his buddy. We had arguments in the hotel room. We also spent entire nights in bed and I told her my dreams. I told her about the big snake of the world that was coiled in the earth like a worm in an apple and would someday nudge up a hill to be thereafter known as Snake Hill and fold out upon the plain, fifty miles long and devouring as it went along. I told her this Snake was Satan. "What's going to happen?" she squealed, meanwhile she held me by the cock. "A saint called Dr. Sax will destroy it with secret herbs which he is at this very moment cooking up in his underground shack somewhere in America. It may also be disclosed that the Snake is just a husk of doves; when the Snake dies great clouds of seminal-gray doves will flutter out and bring tidings of peace around the world." I was out of my mind with hunger and bitterness. One night Louanne disappeared with a niteclub owner. I was waiting for her by appointment in a doorway across the street, at Larkin and Geary, hungry, when she suddenly stepped out of the foyer of the fancy apt. house with her girlfriend, the niteclub owner and a greasy old man with a roll. Originally she'd just gone in to see her girlfriend. I saw what a whore she was. She was afraid to give me the sign though she saw me in that engaged doorway. She walked on little whore-feet and got in the Cadillac and off they went. Now I had nobody, nothing. I walked around picking butts from the street. I passed a fish 'n' chip joint on Market Street and suddenly the woman in there gave me a terrified look as I passed; she was the proprietress; she apparently thought I was coming in there with a gun to holdup the joint. I walked on a few feet. It suddenly occurred to me this was my mother of a hundred and fifty years ago in England and that I was her footpad son returning from gaol to haunt her honest labours in the hashery. I stopped frozen with ecstasy on the sidewalk. I looked down Market Street. I didn't know whether it was that or Canal Street in New Orleans: it led to water, ambiguous universal water, just like 42nd street New York leads to water, and you never know where you are. I thought of Al Hinkle's ghost on Times Square. I was delirious. I wanted to go back and leer at my strange Dickensian mother in the hash joint. I tingled all over from head to foot. It seemed I had a whole host of memories leading back to 1750 in England and that I was in San Francisco now only in another life and in another body. "No," that woman seemed to say with that terrified glance "don't come back and plague your honest hardworking mother. You are no longer like a son to me- - and like your father, my first husband 'ere this kindly Greek took pity on me" (the proprietor was a Greek with hairy arms) "you are no good, inclined to drunkenness and routs and final disgraceful robbery of the fruits of my 'umble labours in the hashery. Oh son! did you not ever go on your knees and pray for deliverance for all your sins and scoundrel's acts? Lost boy!- -depart! do not haunt my soul, I have done well forgetting you. Reopen no old wounds, be as if you had never returned and looked in to me- -to see my labouring humilities, my few scrubbed pennies---hungry to grab, quick to deprive, sullen, unloved, meanminded son of my flesh. Son! Son!" It made me think of the Big Pop vision in Gratna with Bill. And for just a moment I had reached the point of ecstasy that I always wanted to reach and which was the complete step across chronological time into timeless shadows, and wonderment in the bleakness of the mortal realm, and the sensation of death kicking at my heels to move on, with a phantom dogging its own heels, and myself hurrying to a plank where all the Angels dove off and flew into infinity. This was the state of my mind. I thought I was going to die the very next moment. But I didn't, and walked four miles and picked up ten long butts and took them back to my hotel room and poured their tobacco in my old pipe and lit up. That was the way Neal found me when he finally decided I was worth saving. He took me home to Carolyn's house. "Where's Louanne man?" "The whore ran off." Carolyn was a relief after Louanne; a wellbred polite young woman and she was aware of the fact that the eighteen dollars Neal had sent her was mine. I relaxed a few days in her house. From her livingroom window in the wooden tenement on Liberty Street you could see all of San Francisco burning green and red in the rainy night. Neal did the most ridiculous thing of his career the few days I was there. He got a job demonstrating a new kind of pressure cooker in the kitchens of homes. The salesman gave him piles of samples and pamphlets. The first day Neal was a hurricane of energy. I drove all over town with him as he made appointments. The idea was to get invited socially to a dinner party and then leap up and start demonstrating the pressure cooker. "Man" cried Neal excitedly "this is even crazier than the time I worked for Sinex. Sinex sold encyclopedias in Oakland. Nobody could turn him down. He made long speeches, he jumped up and down, he laughed, he cried. One time we broke into an Okie house where everybody was getting ready to go to a funeral. Sinex got down on his knees and prayed for the deliverance of the deceased soul. All the Okies started crying. He sold a complete set of encyclopedias. He was the maddest guy in the world.

I wonder where he is. We used to get next to pretty young daughters and feel them up in the kitchen. This afternoon I had the gonest housewife in her little kitchen- -arm around her demonstrating. Ah! Hmm! Wow!" "Keep it up Neal," I said, "maybe someday you'll be mayor of San Francisco." He had the whole cookpot spiel worked out; he practised on Carolyn and I in the evenings. One morning he stood naked looking at all San Francisco out the window as the sun came up. He looked like someday he'd be the pagan mayor of San Francisco. But his energies ran out. One rainy afternoon the salesman came around to find out what Neal was doing. Neal was sprawled on the couch. "Have you been trying to sell these?" "No" said Neal "I have another job coming up." "Well, what are you going to do about all these samples?" "I don't know." In a dead silence the salesman gathered up his sad pots and left. I was sick and tired of everything and so was Neal. But one night we suddenly went mad together again; we went to see Slim Gaillard in a little Frisco niteclub. Slim Gaillard is a tall thin Negro with big sad eyes who's always saying "Right-orooni" and "How 'bout a little bourbon-orooni." In Frisco great eager crowds of young semi-intellectuals sit at his feet and listen to him on piano, guitar and bongo drums. When he gets warmed up he takes off his shirt and undershirt and really goes. He does and says anything that comes into his head. He'll sing "Cement Mixer, Put-ti Put-ti" (which he wrote) and suddenly slow down the beat and brood over his bongos with fingertips barely tapping the skin as everybody leans forward breathlessly to hear; you think he'll do this for a minute or so but he goes right on, for as long as an hour, making an imperceptible little noise, like Al Hinkle did, with the tip of his fingernails, getting smaller and smaller all the time till you can't hear it any more and sounds of traffic come in the open door. Then he slowly gets up and takes the mike and says, very slowly, "Great-orooni...fine-orooni....hello-orooni...bourbon-orooni...all-orooni....how are the boys in the front row making out with their girls-orooni...orooni...orooni... oroonirooni..." He keeps this up for fifteen minutes, his voice getting softer and softer till you can't hear. His great sad eyes scan the audience. Neal stands in the back saying "God! Yes!" and clasping his hands in prayer and sweating. "Jack, Slim knows time, he knows time." Slim sits down at the piano and hits two notes, two c's, then two more, then one, then two and suddenly the big burly bassplayer wakes up from a tea-reverie and realizes Slim is playing "C-Jam Blues" and he slugs in his big forefinger on the string and the big booming beat begins and everybody starts rocking and Slim looks just as sad as ever, and they blow jazz for half an hour, and then Slim goes mad and grabs the bongos and plays tremendous rapid Cuban beats and yells crazy things in Spanish, in Arabic, in Peruvian dialect, in Mayan, in every language he knows and he knows innumerable languages. Finally the set is over; each set takes two hours. Slim Gaillard goes and stands against a post looking sadly over everybody's head as people come and talk to him. A bourbon is slipped into his hand. "Bourbon-orooni---thank you orooni..." Nobody knows where Slim Gaillard is. Neal once had a dream that he was having a baby and his belly was all bloated up blue as he lay on the grass of a California hospital. Under a tree, with a group of colored men, sat Slim Gaillard. Neal turned despairing eyes to him. Slim said "There you go-orooni." Now Neal approached him, he approached his God, he thought Slim was God, he shuffled and bowed in front of him and asked him to join us. "Right-orooni" says Slim; he'll join anybody but he won't guarantee to be there with you in spirit. Neal got a table, bought drinks, and sat stiffly in front of Slim. Slim dreamed over his head. Not a word was spoken. Every time Slim said "orooni" Neal said "Yes!" I sat there with these two madmen. Nothing happened. To Slim Gaillard the whole world was just one big Orooni. That same night I dug Lampshade on Fillmore and Geary. Lampshade is a crazy big colored guy who comes staggering into musical Frisco saloons with coat hat and scarf and jumps on the bandstand and starts singing: the veins pop in his forehead: he heaves back and blows a big foghorn blues out of every muscle in his soul. He yells at people while he's singing. He drinks like a fish. His voice booms over everything. He grimaces, he writhes, he does everything. He came over to our table and leaned over us and said "Yes!" and then he staggered out to the street to hit another saloon. Then there's Connie Jordan, a madman who sings and flips his arms and ends up splashing sweat on everybody and kicking over the mike and screaming like a woman; and you see him late at night, exhausted, listening to wild jazz sessions at Jackson's Hole with big round eyes and limp shoulders, a big gooky stare into space and a drink in front of him. I never saw such crazy musicians. Everybody in Frisco blew. It was the end of the continent, they didn't give a damn. That summer I was to see much more of it until the very walls shuddered and cracked. Neal and I goofed around San Francisco in this manner until I got my next G.I. check and got ready to go back home. What I accomplished by coming to Frisco I don't know. Carolyn wanted me to leave. Neal didn't care one way or the other. I bought a loaf of bread and meats and made myself ten sandwiches to cross the country with again; they were all going to go rotten on me by the time I got to Dakota. The last night Neal went mad and found Louanne somewhere downtown and we got in the car and drove all over Richmond across the bay hitting Negro jazz shacks in the oil flats. Louanne went to sit down and a colored guy pulled the chair out from under her. The gals approached her in the john with propositions. I was approached too. Neal was sweating around. It was the end, I wanted to get out. At dawn I got on my New York bus and said goodbye to Neal and Louanne. They wanted some of my sandwiches. I told them no. It was a sullen moment. We were all thinking we'd never see each again and we didn't care. That was that. I started back all the way across this groaning continent with my ten sandwiches and a couple of dollars and got back to New York just in time to see Ed White, Bob Burford and Frank Jeffries off on the Queen Mary for France, never dreaming that the following year I would be with Neal and Jeffries both on the craziest trip of all. Moreover you would think a bus trip such as I took from Frisco to New York would be uneventful and I'd get home in one piece and could relax. Not so; in North Dakota the bus got stuck in a tremendous badlands blizzard that piled up the road ten feet high; the back machinery blew up and burned as

I slept; the bus became frozen so that the passengers had to spend the night in a diner or freeze and nevertheless I slept unnoticed in the bus and felt perfect when I woke up, and slept right straight through the repairs in a Fargo garage. In Butte Montana I got involved with drunken Indians; spent all night in a big wild saloon that was the answer to Bill Burroughs' quest for the ideal bar; I made a few bets on the wall, got drunk; I saw an old card dealer who looked exactly like W.C. Fields and made me cry thinking of my father. There he was, fat with a bulbous nose, wiping himself with a backpocket handkerchief, green visor, wheezing asthmatically in the Butte winter night games, till he finally packed off with his old dog to sleep another day. He was a blackjack dealer. I also saw a ninety year old man called Old John who played cards with slitted eyes and had been doing so they told me for the last seventy years in the Butte night. In Big Timber I saw a young cowboy who'd lost an arm in the war and sat with the old men in a winter afternoon inn looking with longing eyes at the boys loping by outside in the great Yellowstone snows. In Dakota I saw a rotary plow hit a brand new Ford and send it scattering in a million pieces over the plain, like sowing for the Spring. In Toledo Ohio I got off the bus and hitch hiked up to Detroit Michigan to see my first wife. She wasn't there and her mother wouldn't lend me two bucks to eat with. I sat fuming with rage on the floor of the Detroit Greyhound bus station men's room. I sat among the bottles. Preachers approached me with stories of the Lord. I spent my last dime on a cheap meal in Detroit skid row. I called up my wife's father's new wife and she wouldn't even see me. My whole wretched life swam before my weary eyes, and I realized no matter what you do it's bound to be a waste of time in the end so you might as well go mad. All I wanted was to drown my soul in my wife's soul and reach her through the tangle of shrouds which is flesh in bed. At the end of the American road is a man and a woman making love in a hotel room. That's all I wanted. Her relatives were conspiring to keep us separated; not that they were wrong but they felt I was a bum and would only reopen old wounds in her heart. Actually she was in Lansing Michigan that night, a hundred miles away, and I was lost. All I wanted and all Neal wanted and all anybody wanted was some kind of penetration into the heart of things where, like in a womb, we could curl up and sleep the ecstatic sleep that Burroughs was experiencing with a good big mainline shot of M. and advertising executives were experiencing with twelve Scotch & Sodas in Stouffers before they made the drunkard's train to Westchester---but without hangovers. And I had many a romantic fancy then, and sighed at my star. The truth of the matter is, you die, all you do is die, and yet you live, yes you live, and that's no Harvard lie. In Pennsylvania I had to get off the bus and steal apples in a countrytown store or starve. I staggered back East in search of my stone, got home and ate everything in the icebox again, only now it was a refrigerator, fruit of my 1947 labors, and that in some measure was the progress of my life. Then came the big ship of the world: I went to school and met Mrs. Holmes in the lobby, John Holmes' mother whom I'd just seen as I went through Tucson, and she said her son was seeing off some friends of mine on the Queen Mary. I didn't have a nickel. I walked three miles to the pier and there were John Holmes, his wife and Ed Stringham standing around waiting to be admitted to the gangplank. We rushed onboard and found Ed White, Bob Burford and Frank Jeffries drinking whiskey in their stateroom with Allen Ginsberg who had brought it (together with his latest poems) and others. Not only that but Hal Chase was on the ship, and the ship was so big that we never saw him; and Lucien Carr was on the ship, but he was seeing another party of people off and didn't even know we were there. Mad Burford dared me to stowaway and go to France with them. I accepted the dare, I was drunk. We held up the elevator and were told that Somerset Maugham, the famous writer, was fuming because of this. We saw Truman Capote, supported by two old ladies, staggering on the ship in tennis sneakers. Americans rushed pellmell through narrow corridors drunk. It was the Great Ship of the World, it was too big, everybody was on it and everybody was looking for everyone else and couldn't find. Pier 69. John Holmes' wife insisted I would not stowaway and dragged me off the ship by the ear. I played football among the warehouse crates. It was the end of another era. It was the second ship I had missed in two years, one on both coasts, the Korean ship and this Queen Mary Francebound ship, and the reason for this was because I was doomed for the road and the ragged investigation of my native country with the crazy Neal. After all that happened you wouldn't believe it, but it was I that went and saved Neal in his hour of broken need within a matter of months. It was worth it, for thereafter Neal became great. BOOK THREE:- In the Spring of 1949 I suddenly came into a wonderful thousand dollar check from a New York company for the work I did. With this I tried to move my family---that is to say, my mother, sister, brother-in-law and their child---to a comfortable home in Denver. I myself traveled to Denver to get the house, taking great pains not to spend over a dollar for food all the way. In one day, hustling and sweating around the May-time mountain town, and with the invaluable assistance of Justin W. Brierly, I found the house, paid the first two months' rent on it and sent them a wire in New York telling them to come in. I paid the moving bill, $350.00. But it all fell through. They didn't like Denver and they didn't like living in the country. My mother was the first to go back; then finally my sister and her husband went back. Here I made an attempt to settle down those I love in a more or less permanent homestead from which all human operations could be conducted to the satisfaction of all parties concerned. I believed in a good home, in sane and sound living, in good food, good times, work, faith and hope. I have always believed in these things. It was with some amazement that I realized I was one of the few people in the world who really believed in these things without going around making a dull middleclass philosophy out of it. I was suddenly left with nothing in my hands but a handful of crazy stars. For this I had abstained from taking a long-promised voyage to France to join the boys; for this I had put aside a number of secret desires of mine, such as rejoining my wife in Detroit, or suddenly marrying a wild Puerto Rican gal in New York and settling down to homelife in the tenements. Everything had happened and I was a thousand dollars poorer. I never dreamed I'd have a thousand dollars anyway. It was all gone in a matter of weeks. I stood poised on the great western plain and didn't know what to do. I said to myself "Well I might as well go be mad again" and I made preparations to go get Neal in San Francisco and see what he was doing now. I tried honest ways to get the money together for the voyage to the Coast. One morning at three A.M. I got up and hitch hiked down from my house out Alameda Boulevard Denver six miles into town; only thing is I didn't get any rides and I just plainly hiked it. I arrived at the Denargo Fruit Wholesale Markets before daybreak, dogtired. This was the place I had almost worked in 1947 with Eddy my roadbuddy. I was hired immediately. There then began a day of labor that I shall never forget. I worked from 4 o'clock in the morning clear to six o'clock in the evening, and at the end of that day I was paid eleven dollars and some change. And the work was so hard that I quickly developed Charley Horses in my arms and almost had to scream to go on. Of course I was soft compared to the Japanese fellows who worked side by side with me; their muscles were attuned to this onerous business of dragging a fruit-wagon loaded eight crates high and having to balance it and pull it with arms backward outstretched and if you make one mistake you ruin a whole load of fruit and do it on your own poor head. I cut around all day long with these muscular Nisei and swore and swore. At one point we had to stick a gadget under the wheels of a great box-car and advance it down the tracks at the rate of half-an-inch a yank on the lever---a hundred foot down the line. I myself unloaded a box-car and a half of fruit-crates in the entire day, interrupted only by one trip to the Denver wholesale houses where I lugged watermelon crates over the icy floor of a boxcar into the blazing sun of an ice-splattered truck and developed a mean sneeze. It was okay with me once again I wanted to get to San Francisco, everybody wants to get to San Francisco and what for? In God's name and under the stars what for? For joy, for kicks, for something burning in the night. The other fellows each loaded three boxcars apiece and I was half as fast, consequently the boss felt I was not a fit prospect for his profitable scheme and fired me without saying as much, as I made my feelings apparent and said I would never come back. Then I staggered to Larimer street with my eleven dollars and got drunk in Jiggs' buffet bar across the street from the Windsor Hotel where Neal Cassady had lived with his father Old Neal Cassady in the depression Thirties. And as of yore I looked everywhere for the father of Neal Cassady. Nowhere to be found. Either you find someone who looks like your father in places like Montana, or you look for a friend's father where he is no more, that's what you do. Then in spite of myself, the morning disclosed a woman's bare leg wrapped in silk stockings, and in that stocking was a hundred dollar bill, and she gave it to me and said "You've been talking of a trip to Frisco; that being the case take this and go and have your fun." So all my problems were solved and I got a Travel Bureau car for eleven dollars gas-fare to Frisco and zoomed over the land to Neal. Two fellows were driving this car; they said they were pimps. Two other fellows were passengers with me. We sat tight and bent our minds to the goal. As we crossed the Colorado-Utah border I saw God in the sky in the form of huge sunburning clouds above the desert that seemed to say to me "The day of wrath will come." Ah well, alackaday, I was more interested in some old rotted covered wagons and pool tables sitting in the Nevada desert near a Coca Cola stand and where there were huts with the weatherbeaten signs still flapping in the haunted shrouded desert wind, saying, "Rattlesnake Bill lived here" or "Brokenmouth Annie holed up for years." Yes, zoom! In Salt Lake City the pimps checked up on their girls and we drove on. Before I knew it, once again I was seeing the fabled city of San Francisco stretched on the Bay in the middle of the night. I ran immediately to Neal. He had a house on Russian Hill now. I was burning to know what was on his mind and what would happen now, for there was nothing behind me any more, all my bridges were gone and I didn't give a damn about anything at all. I knocked on his door at two o'clock in the morning. He came to the door stark naked and it might just have been President Truman knocking for all he cared. He received the world in the raw. "Jack!" he said with genuine awe.

"I didn't think you'd actually do it. You've finally come to me." "Yep" I said "Everything fell apart in my family. How are things in yours?" "Not so good, not so good. But we've got a million things to talk about. Jack the time has FI-NALLY come for us to talk and get with it." We agreed it was about time and went in. Now my arrival was somewhat like the arrival of the strange and most evil Angel in the home of the snow-white fleece, as Neal and I began talking excitedly in the kitchen downstairs and this brought forth sobs from upstairs. Everything I said to Neal was answered with a wild whispering shuddering "YES!" Carolyn knew what was going to happen. Apparently Neal had been quiet a few months; now the angel had arrived and he was going mad again. "What's the matter with her?" I whispered. He said "She's getting worse and worse, man, she cries and makes tantrums, won't let me out to see Slim Gaillard, gets mad every time I'm late, then when I stay home she won't talk to me and says I'm an utter beast." He ran upstairs to soothe her. I heard Carolyn yell "You're a liar, you're a liar, you're a liar!" I took the opportunity to examine the very wonderful house they had. It was a two-story crooked rickety wooden cottage in the middle of tenements right on top of Russian Hill with a view of the Bay; it had four rooms, three upstairs and one immense sort of basement kitchen downstairs. The kitchen door opened onto a grassycourt where washlines were. In back of the kitchen was a storage room where Neal's old shoes still were caked an inch thick with Texas mud from the night the Hudson got stuck at Hempstead near the Brazos River. Of course the Hudson was gone, Neal hadn't been able to make further payments on it. He had no car at all now. Their second baby was accidentally coming. It was a horrible tragedy to hear Carolyn sobbing so. We couldn't stand it and went out to buy beer and brought it back to the kitchen. Carolyn finally went to sleep or spent the night staring blankly at the dark. I had no idea what was really wrong except perhaps Neal had driven her mad after all. After my last leaving of Frisco he had gone crazy over Louanne again and spent months haunting her apartment on Divisadero where every night she had a different sailor in and he peeked down through her mail-shot which opened up on the bed. There he saw Louanne sprawled in the mornings with a boy. He trailed her around town. He wanted absolute proof that she was a whore. He loved her, he sweated over her. Finally he got hold of some bad s- - t, as it's called in the trade, green uncured marijuana, quite by mistake, and smoked too much of it. "The first day" said Neal "I lay rigid as a board in bed and couldn't move or say a word. I just looked straight up with my eyes open wide. I could hear buzzings in my head and saw all kinds of wonderful technicolor visions and felt wonderful. The second day everything came to me, EVERYTHING I'd ever done or known or read or heard of or conjectured came back to me and rearranged itself in my mind in a brand new logical way. Yes, I said, yes, yes, yes. Not loud. Just yes, real quiet and because I could think of nothing else to say. These green tea visions lasted until the third day. I had understood everything by then, my whole life was decided, I knew I loved Louanne, I knew I had to find my father wherever he is and save him, I knew you were my buddy, I knew how Great Allen is. I knew a thousand things about everybody everywhere. Then the third day I began having a terrible series of waking nightmares and they were so absolutely horrible and grisly and green that I just lay there doubled up with my hands around my knees saying Oh, Oh, Ah, Oh…The neighbors heard me and sent for a doctor. Carolyn was away with the baby visiting her folks. The whole neighborhood was concerned. They came in and found me lying on the bed with my arms stretched out forever. Jack I ran to Louanne with some of that tea. And do you know that the same thing happened to that dumb little cunt---the same visions, the same logic, the same final decision about everything, the view of all truths in one painful lump leading to nightmares and pain. Then I knew I loved her so much I wanted to kill her. I ran home and beat my head on the wall. I ran to Al Hinkle, he's back in Frisco with Helen, I asked him about a brakeman who has a gun, I went to the brakeman, I got the gun, I ran to Louanne, I looked down the mailslot, she was sleeping with a sailor, I came back in an hour, I barged in, she was alone---and I gave her the gun and told her to kill me. She held the gun in her hand the longest time. I asked her for a sweet dead pact. She didn't want. I said one of us had to die. She said no. I beat my head on the wall. She talked me out of it." "Then what happened?" "That was months ago---after you left. She finally married one of the sailors, dumb sonofabitch has promised to kill me if he finds me, if necessary I shall have to defend myself and kill him and I'll go to San Quentin, 'cause Jack one more rap of ANY kind and I go to San Quentin for life---that'll be the end of me. Bad hand and all." He showed me his hand. I hadn't noticed in the excitement that he had really suffered a terrible accident with his hand. "I hit Louanne on the brow on Feb. 26 at six o'clock in the evening the last time we met and the last last time we decided everything. Now listen to this: my thumb only deflected off her brow and she didn't even have a bruise and in fact laughed, but _my_ end, my thumb got infected and a poorass doctor made a bad job of fixing it and finally I had a touch of gangrene in it and they had to amputate a cunthair tip off the end." He unwrapped the bandages and showed me. The flesh, about half an inch, was missing under the nail. "It got from worse to worse. I had to support Carolyn and Cathy Ann and had to work as fast as I could at Goodyear tire company hauling big hundred pound tires from the floor to the top of the cars. I could only use my good hand but I kept banging the bad one. I broke it and they reset it and stuck a pin in it and it's getting all infected and swoled again. All these heebyjeebies!" he laughed "and I've never felt better and finer and happier with the world and to see little lovely children playing in the sun and I am so glad to see you my fine gone wonderful Jack and I know, I KNOW everything will be allright." He congratulated me on my thousand dollars, which was no more now. "We know life, now Jack, we're growing older each of us little by little and are coming to know things. What you tell me about your family I understand well, I've always dug your feelings and now in fact you're ready to hook up with a real great girl if you can only find her and cultivate her and make her mind your soul as I have tried so hard to do with these damned women of mine. Shit! shit! shit!" He yelled. And in the morning Carolyn threw the both of us out baggage and all, right out on the street. It began when we called Bill Tomson, old Denver Bill in the afternoon and had him come over for beer, while Neal, who couldn't work on account of his hand, minded the baby and did the dishes and the wash in the backyard but did a sloppy job of it in his excitement. Tomson agreed to drive us to Marin City to look for Henri Cru. (Neal never gave cute names to perfectly normal drab pursuits.) Carolyn came in from work at the dentist's office and gave us all the sad and dirty look of a harassed woman's life. I tried to show this woman that I had no mean intentions concerning her homelife by saying hello to her and talking as warmly as I could but she knew it was a con and maybe one I'd learned from Neal and only gave a brief smile. In the morning there was a terrible scene: she lay on the bed sobbing and writhing and in the midst of this I suddenly had the need to go to the bathroom and the only way I could get there was through her room. "Neal, Neal" I cried "where's the nearest bar!" "Bar?" he said surprised; he was washing his hands in the kitchen sink downstairs. He thought I wanted to get drunk. I told him my dilemma and he said "Go right ahead, she does that all the time." No, I couldn't do that. I rushed out to look for a bar; I walked uphill and downhill in a vicinity of four blocks on Russian Hill and found nothing but laundromats, cleaners, soda fountains, beauty parlors, haberdashers and hardware. I rushed back to the crooked little house determined to save my soul. They were yelling at each other as I slipped through with a feeble smile and locked myself in the bathroom. A few moments later Carolyn was throwing Neal's things on the livingroom floor and telling him to pack. To my amazement I saw a full length oil painting of Helen Hinkle over the sofa. I suddenly realized that all these women were spending months of loneliness and womanliness together chatting about the madness of the men. I heard Neal's maniacal giggle across the house, together with the wails of his baby. The next thing I knew he was gliding around the house like Groucho Marx with his poor broken thumb wrapped in a huge white bandage sticking up like a beacon that stands motionless above the frenzy of the waves. Once again I saw his pitiful huge battered trunk with socks and dirty underwear sticking out: he bent over it throwing everything he could find in it. Then he got his suitcase. This suitcase was the beatest suitcase in the U.S.A. It consisted of paper with designs on it making it look like leather and suspicious-looking hinges of some kind pasted on. A great rip ran down the top: Neal lashed on a rope. Then he grabbed his seabag and threw things into that. I got my suitcase, stuffed it, and as Carolyn lay abed in the room saying "Liar! Liar! Liar!" we leaped out of the house and struggled down the street to the nearest cable car---a mass of men and suitcases with that enormous bandaged thumb sticking up in the air. That thumb became the symbol of Neal's final development. He no longer cared about anything (as before) but now he also <u>cared</u> <u>about</u> <u>everything</u> <u>in</u> <u>principle,</u> and that is to say, it was all the same to him and he belonged to the world and there was nothing he could do about it. He stopped me in the middle of the street. "Now man, I know you're probably real bugged, you just got to town and we get thrown out the first day and you're wondering what I've done to deserve this and so on---together with all horrible appurtenances---hee hee hee!---but look at me. Please Jack, look at me." I looked at him. He was wearing a T-shirt, torn pants hanging down his belly, tattered shoes; he had not shaved, his hair was wild and bushy, his eyes bloodshot, and that tremendous bandaged thumb stood supported in midair at heart-level (he had to hold it up that way) and on his face was the goofiest grin I ever saw. He stumbled around in a circle and looked everywhere. "What do my eyeballs see? Ah---the blue sky. Long-fellow!" He swayed and blinked. He rubbed his eyes. "Together with windows---have you ever dug windows? Now let's talk about windows. I have seen some really crazy windows that made faces at me and some of them had shades drawn and so they winked." Out of his seabag he fished out a copy of Eugene Sue's "Paris---" and adjusting the front of his T-shirt began reading on the streetcorner with a pedantic air. "Now really Jack let's dig everything as we go along..." He forgot about that in an instant and looked around blankly. I was glad I had come, he needed me now.

"Why did Carolyn throw you out? what are you going to do?" "Eh?" he said. "Eh? Eh?" We racked our brains for where to go and what to do. I had a fairly good career underway in NY and I realized it was up to me to help Neal. Poor, poor Neal---the Devil himself had never fallen further; in idiocy, with infected thumb, surrounded by the battered suitcases of his motherless feverish life across America and back numberless times, an undone bird, a broken turd, name your price and take your change. "Let's walk to New York" he said "and as we do so let's take stock of everything along the way---yass." I took out my money and counted it; I showed it to him. 2x "I have here" I said "the sum of eighty three dollars and change and if you come with me let's go to New York---and after that let's go to Italy." "Italy?" he said. His eyes lit up. "Italy yass---how shall we get there, dear Jack?" I pondered this. "I'll make some more money, I'll get another thousand dollars. We'll go dig all the crazy women in Rome, Paris, all those places; we'll sit at sidewalk cafes; we'll catch up with Burford White and Jeffries and live in whore houses. Why not go to Italy?" "Why yass" said Neal and then realized I was serious and looked at me out the corner of his eye for the first time, for I'd never committed myself before with regard to his burdensome existence, and that look was the look of a man weighing his chances at the last moment before the bet. There was triumph and insolence in his eyes, a devilish look, and he never took his eyes off mine for the longest time. I looked back at him and blushed. I said "What's the matter?" I felt wretched when I asked it. He made no answer but continued looking at me with the same wary insolent side-eye. I tried to remember everything he'd done in his life and if there wasn't something back there to make him suspicious of something now. Resolutely and firmly I repeated what I said- -"Come to NY with me, I've got the money." I looked at him; my eyes were watering with embarrassment and tears. Still he stared at me. Now his eyes were blank and looking through me. It was probably the pivotal point of our friendship when he realized I had actually spent some hours thinking about him and he was trying to place that in his tremendously involved and tormented mental categories. Something clicked in both our souls. In mine it was suddenly concern for a man who was years younger than I, five years, & whose fate was wound with mine across the passage of the shrouded years; in his it was a matter that I can only ascertain from what he did afterwards. He became extremely joyful and said everything was settled. "What was that look?" I asked. He was pained to hear me say that. He frowned. Rarely Neal frowned. We both felt perplexed and uncertain of something. We were standing on top of Russian Hill on a beautiful sunny day in San Francisco; our shadows fell across the sidewalk. Out of the tenement next to Carolyn's house filed eleven Greek men and women who instantly lined themselves up on the sunny pavement while another backed up across the narrow street and smiled at them over a camera. We gaped at these ancient people who were having a wedding party for one of their daughters probably the thousandth in an unbroken dark generation of smiling in the sun. They were well dressed, and they were strange. Neal and I might have been in Cyprus for all of that. Gulls flew overhead in the sparkling air. "Well" said Neal in a very shy and sweet voice "shall we go?" "Yes" I said "let's go to Italy." And so we picked up our bags, he the trunk with his one good arm and I the rest, and staggered to the cable-car stop; in a moment rolled down the hill with our legs dangling to the sidewalk from the jiggling shelf, two brokendown heroes of the western night and more to go. First thing, we went to a bar down on Market street and decided everything---that we would stick together and be buddies till we die. Neal was very quiet and seemed a little subdued and preoccupied looking at the old bums in the saloon that reminded him of his father. "I think he's in Denver...this time we must absolutely find him, he may be in County Jail, he may be around Larimer street again, but he's to be found. Agreed?" Yes, it was agreed; we were going to do everything we'd never done and had been too silly to do in the past. Then we promised ourselves two days of kicks in San Francisco before starting off, and of course the agreement was to go by Travel Bureau in share-the-gas cars and save as much money as possible for what we were going to do across the land. We were also going to Detroit for me to fetch Edie and make up my mind about her once and for all. Neal claimed he no longer needed Louanne tho he still loved her. We both agreed he would make out in New York and as it turned out he did and got married again: but more of that after 3,000 miles and many days and nights. We stashed our gear in a Greyhound bus locker for ten cents, Neal put on his pinstripe suit with a sports shirt, and we took off for Bill Tomson's who was going to be our chauffeur for 2-day Frisco kicks. Bill Tomson agreed over the phone to do so. He arrived at the corner of Market and 3rd shortly thereafter and picked us up. Bill was now living in Frisco, working as a clerk and married to a pretty little blonde called Helena. Neal confided in me that her nose was too long---this was his big point of contention about her, for some strange reason---and her nose wasn't too long at all. This must have reached back to the days when he stole Carolyn from Bill in the Denver hotel room. Bill Tomson is a thin dark handsome kid with a pinsharp face and combed hair that he keeps shoving back from the sides of his head. He has an extremely earnest approach and a big smile. But evidently his wife Helena had wrangled with him over the chuffering idea- - and determined to make a stand as the man of the house (they lived in a little room) he nevertheless stuck by his prom-ise to us, but with consequences. His mental dilemma resolved itself in a bitter silence. He drove Neal and I all over Frisco at all hours of day and night and never said a word; all he did was go through red lights and make sharp turns on two wheels and this was telling us the shifts to which we'd put him. He was midway between the challenge of his new wife and the challenge of his old Denver poolhall gang leader. Neal was completely pleased and of course unperturbed by the driving. We paid absolutely no attention to Bill and sat in the back and yakked. The next thing was to go to Marin City to see if we could find Henri Cru. I noticed with some wonder that the old ship Adm. Freebee no longer stood in the bay; and then of course Henri was no longer in the second-to-last compartment of the shack in the canyon. A beautiful colored girl opened the door instead; Neal and I talked to her a great deal. Bill Tomson waited in the car reading Eugene Sue's

"Paris ---". I took one last look at Marin City and knew there was no sense trying to dig up the involved past; instead we decided to go see Helen Hinkle about sleeping accommodations. Al had left her again, was in Denver, and damned if she still didn't plot to get him back. We found her sitting on the Oriental-type rug of her fourroom tenement flat on upper Mission crosslegged with a deck of fortune cards. I saw sad signs that Al Hinkle had lived here a while and then left out of stupors and disinclinations only. "He'll come back" said Helen "that guy can't take care of himself without me---it was Jim Holmes who did it this time." She gave a furious look at Neal and Bill Tomson. "All the time before he came Al was perfectly happy and worked and we went out and had wonderful times. Neal you know that. Then they'd sit in the bathroom for hours, Al in the bathtub and Holmes on the seat and talk and talk and talk---such silly things." Neal laughed. For years he was the chief prophet of that gang and now they were learning his technique. Jim Holmes had grown a beard and his big sorrowful blue eyes had come looking for Al Hinkle in Frisco; what happened, he (actually and no lie) had his small finger amputated in a Denver mishap and collected a goodly sum of money. For no reason under the sun they decided to give Helen the slip and go to Maine--- this too is no lie, Portland Maine, where apparently Holmes had an aunt of some kind. So they were now either in Denver going through or already in Portland. "When Jim's money runs out Al'll be back" said Helen looking at her cards. "Damn fool...he doesn't know anything and never did. All he has to do is know that I love him." Helen Hinkle looked like the daughter of the Greeks with the sunny camera as she sat there on the rug, her long hair streaming to the floor, plying the tellingcards. I got to like her. We even decided to go out that night and hear jazz and Neal would take a six foot blonde that lived down the street, Julie. "In that case may I leave now?" said Tomson sassily, and we told him to go ahead but be ready for the next day. And that night Helen, Neal and I went to get Julie. This girl had a basement apartment, a little daughter and an old car that barely ran and which Neal and I had to push down the street as the girls jammed at the starter. I heard them giggle about me "Jack's just come in from a long trip---he has to be relieved." We went to Helen's and there everybody sat around---Julie, her daughter, Helen, Bill Tomson, Helena Tomson---all sullen in the overstuffed furniture as I stood in a corner neutral in Frisco problems and Neal stood in the middle of the room with his balloon-thumb in the air breast-high, giggling. "Gawd damn" he said "we're all losing our fingers...hawr hawr hawr." "Neal why do you act so foolish?" said Helen. "Carolyn called and said you left her. Don't you realize you have a daughter." "He didn't leave her, she kicked him out!" I said breaking my neutrality. They all gave me dirty looks; Neal grinned. "And with that thumb what do you expect the poor guy to do." I added. They all looked at me: particuarly Helena Tomson lowered a mean gaze on my flesh. It wasn't anything but a sewing circle and the center of it was the culprit, Neal---responsible perhaps for everything that was wrong. I looked out the window at the buzzing night-street of Mission; I wanted to get going and hear the great jazz of Frisco, and remember this was only my second night in town, everything had happened aheap. "I think Louanne was very very wise leaving you Neal. For years now you haven't any sense of responsibility for anyone. You've done so many awful things I don't know what to say to you." And in fact that was the point and they all sat around just looking at Neal with lowered and hating eyes and he just stood on the carpet in the middle of them and giggled---he merely giggled. He made a little dance. His bandage was getting dirtier all the time, it began to flop and unroll. I suddenly realized that Neal was by virtue of his enormous series of sins becoming the Idiot...the Imbecile...the Saint of the Lot. "You have absolutely no regard for anybody but yourself and your damned kicks. All you think about is what's hanging between your legs and how much money or fun you can get out of people and then you just throw them aside...Not only that but you're silly about it. It never occurs to you that life is serious and there are people trying to make something decent out of it instead of just goofing all the time." That's what Neal was, the HOLY GOOF. "Carolyn is crying her heart out tonight but don't think for a minute she wants you back, she said she never wanted to see you again and she said it was to be final this time. Yet you stand here and make silly faces and I don't think there's a care in your heart." This was not true, I knew better and I could have told them all right there. I didn't see any sense in trying it. These accusations were the same that had been levelled at me many a time in my own life in the east. I longed to go and put my arm around Neal and say "Now look here all of you, remember just one thing, this guy has his troubles too and another thing he never complains and he's given all of you a damned good time just being himself and if that isn't enough for you then send him to the firing squad, that's apparently what you're itching to do any-way.." Nevertheless Helen Hinkle was the only one in the gang who wasn't afraid of Neal and who could sit there calmly, with her face hanging out, telling him off in front of everybody. There were earlier days in Denver when Neal had everybody sit in the dark with their girls and just talked- -and talked- - and talked---with a voice that was once hypnotic and strange and was said to make the girls come across by sheer force of persuasion and the content of what he said. This was when he was fifteen, sixteen. Now his disciples were married and the wives of his disciples had him on the carpet for the sexuality and the life he had helped burgeon---this may be a little thick. I listened fur-ther. "Now you're going east with Jack and what do you think you're going to accomplish by that? Carolyn has to stay home and mind the baby now you're gone---how can she keep her dentist job---and she never wants to see you again and I don't blame her. If you see Al along the road you tell him to come back to me or I'll kill him." Just as flat as that. It was the saddest and sweetest night. Then a complete silence fell over everybody and when once Neal would have talked his way out, he now just fell silent himself, but standing, in front of everybody, in full sight, ragged and broken and idiotic, right under the lightbulbs, his bony mad face covered with sweat and throbbing veins, saying "Yes, yes, yes" as though tremendous revelations were pouring into him all the time now, and I am convinced they were, and the others suspected as much and were frightened. What was he knowing? He tried all in his power to tell me what he was knowing, and they envied that about me, my position at his side, defending him and drinking him in as they once tried to do. Then they looked at me. What was I, a stranger, doing on the West Coast this fair night. I recoiled from the thought. "We're going to Italy" I said; I washed my hands of the whole matter. Then too there was a strange air of maternal satisfaction in the air, for the girls were really looking at Neal like a mother looks at the dearest and most errant child, and he with his sad thumb and all his revelations knew it well and that was why he was able, in breathless silence, to get up from the chair, stand a moment, and walk out of the apartment without a word, to wait for us downstairs as soon as we'd made up our minds about TIME. This was what we sensed about the ghost on the sidewalk. I looked out the window. He was alone in the doorway digging the street. Bitterness, recriminations, advice, morality, sadness, it was all behind him and ahead of him was the ragged and ecstatic joy of pure being. "Come on Helen, Julie, let's go hit the jazz joints and forget it. Neal will be dead someday. Then what can you say to him." "The sooner he's dead the better" said Helen, and she spoke officially for almost everyone in the room. "Very well then" I said, "but now he's alive and I'll bet you want to know what he does next and that's because he's got the secret that we're all busting to find and he's got splitting his head wide open and if he goes mad don't worry it won't be your fault but the fault of God." They objected to this; they said I really didn't know Neal; they said he was the worst scoundrel that ever lived and I'd find out someday to my regret. I was amused to hear them protest so much. Bill Tomson rose to the defense of the ladies and said he knew Neal better than anybody and all Neal was, was just a very interesting and even amusing conman, and Ah but that was a bit too thick for me because if you're going to be respectable be so, and if not, don't be so, and make no halfway bones about it, and this I sought to say. It was a dig at their shoddy routines and cons, past and present, which fortunately they didn't get and where did I stand but on the verge of the moon, why talk? I went out to find Neal and we had a brief talk

about it. "Ah man don't worry, everything is perfect and fine." He was
rubbing his belly and licking his lips. The girls came down and we
started out on our big night, once more pushing the car down the
street till we had it running so fast it got away from us and the girls
didn't come back till they hailed a car willing to push them back to
us wandering around laughing in the dark. "Wheeoo! let's go!" cried
Neal, and we jumped in the back seat and clanked to Howard Street,
meanwhile hiding so the fellows who were pushing the girls and had
come around the corner to find them again would push us all the way
to Howard street thinking they had a chance for dates. They were disappointed when the motor started up and Julie made a few fast turns
and got us to Howard street minus the boys. Out we jumped in the
warm mad night hearing a wild tenorman bawling horn across the
way going "EE-YAH! EE-YAH! EE-YAH!" and hands clapping to the
beat and folks yelling "Go, go, go!" Far from escorting the girls into
the place Neal was already racing across the street with his thumb in
the air yelling "Blow, man, blow!" A bunch of colored men in Saturday night suits were whooping it up in front. It was a sawdust saloon,
all wood, with a small bandstand near the john on which the fellows
huddled with their hats on blowing over people's heads, a crazy place,
not far from Market street, in the dingy back of it, near Mission and
the big bridge causeway; crazy floppy women wandered around sometimes in their bathrobes, bottles clanked in alleys. In back of the joint
in a dark corridor beyond the splattered toilets scores of men and
women stood against the wall drinking wine-bolly-olly and spitting
at the stars. The behatted tenorman was blowing at the peak of a
wonderfully satisfactory free idea, a rising and falling riff that went
from "EE-yah!" to a crazier "EE-de-lee-yah!" and blasted along to the
rolling crash of butt-scarred drums hammered by a big brutal Negro
with a bullneck who didn't give a damn about anything but punishing his tubs, crash, rattle-ti-boom crash. Uproars of music and the
tenorman <u>had it</u> and everybody knew he had it. Neal was clutching
his head in the crowd and it was a mad crowd. They were all urging
that tenorman to hold it and keep it with cries and wild eyes; and he

was raising himself from a crouch and going down again with his horn, looping it up in a clear cry above the furor. A six foot skinny Negro woman was rolling her bones at the man's hornbell, and he just jabbed it at her, "Ee! ee! ee!" He had a foghorn tone; his horn was taped; he was a shipyard worker and he didn't care. Everybody was rocking and roaring. Helen and Julie with beer in their hands were standing on their chairs shaking and jumping. Groups of colored guys stumbled in from the street falling over each other to get there. "Stay with it man!" roared a man with a foghorn voice, and let out a big groan that must have been heard clear out in Sacramento, ah-haa! "Whoo!" said Neal. He was rubbing his chest, his belly, the sweat splashed from his face. Boom, kick, that drummer was kicking his drums down the cellar and rolling the beat upstairs with his murderous sticks, rattlety boom! A big fat man was jumping on the platform making it sag and creak. "Yoo!" The pianist was only pounding the keys with spreadeagled fingers, chords, at intervals when the great tenorman was drawing breath for another blast, Chinese chords, shuddering the piano in every timber, chink and wire, boing! The tenorman jumped down from the platform and just stood in the crowd blowing around; his hat was over his eyes; somebody pushed it back for him. He just hauled back and stamped his foot and blew down a hoarse, baughing blast, and drew breath, and raised the horn and blew high wide and screaming in the air. Neal was directly in front of him with his face lowered to the bell of the horn, clapping his hands, pouring sweat on the man's keys, and the man noticed and laughed in his horn a long quivering crazy laugh and everybody else laughed and they rocked and rocked; and finally the tenorman decided to blow his top and crouched down and held a note in high C for a long time as everything else crashed along and the cries increased and I thought the cops would come swarming from the nearest precinct. It was just a usual Saturday night goodtime, nothing else. The clock on the wall quivered and shook; nobody cared about that thing. Neal was in a trance. The tenorman's eyes were fixed straight on him; he had found a madman who not only understood but cared and wanted to understand more and much more than there was, and they began duelling for this; everything came out of the horn, no more phrases, just cries, cries, "Baugh" and down to "Beep!" and up to "EEEEE!" and down to clinkers and over to sideways echoing horn-sounds. He tried everything, up, down, sideways, upside down, horizontal, thirty degrees, forty degrees and finally he fell back in somebody's arms and gave up and everybody pushed around and yelled "Yes! Yes! He blowed that one!" Neal wiped himself with his handkerchief. Then up stepped Freddy on the bandstand and asked for a slow beat and looked sadly out the open door over people's heads and began singing "Close Your Eyes." Things quieted down a minute. Freddy wore a tattered suede jacket, a purple shirt, cracked shoes and zoot pants without press: he didn't care. He looked like a Negro Hunkey. His big brown eyes were concerned with sadness, and the singing of songs slowly and with long thoughtful pauses. But in the second chorus he got excited and grabbed the mike and jumped down from the bandstand and bent to it. To sing a note he had to touch his shoe-tops and pull it all up to blow, and he blew so much he staggered from the effect, and only recovered himself in time for the next long slow note. "Mu-u-u-u-sic pla-a-a-a-a-ay!" He leaned back with his face to the ceiling, mike held at his fly. He shook, he swayed. Then he leaned in almost falling with his face against the mike. "Ma-a-a-ake it dream-y for dan-cing"---and he looked at the street outside with his lips curled in scorn---"while we go ro-man-n-n-cing" he staggered sideways---- "Lo-o-o-ove's holi-da-a-ay"---he shook his head with disgust and weariness at the whole world----"Will make it seem"---what would it make it seem?---everybody waited, he mourned--- "O---kay." The piano hit a chord. "So baby come on just clo-o-oose your ey-y-y-y-y-yes"---his mouth quivered, he looked at us, Neal and I, with an expression that seemed to say "Hey now, what's this thing we're all doing in this sad brown world"----and then he came to the end of his song, and for this there had to be elaborate preparations during which time you could send all the messages to Garcia around the world twelve times and what difference did it make to anybody because here we were dealing with the pit and prunejuice of poor beat life itself in the Godawful streets of man, so he said and sang it, "Close--- your----" and blew it way up to the ceiling and thru to the stars and on up--- "Ey-y-y-y-y-es" and staggered off the platform to brood. He sat in the corner with a bunch of boys and paid no attention to them. He looked down and wept. He was the greatest. Neal and I went over to talk to him. We invited him out to the car. In the car he suddenly yelled "Yes! ain't nothing I like better than good kicks! Where do we go?" Neal jumped up and down in the seat giggling maniacally. "Later! later!" said Freddy. "I'll get my boy to drive us down to Jackson's Hole, I got to sing. Man I _live_ to sing. Been singing Close Your Eyes for two weeks- -I don't want to sing nothing else. What are you boys up to?" We told him we were going to New York in two days. "Lord, I ain't never been there and they tell me it's real jumping town but I ain't got no cause complaining where I am. I'm married you know." "Oh yes?" said Neal lighting up. "And where is the darling tonight." "What do you _mean_" said Freddy looking at him out of the corner of his eye. "I tole you I was _married_ to her didn't I?" "Oh yes, Oh yes" blushed Neal. "I was just asking. Maybe she has friends? or sisters? A ball, you know, I'm just looking for a ball." "Yah, what good's a ball, life's too sad to be balling all the time" said Freddy lowering his eye to the street. "Shh-eee-it!" he said. "I ain't got no money and I don't care tonight." We went back in for more. The girls were so disgusted with Neal and I for gunning off and jumping around that they had left and gone to Jackson's hole on foot; the car wouldn't run anyway. We saw a horrible sight in the bar: a white hipster fairy had come in wearing a Hawaiian shirt and was asking the big drummer if he could sit in. The musicians looked at his shirt suspiciously. "Do you blow?" He said he did, mincing. They looked at each other and said "Yeah, yeah, that's what the man does, shh-eee-eet!" So the fairy sat down at the tubs and they started the beat of a jump number and he began stroking the snares with soft goofy bop brushes, swaying his neck with that complacent Reichianalyzed ecstasy that doesn't mean anything except too much T and soft foods and goofy kicks on the cool order. But he didn't care. He smiled joyously into space and kept the beat, tho softly, and with bop subtleties, a giggling rippling background for big solid foghorn blues the boys were blowing unawares of him. The big Negro bullneck drummer sat waiting for his turn. "What that man doing?" he said. "Play the music!" he said. "What in hell!" he said. "Shh-ee-eet!" and looked away disgusted. Freddy's boy showed up: he was a little taut Negro with a great big Cadillac. We all jumped in. He hunched over the wheel and blew the car clear across Frisco without stopping once, seventy miles per, right through traffic and nobody even noticed him he was so good. Neal was in ecstasies. "Dig this guy, man! dig the way he sits there and don't move a bone and just balls that jack and can talk all night while he's doing it, only thing is he doesn't bother with talking, he lets freddy do that, and Freddy's his boy and tells him about life, listen to them, O man the things, the things I could---I wish---O yes...let's go, let's not stop, Go now! Yes!" And Freddy's boy wound around a corner and bowled us right in front of Jackson's Hole and was parked. A cab pulled up: out of it jumped a skinny withered little Negro preacherman who threw a dollar at the cabby and yelled "Blow!" and ran into the club pulling on his coat (just come out of work) and dashed right through the downstairs bar yelling "Go, go, go!" and stumbled upstairs almost falling on his face and blew the door open and fell into the jazzsession room with his hands out to support him against anything he might fall on, and he fell right on Lampshade who was reduced to working as a waiter in Jackson's Hole this season, and the music was there blasting and blasting and he stood transfixed in the open door screaming "Go man go!" And the man was a little short Negro with an alto horn that Neal said obviously lived with his grandmother just like Jim Holmes, slept all day and blew all night and blew a hundred choruses before he was ready to jump for fair, and that's what he was doing. "It's Allen Ginsberg!" screamed Neal above the fury. And it was. This little grandmother's boy with the taped up alto had beady glittering eyes, small crooked feet, spindly legs and he hopped and flopped with his horn and threw his feet around and kept his eyes transfixed on the audience (which was just people laughing at a dozen tables, the room thirty by thirty feet and low-ceiling) and he never stopped. He was very simple in his ideas. Ideas meant nothing to him. What he liked was the surprise of a new simple variation of a chorus. He'd go from… "ta-tup-tader-rara…ta-tup-tade-rara".. repeating and hopping to it and kissing and smiling into his horn---and then to "ta-tup-EE-da-de-dera-RUP! ta-tup-EE-da-de-dera-RUP!" and it was all great moments of laughter and understanding for him and everyone else who heard. His tone was clear as a bell, high, pure, and blew straight in our faces from two feet away. Neal stood in front of him oblivious to everything else in the world with his head bowed, his hands socking in together, his whole body jumping on his heels and the sweat, always the sweat pouring and splashing down his tormented collar to literally lie in a pool at his feet. Helen and Julie were there and it took us five minutes to realize it. Whoo, Frisco nights, the end of the continent and the end of doubt, all dull doubt and tomfoolery, goodbye. Lampshade was roaring around with his trays of beer: everything he did was in rhythm: he yelled at the waitress with the beat: "Hey now babybaby, make a way, make a way, it's Lampshade coming your way" and he hurled by her with the beers in the air and roared through the swinging doors in the kitchen and dance with the cooks and come sweating back. Connie Jordan sat absolutely motionless at a corner table with an untouched drink in front of him, staring gook-eyed into space, his hands hanging at his sides till they almost touched the floor, his feet outspread like lolling tongues, his body shriveled into absolute weariness and entranced sorrow and what-all was on his mind: a man who knocked himself out every evening and let the others put the quietus to him in the night. Everything swirled around him like clouds. And that little grandmother's alto, that little Allen Ginsberg hopped and monkeydanced with his magic horn and blew two hundred choruses of blues each one more frantic than the other and no signs of failing energy or willingness to call anything a day. The whole room shivered. It has since been closed down, naturally. On the corner of Fifth and Howard an hour later I stood with Ed Saucier a San

Francisco alto man who waited with me while Neal made a phone call in a saloon to have Bill Tomson pick us up. It wasn't anything much, we were just talking, except that suddenly we saw a very strange and insane sight. It was Neal. He wanted to give Bill Tomson the address of the bar so he told him to hold the line a minute and ran out to see, and to do this he had to rush pellmell through a long bar of brawling drinkers in white shirts, go to the middle of the street and look at the post signs. He did this, crouched low to the ground like Groucho Marx, his feet carrying him with amazing swiftness and came out of the bar like an apparition with his baloon thumb stuck up in the night and came to whirling stop in the middle of the road looking everywhere above him for the signs. They apparently were hard to see in the dark and he spun a dozen times in the road, thumb upheld, in a wild anxious silence. So anybody coming along the street would see this: a wild-haired person with a balooning thumb held up like a great goose of the sky spinning and spinning in the dark, the other hand distractedly inside his pants. Ed Saucier was saying "I blow a sweet tone wherever I go and if people don't like it ain't nothing I can do it about it. Say man, that buddy of yours is a crazy cat, looka him over there" ---and we looked. There was a big silence everywhere as Neal saw the signs and rushed back in the bar practically going under someone's legs as they came out and gliding so fast through the bar a second time that everybody had to make a double take to see him. A moment later Bill Tomson showed up and with the same amazing swiftness Neal glided across the street and into the cardoor without a sound. We were off again. "Now Bill I know you're all hungup with your wife about this thing but we absolutely must make Thornton and Gomez in the incredible time of three minutes or everything is lost. Ahem! Yes! (cough-cough) In the morning Jack and I are leaving for NY and this is absolutely our last night of kicks and I know you won't mind." No, Bill Tomson didn't mind: he only drove through every red light he could find and hurried us along in our foolishness. At dawn he went back to bed. Neal and I ended up with a colored guy called Walter who invited us to his home for a bottle of beer. He lived in the tenements in back of Howard. His wife was asleep when we came in. The only light in the apartment was the bulb over her bed. We had to get up on a chair and unscrew the bulb as she lay smiling beneath us. She was about 15 years older than Walter and the sweetest woman in the world. Then we had to plug in the extension over her bed and she smiled and smiled. She never asked Walter where he'd been, what time it was, nothing. Finally we were set in the kitchen with the extension and sat down around the humble table to drink the beer and tell the stories. We told Walter to tell us his story. He said he was in a whore house in LA where they had a monkey at the entrance that you had to place a bet with and if you lost the monkey gave it to you up the back. If you won a girl was yours for free. He insisted this was a true story. "That monkey" he said "ain't never seen such a monkey. Place the bet in the cage, you know, and monkey roll the cage and dice come out. Man lose a bet to that monkey and gits himself britched. I ain't telling you no lie. That's the monkey." Neal and I were delighted with the story. Then it was time to leave and move the extension back to the bedroom and screw back the bulb. Walter's wife smiled and smiled as we repeated the thing all over again. She never said a word. Out on the dawn street Neal said "Now you see, man, there's a REAL woman for you. Never a harsh word, never a complaint, her old man can come in any hour of the night with anybody and have talks in the kitchen and drink the beer and leave any old time. This is a man, and that's his castle." He pointed up at the tenement proudly. We stumbled off. The big night was over. A cruising car followed us suspiciously for a few blocks. We bought fresh buns in a bakery and ate them in the gray ragged street. A tall bespectacled well-dressed fellow came stumbling down the street with a Negro in a truckdriving cap. They were a strange pair. A big truck rolled by and the Negro pointed at it excitedly and tried to express his feeling. The tall white man furtively looked over his shoulder and counted his money. "It's Bill Burroughs!" giggled Neal. "Counting his money and worried about everything, and all that other boy wants to do is talk about trucks and things he knows." We followed them awhile. We had to sleep: Helen Hinkle was out of the question. Neal knew a railroad brakeman called Henry Funderburk who lived with his father in a hotel room on 3rd Street. Originally he'd been on good terms with them but lately not so, and the idea was for me to try persuading them to let us sleep on their floor. It was horrible. I had to call from a morning diner. The old man answered the phone suspiciously. He remembered me from what his son had told him. To our surprise he came down to the lobby and let us in. It was just a sad old brown Frisco hotel. We went upstairs and the old man was kind enough to give us the entire bed. "I have to get up anyway" he said and retired to the little kitchenette to brew coffee. He began telling stories about his railroading days. He reminded me of my father. I stayed up and listened to the stories. Neal, not listening, was washing his teeth and bustling around and saying "Yes that's right," to everything he said. Finally we slept; and in the morning Henry came back from the Bakersfield run and took the bed as Neal and I got up. Now old Mr. Funderburk dolled himself up for a date with his middleaged sweetheart. He put on a green tweed suit, a cloth cap same material, and stuck a flower in his lapel. "These romantic old brokendown Frisco brakemen live sad but eager lives of their own" I told Neal in the toilet. "It was very kind of him to let us sleep here." "Yass, yeass" said Neal not listening. He rushed out to get a Travel Bureau car. My job was to hurry to Helen Hinkle's for our bags. She was sitting on the floor with her fortunetelling cards. "Well goodbye Helen and I hope everything works out fine." "When Al gets back I'm going to take him to Jackson's Hole every night and let him get his fill of madness. Do you think that'll work Jack? I don't know what to do." "What do the cards say?" "The ace of spades is far away from him. The heart cards always surround him - - the queen of hearts is never far. See this jack of spades? - - that's Neal, he's always around." "Well we're leaving for New York in an hour." "Someday Neal's going to go on one of these trips and never come back." She let me take a shower and shave and then I said goodbye and took the bags downstairs and hailed a Frisco taxi-bus, which is an ordinary taxi that runs a regular route and you can hail it from any corner and ride to any corner you want for about fifteen cents, cramped in with other passengers like on a bus but talking and telling jokes like in a private car. Mission street that last day in Frisco was a great riot of construction work, children playing, whooping Negroes coming home from work, dust, excitement, the great buzzing and vibrating hum of what is really America's most excited city---and overhead the pure blue sky and the joy of the foggy sea that always rolls in at night to make everybody hungry for food and further excitement. I hated to leave; my stay lasted sixty odd hours. With frantic Neal I was rushing through the world without a chance to see it. In the afternoon we were buzzing towards Sacramento and eastward again. The car belonged to a tall thin fag who was on his way home to Kansas and wore dark glasses and drove with extreme care; the car was what Neal called a "fag Plymouth," it had no pickup and no real power. "Effeminate car!" whispered Neal in my ear. There were two other passengers, a couple, typical halfway tourists who wanted to stop and sleep everywhere. The first stop would have to be Sacramento which wasn't even the faintest beginning of the trip to Denver. Neal and I sat alone in the backseat and left it up to them and talked. "Now man that alto man last night had IT---he held it once he found---I've never seen a guy who could hold so long." I wanted to know what "IT" meant. "Ah well" laughed Neal "now you're asking me im-pon-de-rables - -ahem! Here's a guy and everybody's there, right? Up to him to put down what's on everybody's mind. He starts the first chorus, he lines up his ideas, people yeah, yeah but get it, and then he rises to his fate and has to blow equal to it. All of a sudden somewhere in the middle of the chorus he GETS IT---everybody looks up and knows; they listen; he picks it up and carries. Time stops. He's filling empty space with the substance of our lives. He has to blow across bridges and come back and do it with such infinite feeling for the tune of the moment that everybody knows it's not the tune that counts but IT---" Neal could go no further; he was sweating telling about it. Then I began talking; I never talked so much in all my life. I told Neal that when I was a kid and rode in cars I used to imagine I held a big scythe in my hand and cut down all the trees and posts and even sliced every hill that zoomed past the window. "Yes! yes!" Yelled Neal. "I used to do it too only different scythe - -tell you why. Driving across the west with the long stretches my scythe had to be immeasurably longer and it had to curve over distant mountains slicing off their tops and reach another level to get at further mountains and at the same time clip off every post along the road, regular throbbing poles. For this reason--- O man I have to tell you, NOW, I have IT, I have to tell you the time my father and I and a raggedy bum from Larimer street took a trip to Nebraska in the middle of the depression to sell flyswatters. And how we made them, we bought pieces of ordinary regular old screen and pieces of wire that we twisted double and little pieces of blue and red cloth to sew around the edges and all of it for a matter of cents in a Five and Ten and made thousands of flyswatters and got in the old bum's jaloppy and went clear around Nebraska to every farmhouse and sold them for a nickel apiece- -mostly for charity the nickels were given us, two bums and a boy, apple pies in the sky and my old man in those days was always singing Hallejuh I'm a Bum, Bum Again. And man now listen to this after two whole weeks of incredible hardship and bouncing around and hustling in the heat to sell these awful makeshift flyswatters they started to argue about the division of the proceeds and had a big fight on the side of the road and then made up and bought wine and began drinking wine and didn't stop for five days and five nights while I huddle and cry in the background and when they were finished every last cent was spent and we were right back where we started from, Larimer street. And my old man was arrested and I had to plead at court to the judge to let him go 'cause he was my Pa and I had no mother, Jack I made great mature speeches at the age of eight in front of interested lawyers and that's when Justin Brierly first heard of me because then he was just beginning to take interest in founding a special juvenile court with particular humane emphasis on the problems of beat children in and around Denver and the Rocky Mountain district..." We were hot; we were going east; we were excited. "Let me tell you more" I said "and only as a parenthesis within what you're saying and to conclude my last thought... As a child lying back in my father's car in the back seat I also had a vision of myself on a white horse riding alongside over every possible obstacle that presented itself: this included dodging posts, hurling around houses, sometimes jumping over when I looked too late, running over hills, across sudden squares with traffic that I had to dodge thru incredibly..." "Yes! yes! yes!" breathed Neal ecstatically "only difference with me was, I myself ran, I had no horse, you were a eastern kid and dreamed of horses, of course we won't assume such things as we both know they are really dross and literary ideas, but merely, that I in my perhaps wilder schizophrenia actually RAN on foot along the car and at incredible speeds sometimes ninety making it over every bush and fence and farmhouse and sometimes taking quick dashes to the hills and back without losing a moment's ground.." We were telling these things and both sweating. We had completely forgotten the people up front who had begun to wonder what was going on in the backseat. At one point the driver said "For God's sakes you're rocking the boat back there." Actually we were, the car was swaying as Neal and I both swayed to the rhythm and the IT of our final excited joy in talking and living to the blank tranced end of all particulars that had been lurking in our souls all our lives. "Oh man! man! man!" moaned Neal "And it's not even the beginning of it...and now here we are at last going East together, we've never gone East together Jack, think of it, we'll dig Denver together and see what everybody's doing altho that matters little to us the point being that we know what IT is and we know TIME and we know that everything is really fine." Then he whispered, clutching my sleeve, sweating: "Now you just dig them in front..They have worries, they're counting the miles, they're thinking about where to sleep tonight, how much money for gas, the weather, how they'll get there...and all the time they'll get there anyway you see. But they need to worry, their souls really won't be at peace unless they can latch on to an established and proven worry and having once found it they assume facial expressions to fit and go with it, which is, you see, unhappiness, a false really false expression of concern and even dignity and all the time it all flies by them and they know it and that TOO worries them NO End. Listen! listen! 'Well now' he mimicked 'I don't knaow---maybe we shouldn't get gas in that station, I read recently in a Petroleum magazine that this kind of gas has a great deal of GOOK in it and someone once told me it even had LOON in it and I don't knaow, well I just don't feel like it anyway...' Man you dig all this"---he was poking me furiously in the ribs to understand. I tried my wildest best. Bing, bang, it was all Yes Yes Yes in the backseat and the people up front were mopping their brows with fright and wishing theyd never picked us up at Travel Bureau. It was only the beginning too. After a wasted night in Sacramento the fag slyly bought a room in a hotel and invited Neal and I to come up for a drink, while the couple went to sleep at relatives, and in the hotel room Neal tried everything in the books to get money from the fag, submitting finally to his advances while I hid in the bathroom and listened. It was insane. The fag began by saying he was very glad we had come along because he liked young men like us, and would we believe it but he really didn't like girls and had recently concluded an affair with a man in Frisco in which he had taken the male role and the man the female role. Neal plied him with businesslike questions and nodded eagerly. The fag said he would like nothing better but to know what Neal thought about all this. Warning him first that he had once been a hustler in his youth, Neal proceeded to handle the fag like a woman, tipping him over legs in the air and all and gave him a monstrous huge banging. I was so non-plussed all I could do was sit and stare from my corner. And after all that trouble the fag turned over no money to us, tho he made vague promises for Denver, and on top of that he became extremely sullen and I think suspicious of Neal's final motives. He kept counting his money and checking on his wallet. Neal threw up his hands and gave up. "You see man, it's better not to bother. Give them what they secretly want and they of course immediately become panic-stricken." But he had sufficiently conquered the owner of the Plymouth to take over the wheel without remonstration, and now we really traveled. We left Sacramento at dawn and were crossing the Nevada desert by noon after a hurling passage of the Sierras that made the fag and the tourists cling to each other in the backseat. We were in front, we took over. Neal was happy again. All he needed was a wheel in his hand and four on the road. He talked about how bad a driver Bill Burroughs was and to demonstrate---"Whenever a huge big truck like that one coming loomed into sight it would take Bill infinite time to spot it, cause he couldn't SEE, man he can't SEE-- 2---" he rubbed his eyes furious to show----"And I'd say whoop, lookout, Bill a truck, and he'd say 'Eh? What's that you Say Neal?' 'Truck! truck!' and at the VERY last MOMENT he would go up to the truck like this"---and Neal hurled the Plymouth head-on at the truck roaring our way, wobbled and hovered in front of it a moment, the truckdriver's face growing white before our eyes, the people in the backseat subsiding in gasps of horror, and swung away at the last moment- "like that you see, exactly like that, that's how bad he was." I wasn't scared at all: I knew Neal. The people in the backseat were speechless. In fact they were afraid to complain: God knows what Neal would do, they thought, if they should ever complain. He balled right across the desert in this manner, demonstrating various ways of how not to drive, how his father used to drive jaloppies, how great drivers made curves, how bad drivers hove over too far in the beginning and had to scramble at the curve's end, and so on. It was a hot sunny afternoon. Reno, Battle Mountain, Elko, all the towns along the Nevada road shot by one after another and at dusk we were in the Salt Lake flats with the lights of Salt Lake City infinitesimally glimmering almost a hundred miles across the mirage of the flats, twice-showing, above and below the curve of the earth, one clear, one dim. I told Neal that the thing that bound us all together in this world was invisible: and to prove it pointed to long lines of telephone poles that curved off out of sight over the bend of a hundred miles of salt. His floppy bandage, all dirty now, shuddered in the air; his face was a light---"Oh yes man, dear God, yes, yes!" Suddenly he collapsed. I turned and saw him huddled in the corner of the seat sleeping. His face was down on his good hand and the bandaged hand, automatically and dutifully remained in the air. The people in the front seat sighed with relief. I heard them whispering mutiny. "We can't let him drive any more, he's absolutely crazy, they must have let him out of an asylum or something." I rose to Neal's defense and leaned forward to talk to them. "He's not crazy, he'll be allright, and don't worry about his driving, he's the best in the world." "I just can't stand it" said the girl with a suppressed hysterical whisper. I sat back and enjoyed nightfall on the desert and waited for poorchild Angel Neal to wake up again. He woke up just as we were on a hill overlooking Salt Lake City's neat patterns of light (the tourists wanted to see a famous hospital up there) and opened his eyes to the place in this spectral world where he was born unnamed and bedraggled years ago. "Jack, Jack, look, this is where I was born, think of it! People change, they eat meals year after year and change with every meal. EE! Look!" He was so excited it made me cry. Where would it all lead? The tourists insisted on driving the car the rest of the way to Denver. Okay, we didn't care. We sat back and talked. In any case they got too tired in the morning and Neal took the wheel in the Eastern Colorado desert at Craig. We spent almost the entire night crawling cautiously over Strawberry Pass in Utah and lost immeasurable time. They went to sleep. Neal headed pellmell for the mighty wall of Berthoud Pass that stood a hundred miles ahead on the roof of the world, a tremendous Gibraltarian door shrouded in clouds. He took Berthoud Pass like a duck on a June bug---same as Tehatchapi, cutting off the motor, floating it, passing everybody and never halting the rhythmic advance that the mountains themselves intended, till we overlooked the great hot plain of Denver again---as I'd first seen it after Central City with the kids---and Neal was home. It was with a great deal of silly relief that these people let us off the car at the corner of 27th and Federal. Our battered suitcases were piled on the sidewalk again; we had longer ways to go. But no matter, the road is life. Now we had a number of circumstances to deal with in Denver and they were of an entirely different order than 1947. We could either get another TB car at once or stay a few days for kicks and look for his father: we decided this. My idea was for Neal and I to live at the house of the woman who had given me the money to go to Frisco. But Justin Brierly knew we were coming through together and had already warned her against "Jack's friend from Frisco" and so when I called on the phone first thing (from the gas station where we were left off) she immediately made it known to me she wouldn't have anything to do with Neal in her house. When I told Neal this he instantly realized he was back in the same old Denver that had never given him any quarter, for in Frisco at least he had found himself a hometown where he was treated like everyone else. In Denver his reputation was too much. I racked my brain for what to do. I finally hit on the idea of having Neal stay at the home of some Okies I knew out on Alameda Blvd. where I had lived briefly with my family, and I would stay with the woman. A darkness came across Neal's face, and from that moment on in Denver he reverted to his youthful days of violence and bitterness. It was him against Denver as long as we were there. When I fully understood this I left the woman's house and went to live with Neal at the Okie woman's house and even then my watchfulness had little effect. First things first: we decided before I went to the woman's house to eat and have a last brief talk in a restaurant. We were both exhausted and dirty. In the john I was taking a leak in a urinal and stepped out before I was finished and aimed to the other urinal, momentarily halting the flow and saying to Neal "Dig this trick." "Yes man it's a very good trick but awful on your kidneys and because you're getting a little older now everytime you do this eventually years of misery in your old age, awful kidney miseries for the days when you sit in parks." It made me mad. "Who's old? I'm not much older than you are!" "I wasn't saying that, man!" "Ah shit," I said "you're always making cracks about my age. I'm no old fag like that sonofabitch, you don't have to warn me about MY kidneys." We went back to the booth and just as the waitress set down the hot roast beef sandwiches---and where ordinarily Neal would have leaped to wolfe the food at once--- I said to cap my anger "And I don't want to hear any more of it."---and suddenly Neal's eyes grew tearful and he got up and left his food steaming there and walked out of the restaurant. I wondered if he was just wandering off forever. I didn't care I was so mad---I had flipped momentarily and turned it down on Neal. But the sight of his uneaten food made me sadder than anything in years. "I shouldn't have said that...he likes to eat so much..he's never left his food like this..What the hell. That's showing him anyway." Neal stood outside the restaurant for exactly five minutes and then came back and sat down. "Well" I said "What were you doing out there? Knotting up your fists, cursing me, thinking up new gags about my kidneys." Neal mutely shook his head. "No man, no man, you're all completely wrong. If you want to know, well---" "Go ahead, tell me." I said all this and never looked up from my food: I felt like a beast. "I was crying" said Neal. "Ah hell you never cry." "You say that? Why do you think I don't cry?" "You don't die enough to cry." Every one of these things I said was a knife at myself. Everything I had ever secretly held against Neal was coming out: how ugly I was and what filth I was discovering in the depths of my own impure psychologies. Neal was shaking his head, "No man, I was crying." "Go on, I bet you were so mad you had to leave." "Believe me, Jack, really do believe me if you've ever believed anything about me." I knew he was telling the truth and yet I didn't want to bother with the truth and when I looked up at him I think I was cock-eyed from cracked intestinal twistings in my awful soul. Then I knew I was wrong. "Ah manNealI'm sorry, I never acted this way before with you. Well now you know me. You know I don't have close relationships with anybody much.. I don't know what to do with these things. I hold things in my hand like they was pieces of turd and don't know where to put it down. Let's forget it." The holy con man began to eat. "It's not my fault! it's not my fault!" I told him. "Nothing in this lousy world is my fault, don't you see that? I don't want it to be and it can't be and it WON'T be." "Yes man, yes man. But please harken back and believe me." "I do believe you, I do." This was the sad story of that afternoon. All kinds of tremendous complications arose that night when Neal went to stay with the Okie family. These had been neighbors of mine. The mother was a wonderful woman in jeans who drove trucks to support her kids, five in all, her husband having left her years before when they were traveling around the country in a trailer. They had rolled all the way from Indiana to LA in that trailer. After many a goodtime and a big Sunday afternoon drunk in crossroads bars and laughter and guitarplaying in the night the big lout had suddenly walked off across the dark field and never returned. Her children were wonderful. The eldest was a boy, who wasn't around that summer but in a camp for delinquent kids in the mountains; next was a lovely 14-yr.-old daughter who wrote poetry and picked flowers in the fields and wanted to grow up and be an actress in Hollywood, Nancy by name; then came the little ones, little Billy who sat around the campfire at night and cried for his "Pee-tater" before it was half roasted, and little Sally who made pets of worms, horny toads, beetles and anything that crawled and gave them names and places to live. They had four dogs. They lived their ragged and joyous lives on the little new-settlement street where my house had been and were the butt of the neighbors' semi-respectable sense of propriety only because the poor woman's husband had left her and because they littered up the yard like humans. At night all the lights of Denver lay like a great wheel on the plain below, for the house was in that part of the west where the mountains roll down foothilling to the plain and where in primeval times soft waves must have washed from sea-like Mississippi to make such round and perfect stools for the island-peaks like Berthoud and terrible Pike and Estes mount. Neal went there and of course he was all sweats and joy at the sight of them especially Nancy but I warned him not to touch her, and probably didn't have to. The woman was a great man's woman and took to Neal right away but she was bashful and he was bashful. The result was uproaring beerdrinking in the littered livinroom and music on the phonograph. The complications rose like clouds of butterflies: the woman, Johnny everyone called her, was finally about to buy a jaloppy as she had been threatening to do for years, and had recently come into a few bucks towards one. (Meanwhile, remember, I was lolling at the woman's house and drinking Scotch.) Neal immediately took over the responsibility of selecting and naming the price of the car, because of course he wanted to use it himself so as of yore he could pick up girls coming out of high school in the afternoons and drive them up to the mountains. Poor innocent Okie Johnny was always agreeable to anything. The following afternoon Neal called up from the country and said "Man I don't want to bother you but I swear and swear my shoes are no longer wearable, I absolutely need another pair of shoes, what shall we do?" By a wonderful coincidence I had a pair of old shoes sitting around Clementine's closet. I said to her, holding the phone, "Listen Neal absolutely needs shoes- -I'm going to give him the old pair. How about letting him come over and pick them up?" "No, definitely no" she said and how forewarned can you get but we agreed that I could meet him on the corner down the street and hand them over. "Yass, o yass" said Neal sensing all this, and he hitched in from the country and met me half an hour later on the corner. It was a beautiful warm sunny afternoon. I had also been dispatched to get a quart of vanilla ice cream for Clementine's supper party with friends and came to Neal, whom I found playing baseball with a bunch of kids while he waited, carrying an old pair of shoes in a brown paper bag and a quart of vanilla ice cream. "There you are man---oh yes, oh yes vanilla ice cream, lemme taste." I put the ice cream on the ground and began firing high hard ones at the kid catcher, then I took over the catcher's mitt and squatted by the lubrication pit of the gas station and Neal fired some in. We were having a great time. We showed the kids how to fashion curves and make them drop. Then we played high flies and Neal went scattering among the traffic of 27th St. with his thumb stuck breast-high like a shield and the glove upheld for the flyball that dribbled down through branches and leaves of high old trees. Suddenly I noticed the ice cream was melting. "Say Neal what am I, a con man? I think I'll move in with you and Johnny tonight." "Why of course man, what did you do it in the first place for?" "I thought I had some loyalty I owed Clementine---she gave me money to go to Frisco. I don't know." I didn't know what I was doing. Neal and I shook hands on the corner and made a meet for eight o'clock in the Glenarm bar, the old hangout near the poolhall. I went back to Clementine and told her I was leaving for NY that night. She made a tremendous fried chicken dinner and for dessert strawberry pie with vanilla a la mode. I liked this woman and you can see why I owed her some attention. She was wise, too. "If you're not really leaving for NY tonight come back any time and we'll have a drink." I rushed off guiltily. Things are so hard to figure when you live from day to day in this feverish and silly world. Neal was very excited that night because his brother Jack Daly was meeting us at the bar. He was wearing his best suit and beaming all over. "Now listen Jack, I must tell you about my brother Jack---he's really my stepbrother, my mother's son before she married Old Neal in Missouri." "By the way have you looked for your father." "This afternoon man I went down to Jigg's buffet where he used to pour draft beer in tender befuddlement and get hell from the boss and go staggering out- -no- -and I went to the old barbershop next to the Windsor- -no, not there---Old fellow told me he thought he was- -Imagine!- - working in a railroad cookshack for the BOSTON & MAINE in New England! But I don't believe him, they make up fractious stories for a dime. Now listen to hear. In my childhood Jack Daly my stepbrother was my absolute hero. He used to bootleg whiskey from the mountains and one time he had a tremendous fist fight with his other brother that lasted two hours in the yard and had the women screaming and terrified- - We used to sleep together. The one man in the family who took tender concern for me. And tonight I'm going to see him again for the first time in seven years, he just got back from Kansas City." "And what's the pitch?" "No pitch man, I only want to know what's been happening in the family---I have a family, remember---and most particuarly, Jack, I want him to tell me things that I've forgotten in my childhood, I want to remember, remember, I do!" I never saw Neal so glad and excited. While we waited for his brother in the bar he talked to a lot of younger Glenarm Denver downtown hustlers of the new day and checked on new gangs and goings-on.

Then he made inquiries after Louanne, since she'd been in Denver recently. I sat over a glass of beer remembering Denver 1947 and wondering. Then Jack Daly arrived---a wiry curly-haired man of thirty five with work-gnarled hands. Neal stood in awe before him. "No," said Jack Daly "I don't drink any more." "See? see?" whispered Neal in my ear "he doesn't drink any more and he used to be the biggest whiskeyleg in town; he's got religion now, he told me over the phone, dig him, dig the change in a man.. my hero has become so strange." Jack Daly was suspicious of his young stepbrother. He took us out for a spin in his old rattly coupe and in the car first thing he made his position clear as regards Neal. "Now look Neal, I don't believe you any more or anything you're going to try to tell me---I came to see you tonight because there's a paper I want you to sign for the family. Your father is no longer mentioned among us and we want absolutely nothing to do with him, and I'm sorry to say with you either any more." I looked at Neal. His face dropped and darkened. "Yass, yass" he said. The brother condescended to drive us around and even bought us ice cream pops. Nevertheless Neal plied him with innumerable questions about the past and he supplied the answers and for a moment Neal almost began to sweat again with excitement. Oh where was his raggedy father that night? The brother dropped us off at the sad lights of a carnival on Alameda blvd. at Federal. He made an appointment with Neal for the paper-signing next afternoon and left. I told Neal I was sorry he had nobody in the world to believe him. "Remember that I believe in you. I'm infinitely sorry for the foolish grievance I held against you yesterday afternoon." "Allright man, it's agreed" said Neal. We dug the carnival together. There were merry-gorounds, sad ferris wheels, popcorn, roulette wheels, sawdust and hundreds of young Denver kids in Levis wandering around. Dust rose to the stars together with every sad music on earth. Neal was wearing extremely tight Levis and a T. Shirt and looked suddenly like a real Denver character again. There were motorcycle kids with visors and mustaches and beaded jackets hanging around the shrouds in back of the tents with pretty girls in Levis and rose shirts. There were a lot of Mexican girls too and one amazing little girl about three feet hi, really a midget, with the most beautiful and tender face in the world who turned to her companion and said "Man let's call up Gomez and get out." Neal stopped dead in his tracks at the sight of her. A great knife stabbed him from the darkness of the night. "Man I love her, I <u>love</u> her.." We had to follow her around for a long time. She finally went across the hi way to make a phonecall in a motel booth and Neal pretended to be looking through the pages of the directory but was really all wound towards her. I tried to open up a conversation with the lovey-doll's friends but they paid no attention to us. Gomez arrived in a rattly truck - - just like Dah-you-Go Freddy in Fresno- -and took the girls off. Neal stood in the road clutching his breast. "Oh man, I almost died.." "Why didn't you talk to her?" "I can't, I can't…" We decided to buy some beer and go up to Okie Johnnie's and play records. We hitched on the road with a bag of beercans. Little Nancy Johnny's 14-yr-old dotter was the prettiest girl in the world and was about to grow up into a gone woman. Best of all were her long tapering sensitive fingers that she used to talk with. Neal sat in the furthest corner of the room watching her with slitted eyes and saying "Yes, yes, yes." Nancy was aware of him; she turned to me for protection. Previous months of that summer I had spent a lot of time with her talking about books and little things she was interested in and to be utterly truthful the mother was harboring our marriage in her mind in a few future years. I would have liked the idea, too, the only thing wrong with it being I felt responsibility towards the whole family and of course I didn't have the money to undertake any such mad scheme---the end would have been driving around the country in a trailer and working and my having a more mature relationship with the mother and a lovey-dovey one with the daughter. I wasn't quite ready for the strain of real abysmal drowning in the pit of night which it would have been. Nothing happened that night; we went to sleep. Everything happened the next day. In the afternoon Neal and I went to downtown Denver for our various chores and to see the Travel Bureau for a car to New York. I called Justin W. Brierly and he arranged to meet me and Neal for an afternoon talk. He drove up in his frantic Oldsmobile with the powerful spotlight and stepped out, Panama-hatted and Palm-Beach suit, and said "Well well well, Happy New Year." With him was Dan Burmeister a tall curly headed college boy who despised Neal and knew him from years back. Neal and Brierly met face to face for the first time since the evening in New York when Allen Ginsberg had bowed to his poetry. "Well Neal you look much older" said Brierly over his shoulder. "What have you been doing with yourself." "Oh same old thing, you know. Now I wonder if you could drive me to St. Luke's hospital so I could have this thumb looked after and you can have yr. talk with Jack." "Why that's fine" said Brierly. The idea had been for all of us to talk---and the idea of the thumb was new to me. Neal just didn't want to bother, nor did Brierly. Child and master had come to the end of their road. Neal whispered in my ear "Have you noticed he has to wear dark glasses now to conceal those awful rings under his eyes, and how pale and watery they've become and sort of red and sickly?" I sat in my neutral position. When I was alone with Burmeister and Brierly they began dissecting Neal and asking me why I bothered with him. "I think he's a great guy- -I know what you're going to say---You know that I tried to straighten out my family---" I didn't know what to say. I felt like crying, Goddamit everybody in the world wants an explanation for your acts and for your very being. We switched the subject and talked of other things. Ed White was still in Paris, so was Bob Burford who'd sent for his Denver sweetheart to come and marry him there, and so was Frank Jeffries. "Jeffries is in the South of France living in a whore house, you know, and having a very wonderful time. Of course Ed is amusing himself in the museums and elsewhere as ever." They watched me keenly wondering what I had to do with Neal. "And how is Clementine?" they asked, slyly. "Someday Neal will prove himself to be a great man or a great idiot" I said. "My interest in Neal is the interest I might have had in my brother that died when I was five years old to be utterly straight about it. We have a lot of fun together and our lives are fuckt up and so there it stands. Do you know how many states we've been in together?" I got all joyful and began telling them the stories. I rejoined Neal in the late afternoon and we started out for Okie Johnny's, up Broadway, where Neal suddenly sauntered into a sports goods store, calmly picked up a softball on the counter, and came out popping it up and down in his palm. Nobody noticed, nobody ever notices such things. It was a drowsy hot afternoon. We played catch as we went along. "We'll get a Travel Bureau car for sure tomorrow." Clementine had given me a big quart of Old Granddad Bourbon. We started drinking it at Johnny's house. Across the cornfield in back lived a beautiful young chick that Neal had been trying to make ever since he arrived. Trouble was brewing. He threw too many pebbles in her window and frightened her. As we drank the bourbon in the littered livingroom with all its dogs and scattered toys and sad talk Neal kept running out the back kitchen door and crossing the cornfield to throw pebbles and whistle. Once in a while Nancy went out to peek. Suddenly Neal came back pale. "Trouble, m'boy. That gal's mother is after me with a shotgun and she got a gang of hi school kids to beat me up from down the road." "What's this? Where are they?" "Across the cornfield m'boy." Neal was drunk and didn't care. We went out together and crossed the cornfield in the moonlight. I saw groups of people on the dark dirt road. "Here they come!" I heard. "Wait a minute" I said "What's the matter please?" The mother lurked in the background with a big shotgun across her arm. "That damn friend of yours been annoying us long enough---I'm not the kind to call the law---if he comes back here once more I'm gonna shoot and shoot to kill." The hischool boys were clustered with their fists knotted. I was so drunk I didn't care either but I soothed everybody some. I said "He won't do it again, I'll watch him, he's my brother and listens to me. Please put your gun away and don't bother about anything." "Just one more time!" she said firmly and grimly across the dark. "When my husband gets home I'm sending him after you." "You don't have to do that, he won't bother you any more, understand, now be calm and it's okay." Behind me Neal was cursing under his breath. The girl was peeking from her bedroom window. I knew these people from before and they trusted me enough to quiet down a bit. I took Neal by the arm and back we went over the moony corn-rows. "Woo-hee!" he yelled. "I'm gonna git drunk tonight." We went back to Johnny and the kids. Suddenly Neal got mad at a record little Nancy was playing and broke it over his knee: it was a hillbilly record. There was an early Dizzy Gillespie there that he valued- -I'd given it to Nancy before- -and I told her as she wept to take it and break it over Neal's head. She went over and did so. Neal gaped dumbly. We all laughed. Everything was all right. Then Johnny wanted to go out and drink beer in the roadhouse saloons. "Lessgo!" yelled Neal. "Now dammit if you'd bought that car I showed you Tuesday we wouldn't have to walk." "I didn't like that damn car!" yelled Johnny. Little Billy was frightened: I put him to sleep on the couch and trussed the dogs on him. Johnny drunkenly called a cab and suddenly while we were waiting for it a phonecall came for me from Clementine. Clementine had a middleaged boyfriend who hated my guts, naturally, and earlier that afternoon I had written a letter to Bill Burroughs who was now in Mexico City relating the adventures of Neal and I and under what circumstances we were staying in Denver. I wrote: "I'm staying with a woman and having a right good time." I foolishly gave this letter to the middleaged boyfriend to mail, right after the fried chicken supper. He surreptitiously opened it, read it, and took it at once to Clementine to prove to her that I was a conman. Now she was calling me tearfully and saying she'd never want to see me again. Then the triumphant middleaged boyfriend got on the phone and began calling me a bastard. As the cab honked outside and the kids cried and the dogs barked and Neal danced with Johnny I yelled every conceivable curse I could think over that phone and added all kinds of new ones and in my drunken frenzy I told everybody over the phone to go to hell and slammed it down and went out to get drunk. We stumbled over each other to get out of the cab at the road-house---a hillbilly roadhouse near the hills---and went on and ordered beers. Everything was collapsing, and to make things inconceivably more frantic there was an ecstatic spastic fellow in the bar who threw his arms around Neal and moaned in his face and Neal went mad again with sweats and insanity, and to further the unbearable confusion Neal rushed out the next moment and stole a car right from the driveway and took a dash to downtown Denver and came back with a newer better one. Suddenly in the bar I looked up and saw cops and people were milling around the driveway in the headlights of cruisers talking about the stolen car. "Somebody's been stealing cars left and right here!" the cop was saying. Neal stood right in back of him listening and saying "Ah yass, ah yass." The cops went off to check. Neal came in the bar and rocked back and forth with the poor spastic kid who had just gotten married that day and was having a tremendous drunk while his bride waited somewhere. "Oh man, this guy is the greatest in the world!" yelled Neal. "Jack, Johnny, I'm going out and get a real good car this time and we'll all go and with Albert too" (the spastic saint) "and have a big drive in the mountains." And he rushed out. Simultaneously a cop rushed in and said a car stolen from downtown Denver was parked in the driveway. People discussed it in knots. From the window I saw Neal jump into the nearest car and roar off, and not a soul noticed him. A few minutes later he was back in an entirely different car, a brand new Plymouth. "This one is a real beaut!" he whispered in my ear. "The other one coughed too much--- I left it at the crossroads...saw that lovely parked in front of a farmhouse. Took a spin in Denver. Come on man let's ALL go riding." All the bitterness and madness of his entire Denver life was blasting out of his system like daggers from his poors. His face was red and sweaty and mean. "No, I ain't gonna have nothing to do with stolen cars." "Aw come on man! Albert'll come with me, won't you Albert?" And Albert---a thin dark-haired holy-eyed moaning foaming lost soul--- leaned on Neal and groaned and groaned for he was sick suddenly and for some odd intuitive reason he became terrified of Neal and threw up his hands and drew away with terror writhing in his face. Neal bowed his head and sweated. He ran out and drove away. Johnny and I found a cab in the driveway and decided to go home. As the cabby drove us home up the infinitely dark Alameda boulevard along which I had walked many and many a lost night the previous months of the summer, singing and moaning and eating the stars and dropping the juices of my heart drop by drop on the hot night tar, Neal suddenly hove up behind us in the stolen Plymouth and began tooting and tooting and crowding us over and screaming. The cabby's face grew white. "Just a friend of mine" I said. Neal got disgusted with us and suddenly shot ahead ninety miles an hour and we watched his sad red tail-light vanishing towards the unseen mountains throwing spectral dust across the exhaust. Then he turned in at Johnny's road and almost filled the ditch and took another right and pulled up in front of the house; just as suddenly took off again, U-turned and went back towards town as we got out of the cab and paid the fare. A few moments later as we waited anxiously in the dark yard he returned with still another car, a battered coupe, stopped it in a cloud of dust in front of the house and just staggered out and went straight into the bedroom and flopped dead drunk on the bed. And there we were with a stolen car right on our doorstep. I had to wake him up, I couldn't get the car started myself and dump it somewhere far off. He stumbled out of bed wearing just his jockey shorts and we got in the car together---while the kids giggled from the windows---and went bouncing and flying straight over the corn-rows at the end of the road till finally the car couldn't take any more and stopped dead under an old cottonwood near the old mill. "Can't go any further" said Neal simply and got out and started walking back over the cornfield, about a half mile, in his shorts. We got back to the house and he went to sleep. Everything was in a horrible mess, all of Denver, Clementine, cars, children, poor Johnny, the livingroom splattered with beer and cans and I simply went to sleep myself. A cricket kept me awake for sometime. At night in this part of the West the stars, as I had seen them in Wyoming, are big as Roman Candles and as lonely as the Prince who's lost his ancestral home and journeys across the spaces trying to find it again, and knows he never will. So they slowly wheeled the night and then long before ordinary dawn the great red sun appeared far over entire territorial areas of dun land towards

West Kansas and the birds sang above Denver. Where were the old Denver Birds, the ones I understood? Horrible nauseas possessed Neal and I in the morning. First thing he did was go out across the cornfield to see if the car would carry us East. I told him no go but he went anyway. He came back pale. "Man, that's a detective's car and every precinct in town knows my fingerprints from the year that I stole five hundred cars. You see what I do with them, I just wanta ride man! I gotta go! Listen, we're going to wind up in jail if we don't get out of here this very instant." "You damned right" I said and we began packing faster than our hands could go. Dangling neckties and shirt tails we said quick goodbyes to our sweet little family and stumbled off towards the protective road where nobody would know. Little Nancy was crying to see us, or me, or whatever it was, go---and Johnny was courteous, and I kissed her and apologized. "He sure is a crazy one," she said "he reminds me of my husband that run away. Just exactly the same guy. I sure hope my Mickey don't grow up that way, they all do now." Mickey was her son, the one in delinquent school. "Tell him not to steal coca cola cases" I said "He told me that's what he was doing and that's the way he'll innocently start till the cops start beating him up." And I said goodbye to little Sally who had her pet beetle in her hand, and little Billy was asleep. All this in the space of seconds, in a lovely Sunday morning dawn, as we stumbled off with our wretched baggage across the nauseas of the night before. We hurried. Every minute we expected a cruising car to suddenly appear from around a country bend and come sloping for us. "If that woman with the shotgun ever finds out we're cooked" said Neal. "We MUST get a cab" I said "Then we're safe." We tried to wake up a farm family to use their phone but the dog drove us away. Every minute things became more dangerous, the coupe would be found wrecked in the corn by any early-rising country man. One lovely old lady let us use her phone finally and we called a downtown Denver cab but he didn't come. We stumbled on down the road. Early morning traffic began, every car looking like a cruiser. Then we suddenly saw the cruiser coming and I knew it was the end of my life as I had known it and that it was entering a new and horrible stage of jails and iron sorrows, such as Egyptian kings must know in the drowsy afternoon when the fight is up in the reeds of the mires. But the cruiser was our taxi and from that moment on we flew East and had to. At the Travel Bureau there was a tremendous offer for someone to drive a 47 Cadillac limousine to Chicago. The owner had been driving up from Mexico with his family and got tired and put them all on a train. All he wanted was identification and for the car to get there. I showed the man- -a squat Italian Chicago baron---my papers and assured him everything would come off right. I told Neal "And don't fuck up with this car." Neal was jumping up and down with excitement to see it. We had to wait an hour. We lay on the grass near the church where in 1947 I had passed some time with panhandling hoboes after seeing Ruth G. home and there I fell asleep from sheer horror and exhaustion with my face to the afternoon birds. But Neal hustled right around town. He drew up a talking acquaintance with a waitress in a luncheonette and as of yore, when he had her alone outside, persuaded her the sun and the moon and she innocently accepted and must have been an impulsive girl. In any case Neal made a date to take her driving in his Cadillac that afternoon, and came back to wake me with the news. Now I felt better. I rose to the new complications. When the Cadillac arrived Neal instantly drove off with it "to get gas" and the Travel Bureau man looked at me and said "When's he coming back. The passengers are all ready to go and waiting." He showed me two Irish boys from an Eastern Jesuit school waiting with their suitcases on the benches. "He just went for gas. He'll be right back." I cut down to the corner and watched Neal as he waited for the waitress, who had been changing in her room on the corner of 17th and Grant, in fact I could see her from where I stood in front of her mirror primping and fixing her silk stockings and I wished I could go along with them. She came running out of the hotel and jumped in the Cadillac. I wandered back to reassure the TB boss and the passengers. From where I stood in the door I saw a faint flash of the Cadillac crossing Cleveland Place with Neal, T-shirted and joyous, fluttering his hands and talking to the girl and hunching over the wheel to go as she sat sadly and proudly beside him. They went to a parking lot in broad daylight, parked near the brickwall at the back (a lot Neal had worked in) and there, he claims, he laid her in nothing flat; not only that but persuaded her to follow us East as soon as she had her pay on Friday, come by bus, and meet us at John Holmes' apt. on Lex avenue New York. She agreed to come; her name was Beverly. Thirty minutes and Neal roared back, deposited the girl at her hotel, with kisses, farewells, promises, and zoomed right up to the TB to pick up the crew. "Well it's about time!" said the Broadway Sam TB boss. "I thought you'd gone off with that Cadillac." "It's my responsibility" I said "don't worry"---and said that because Neal was in such obvious frenzy everybody could guess his madness and complete uncare. Neal became businesslike and coughing and assisted the Jesuit boys with their baggage. They were hardly seated, and I had hardly waved good-bye to Denver, before he was off, the big motor thrumming with immense birdlike power. Not two miles out of Denver the speedom-eter broke because Neal was pushing well over 110 miles an hour. "Well no speedometer, I won't know how fast I'm going, I'll just ball that jack to Chicago and tell by time." It didn't seem we were even going seventy but all the cars fell from us like dead flies on the straightaway hiway leading up to Greeley. "Reason why we're going northeast is because, Jack, we must absolutely visit Ed Uhl's ranch in Sterling, you've got to meet him and see his ranch and this boat cuts so fast we can make it without any time-trouble and get to Chicago long before that man's train." Okay, I was for it. It began to rain but Neal never slackened. It was a beautiful big limousine, the last of the old-style limousines, black, with a big elongated square body and whitewall tires and probably bulletproof windows. The Jesuit boys---St. Bonaventura---sat in the back gleeful and glad to be underway, and they had no idea how fast we were going. They tried to talk but Neal said nothing and took off his T-shirt and just drove the rest of the way barechested. "Oh that Beverly is a sweet gone little gal---she's going to join me in NY---we're going to get married as soon as I can get divorce papers from Carolyn---everything's jumping Jack and we're off. Yes!" The faster we left Denver the better I felt and we were doing it <u>fast.</u> It grew dark when we turned off the hiway at Junction and hit a dirt road that took us across dismal E. Colorado plains to Ed Uhl's ranch in the middle of Coyote Nowhere. But it was still raining and the mud was slippery and Neal slowed to seventy, but I told him to slow even more or we'd slide, and he said "Don't worry, man, you know me." "Not this time" I said "You're really going much too fast." And just as I said that we hit a complete left turn in the hiway and Neal socked the wheel over to make it but the big car skidded in the greasy mud and wobbled hugely. "Lookout!" yelled Neal who didn't give a damn and wrestled with his Angel a moment and the worse that happened we ended up backass in the ditch with the front out on the road. A great stillness fell over everything. We heard the whining wind. We were suddenly in the middle of the wild prairie. There was a farmhouse a quarter mile up the road. I couldn't stop swearing I was so mad and disgusted with Neal. He said nothing and went off to the farmhouse in the rain, with a coat, to see for help. "Is he your brother?" the boys asked in the back seat. "He's a devil with a car isn't he?---and according to his story he must be with the women." "He's mad" I said "an yes, he's my brother." I saw Neal coming back with the farmer in his tractor. They hooked chains on and the farmer hauled us out of the ditch. The car was muddy brown, a whole fender was cracked. With the speedometer already broken it was only the beginning. The farmer charged us five dollars. His daughters watched in the rain. The prettiest, shyest one hid far back in the field to watch and she had good reasons because she was absolutely and finally the most beautiful girl Neal and I ever saw in all our lives. She was about sixteen, and had a plains complexion like wild roses, and the bluest eyes, and most lovely hair, and the modesty and quickness of a wild antelope. Every look from us and she flinched. She stood there with the immense winds that blew clear down from Saskatchewan knocking her hair about her lovely head like shrouds, living curls of them. She blushed and blushed. We finished our business with the farmer, took one last look at the prairie rose, and drove off, slower now, till dark came and Neal said Ed Uhl's ranch was dead ahead. "Oh a girl like that scares me" I said. "I'd give up everything and throw myself at her mercy and if she didn't want me I'd just as simply go and throw myself off the edge of the world." The Jesuit boys giggled. They were full of corny quips and eastern college talk and had nothing, positively nothing on their bird-beans except a lot of Aquinas for stuffing for their pepper. Neal and I paid absolutely no attention to them. As we crossed the muddy plains he told stories about his cowboy days, he showed us the stretch of road where he spent an entire morning riding; and where he'd done fence mending as soon as we hit Uhl's property, which was immense; and where old Uhl, Ed's father, used to come clattering on the rangeland grass chasing a heifer and howling. "Git im, git im goddammit!" He sounded as mad as Kells Elvins' paretic father. "He had to have a new car every six months" said Neal "He just didn't care. When a stray got away from us he'd drive right after it as far as the nearest waterhole and then get out and run after it on foot. Counted every cent he ever made and put it in a pot. A mad old rancher. I'll show you some of his old wrecks near the bunkhouse. This is where I came on probation after my last hitch in a joint. This is where I lived when I wrote those letters you saw to Hal Chase." We turned off the road and wound across a path through the winter pasture. A great mournful group of whitefaced cows suddenly milled across our headlights. "There they are! - -Uhl's cows! We'll never be able to get through them. We'll have to get out and whoop 'em up! Hee hee hee!!" But we didn't have to do that and only inched along through them sometimes gently bumping as they milled and mooed like a sea around the cardoors. Beyond we saw the lonely lights of Ed Uhl's ranchouse. Around these lonely lights stretched hundreds and hundreds of miles of plains with nothing on them but twenty or so ranchouses like his. The kind of utter darkness that falls on a prairie like that is inconceivable to an Easterner. There were no stars, no moon, no light whatever except the light of Mrs. Uhl's kitchen. What lay beyond the shadows of the yard was an endless view of the world that you wouldn't be able to see till dawn. After knocking on the door and calling out in the dark for Ed Uhl who was milking cows in the barn I took a short careful walk into that darkness, about twenty feet and no more. Me seems I heard coyotes. Uhl said what I heard was probably one of his father's wild horses whinnying in the distance. Ed Uhl was about our age, tall, rangy, spike-teeth, laconic. Neal had made a great story in the car about how he used to bang Ed's wife before he married her. He and Neal used to stand around on Curtis st. corners and whistle at girls. Now he took us graciously into his gloomy brown unused parlor and fished around till he found dull lamps and lit them and said to Neal "What in the hell happened to yore thumb?" "I socked Louanne and it got infected so much they had to amputate the end of it." "What in the hell did you go and do that for?" I could see he used to be Neal's older brother. He shook his head; the milk pail was still at his feet. "You always been a crack-brained sonofabitch anyhow." Meanwhile his young wife prepared a magnificent spread in the big ranch kitchen. She apologized for the peach ice cream. "It ain't nothing but cream and peaches froze-up together." Of course it was the only real ice cream I ever had in my whole life. She started sparsely and ended up abundantly; as we ate new things appeared on the table. She was a well built blonde but like all women who live in the wide spaces she complained a little of the boredom. She enumerated the radio programs she usually listened to at this time of night. Ed Uhl sat just staring at his hands. Neal ate voraciously. He wanted me to go along with him in the fiction that I owned the Cadillac, that I was a very rich man and Neal was my friend and chauffeur. It made no impression on Ed Uhl. Every time the stock made sounds in the barn he raised his head to listen. "Well I hope you boys make it to New York." Far from believing that tale about my owning the Cadillac he was convinced Neal had stolen it. We stayed at the ranch about an hour. Ed Uhl had lost faith in Neal just like Jack Daly---he only looked at him warily when he looked. There were riotous days in the past when they had stumbled around the streets of Laramie Wyoming arm-in-arm when the haying was over and this was dead and gone. Neal hopped in his chair convulsively. "Well yes, well yes, and now I think we'd better be cutting along because we gotta be in Chicago by tomorrow night and we've already wasted several hours." The college boys thanked Uhl graciously and we were off again. I turned to watch the kitchen light recede in the sea of night. Then I leaned ahead. In no time at all we were back on the highway and that night I saw the entire state of Nebraska unroll perceptibly before my eyes. A hundred and ten miles an hour straight through, an arrow road, sleeping towns, no traffic, and the Union Pacific streamliner falling behind us in the moonlight. I wasn't frightened at all that night; it was the next day when I saw how fast we were going that I gave it up and went in the back seat to shut my eyes. Now in the moony night it was perfectly legitimate to go 110 and talk and have all the Nebraska towns---Ogallala, Gothenburg, Kearny, Grand Island, Columbus---unreel with dreamlike rapidity as we roared ahead and talked. It was a magnificent car, it could hold the road like a boat holds water. Gradual curves were its singing ease. But Neal was punishing this car and by the time we got to Chicago, not the next night but when it was still daylight, the rods were all but gone. "Ah man what a dreamboat" sighed Neal. "Think if you and I had a car like this what we could do. Do you know there's a road that goest down Mexico and all the way to Panama?- -and maybe all the way to the bottom of South America where the Indians are seven feet tall and eat cocaine on the mountainside? Yes! You and I, Jack, we'd dig the whole world with a car like this because man the road must eventually lead to the whole world. Ain't nowhere else it can go? Right? Oh and are we going to cut around old Chi with this thing! Think of it Jack I've never been to Chicago in all my life." "We'll come in there like gangsters in this Cadillac!" "Yes! And girls!---we can pick up girls, in fact Jack I've decided to make extra special fast time so we can have an entire evening to cut around in this thing. Now you just relax and I'll ball the jack all the way." "Well how fast are you going now?" "A steady one-ten I figure---you wouldn't notice it. We've still got all Iowa in the daytime and then I'll make that old Illinois in nothing flat." The boys fell asleep and we talked and talked all night. It was remarkable how Neal could go mad and then suddenly the next day just calmly and sanely continue with his soul---which I think is wrapped in a fast car, a coast to reach, and a woman at the end of the road---as tho nothing happened. "I get like that every time in Denver now---I can't make that town any more. Gooky, gooky, Neal's a spooky. Zoom!" We went thru a ghostlike town and resumed. I told him I had been over this Nebraska road before in 47. He had too. "Jack when I was working for the New Era Laundry in Los Angeles 1945 I made a trip to Indianapolis Indiana for the express purpose of seeing the Memorial Day races hitch hiking by day and stealing cars by night to make time. I was coming thru one of these towns we passed with a set of license plates under my shirt when a sheriff picked me up on suspicion. I made the most magnificent speech in my life to get out of that---telling him I was torn between a vision of Jesus and my old habits of stealing cars and had picked up the plates only to weigh the issue in my hand, of course that didn't work until I started crying and beating my head on the desk and I meant it, I meant it! that's the point---real awful feelings possessed me and at the same time every moment wasted made me later and later for the races. Of course I missed them, damn it, they sent me back to Denver on probation and everything was cleared there. The following Fall I did the same thing again to see the Notre Dame-Ohio State game in South Bend Indiana- -no hitch that time and Jack I had just the money for the ticket and didn't eat anything all the way up and back except for what I could panhandle from all kinds of crazy cats I met on the road and at the game and so on. How mad I was then!---I was probably the only guy in the world who went to such trouble to see an old ballgame and trying to gun cunts along the way." I asked him the circumstances of his being in LA 1945. "I was arrested in California, you know. The name of the joint won't mean anything to you but it was___ ___absolutely the worst place I've been in. I had to escape---I pulled the greatest escape in my life speaking of escapes you see in a general way. Well I got out and had to walk across the woods with the fear if they caught me they'd really give it to me---I mean rubber hoses and the works and probably accidental death. I had to get rid of my joint clothes and sneaked the neatest theft of a shirt and pants from a gas station, arriving in LA clad as gas attendant and walked to first station I saw and got hired and got myself a room and changed name and spent an exciting year in LA including a whole gang of new friends and some really great girls, that season ending when we were all driving on Hollywood boulevard one night and I told my buddy to steer the car while I kissed my girl- -I was at the wheel, see---and HE DIDN'T HEAR ME and we ran smack into a post but only going twenty and I broke my nose. You've seen before my nose...the crooked Grecian curve up here. After that I went to Denver and met Louanne in a sodafountain that spring. Oh man she was only fifteen and wearing Levis and just waiting for someone to pick her up. Three days and three nights of talk in the Ace Hotel, third floor, southeast corner room, a holy memento room and sacred scene of my days---she was so sweet then, so young, so whorish, so mine. Ah man I get older and older. Hup! hup! look at those old bums by the track there with a fire." He almost slowed down. "You see, I never know whether my father's there or not." There were some figures by the tracks reeling in front of a woodfire. "I never know whether to ask. He might be anywhere." We drove on. Somewhere behind us or in front of us in the huge night his father lay drunk under a bush, and no doubt about it---spittle on his chin, piss on his pants, molasses in his ears, goo in his nose, maybe blood on his hair and the moon shining down on him. I took Neal's arm. "Ah man, we're sure going home now." New York was going to be his permanent home for the first time. He jiggled all over he couldn't wait fast enough. "And think, Jack, when we get to Pennsy we'll start hearing that gone Eastern bop on the disc jockeys. Geeyah, roll old boat roll!" That magnificent car made the wind roar; it made the plains unfold like a roll of paper; it cast hot tar from itself with deference---an imperial boat. Long after we'd left the great sage spaces of the Sandhills it bruited its immense snout bearing the dust of same through dews of Nile-like valleys and early morn. I opened my eyes to a fanning dawn; we were hurling up to it. Neal's rocky dogged face as ever bent over the dashlight with a bony purpose of its own. "What are you thinking Pops?" "Ah-ha, ah-ha same old thing, y'know---gurls gurls gurls. Together also with a flitting thought & vagrant dreams-bedeviled with broken promises- -hup! ahem!" There was nothing to say in a good boat like that. I went to sleep and woke up to the dry hot atmospheres of July Sunday morning in Iowa, and still Neal was driving and driving and had not slackened his speed the least bit except the curvy corndales of Iowa at a minimum of 80 and the straightaway 110 as usual unless bothways traffic forced him to fall in line at a crawling and most miserable 60. When there was a chance he shot ahead and passed cars by the half-dozen and left them behind in a cloud of dust. A mad guy in a brand new Buick saw all this on the road and decided to race us. When Neal was just about to pass a pas-sel he shot by us without warning and howled and tooted his horn and flashed the tail lights for challenge. We took off after him like a bird dog. "Now wait" laughed Neal "I'm going to tease that sonofa-bitch for a dozen miles or so. Watch." He let the Buick go way ahead and then accelerated and caught up with it most impolitely. Mad Buick went out of his mind: he gunned up to 100. We had a chance to see who he was. He seemed to be some kind of Chicago hipster traveling with a woman old enough to be, and probably actually his mother. God knows if she was complaining but he raced. His hair was dark and wild, an Italian from Old Chi; he wore a sports shirt. There was probably an idea in his mind that we were a new gang from LA invading Chicago, maybe some of Mickey Cohen's men, because the limousine looked every bit the part and the license plates were Cali-fornia. Mainly it was just road kicks. He took terrible chances to stay ahead of us, he passed cars on curves and barely got back in line as a truck wobbled into view and loomed up huge. Eighty miles of Iowa we unreeled in this fashion and the race was so interesting that I had no opportunity to be frightened. Then the mad guy gave up, pulled up at a gas station, probably on orders from the old lady, and as we roared by he waved gleefully and acknowledged everything. On we sped, Neal bare-chested, I with my feet on the dashboard, and the college boys sleeping in the back. We stopped to eat breakfast at a diner run by a white haired lady of the land who gave us extra large portions of potatoes as churchbells rang in the nearby town. Then off again. "Neal don't drive so fast in the daytime." "Don't worry man I know what I'm doing." I began to flinch. Neal came up on lines of cars like the Angel of Terror. He almost rammed them along as he looked for an opening. He teased their bumpers, he eased and pushed and craned around to see the curve, then the huge car leaped to his touch and passed and always by a hair we made it back to our side as other lines filed by in the opposite direction and I shuddered. I couldn't take it any more. It is only seldom that you find a long Nebraskan straightaway in Iowa and when we finally hit one Neal made his usual 110 and I saw flashing by outside several scenes that I remembered from 1947---a long stretch where Eddy and I had been stranded two hours. All that old road of my past unreeling dizzily as if the cup of life had been overturned and everything gone mad. My eyes ached in nightmare day. "Ah shit Neal, I'm going in the backseat, I can't stand it any more, I can't look." "Hee hee hee!" tittered Neal and he passed a car on a narrow bridge and swerved in dust and roared on. I jumped in the backseat and curled up to sleep. One of the boys jumped in front for the fun. Great paranoiac horrors that we were going to crash this very morning took hold of me and I got down on the floor and closed my eyes and tried to go to sleep. As a seaman I used to think of the waves rushing beneath the shell of the ship and the bottomless deeps thereunder---now I could feel the road some twenty inches beneath me unfurling and flying and hissing at incredible speeds and on and on across the groaning continent. When I closed my eyes all I could see was the road unwinding into me. When I opened them I saw flashing shadows of trees vibrating on the floor of the car. There was no escaping it. I resigned myself to all. And still Neal drove, he had no thought of sleeping till we got to Chicago. In the afternoon we crossed old Des Moines again. Here of course we got snarled in traffic and had to go slow and I got back in the front seat. A strange pathetic accident took place. A fat colored man was driving with his entire family in a sedan in front of us; on the rear bumper hung one of those canvas desert waterbags they sell tourists in the desert. He pulled up sharp, Neal was talking to the boys in the back and didn't notice, and we rammed him at 15 miles an hour smack on the waterbag which burst like a boil and squirted water in the air. No other damage except a bent fender. Neal and I got out to talk to him. The upshot of it was an exchange of addresses and some talk, and Neal not taking his eyes off the man's wife whose beautiful brown breasts were barely concealed inside a floppy cotton blouse. "Yass, yass." We gave him the address of our Chicago baron and went on. The other side of Des Moines a cruising car came after us with the siren growling with orders to pull over. "Now what!" The cop came out. "Were you in an accident coming in?" "Accident? We broke a guy's waterbag at the junction." "He says he was hit and run by a bunch in a stolen car." This was one of the few instances Neal and I knew of a Negro acting like a suspicious old fool. It so surprised us we laughed. We had to follow the patrolman to the station and there spent an hour waiting in the grass while they telephoned Chicago to get the owner of the Cadillac and verify our position as hired drivers. Mr. Baron said, according to our cop: "Yes that's my car but I can't vouch for anything else those boys might have done." "They were in a minor accident here in Des Moines." "Yes, you've already told me that---what I meant was, I can't vouch for anything they might have done in the past." No dope. Everything was straightened out and we roared on. In the afternoon we crossed drowsy old Davenport again and the low-lying Mississippi in her sawdust bed; then Rock Island, a few minutes of traffic, the sun reddening and sudden sights of lovely little tributary rivers flowing softly among the magic trees and greeneries of mid-American Illinois. It was beginning to look like the soft sweet East again; the great dry West was accomplished & done. The state of Illinois unfolded before my eyes in one vast movement that lasted a matter of hours as Neal balled straight across at the same speed and in his tiredness was taking greater chances than ever. At a narrow bridge that crossed one of these lovely little rivers he shot precipitately into an almost impossible situation. Two slow cars were bumping over the bridge: coming the other way was a huge truck-trailer with a driver who was making a close estimate of how long it would take the slow cars to negotiate the bridge, and his estimate was, to just keep going and by the time he got there they'd be over. There was absolutely no room for such a truck and cars going the other direction on the bridge. Behind the truck cars pulled out and peeked for an opening. In front of the slow cars even slower cars were pushing along. The road was crowded and exploding to pass. In the middle of this mess was the almost one-way narrow bridge. Neal came down on all this at 110 miles an hour and never hesitated. He passed the slow cars, made a slight mistake and almost hit the left rail of the bridge, was going head-on for the unslowing truck, cut right sharply, almost hitting the first slow car, and had to cut back in line with another car pulling out from behind the truck to look, toot the horn, push him back, and all in a matter of two seconds flashing by and leaving nothing worse than a cloud of dust instead of a horrible five-way crash with cars lurching in every direction and the great truck humping its back to die in the fatal red afternoon of Illinois with its dreaming fields. I couldn't get it out of my mind, also, that Stan Hasselgard the famous bop clarinetist had died in an Illinois car-crash, probably on a day like this. I went to the backseat again. The boys stayed in the back too now. Neal was bent on Chicago before night-fall. At a road-rail junction we picked up two hoboes who rounded up a halfbuck between them for gas. A moment before sitting around track by the watertower polishing off the last of the wine, now they found themselves in a muddy but unbowed and splendorous Cadillac limousine headed for Chicago in precipitous haste. In fact the old boy up front who sat next to Neal never took his eyes off the road and prayed his poor bum prayers, I tell you. "Well" the only thing they said "we never knew we'd get to Chicaga so fast when we left the gang last night." As we passed drowsy Illinois towns where the people are so conscious of Chicago gangs that pass like this in limousines

334

every day, we offered a real strange sight: six unshaven men, the driver barechested, me in the backseat holding on to a strap and my head leaned back on the cushion looking at the countryside with an imperious eye---just like a new California gang coming in to contest the spoils of Chicago, or at least, the young lieutenants and chauffeurs and gunsels thereof. When we stopped for cokes and gas at a smalltown station people came out to stare at us but they never said a word and I think made mental notes of our descriptions and heights in case of futureneed. To transact business with the girl who ran the gaspump Neal merely threw on his T. Shirt like a scarf and was curt and abrupt as usual and got back in the car and off we roared again. Pretty soon the redness turned purple, the last of the enchanted rivers flashed by, and we saw distant smokes of Chicago beyond the drive. We had come from Denver to Chicago, 1028 miles according to the Rand-McNally mileage chart, in exactly 23 hours counting the two hours we wasted in the Colorado ditch and at the Ed Uhl ranch eating, and the hour with the police in Iowa, for a mean total of 20 averaging 51 across the land with one driver, and 59 counting the extra 150 miles out of the way for Sterling. (or 1178 mis. in all). Which is a kind of crazy record in the night. The great metropolis of Chicago glowed red before our eyes. We were suddenly on Madison street among hordes of hoboes some of them sprawled out on the street with their feet in the curb, as hundreds of others milled in the doorways of saloons and alleys. "Wup! wup! look sharp for old Neal Cassady there, he may be in Chicago by accident this year." We let out the hoboes on this street and proceeded to downtown Chicago. Screeching trolleys, newsboys, gals cutting by, the smell of fried food and beer in the air, neons winking- -"We're back in the bigtown Jack! Whooee!" First thing to do was park the Cadillac in a good dark spot and wash up and dress for the night. Across the street from the YMCA we found a redbrick alley between buildings where we stashed the Cadillac with her snout pointed to the street and ready to go, then followed the college boys up to the Y where they got a room and allowed us the privilege of using their facilities for an hour. Neal and

I shaved and showered, I dropped my wallet in the Hall, Neal found it and was about to sneak it in his shirt when he realized it was ours and was right disappointed. Then we said goodbye to those boys who were glad they'd made it in one piece and took off to eat in a cafeteria. Old brown Chicago with the glooms that shroud the Els and the sullen whores that cut along and the strange semi-eastern, semi-western types going to work and spitting: Neal stood in front of the cafeteria rubbing his belly and taking it all in. He wanted to talk to a strange middleaged colored woman who had come into the cafeteria with a story about how she had no money but she had buns with her and would they give her butter. She came in flapping her hips, was turned down, and went out flipping her ass. "Whoo!" said Neal. "Let's follow her down the street, let's take her to the old Cadillac in the alley. We'll have a ball the three of us." But we forgot that and headed straight for No. Clark street, after a spin in the Loop, to see the hootchikootchy joints and hear the bop. And what a night it was. "Oh man" said Neal to me as we stood in front of a bar "dig these old Chinamen that cut by Chicago. What a weird town---whee! And that woman in that window up there, just looking down with her big breasts hanging from her nightgown. Just big wide eyes waiting. Wow! Jack we gotta go and never stop going till we get there." "Where we going man?" "I don't know but we gotta go." Then here came a gang of young bop musicians carrying their instruments out of cars. They piled right into a saloon and we followed them. They set themselves up and started blowing. There we were! The leader was a slender drooping curly-haired pursy-mouth tenorman, thin of shoulder, draped loose in a sports shirt, cool in the warm night, self-indulgence written in his eyes, who picked up his horn and frowned in it and blew cool and complex and was dainty stamping his foot to catch ideas and ducked to miss others---and said "Blow" very quietly when the other boys took solos. The leader, the encourager, the schoolmaker in the great formal school of underground American music that would someday be studied all over the universities of Europe and the World. Then there was Prez, a husky handsome blond like a freckled boxer, meticulously wrapped inside his sharkskin plaid suit with the long drape and the collar falling back and the tie undone for exact sharpness and casualness, sweating and hitching up his horn and writhing into it, and a tone just like Prez Lester Young himself. "You see man Prez has the technical anxieties of a money-making musician, he's the only one who's well dressed, see him grow worried when he blows a clinker, but the leader that cool cat tells him not to worry and just blow and blow---the mere sound and serious exuberance of the music is all HE cares about. He's an artist. He's teaching young Prez the boxer. Now the others dig!!" The third sax was an alto, 18 year old cool contemplative Charley Parker-type Negro from high school---with a broadgash mouth---taller than the rest--- grave---raised his horn and blew into it quietly and thoughtfully and elicited birdlike phrases and architectural Miles Davis logics. These were the children of the great bop innovators. Once there was Louis Armstrong blowing his beautiful top in the muds of New Orleans; before him the mad musicians who had paraded on official days and broke up their Sousa marches into ragtime. Then there was swing, and Roy Eldridge vigorous and virile blasting the horn for everything it had in ways of power and logic and subtlety---leaning to it with glittering eyes and a lovely smile and sending it out broadcast to rock the jazzworld. Then had come Charley Parker---a kid in his mother's woodshed in Kansas City, blowing his taped-up alto among the logs, practising on rainy days, coming out to watch the old swinging Basie and Benny Moten band that had Hot Lips Page and the rest---Charley Parker leaving home and coming to Harlem, and meeting mad Thelonius Monk and madder Gillespie....Charley Parker in his early days when he was flipped and walked around in a circle while playing. Somewhat younger than Lester Young, also from KC, that gloomy saintly goof in whom the history of jazz was wrapped: for when he held his horn high and horizontal from his mouth he blew the greatest; and as his hair grew longer and he got lazier and turned to junk, his horn came down halfway; till it finally fell all the way and today wearing his thicksoled shoes so that he can't feel the sidewalks of life his horn is held weakly against his chest and he blows cool and easy getout phrases and has given up. Here were the children of the American bebop night. Stranger flowers yet---for as the Negro alto mused over everyone's head with dignity, the young tall slender blond kid from Curtis street Denver, Levis and studded belt, sucked on his mouthpiece while waiting for the others to finish; and when they did he started, and you had to look around to see where the solo was coming from, for it came from angelical smiling lips upon the mouthpiece and it was a soft sweet fairytale solo on an alto. A fag alto had come into the night. What of the others and all the soundmaking- - there was the bassplayer, wiry redhead with wild eyes jabbing his hips at the fiddle with every driving slap, at hot moments his mouth hangs open trancelike. "Man there's a cat who can really fuck his girl." The sad dissipated drummer, like our white hipster in Frisco Howard st., completely goofed, staring into space, chewing gum, wide-eyed, rocking the neck with Reich kick and complacent ecstasy. The piano---a big husky Italian truckdriving kid with meaty hands, a burly and thoughtful joy. They played an hour. Nobody was listening. Old No. Clark bums lolled at the bar, whores screeched in anger. Secret Chinamen went by. Noises of hootchykootchy interfered. They went right on. Out on the sidewalk came an apparition---a 16 yr. old kid with a goatee and a trombone case. Thin as rickets, madfaced, he wanted to join this group and blow with them. They knew him from before and didn't want to bother with him. He crept into the bar and surreptitiously undid his trombone and raised it to his lips. No opening. Nobody looked at him. They finished, packed up and left for another bar. They were gone. The boy has his horn out, assembled it and polished the bell and no one cares. He wants to jump, skinny Chicago Kid. He slaps on his dark glasses, raises the trombone to his lips alone in the bar, and goes "Baugh!" Then he rushes out after them. They won't let him play with them, just like the sandlot football team in back of the gastank. "All these guys live with their grandmothers just like Jim Holmes and our Allen Ginsberg alto" said Neal. We rushed after the whole gang. They went into Anita O'Day's club and there unpacked and played till nine o'clock in the morning. Neal and I were there with beers. At intermissions we rushed out in the Cadillac and tried to pick up girls all up and down Chicago. They were frightened of our big scarred prophetic car. We rushed back, we rushed out again. In his mad frenzy Neal backed up smack on hydrants and tittered maniacally. By nine o'clock the car was an utter wreck; the brakes weren't working any more; the fenders were stove in; the rods were rattling. It was a muddy boot and no longer a shiny limousine. It had paid the price of the night. "Whee!" The boys were still blowing at Neets'. And suddenly Neal stared into the darkness of a corner beyond the bandstand and said "Jack, God has arrived." I looked. Who was sitting in the corner with Denzel Best and John Levy and Chuck Wayne the onetime cowboy guitarist? GEORGE SHEARING. And as ever he leaned his blind head on his pale hand and all ears opened like the ears of an elephant listened to the American sounds and mastered them for his own English summer's night-use. Then they urged him to get up and play. He did. He blew innumerable choruses replete with amazing chords that mounted higher and higher till the sweat splashed all over the piano and everybody listened in awe and fright. They led him off the stand after an hour. He went back to his dark corner, old God Shearing, and the boys said "There ain't nothing left after that." But the slender leader frowned. "Let's blow anyway." Something would come of it yet. There's always more, a little further--it never ends. They sought to find new phrases after Shearing's explorations; they tried hard. They writhed and twisted and blew. Every now and then a clear harmonic cry gave new suggestions of a tune that would someday be the only tune in the world and which would raise men's souls to joy. They found it, they lost, they wrestled for it, they found it again, they laughed, they moaned----and Neal sweated at the table and told them to go, go, go. At nine o'clock in the morning everybody, musicians, girls in slacks, bartenders, and the one little skinny unhappy trombonist staggered out of the club into the great roar of Chicago day to sleep until the wild bop night again. Neal and I shuddered in the raggedness. It was now time to return the Cadillac to the owner, who lived out on Lake Shore drive in a swank apartment with the enormous garage underneath managed by oil-scarred Negroes who had to sleep nights to hold their jobs and couldn't stay up all night with the bop. We drove out there and swung the muddy heap into its berth. The mechanic did not recognize the Cadillac. We handed the papers over. He scratched his head at the sight of it. We had to get out fast. We did. We took a bus back to downtown Chicago and that was that. And we never heard a word from our Chicago Baron about the condition of his car, in spite of the fact that he had our addresses and could have complained. It was simply that he had a lot of money and didn't care what kind of fun we had with his car which might have been only one of many in his stable. It was time for us to move on to Detroit and conclude the final thing in our disordered life together on the road. "If Edie's willing she'll come straight back to NY with us. We'll get an apartment in town and if that Beverly Denver girl of yurs. actually does follow you we'll be all set with our women and go out and get jobs and eventually if I make any more money we'll do exactly as we said in the trolley car, we'll go to Italy." "Yes man, let's go!" We took a bus to Detroit, our money was now running quite low. We lugged our wretched baggage through the station. By now Neal's thumb bandage was almost as black as coal and all unrolled. We were both as miserable looking as anybody could be after all the things we'd done. Exhausted Neal fell asleep in the bus that roared across the state of Michigan. I took up a conversation with a pretty country girl wearing a lowcut cotton blouse that displayed the beautiful suntan on her breast tops. I was on my way to see my wild former wife, I wanted to test other girls and see what they had to offer me. She was dull. She spoke of evenings in the country making popcorn on the porch. Once this would have gladdened my heart but because her heart was not glad when she said it I knew there was nothing in it but the idea of what one should do. "And what else do you do for fun?" I tried to bring up boyfriends and sex. Her great dark eyes surveyed me with emptiness and a kind of chagrin that reached back generations and generations in her blood from not having done what was crying to be done...whatever it was, and everybody knows what it was. "What do you want out of life?" I wanted to take her and wring it out of her. She didn't have the slightest idea what she wanted. She mumbled of jobs, movies, going to her grandmother's for the summer, wishing she could go to New York and visit the Roxy, what kind of outfit she would wear---something like the one she wore last Easter, white bonnet, roses, rose pumps and leather gabardine coat. "What do you do on Sunday afternoons?" I asked. She sat on her porch. The boys went by on bicycles and stopped to chat. She read the funny papers, she reclined on the hammock. "What do you do on a warm summer's night?" She sat on the porch, she watched the cars go by in the road. She and her mother made popcorn. "What does your father do on a summer's night?" He works, he has an all-night shift at the boiler factory. "What does your brother do on a summer's night." He rides around on his bicycle, he hangs out in front of the sodafountain. "What is he aching to do? What are we all aching to do? What do we want?" She didn't know. She yawned. She was sleepy. It was too much. Nobody could tell. Nobody would ever tell. It was all over. She was eighteen and most lovely, and lost. And Neal and I, ragged and dirty like as if we had lived off locust, stumbled out of the bus in Detroit and went across the street and got a cheap hotel with the bulb hanging from the ceiling and raised the brown torn shade and looked out on the brickalley. Right beyond the furthest garbage pails something awaited us...Two gone women in slacks ran the place. We thought it was a whore house. Rules were printed and tacked on every slatwall in the joint. "Have consideration for fellow tenants and don't hang wash in here." Don't do this, don't do that. Neal and I went out and ate a meatloaf meal in a bum cafeteria and started walking to my wife's house five miles up Mack Avenue in the vast Detroit dusk. I had called her and she wasn't in yet. "We'll wait for her if necessary all night on the lawn." "Right man, now I'm following with you and you lead the way." At ten o'clock that night we were still wrapped in conversation when a cruising car pulled up and two cops got out with pads and told us to get up. There had been a complaint about two hoodlums casing a house from a lawn across the street and talking in loud voices. "You got us all wrong officer, that house is my former wife's house and we're waiting for her to come home." "Who's this fellow with you?" "That's my friend. We come in from California on the way to NY and my wife is coming with us." "I thought you said she was your former wife." "The marriage was annulled but we may get married again." Hesitantly the cops went off, but they told us to get the hell out of the neighborhood. We went to a bar and waited there. The cops had already talked to the bartender and told him the whole story, so as to keep his eye on us. Neal went back to Edie's house after an hour to check on what was happening and horror of horrors, the cops had knocked on the door and talked to her mother and told her what I was doing. She had no use for me. She had gotten herself a new husband, a middleaged paint manufacturer, and didn't want any more trouble with the likes of my kind. She disclaimed all responsibility for what I might do in Detroit. Not only that they got her up out of bed. Neal and I decided to go back downtown and lay low. When Edie came back from somewhere in Detroit late that night she was amazed to hear the news. In the morning she herself was at the phone when I called. "You and that crazy friend of yours come on out right away. I'll be waiting on the corner with the kids." The kids turned out to be wild young rock-in-the-belly socialite juvenile delinquents, and here she was about 27 years old and still as goofy as ever. The moment I saw her I knew I'd never go back to her: she was fat, her hair was clippt short, she wore overalls and munched on candy with one hand and drank beer with the other. She paid no attention to Neal and I, her old trick, just talked and giggled with the kids. However she fed us well, her mother was out, we raided a roast for fair. Then we went rattling around in the kids' hotrod for no especial reason. They were crazy kids: sixteen years old and already in trouble with the cops with speeding tickets and whatnot.. "What you come back to Detroit for Kerouac?" "I don't know, I wanted to see you." "Well if we're gonna get married and all that stuff

342

again I want a maid this time." That clinched it. "I don't want to wash dirty dishes, let somebody else do it." "Ain't you got a pretty soul?" "Souls don't mean nothing to me Kerouac, cut that juvenile talk and talk facts." "You can stuff your facts up." "Ah-ha, same old fool." This was our lovey-dovey talk. Neal listened and looked sharply. "You know the trouble with her?" he told me. "She's got a rock in her belly, she got a weight in there that just pushes and vibrates against her stomach and won't let her come down and talk. She won't do anything for the rest of her life except goof and goof all the time and you'll never get anywhere with her." That was a pretty fair estimate. Still I had such regard for her from the past I didn't want to leave Detroit right away. I wanted to have it out with her. That night she got a girlfriend for Neal, but the girlfriend couldn't shake her own boyfriend and all five of us went out in Edie's car to hear jazz in Hastings street Detroit colored section. It's a sullen town. A group of Negroes passt us on the street and said "Sure is a lot of white people around here." We were back East sure enough. Neal shook his head sadly. "Man, it ain't nice around here. This is one hell of a town." Detroit is actually one of the worst towns possible in America. Its nothing but miles and miles of factories and the downtown section is no bigger than Troy N.Y except the population is way up in the millions. Everybody thinks about money, money, money. But down on Hastings st. the boys were blowing. A great big baritone sax that Neal and I had seen actually before in Jackson's Hole Frisco that winter was on the stand, but the stand was elevated over the bar, where the girls danced, and the whole idea was dance not music. Nevertheless old baritone blew and rocked his big horn on a fast blues. And poor Edie, she sat at the bar with her little hands knotted into childish fists, holding them up before her face with glee to hear it. And suddenly she said to me in the uproar "Hey! That Neal has a great soul." I said "How did you know that?" Then I knew Edie was as great as ever but that there was something between us now and we'd never make it together. I was pretty sad. That something was the years apart---she had changed, changed friends, ways of spending evenings, interests, all that and had let herself fall into complete self-indulgence and uncare. But that old spark was still there. Only a matter of months earlier Hunkey had visited her in Detroit and left a whole passel of fine shirts in her house where he'd stayed a few days complaining until her mother threw him out. Hunkey was in Sing Sing now, stashed away for years among the bongo cans Puerto Rican prisoners make for sunset pleasures in steel halls. She gave me one of his shirts; my new wife wears it now; a beautiful fine shirt, typical of Hunkey. I wanted to make love to Edie for the last time but she wouldn't have it. We drove to the Lake, alone, leaving Neal at the hotel where the whore proprietors in slacks had refused letting Edie in for talk and beerdrinking ("We don't run that kind of place!") and Edie told them to go to hell. At the lake we sat in the car like ordinary lovers. I said "What about you and I trying it for the first time or the last time or whatever you want." "Don't be silly." I got mad and jumped out of the car and slammed the door and went off to "brood" by the water. This had always worked before, she always followed and soothed me. But now she simply shifted to reverse, backed out and drove home to go to sleep, leaving me with seven miles of Detroit night to walk in because there wasn't a bus running anywhere. I walked back four miles to the nearest trolley line. It was like the walks I had taken on dark Alameda boulevard in Denver when I used to beat my head on the tar that shimmered in the starlight. It was all over, Neal said we might as well go to NY. I wanted to give it one last try. We went to Edie's the following afternoon and spent another goofy five hours with the crazy kids and devouring food from the icebox while her mother was at work. Then Edie told us to wait in the Mack Ave. bar same one with the inquisitive bartender, till she joined us there. Just as we rounded the corner I looked back and saw her waving at a car in the street and slipping from the front door into it. The car backed so as not to come our way and vanished. I said "What the hell is that? Was that Edie getting in that car? Isn't she going to meet us here?" Neal was silent. We waited an hour and then he put his arm around me and said "Jack you don't want to believe but don't you see what happened? It's never occurred to you that she has a boy, a lover in Detroit, he came to get her just now. You wait here you'll wait all night." "She was never like that!" "You don't get to know women even after a million years with them. It's just like Louanne, man, they're all whores---and you know that I mean by whore something entirely different than what the word means. They just turn their minds away from you and like changing fur coats they don't care any more. Women can forget what men can't. She's forgotten you, man. You don't want to believe it." "I can't." "You saw her with your own eyes didn't you?" "I guess I did." "She slipped off with him. Real bitchy too, she won't even tell you the slightest what's on her mind. Oh man, I know these women, I've been watching her these two days and I know, I KNOW." Summer was over. We stood on the sidewalk in front of the bar---and what the hell were we doing in Detroit?---and it grew cold. It was the first cold dusk since the Spring. We huddled in our T-Shirts. "Ah man I know how you feel. And we've settled our lives on this grip---I've done with Carolyn, I'm long done with Louanne, and now you're done with Edie. We'll go to NY and start all over again. I loved Louanne with every fibre in my bones, man, and I got the same treatment you're getting." Nevertheless I walked back to her house to see if she was there. Her mother was home now, I saw her in the kitchen window. This was an era in my life all washed up. I agreed with Neal. "People change, man, that's what you gotta know." "I hope you and I'll never change." "We know, we know." We got on a trolley and rode to downtown Detroit, and suddenly I remembered that Louis Ferdinand Celine had once rode on the same trolley with his friend Robinson, whoever Robinson was if not likely Celine himself; and Neal was like myself, for I'd had a dream of Neal the night before in the hotel, and Neal was me. In any case he was my brother and we stuck together. We couldn't afford another night in the hotel room so we stashed our gear in a Greyhound locker and decided to stay up in an all night movie on Skid Row. It was too cold for parks. Hunkey had been here on Detroit skidrow, he had dug every shooting gallery and allnight movie and every brawling bar with his dark eyes many a time. His ghost haunted us. We'd never find him on Times Square again. We thought maybe by accident Old Neal Cassady was here too---but he was not. For 35c each we went into the beatup old movie and sat down in the balcony, till morning when we were shooed downstairs. The people who were in that allnight movie were the end. Beat Negroes who'd come up from Alabama to work in car factories on a rumor; old white bums; young longhaired hipsters who'd reached the end of the road and were drinking wine; whores, ordinary couples and housewives with nothing to do, nowhere to go, nobody to believe in. If you sifted all Detroit in a wire basket the beater solid core of dregs couldn't be better gathered. The picture was singing cowboy Roy Dean and his gallant white Horse Bloop, that was number one; number two doublefeature film was Geo. Raft, Sidney Greenstreet and Peter Lorre in a picture about Istanbul. We saw both of these things six times each during the night. We saw them waking, we heard them sleeping, we sensed them dreaming, we were permeated completely with the strange gray Myth of the West and the weird dark Myth of the East when morning came. All my actions since then have been dictated automatically to my subconscious by this horrible osmotic experience. I heard big Greenstreet sneer a hundred times; I heard Peter Lorre make his sinister come-on, I was with Geo. Raft in his paranoiac fears; I rode and sang with Roy Dean and shot up the rustlers innumerable times. People slugged out of bottles and turned around and looked everywhere in the dark theater for something to do, somebody to talk to. In the head everybody was guiltily quiet, nobody talked. In the gray dawn that puffed ghostlike about the windows of the theater and hugged its eaves I was sleeping with my head on the wooden arm of a seat as six attendants of the theater converged with their nights' total of swept-up rubbish and created a huge dusty pile that reached to my nose as I snored head down---till they almost swept me away too. This was reported to me by Neal who was watching from ten seats behind. All the cigarette butts, the bottles, the matchbooks, the come and the gone was swept up in this pile. Had they taken me with it Neal would have never seen me again. He would have to roam the entire United States and look in every garbage pail from coast to coast before he found me embryonically convoluted among the rubbishes of my life, his life and the life of everybody concerned and not concerned. What would I have said to him from my rubbish womb. "Don't bother me, man, I'm happy where I am. You lost me one night in Detroit in August 1949. What right have you to come and disturb my reverie in this pukish can." In 1942 I was the star in one of the filthiest dramas of all time. I was a seaman, and went to the Imperial Cafe on Scollay Square in Boston to drink. I drank 60 glasses of beer and retired to the toilet, where I wrapped myself around the toilet bowl and went to sleep. During the night at least a hundred sailors, seamen and assorted civilians came in and pissed and puked on me till I was unrecognizably caked. What difference does it make after all?---anonymity in the world of men is better than fame in heaven, for what's heaven? what's earth? all in the mind. Gibberishly Neal and I stumbled out of this horror-hole at dawn and went to find our Travel Bureau car. The end had come. There was nothing left but despair. After spending a good part of the morning in Negro bars and chasing gals and listening to jazz records on jukeboxes, we finally got our car and were instructed to go out to the man's home with our gear and be ready to go. Neal and I sat in a park resting on the grass. Neal was looking at me. "Say man do you know you're going to have trouble with your ears in a few years?" "What are you talking about?" "You've got brown in your ears, that's a bad sign." It wasn't my fault, I wouldn't even discuss it. "What do you want me to do about it?" I yelled. "Did I make the world? Did I perpetrate or even hint it?" Then I rubbed my small finger into my ear and noticed Neal was right. It was very sad. Everything was falling apart by degrees. We reclined in the grass and looked at the blue sky. Trolleys screeched all around us. In the afternoon we learned we'd have to wait another day, and that evening I called Edie again and this time she showed up with a case of beer in back of her car and we went out to hear jazz again. She had positively nothing to say about hanging us up the night before; she hardly realized she'd done

347

it. "Oh has she got the rock in the belly!" whispered Neal. She sped through a red light on Hastings Street and instantly a cruising car overtook us and ordered us to stop. Neal and I hopped out with our hands up. That's how wretched we'd become by now. The cops immediately frisked us. We had nothing on but T Shirts. They patted us and felt everywhere and scowled and were dissatisfied. "Goddam it" Edie said "I never get in cop trouble when I'm alone. Listen here you guys do you know who my father is? I won't have any of this bull!" "What are you doing with that case of beer in back of the car?" "It's none of yr. good goddam business." "It so happens you went through a redlight young lady." "So?" You never saw anybody sassier with the cops. As for Neal and I we were completely inured to it. We followed the cops to the station house and gave ourselves over to the desk. Neal even got excited and told stories to the Sgt. Edie was making important phonecalls and getting all her relatives lined up behind her. She turned on me with fury. "Kerouac it's always you when there's cops, you and that damn friend of yrs. look like a couple of 1st class hoodlums. I'll have nothing absolutely nothing to do with you any damned more." "That's allright" I said "Yr. mother said I shouldn't reopen any old wounds, she said I was a bum." "And do you know she's right?" Neal and I were delighted to be in the police station, it was just like home, we had a wonderful time. The cops were sort of pleased with us. Another step and we'd be getting the hose in the backroom and screaming with delight---maybe. Edie thoroly frightened the entire precinct with her socialite sassy insults and threats and we were all let free and went off to drink the case of beer. In a dizzy dream she left and went home and I've never seen her again. In the following afternoon Neal and I struggled five miles in local buses with all our beat gear and got to the home of the man who was going to charge us $4 apiece for the ride to NY. He was a middleaged blond fellow with glasses, with a wife and kid and a good home. We waited in the yard while he got ready. His lovely wife in cotton kitchen dress offered us coffee but we were too busy talking. By this time Neal was so exhausted and out of his mind that everything he saw delighted him. He was reaching a pious frenzy. He sweated and sweated. The moment we were in the new Chrysler and off to New York the poor man realized he had contracted a ride with two maniacs, but he made the best of it and in fact got used to us just as we passed the Briggs Stadium and talked about next year's Detroit Tigers. In the misty night we crossed Toledo and went onward across old Ohio. I realized I was beginning to cross and re-cross towns in America as though I was a traveling salesman---ragged travellings, bad stock, rotten beans in the bottom of my bag of tricks, nobody buying. The man got tired near Pennsylvania and Neal took the wheel and drove clear the rest of the way to New York and we began to hear the Symphony Sid show on the radio with all the latest bop and now we were entering the great and final city of America. We got there in early morning. Times Square was being torn up, for NY never rests. We looked for Hunkey automatically as we passed. In an hour we were out at my mother's new flat on Long Island where the Detroit man wanted to clean up, and she herself was busily engaged with painters who were friends of the family arguing with them about the price as we stumbled up the stairs from San Francisco. "Jack" said my mother "Neal can stay here a few days and after that he has to get out, do you understand me?" The trip was over. Neal and I took a walk that night among the gas tanks and railroad bridges and foglamps of Long Island. I remember him standing under a streetlamp. "Just as we passed that other lamp I was going to tell you a further thing, Jack but now I am parenthetically continuing with a new thought and by the time we reach the next I'll return to the original subject, agreed?" I certainly agreed. We were so used to traveling we had to walk all over Long Island but there was no more land, just the Atlantic Ocean and we could only go so far. We clasped hands and agreed to be friends forever. Not five nights later we went to a party in New York and I saw a girl called Diane and I told her I had a friend with me that she ought to meet sometime. I was drunk and told her he was a cowboy. "Oh I've always wanted to meet a cowboy." "Neal?" I yelled across the party, which included Jose Garcia Villa the poet, Walter Adams, Victor Tejeira the

Venezualan poet, Jinny Baker a former love of mine, Allen Ginsberg, Gene Pippin and innumerable others---"come over here man." Neal came bashfully over. An hour later in the drunkenness of the party with which of course he had nothing to do he was kneeling on the floor with his chin on her belly and telling her and promising her everything and sweating. She was a big sexy brunette, as Villa said "Something straight out of Degas" and generally like a beautiful Parisian whore. The next day Neal was living with her; in a matter of months they were dickering with Carolyn in San Francisco by long-distance telephone for the necessary divorce papers so they could get married. Not only that, but another few months later Carolyn gave birth to Neal's second baby, the result of a few nights understanding just before I got there. And another matter of months and Diane had a baby. Together with one illegitimate child in Colorado somewhere, Neal was now the father of four little ones and didn't have a cent and was all troubles and ecstasy and speed as ever. Came the time when I finally went West alone with some new money with the intention of sinking down to Mexico and spending it there, and Neal---threw everything up and came to join me. It was our last trip and it ended among the banana trees that we always knew were at the end of the road.

BOOK FOUR:-

As I say, I came into some new money and---once I straightened out my mother with rent for the rest of the year---nothing to do, nowhere to go. I would never have gone off again except for two things. One: a woman who fed me lobsters, mushroom-on-toast and Spring asparagus in the middle of the night in her apartment in NY but gave me a bad time otherwise. Two: whenever Spring comes to NY I can't stand the suggestions of the land that come blowing over the river from New Jersey and I've got to go. So I went. For the first time in our lives I said goodbye to Neal in New York and left him there. He worked in a parking lot on Madison and 40th. As ever he rushed around in his ragged shoes and T-shirt and belly-hanging pants all by himself straightening out immense noontime rushes of cars. He darted among fenders, leaped over bumpers, shot behind the wheel and roared off ten feet and humped the car dead-stop; got out, ran clear across the lot, moved five cars off the brickwall in twenty seconds; raced back maniacally, leaped into the offending bottleneck car and whirled it around the lot among zigzagged dead cars to a neat stop in an unobtrusive corner. When usually I came to visit him at dusk there was nothing to do. He stood in the shack counting tickets and rubbing his belly. The radio was always on. "Man have you dug that mad Marty Glickman announcing basketball games---up-to-mid-court-bounce-fake-netshot (pause) swish, two points. Absolutely the greatest announcer I ever heard." He was reduced to simple pleasures like these. He lived with Diane in a coldwater flat in the East Seventies. When he came home at night he took off all his clothes and put on a hiplength Chinese silk jacket and sat in his easy chair to smoke a waterpipe loaded with tea. These were his coming-home pleasures: together with a deck of dirty cards. "Lately I've been concentrating on this deuce of diamonds. Have you noticed where her other hand is? I'll bet you can't tell. Look long and try to see." He wanted to lend me this deuce of diamonds, which depicted a tall mournful fellow and a lascivious sad whore on a bed trying a position. "Go ahead man, I've used it many times!" Diane his wife cooked in the kitchen and looked in with a wry smile. Everything was allright with her. "Dig her? dig her man? That's Diane. See, that's all she does, she pokes her head in the door and smiles. Oh I've talked with her and we've got everything straightened out most beautifully. We're going to go and live on a farm in New Hampshire this summer---station wagon for me to cut back to NY for kicks, nice big house and have a lot of kids in the next few years. Ahem! Harrumph! Egad!" He leaped out of the chair and put on a Willie Jackson record. This was exactly what he had been doing with Carolyn in Frisco. Diane called up the second wife on the phone repeatedly and had long talks with her. They even exchanged letters about Neal's eccentricity. Of course he had to send Carolyn part of his pay every month for support or he'd wind up in jail. To make up lost money he pulled tricks in the lot, a change artist of the first order. I saw him wish a well-to-do-man Merry Christmas so volubly a fivespot in change for twenty was never missed. We went out and spent it in Birdland the bop joint. On a misty night we talked on the corner of Fifth Avenue and 49th, three in the morning. "Well Jack, damn, I wish you weren't going, I really do. It'll be my first time in New York without my old buddy." And he said "New York, I stop over in it, Frisco's my hometown. All the time I've been here I haven't had any girl but Diane---this only happens to me in New York. Damn! But the mere thought of crossing that awful continent again...Jack we haven't talked straight in a long time." In New York we were always jumping around frantically with crowds of friends at drunken parties. It somehow didn't seem to fit Neal. He looked more like himself huddling in the cold misty spray of the rain on empty 5th ave. at night. "Diane loves me. She's told me and promised me I can do anything I want and there'll be a minimum of trouble...You see man, you get older and trouble piles up. Someday you and me'll be coming down an alley together at sundown and looking in the cans to see." "You mean we'll end up old bums?" "Why not man? Of course we will if we want to, and all that. There's no harm ending that way. You spend a whole life of non-interference with the wishes of others including politicians and the rich and nobody bothers you and you cut along and make it your own way." I agreed with him. He was reaching his mature decisions in the simplest direct way. "What's your road, man?---holyboy road, madman road, rainbow road, guppy road, any road. It's an anywhere road for anybody anyhow. Where body how?" We nodded in the rain. This was kind sense. "Sheeit, and you've got to look out for your boy. He ain't a man less he's a jumping man - -do what the doctor say. I'll tell you Jack, straight, no matter where I live my trunk's always sticking out from under the bed, I'm ready to leave or get thrown out. I've decided to leave everything out of my hands. YOU've seen me try and break my ass to make it and YOU know that it doesn't matter and we know time...how to slow it up and walk and dig and just oldfashioned spade kicks, what other kicks are there? We know." We sighed in the rain. It was falling all up and down the Hudson Valley that night. The great world piers of the sea-wide river were drenched in it, old steamboat landings at Poughkeepsie were drenched in it, old Split Rock pond of sources was drenched in it, Vander-whacker Mount was drenched in it, all earth and land and city street was drenched in it. "So" said Neal "I'm cutting along in my life as it leads me. You know I recently wrote to my old man in Denver county jail---I got the first letter in years from him the other day." "Did you?" "Yass, yass..he said he wants to see the babby spelt with two b's when he can get to Frisco. I found a $13 a month coldwater pad on East 40th, if I can send him the money he'll come and live in New York---if he gets here. I never told you much about my sister but you know I have a sweet littlekid sister. I'd like to get her to come and live with me too." "Where is she?" "Well that's just it, I don't know---he's going to try to find her, the old man, but you know what he'll really do." "So he got back to Denver?" "And straight to jail." "Where was he?" "Texas, Texas...so you see man, my soul, the state of things, my posi-tion---you notice I get quieter." "Yes that's true." Neal had grown quiet in New York. He wanted to talk. We were freezing to death in the cold rain. We made a date to meet at my mother's house before I left. He came the following Sunday afternoon. I had a television set. We played one ballgame on the TV, another on the radio, and switched to a third and kept track of all that was happening every moment. "Remember Jack, Hodges is on second in Brooklyn so while the relief pitcher is coming in for the Phillies we'll switch to Giants-Boston and at the same time notice there Di Maggio has a three ball count and the pitcher is fiddling with the resin bag so we quickly find out what happened to Bob Thomson when we left him thirty seconds ago with a man on third. Yes!" Later in the afternoon we went out and played baseball with the kids in the sooty field by the Long Island railyard. We also played basketball so frantically the younger boys said "Take it easy, you don't have to kill yourself." They bounced smoothly all around us and beat us with ease. Neal and I were sweating. At one point Neal fell flush on his face on the concrete court. We huffed and puffed to get the ball away from the boys: they turned and flipped it

353

away. Others darted in and smoothly shot over our heads. We jumped
at the basket like maniacs and the younger boys just reached up and
grabbed the ball from our sweating hands and dribbled away. They
thought we were crazy. Neal and I went back home playing catch from
each sidewalk of the street. We tried extra special catches diving over
bushes and barely missing posts. When a car came by I ran alongside
and flipped the ball to Neal just barely behind the vanishing bumper.
He darted and caught it and rolled in the grass, and flipped it back for
me to catch on the other side of a parked breadtruck. I just made it
with my meat hand and threw it back so Neal had to whirl and back
up and fall on his back across the hedges. This went on. Back in the
house Neal took out his wallet, harrumphed, and handed my mother
the fifteen dollars he owed her from the time we got a speeding ticket
in Washington. She was completely surprised and pleased. We had a
big supper. "Well Neal" said my mother "I hope you'll be able to take
care of your new baby that's coming and stay married this time." "Yes,
yass, yes." "You can't go all over the country having babies like that.
Those poor little things'll grow up helpless. You've got to offer them
a chance to live." He looked at his feet and nodded. In the raw red
dusk we said goodbye, on a bridge, over a superhiway. "I hope you'll
be in NY when I get back" I told him. "All I hope, Neal, is someday
we'll be able to live on the same street with our families and get to
be a couple of oldtimers together." "That's right man---you know that
I pray for it completely mindful of the troubles we both had and the
troubles coming, as your mother knows and reminds me. I didn't
want the new baby, Diane insisted and wasn't careful and we had a
fight. Did you know Louanne got married to a sailor in Frisco and's
having a baby?" "Yes. We're all getting in there now." He took out a
snapshot of Carolyn in Frisco with the new baby girl. The shadow of
a man crossed the child on the sunny pavement, two long trouser legs
in the sadness. "Who's that?" "That's only Al Hinkle. He came back
to Helen, they're gone to Denver now. They spent a day taking pictures." He took out other pictures. I realized these were all the
snapshots which our children would look at someday with wonder,

thinking their parents had lived smooth well-ordered lives and got up in the morning to walk proudly on the sidewalks of life, never dreaming the raggedy madness and riot, of our actual lives, our actual night, the hell of it, the senseless nightmare road. Juices inform the world, children never know. "Goodbye, goodbye." Neal walked off in the long red dusk. Locomotive smokes reeled above him, just like in Tracy, just like in New Orleans. His shadow followed him, it aped his walk and thoughts and very being. He turned and waved coyly, bashfully. He gave me the brakeman's hiball sign, he jumped up and down, he yelled something I didn't catch. He ran around in a circle. All the time he came closer to the concrete corner of the overpass. He made one last signal. I waved back. Suddenly he bent to his life and walked quickly out of site. I gaped into the bleakness of my own days; I had an awful long way to go too. The following midnight I took the Washington bus; wasted some time there wandering around; went out of my way to see the Blue Ridge; heard the bird of Shenandoah and visited Stonewall Jackson's grave; at dusk stood expectorating in the Kanawha and walked the hillbilly night of Charleston West Virginia; at midnight Ashland Kentucky and a lonely girl under the marquee of a closed up show. The dark and mysterious Ohio, and Cincinnati at dawn. Then Indiana fields again, and St. Louis as ever in its great valley clouds of afternoon. The muddy cobbles and the Montana Logs, the broken steamboats, the ancient signs, the grass and the ropes by the river. By night Missouri, Kansas fields, Kansas night-cows in the secret wides, crackerbox towns with a sea for the end of every street; dawn in Abilene. East Kansas grasses become West Kansas rangelands that climb up the hill of the western night. George Glass was riding the bus with me. He had got on at Terre Haute Indiana and now he said to me "I've told you why I hate this suit I'm wearing, it's lousey---but that ain't all." He showed me papers. He had just been released from Terre Haute Federal pen, stealing and selling cars in Cincinnati. A young curly headed kid of 20. "Soon as I get to Denver I'm selling this suit in a pawnshop and getting me Levis. Do you know what they did to me in that prison?---solitary confinement with a bible, I used to sit on it on the stone floor, when they seed I was doing that they took the bible away and brought back a leetle pocket size one so big. Couldn't sit on it so I read the whole bible and testament. Hey hey" he poked me, munching his candy, he was always eating candy because his stomach had been ruined in the pen and couldn't stand anything else---"you know they's some real hot things in that ba-ble." He told me what it was to signify. "Anybody that's leaving jail soon and starts talking about his release date is signifying to the other fellas that have to stay. We take him by the neck and say 'Don't signify with me!' Bad thing, to signify- -y'hear me?" "I won't signify, George." "Anybody signify with me my nose opens up, I get mad enough to kill. You know why I been in jail all my life? Because I lost my temper when I was thirteen years old. I was in a movie with a boy and he made a crack about my mother---you know that dirty word---- and I took out my jack-knife and cut up his throat and woulda killed him if they hadn't drug me off. Judge said, Did you know what you were doing when you attacked your friend. Yessir your honor I did, I wanted to kill the sonofabitch and still do. So I didn't get no parole and went straight to reform school. I got piles too from sitting in solitary. Don't ever go to a Federal pen, they're the worstest. Sheet, I could talk all night it's been so long since I talked to somebody. You don't know how GOOD I feel coming out. You just sitting in that bus when I got on---riding through Terre Haute---what was you thinking?" "I was just sitting there riding." "Me, I was singing. I sat down next to you cause I was afraid to set down next to any gals for fear I go crazy and reach under their dress. I gotta wait a while." "Another hitch in jail and you'll be put away for life---you better take it easy from now." "That's what I intend to do, only trouble is m'nose opens up and I can't tell what I'm doing." He was on his way to live with his brother and sister-in-law; they had a job for him in Colorado. His ticket was bought by the Feds, his destination on the parole. Here was a young kid like Neal had been; his blood boiled too much for him to bear; his nose opened up; but no native strange saintliness to save him from the iron fate. "Be a buddy and watch m'nose don't open up in Denver will you Jack?- -mebbe I can get to my brother's safe." I certainly agreed. When we arrived in Denver I took him by the arm to Larimer street to pawn the penitentiary suit. The old Jew immediately sensed what it was before it was half unwrapped. "I don't want that damn thing here, I get them every day from the Canon City boys." All of Larimer street was overrun with ex-cons trying to sell their prison-spun suits. George ended up with the thing under his arm in a paper bag and walked around in brand new levis and sports shirt. We went to Neal's old Glenarm bar---on the way George threw the suit in an ashcan---and called up Ed White. It was evening now. "Yo?" chuckled Ed White. "Be right over." In ten minutes he came loping into the bar with Frank Jeffries. They were both returned from France and tremendously disappointed with their Denver lives. They loved George and bought him beers. He began spending all his penitentiary money left and right. Again I was back in the soft dark Denver night with its holy alleys and crazy houses. We started hitting all the bars in town, roadhouses out on West Colfax, Five Points Negro bars, the works. Frank Jeffries had been waiting to meet me for years and now for the first time we were suspended together in front of a venture. "Jack, ever since I came back from France I ain't had any idea what to do with myself. Is it true you're going to Mexico? Hot-damn, could I go with you? I can get a hundred bucks and once I get there sign up for the GI Bill in Mexico City College." Okay, it was agreed, Frank was coming with me. He was a rangy bashful shock-haired Denver boy with a big conman smile and slow easy-going Gary Cooper movements. "Hot-damn!" he said and stuck his thumbs on his belt and ambled down the street, swaying from side to side but slowly. His father was having it out with him. He had been opposed to France and now he was opposed to the idea of going to Mexico. Frank was wandering around Denver like a bum because of his fight with his father. That night after we'd done all our drinking and restrained George from getting his nose opened up in Hot Shoppe on Colfax---a fellow came in with two girls and we addressed him as "Hat" and wanted to meet the girls and George leaped for him---Frank scraggled off to sleep in George's hotel room on Glenarm. "I can't even come home late---my father starts fighting with me then he turns on my mother. I tell you Jack I got to get out of Denver quick or I'll go crazy." Well, and I stayed at Ed White's and then later Beverly Burford fixed up a neat little basement room for me and we all ended up there with parties everynight for a week. George vanished off to his brother's at Climax, Colo. and we never saw him again and never will know if anybody's signified with him since and if they've put him away in an iron hall or if he busts his gaskets in the night free. Ed White, Frank, Bev and I spent an entire week of afternoons in lovely Denver bars where the waitresses wear slacks and cut around with bashful loving eyes, not hardened waitresses but waitresses that fall in love with the clientele and have explosive affairs and huff and sweat and suffer from one bar to another; and we spent the same week in nights at Five Points listening to jazz, drinking booze in crazy colored saloons and gabbing till five o'clock in the morn in my basement. Noon usually found us reclined in Bev's backyard among the little Denver kids who played cowboys and Indians and dropped on us from cherry trees in bloom. I was having a wonderful time and the whole world opened up before me because I had no dreams. Frank and I plotted to make Ed White come with us but he was stuck to his Denver life. I spent evenings chatting with Justin W. Brierly in his study. Here he put on his Chinese dressingown and pulled out salted nuts and straight Scotch. "Sit down Jack, and tell me everything about New York. How's Neal? How's Allen? How's Lucien? Do you know where Hal Chase is?- -in Trinidad Colorado on a dig. Have you seen Mr. Hinkle anywhere in the country? What's the latest on yr. friend Burroughs? Burford is still in Paris. Have you been having long talks with Ed? How do you like Jeffries? Is Beverly in good spirits these days?" Justin loved to talk about all of us. "It all describes a wonderful big circle, doesn't it?" he said. "Don't you think it's fun?" He took me out for a ride in his Olds with the big spotlight. We were going down West Colfax when he saw a rickety Mexican jaloppy with headlights off. He turned on his spotlight and put it flush on them, a bunch of Mexican boys. They pulled up fearfully, they thought it was the law. "Aren't your headlights working? Is anything wrong?" called this mad Denver dignitary. "Yes sir, yes sir." they said. "Well" called Brierly "Happy New Year" and because he'd held up traffic for this ridiculous conversation horns were tooting behind. "Oh shut up!" yelled Brierly and shot the car ahead. He pointed his spotlight flush on the richest home in Denver at four o'clock in the morning and explained every room to me as the beams illuminated the interior. People were sleeping in there,---he didn't care. In his study he suddenly fished out an old full-face portrait of Neal when he was sixteen yrs. old. You never saw a chaster face. "See what Neal used to look like? That's why I had faith in him then. Don't worry I saw his possibilities---he just wouldn't learn and so I washed my hands of him." "It's too bad---Neal could have become a big man in the world. On the other hand I like him better the way he is. Big men in the world are unhappy." "You wouldn't say that <u>Neal</u> is happy would you?" "He's ecstatic---if that's more or less than happy." "I should think it's less. Getting all involved with three wives and kids all over the country--- it's absurd." "Go find his mother for him." "Anyway Jack it's been a lot of fun." Brierly grew serious. "Yes I've had a lot of fun and I'd live this life all over again. I'm getting more and more wrapped up in discovering and developing these kids---why I've left my law practice practically go to pot, I've abandoned real estate altogether and next year I think I'll give up my Central City secretaryship. I'm back where I started teaching hi school English." On Brierly's blackboard in High School I saw the names of Carl Sandburg and Walt Whitman scribbled in chalk. A little Negro boy came to him with a problem. He had no time to deliver papers and do his homework all at the same time. Brierly called up his bosses and changed the hours and set everything straight. Boys coming in for vacations from Eastern Universities came to him for summer jobs. He merely picked up the phone and called the Mayor. "Do you happen to remember Bruce Rockwell at Columbia? He's assistant to the mayor now you know---doing very well indeed. He was in your class wasn't he?" He'd been after me. I remember Bruce Rockwell sitting in his room with a major decision to make one May night, which was, go back to Denver or stay in New York in advertising. I was on a bunk with a critical review in my hands. I threw it out of my hands and it landed at his feet. "That's what I think of critics!" I yelled. Bruce Rockwell brooded over his destiny. Suddenly he got up and walked out. He had decided. There was some sort of Gen. MacArthur in him. Now he was assistant to the Mayor and rushing around fogerishly with appointments, golf, cocktail parties, conferences, hurried Martinis in the Brown Hotel and all that; to fatten before his time and get ulcers and go mad in recognized sanity. "No" I said "I think Neal is all right. One of these days he'll go up in a tongue of flame and something'll happen." I was having good times with the Denver kids and lounging around and getting ready to go to Mexico when suddenly Brierly called me one night and said "Well Jack, guess who's coming to Denver?" I had no idea. "He's on his way already, I got this news from my grapevine. Neal bought a car and is coming out to join you." Suddenly I had a vision of Neal, a burning shuddering frightful Angel palpitating towards me across the road, approaching like a cloud, with enormous speed, pursuing me like the Shrouded Stranger on the plain, bearing down on me. I saw his huge face over the plains with the mad bony purpose and the gleaming eyes; I saw his wings; I saw his old jalopy chariot with thousands of sparking flames shooting out from it; I saw the path it burned over the road; it even made its own road and went over the corn, through cities, destroying bridges, drying rivers. It came like wrath to the West. I knew Neal had gone mad again. There was no chance of sending money to either wife if he took all his savings out of the bank and bought a car. Everything was up, the jig and all. Behind him charred ruins smoked. He rushed westward over the groaning and awful continent again and soon he would arrive. We made hasty preparations for Neal. News was that he was going to drive me to Mexico. "Do you think he'll let me come along?" asked Jeff in awe. "I'll talk to him" I said grimly. We didn't know what to expect. "Where will he sleep? What's he going to eat? Are there any girls for him?" It was like the

arrival of Gargantua; preparations had to be made to widen the gutters of Denver and foreshorten certain laws to fit his suffering bulk
and bursting ecstasies. It was like an oldfashioned movie when Neal
arrived. I was in Beverly's crazy house in a golden afternoon. A word
about the house. Her mother was away in France. The chaperone aunt
was old Austice or whatever, she was 75 years old and spry as a
chicken. In the Burford family which stretched from here to Iowa she
was continually shuttling from one house to another and making herself generally useful. At one time she'd had dozens of sons. They were
all gone, they'd all abandoned her. She was old but she was interested
in everything we did and said. She shook her head sadly when we took
slugs of whiskey in the livingroom. "Now you might go out in the
yard for that, young man." Upstairs---it was a kind of boarding house
that summer---boarded a mad guy called Jim who was hopelessly in
love with Beverly. He actually came from Connecticut, from a rich
family they said, and had a career waiting for him there and everything but he preferred being where Bev was. The result was this: in
the evenings he sat in the livingroom with his face burning behind a
newspaper and every time one of us said anything he heard but made
no sign. He particularly burned when Bev said something. When we
forced him to put down the paper he looked at us with incalculable
boredom and suffering. "Eh? Oh yes, I suppose so." He usually said
just that. Austice sat in her corner knitting watching us all with her
birdy eyes. It was her job to be chaperone, it was up to her to see
nobody sweared. Bev sat giggling on the couch. Ed White, Jeffries and
I sprawled around in various chairs. Poor Jim suffered the tortures.
He got up, yawned and said "Well another day another dollar, good-
night" and disappeared upstairs. Bev had no use whatever for him;
she was in love with Ed White. He wriggled like an eel out of her
grasp. We were sitting around like this on a sunny afternoon towards
suppertime when Neal pulled up in front in his jalopy and jumped
out in a tweed suit with vest and watch chain. "Hup! hup!" I heard
out on the street. He was with Bill Tomson who'd just returned from
Frisco with his wife Helena and was living in Denver again. So was

Hinkle and Helen Hinkle, and Jim Holmes. Everybody was in Denver again. I went out on the porch. "Well m'boy" said Neal sticking out his big hand "I see everything is allright on this end of the stick. Hello hello hello" he said to everybody "oh yes, Ed White, Frank Jeffries, how'd'y'do!" We introduced him to Austice. "Oh yass, how'd'y'do. This is m'friend Bill Tomson here, was so kind as to accompany me, harrumph! egad! kaff! kaff! Major Hoople sir," he said sticking out his hand to Jim, who stared at him "yass, yass. Well Jack old man what's the story, when do we take off for Mexico? Tomorrow afternoon? Fine, fine. Ahem! And now Jack I have exactly sixteen minutes to make it to Al Hinkle's house where I am about to recover my old railroad watch which I can pawn on Larimer street before closing time, meanwhile buzzing very quickly and as thoroly as time allows to see if my old man by chance may be in Jiggs' buffet or some of the other bars and then I have an appointment with the barber Brierly always told me to patronize and I have not myself changed over the years and continue with that policy---kaff! kaff!- -At six o'clock SHARP! sharp har me? I want you to be right here where I'll come buzzing by to get you for one quick run to Bill Tomson's house, play Gillespie and assorted bop records, an hour of relaxation prior to any kind of further evening you and Ed and Frank and Bev may have planned for tonight irrespective of my arrival which incidentally was exactly forty-five minutes ago in my old '37 Ford which you see parked out there I made it together with a long pause in Kansas City seeing my stepbrother not Jack Daly but the younger one..." And saying all these things he busily engaged himself in changing from his suitcoat to T-shirt in the livingroom alcove just out of sight of everyone and transferring his watch to another pair of pants that he got out of the same old battered trunk. "And Diane?" I said. "What happened in New York." "Officially Jack this trip is to get a Mexican divorce cheaper and quicker than any kind...I've Carolyn's agreement at last and everything is straight, everything is fine, everything is lovely and we know that we are now not worried about a single thing don't we Jack?" Well, lackadaddy, I'm always ready to follow Neal so we all bustled to the new set of plans and arranged a big night and it was an unforgettable night. There was a party at Al Hinkle's sister's house. Two of his brothers are policemen. They sat there in awe of everything that went on. There was a lovely spread on the table, cakes and drinks. Al Hinkle looked happy and prosperous. "Well are you all set with Helen now?" "Yessir," said Al, "I sure am. I'm about to go to Denver university you know, me and Jim and Bill." "What are you going to take up?" "Oh I don't know right now. Say, Neal gets crazier every year don't he?" "He sure does." Helen Hinkle was there. She was trying to talk to somebody but Neal held the whole floor. He stood before Jeffries White Bev and I who all sat side by side in kitchen chairs along the wall and performed. Al Hinkle hovered nervously behind him. His poor sister was thrust into the background. "Hup! hup!" Neal was saying, tugging at his shirt, rubbing his belly, jumping up and down. "Yass, well---we're all together now and the years have rolled severally behind us and yet you see none of us have really changed, and to prove that I have here a deck of cards with which I can tell very accurate fortunes of all sorts"---It was the dirty deck. Helena Tomson and Bill Tomson sat stiffly in a corner. It was a meaningless party, a complete flop-out. Then Neal suddenly grew quiet and sat in a kitchen chair between Jeff and me and stared straight ahead with rocky doglike wonder and paid no attention to anybody. He simply disappeared for a moment to gather up more energy. If you touched him he would sway like a boulder suspended on a pebble on the precipice of a cliff. He might come crashing down or just sway rocklike. Then the boulder exploded into a sunflower and his face lit up with a lovely smile and he looked around like a man waking up and said "Ah, look at all the nice people that are sitting here with me. Isn't it nice! Jack, how nice." He got up and went across the room hand outstretched to one of the policemen in the party. "How'd'y'do. My name is Neal Cassady? Yes I remember you well. Is everything allright? Well, well. Look at the lovely cake. Oh, can I have some?" Al's sister said yes. "Oh, how wonderful. People are so nice. Cakes and pretty things set out on a table and all for the sake of wonderful little joys and delights. Hmm, it's sweet, so sweet. My. My!" And he stood swaying in the middle of the room eating his cake and looking at everyone with awe. He turned and looked around behind him. Everything amazed him, everything he saw. A picture on the wall made him stiffen to attention. He went up and looked closer, he backed up, he stooped, he jumped up, he wanted to see from all possible levels and angles. He had no idea the impression he was making and cared less. People were now beginning to look at Neal with maternal and paternal affection glowing in their faces. He was finally an Angel, like I always knew he would become, but like any Angel he still had angelic rages and furies and that night when we all left the party and repaired to the Windsor bar in one vast brawling gang Neal became frantically and seraphically drunk. Remember that the Windsor, once Denver's great goldrush hotel and now a bum's flophouse in many respects and a point of interest in the big saloon downstairs where bullet holes were still preserved in the walls, had once been Neal's home. He'd lived here with his father with other bums in one of the rooms upstairs. He was no tourist. He drank in this saloon like the ghost of his father; he slopped down wine, beer and whiskey like water. His face got red and sweaty and he bellowed and hollered at the bar and staggered across the dancefloor where wild western characters danced with floosies and tried to play the piano and threw his arms around ex-cons and shouted with them in the uproar. Meanwhile everybody in our party sat around two immense tables stuck together. There were Justin W. Brierly, Helena and Bill Tomson, a girl from Buffalo Wyoming who was Helena's friend, Frank, Ed White, Beverly, me, Al Hinkle, Jim Holmes and several others, thirteen in all. Brierly was having a great time: he took a peanut machine and set it on the table before him and poured pennies in it and ate peanuts. He suggested we all write something on a penny postcard and mail it to Allen Ginsberg in New York. This we did. There were crazy things written. The fiddle music roared in the Larimer street night. "Isn't it fun?" yelled Brierly. In the men's room Neal and I punched the door and tried to break it but it was an inch thick. I broke my middle finger and didn't even realize it till the next day. We were fumingly drunk. Fifty glasses of beer sat on our table at one time. All you had to do was rush around and sip from each one. Canon City ex-cons reeled and gabbled with us. In the foyer outside the saloon old former prospectors sat dreaming over their canes under the tocking old clock. This fury had been known by them in greater days. This was the bar where Lucius Beebe came once a year in his private railroad champagne car that he parked in the railyard in back. It was mad. Everything swirled. There were scattered parties everywhere. There was even a party in a castle to which we all drove, except Neal who ran off elsewhere, and in this castle we sat at a great Knight's table in the hall and shouted. There was a swimming pool and grottos outside. I had finally found the castle where the great snake of the world was about to rise up. Then in the late night it was just Neal and I and Frank Jeffries and Ed White and Al Hinkle and Jim Holmes in one car and everything ahead of us. We went to Mexican town, we went to Five points, we reeled around. Frank Jeffries was out of his mind with joy. He kept yelling "Sonofa<u>bitch</u>! Hot-<u>damn</u>!" in a high squealing voice and slapping his knees. Neal was mad about him. He repeated everything Frank said and whood and wiped the sweat off his face. "Are we going to get our kicks Jack traveling down to Mexico with this cat Frank! Yes!" It was our last night in holy Denver, we made it big and wild. It all ended up in the basement by candlelight with wine and Austice creeping around upstairs in her nightgown with a flashlight. We even had a colored guy with us now, called himself Gomez. He floated around Five Points and didn't give a damn. When we saw him Bill Tomson called out "Hey is your name Johnny?" Gomez just backed up and passed us once more and said, "Now will you repeat what you said?" "I said are you the guy they call Johnny?" Gomez floated back and tried again. "Does this look a little more like him because I'm trying my best to be Johnny but I just can't find the way." "Well <u>man</u> come on with us!" cried Neal and Gomez jumped in and we were off. We whispered frantically in the basement so as not to wake Austice and Jim upstairs and create confusion with the neighbors. At nine o'clock in the morning everybody had left except Neal and Jeffries who were still yakking and talking like maniacs. People got up to make breakfast and heard strange subterranean voices from next door saying "Yes! yes!" It never ended. Beverly cooked a big breakfast. The time was coming to goof along to Mexico. Neal took the car to the nearest station and had everything shipshape. It was a 37 Ford sedan with the rightside door unhinged and stuck on the frame. The rightside front seat was also broken and you sat there leaning back with your face to the tattered roof. "Just like Min n' Bill" said Neal. "We'll go coughing and bouncing down to Mexico, it'll take us days and days!" I looked over the map. A total of nineteen hundred miles mostly Texas to Laredo, and then another 767 miles through all Mexico to the great city near the Isthmus. I couldn't imagine this trip. It was the most fabulous of all. It was no longer east-west but magic SOUTH. We saw a vision of the entire Western Hemisphere rockribbing clear down to Tierra del Fuega and us flying down the curve of the world into other tropics and other worlds. "Man this will finally take us to IT!" said Neal with definite faith. He tapped my arm. "Just wait and see. Hoo! Whee!" I went with Jeffries concluding the last of his Denver business, and met his poor father who stood in the door of the house saying "Frank---Frank---Frank." "What is it, Dad?" "Don't go." "Oh it's settled, I <u>have</u> to go now; why do you have to do that Pa?" The old man had gray hair and large almond eyes and a tense mad neck. "Frank" he simply said "don't go. Don't make your old father cry. Don't leave me alone again." Frank had explained to me that his father was going mad in recent years. It broke my heart to see all this. "Neal" said the old man addressing me "don't take my Frank away from me. I used to take him to the park when he was a little boy and explain the swans to him. Then his little brother drowned in the same pond. I don't want you to take my boy away." "Father" said Frank "we're leaving now, goodbye." He struggled with his grips. His father took him by the arm. "Frank, Frank, Frank, don't go, don't go, don't go." We fled with our heads bowed and the old man still stood in the doorway of his Den-

366

ver side-street cottage with the beads hanging in the doors and the overstuffed furniture in the parlor. He was as white as a sheet. He was still calling Frank. There was something extremely paralyzed about all his movements and for this reason he did nothing about leaving the doorway but just stood in it muttering the name "Frank" and "don't go" and looking after us anxiously as we rounded the corner. "God Jeff, I don't know what to say." "Never mind!" he moaned. "He's always been like that. I wish you hadn't seen him. My mother's leaving him as soon as she gets straightened out." "That poor old man'll go mad if she leaves him." "She's too young for him anyway" said Frank. We met his mother at the bank where she was surreptitiously drawing money for him. She was a lovely white-haired woman still very young in appearance. She and her son stood on the marble floor of the bank whispering. Frank was wearing a levi outfit jacket and all and looked like a man going to Mexico sure enough. This was his tender existence in Denver and he was going off with the flaming tyro Neal. Neal came popping around the corner and met us just on time. Mrs. Jeffries insisted on buying us all a cup of coffee. "Take care of my Frank" she said "no telling what things might happen in that country." "We'll all watch over each other" I said. Frank and his mother strolled on ahead and I walked in back with crazy Neal: he was telling me about the inscriptions carved on shithouse walls in the east and in the west. "They're entirely different, in the East they make cracks and corny jokes of all kinds; in the West they just write their names, Red O'Hara, Bluffton Montana, came by here, date, the reason being the enormous loneliness that differs just a shade and cunthair as you move across the Mississippi." Well there was a lonely guy in front of us, for Jeffries' mother was a lovely mother and she hated to see her son go but knew he had to go. I saw he was fleeing his father. Here were the three of us---Neal looking for his father, mine dead, Frank fleeing his and going off into the night together. He kissed his mother in the rushing crowds of 17th and she got in a cab and waved at us. Goodbye, goodbye. We got into our old Ford heap and went back to Bev's. Here we spent a planned hour just sitting and talking on the porch with Beverly and Ed under the immense beezing trees of drowsy denver afternoon. And Brierly came to say goodbye. He rolled around the corner in his Olds and we heard his "Merry Christmas" across the heat. He came bustling to us on little business-man feet. "Well well well, ready to go and not a care. How do you feel about this Ed, do you want to go with the boys?" Ed White flipped his hand in the air and just smiled. Beverly was all game to go. She had been hinting it for days. "I wouldn't be in the way" she said. Frank and she had been boyhood-girlhood pals: he used to pull her pigtails and roll hoops in Denver alleys with her brother Bob; later they roared in high schools, the golden high schools of Denver Neal had never made. "Well this is a strange trio indeed" said Brierly "I would never have foreseen it a few years back. Neal, what do you pro-pose to do with these two fellows, do you think you'll drive them to the So. Pole?" "Ah ha, ah ha, yes." Neal looked away. Brierly looked away. All six of us just sat in the hot sun and were silent. "Well" said Brierly "I suppose everything has a meaning. I want to see all of you come back in one piece unless you get lost in the jungle with an Indian girl and end your days sitting in front of a hut making pots. I think you should see Hal in Trinidad on the way down. I can't think of anything else to say except Happy New Year. I'll bet you want to go with them, Beverly? I think you'd better stay in Denver. Isn't that so, Ed? Hmm." Brierly always mused in his soul. Dancingmaster Death picked up his briefcase and got ready to go. "Did you ever hear the story about the midgets who wanted to go up on the giant? It's a very short story. Or the one about---well I think that's enough don't you? Eh?" He looked at all of us and grinned. He straightened his panama hat. "I've got an appointment downtown, I'll have to be say-ing goodbye now." We all shook hands. He was still talking on his way to the car. We couldn't hear him any more but he was still say-ing something. A little boy came by on a tricycle. "Merry Christmas there. Don't you think it might be better if you stayed on the sidewalk, someone might come by and make oatmeal out of you." The little kid shot by in the street with his face pointed to the future. Brierly got in his car, U-turned, and threw a parting sally at the little boy. "When I was your age I was confident too. My mudpies were marvels of architecture. Eh?" Brierly and the little boy disappeared around the corner slowly then we heard him shoot the car ahead to businesslike affairs and he was gone. Then Neal and I and Frank got in the old heap that was waiting for us on the curb and slammed all the loose doors together and turned to say goodbye to Beverly. Ed was riding with us to his house outside town. Beverly was beautiful that day: her hair was long and blond and Swedish, her freckles showed in the sun. She looked exactly like the little girl she had been. There was a mist in her eyes. She might join us later with Ed….but she didn't. Goodbye, goodbye. We roared off. We left Ed in his yard on the plains outside town and raised a cloud of dust. I looked back to watch Ed White recede on the plain. That strange guy stood there for a full two minutes watching US recede on the plain and thinking God knows what sorrowful thoughts. He grew smaller and smaller, till all I could see was a spot---and still he stood motionless with one hand on a washline like a captain with his shrouds and watched us. Neal and Frank sat in front talking excitedly but I was twisted around to see more of Ed White till there was nothing of the human except a growing absence in space, and what space it was, the eastward view towards Kansas that led all the way back to my home in Long Island in a mystery of ever-swallowing spaces. "Ed is still watching us" I told them up front. We took a sudden left and I saw no more of Ed White. I had missed him on the boat and I had missed him here. Now we pointed our rattly snout South and headed for Castle Rock Colorado as the sun turned red and turned the rock of the Mountains to the West to look like a Brooklyn brewery in November dusks. Far up in the purple shades of the rock there was someone walking, walking, but we could not see; maybe that old man with the white hair I had sensed years ago up in the peaks. But he was coming closer to me, if only ever just behind. And Denver receded back of us like the city of salt, her smokes breakingup in the air and dissolving to our sight. It was May: and how can homely afternoons in Colorado with its farms and irrigation ditches and shady dells---the places where little boys go swimming---produce a bug like the bug that bit Frank Jeffries. He had his arm draped over the broken door and was just riding along and talking happily with us when suddenly a bug flew into his arm and imbedded a long stinger in it that made him howl. It had come out of an American afternoon. He yanked and slapped at his arm and dug out the stinger and in a few minutes his arm had begun to swell. He said it hurt. Neal and I couldn't figure what it was. The thing was to wait and see if the swelling went down. Here we were heading for unknown southern lands and barely three miles out of hometown, poor homely old hometown of childhood, a strange feverish exotic bug rose from secret corruptions and sent fear in our hearts. "What is it?" "I've never known of a bug around here that can make a swelling like that." "Damn!" It made the trip seem sinister and doomed. It was a parting farewell from our native land. Did we know our native land so well? We drove on. Frank's arm got worse. We'd stop at the first hospital and have him get a shot of penicillin. We passed Castle Rock, came to Colorado Springs at dark. The great shadow of Pike's Peak loomed to our right. We bowled down the Pueblo hiway. "I've hitched thousands and thousands of times on this road" said Neal. "I hid behind that exact wire fence there one night when I suddenly took fright for no reason whatever." We all decided to tell our stories, but one by one, and Frank was first. "We've a long way to go" preambled Neal "and so you must take every indulgence and deal with every single detail you can bring to mind---and still it won't all be told. Easy, easy," he cautioned Frank who began telling his story "you've got to relax too." Frank swung into his life story as we shot across the dark. He started with his experiences in France but to round out ever-growing difficulties he came back and started at the beginning with his boyhood in Denver. He and Neal compared times they'd seen each other zooming around on bicycles. Frank was nervous and feverish. He wanted to tell Neal everything. Neal was now arbiter, old man, judge, listener, approver, nodder. "Yes, yes, go on please." We passed Walsenburg; suddenly we passed Trinidad where Hal Chase was somewhere off the road in front of a campfire with Ginger and perhaps a handful of anthropologists and as of yore he too was telling his life story and never dreamed we were passing at that exact moment in the hiway headed for Mexico telling our own stories. Oh sad American night! Then we were in New Mexico and passed the rounded rocks of Raton and stopped at a diner ravingly hungry for hamburgers, one of which we wrapped in a napkin not to eat till over the border below. "The whole vertical state of Texas lies before us Jack" said Neal. "As before we made it horizontal. Every bit as long. We'll be in Texas in a few minutes and won't be out till tomorrow night this time and won't stop driving. Think of it." We drove on. Across the immense plain of night lay the first Texas town, Dalhart, which I'd crossed in 1947. It lay glimmering on the dark floor of the earth fifty miles away. The land by moonlight was all mesquite and wastes. On the horizon was the moon. She fattened, she grew huge and rusty, she mellowed and rolled, till the morning-star contended and dews began to blow in our windows----and still we rolled. After Dalhart--- empty crackerbox town---we bowled for Amarillo, and reached it in the morning among windy panhandle grasses that only a few years ago, (1910) waved around a collection of buffalo tents. Now there were of course gas stations and new 1950 jukeboxes with immense ornate snouts and ten-cent slots and awful songs. All the way from Marillo to Childress Texas Neal and I pounded plot after plot of books we'd read into Frank, who asked for it because he wanted to know. At Childress in the hot sun we turned directly south on a lesser road and continued across abysmal wastes to Paducah, Guthrie and Abilene Texas. Now Neal had to sleep and Frank and I sat in the front seat and drove. The old car burned and bopped and struggled on. Great clouds of gritty wind blew at us from shimmering spaces. Frank rolled right along with stories about Monte Carlo and Cagnes-sur-Mer and the blue places near Menton where darkfaced people wandered among white walls. Texas is undeniable: we burned slowly into Abilene and all woke up to look at it. "Imagine living in this town a thousand miles from cities. Whoop, whoop, over there by the tracks, oldtown

Abilene where they shipped the cows and shot it up for gumshoes and drank red-eye. Lookout there!" yelled Neal out the window with his mouth contorted. He didn't care about Texas or anyplace. Redfaced Texans paid him no attention and hurried along the burning sidewalks. We stopped to eat on the hiway south of town. Nightfall seemed like a million miles away as we resumed for Coleman and Brady---the heart of Texas only, wildernesses of brush with an occasional house near a thirsty creek and a fifty mile dirtroad detour and endless heat. "Old dobe Mexico's a long way away" said Neal sleepily from the backseat "so keep her rolling boys and we'll be kissing senoritas b'dawn cause this old Ford can roll if y'know how to talk to her and ease her along---except the backend's about to fall but don't worry about it till we get there. Heeyah!" and he went to sleep. I took the wheel and drove all the way to Fredericksburg, and here again I was crisscrossing the old map again, same place Louanne and I had held hands on a snowy morning in 1949, and where was Louanne now? "Blow!" yelled Neal in a dream and I guess he was dreaming of Frisco jazz and maybe Mexican mambo to come. Frank talked and talked: Neal had wound him up the night before and now he was never going to stop. He was in England by now, relativing adventures hitchhiking on the English road, London to Liverpool, with his hair long and his pants ragged and strange British truckdrivers giving him a lift. We were all redeyed from the continual mistral-winds of old Tex-ass. There was a rock in each of our bellies and we knew we were getting there if only slow. The car only pushed forty with shuddering effort. From Fredericksburg we descended the great western high plains in darkness towards the hot basins of the Rio Grande. San Antone was strait ahead. "Still be long after midnite before we get to Laredo" warned Neal. We were all awake anticipating San Antonio. It grew hotter and hotter in the luscious night as we descended the plains. Moths began smashing our windshield. "Gettin' down into the hot country now boys, the desert rats and the tequila. And this is my first time this far South in Texas" added Neal with wonder. "Gawddamn! this is where my old man comes in the wintertime, sly old bum." Suddenly we were in absolutely tropical heat at the bottom of a five mile long hill and up ahead we saw the lights of old San Antonio. You had the feeling all this used to be Mexican territory indeed. Houses by the side of the road were different, gas stations beater, fewer lamps. Neal delightedly took the wheel to roll us into San Antonio. We entered town in a wilderness of Mexican rickety southern shacks without cellars and old rocking chairs on the porch. We stopped at a mad gas station to get a greasejob. Mexicans were standing around in the hot light of the overhead bulbs that were blackened by valley summerbugs, reaching down into a softdrink box and pulling out beer bottles and throwing the money to the attendant. Whole families lingered around doing this. All around there were shacks and drooping trees and a wild cinnamon smell in the air. Frantic teenage Mexican girls came by with boys. "Hoo!" yelled Neal. "Si! Manana!" Music was coming from all sides, and all kinds of music. Frank and I drank several bottles of beer and got high. We were already almost out of America and yet definitely in it and in the middle of where it's maddest. Hotrods blew by. San Antonio, ah-haa! "Now men listen to me---we might as well goof a couple of hours in San Antone and so we will go and find a hospital clinic for Frank's arm and you and I Jack will cut around and git these streets dug---look at those houses across the street, you can see right into the frontroom and all the purty daughters lying around with True Love magazines, whee! Come, let's go!" We drove around aimlessly awhile and asked people for the nearest hospital clinic. It was near downtown, where things looked more sleek and American, several semi-skyscrapers and many neons and chain drugstores yet with cars crashing through from the dark around town as if there were no traffic laws. We parked the car in the hospital driveway and I went with Frank to see an interne while Neal stayed in the car and changed. The hall of the hospital was full of poor Mexican women, some of them pregnant, some of them sick or bringing their little sick kiddies. It was sad. I thought of poor Bea Franco and what she was doing now. Frank had to wait an entire hour till an interne came along and looked at his swollen arm. There was a name for the type infection he had but none of us bothered to pronounce it. They gave him a shot of penicillin. Meanwhile Neal and I went out to dig the streets of Mexican San Antonio. It was fragrant and soft--- the softest air I'd ever known---and dark, and mysterious, and buzzing. Sudden figures of girls in white bandanas appeared in the dark. Neal crept along and said not a word. "Oh this is too wonderful to do any- thing!" he whispered. "Let's just creep along and see everything. Look! look! a crazy San Antonio pool shack." We rushed in. A dozen boys were shooting pool at three tables, all Mexicans. Neal and I bought cokes and shoved nickels in the jukebox and played Wynonie Blues Harris and Lionel Hampton and Lucky Millinder and jumped. Meanwhile Neal warned me to watch. "Dig now, out of the corner of your eye and as we listen and as we also smell the soft air as you say--- dig the kid, the crippled kid shooting pool at table No. 1, the butt of the joint's jokes, y'see, he's been the butt all his life. The other fel- lows are merciless but they love him." The crippled kid was some kind of malformed midget with a great big beautiful face much too large in which enormous brown eyes moistly gleamed. "Don't you see, Jack? A sanAntonio Mex Jim Holmes, the same story the world over. See they hit him on the ass with a cue? Ha! ha! ha! hear them laugh. You see, he wants to win the game, he's bet four bits. Watch! Watch!" We watched as the angelic young midget aimed for a bankshot. He missed. The other fellows roared. "Ah man" said Neal "and now watch." They had the little boy by the scruff of the neck and were mauling him around, playful. He squealed. He stalked out in the night but not without a backward bashful sweet glance. "Ah man, I'd love to know that gone little cat and what he thinks and what kind of girls he has---Oh man, I'm high on this air!" We wandered out and nego- tiated several dark mysterious blocks. Innumerable houses hid behind verdant almost jungle-like yards; we saw glimpses of girls in front rooms, girls on porches, girls in the bushes with boys. "I never knew this mad San Antonio! Think what Mexico'll be like! Lessgo! lessgo!" We rushed back to the hospital. Frank was ready and said he felt much better. We put our arms around him and told him everything we'd done. And now we were ready for the last 150 miles to the magic border. We leaped into the car and off. I was so exhausted by now I slept all the way to Laredo and didn't wake up till they were parking the car in front of a lunchroom at two o'clock in the morning. "Ah" sighed Neal "the end of Texas, the end of America, we don't know no more." It was tremendously hot: we were all sweating buckets. There was no night dew, not a breath of air, nothing, except billions of moths smashing at bulbs everywhere and the low rank smell of a hot river in the night nearby---the Rio Grande, that begins in cool Rocky Mountain dales and ends up fashioning world-valleys to mingle its heats with the Mississippi muds in the great Gulf. Laredo was a sinister town that morning. All kinds of cabdrivers and border rats wandered around looking for opportunities. There weren't many, it was too late. It was the bottom and dregs of America where all the heavy villains sink, where disoriented people have to go to be near a specific elsewhere they can slip in unnoticed. Contraband brooded in the heavy syrup air. Cops were redfaced and sullen and sweaty, no swagger. Waitresses were dirty and disgusted. Just beyond you could feel the enormous presence of the whole continent of Mexico and almost smell the billion tortillas frying and smoking in the night. We had no idea what Mexico would really be like. We were at sea level again and when we tried to eat a snack we could hardly swallow it. We left our food on plates: I wrapped it up in napkins for the trip anyway. We felt awful and sad. But everything changed when we crossed the mysterious bridge over the river and our wheels rolled on official Mexican soil tho it wasn't anything but a carway for border inspection. Just across the street Mexico began. We looked with wonder. To our amazement it looked exactly like Mexico. It was three in the morning and fellows in strawhats and white pants were lounging by the dozen against battered pocky storefronts. "Look...at...those... cats!" whispered Neal. "Oo" he breathed softly, "wait, wait." The Mexican officials came out grinning and asked please if we would take out our baggage. We did. We couldn't take our eyes from across the street. We were longing to rush right up there and get lost in those mysterious Spanish streets. It was only Nuevo Laredo but it looked like Barcelona. "Man those guys are up all night" whispered Neal. We hurried to get our papers straightened. We were warned not to drink tapwater now we were over the border. The Mexicans looked at our baggage in a desultory way. They weren't like officials at all. They were lazy and tender. Neal couldn't stop staring at them. "See how the <u>cops</u> are in this country. I can't believe it!" He rubbed his eyes. "I'm dreaming." Then it was time to change our money. We saw great stacks of pesos on a table and learned that eight of them made an American buck, or thereabouts. We changed most of our money and stuffed the big rolls in our pockets with delight. Then we turned our faces to Mexico with bashfulness and wonder as those dozens of Mexican cats watched us from under their secret hatbrims in the night. Beyond was music and all night restaurants with smoke pouring out of the door. "Whee" whispered Neal very softly. "Thassall!" grinned a Mexican official. "You boys all set. Go ahead. Welcome Mexico. Have good time. Watch you money. Watch you driving. I say this to you personal, I'm Red, everybody call me Red. Ask for Red. Eat good. Don't worry. Everything fine." "Yes-yes-<u>yes</u>!" squealed Neal and off we went across the street into Mexico on soft feet. We left the car parked and all three of us abreast went down the Spanish street into the middle of the dull brown lights. Old men sat on chairs in the night and looked like Oriental junkies and oracles. No one was actually looking at us yet everybody was aware of everything we did. We turned sharp left into the smoky lunchroom and went in to music of campo guitars on an American Thirties jukebox. Shirtsleeved Mexican cabdrivers and strawhatted Mexican hipsters sat at stools devouring shapeless messes of tortillas, beans, tacos, whatnot. We bought three bottles of cold beer---told at once "Cerveza" was the name for beer---for about thirty cents or ten cents each. We bought packs of Mexican cigarettes for six cents each. We gazed and gazed at our wonderful Mexican money that went so far and played with it and looked around and smiled at everyone. Behind us lay the whole continent of America and everything Neal and I had previously known about life, and life on the road. We had finally found the magic land at the end of the road and we never dreamed the extent of the magic either. "<u>Think</u> of these cats staying up all hours of the night" whispered Neal. "And think of this big continent ahead of us with those enormous Sierra Madre mountains we saw in the movies and the jungles all the way down and a whole desert plateau as big as ours and reaching clear down to Guatemala and God knows where, whoo! What'll we do? what we'll do? Let's move!" We got out and went back to the car. One last glimpse of America across the hot lights of the Rio Grande bridge. We turned our back and fender to it and roared off. Instantly we were out in the desert and there wasn't a light or a car for fifty miles across the flats. And just then dawn was coming over the Gulf of Mexico and we began to see the ghostly shapes of Yucca cactus and Organpipe on all sides. "What a wild country!" I yelped. Neal and I were completely awake. In Laredo we'd been half dead. Frank, who'd been to foreign countries before just calmly slept in the backseat. Neal and I had the whole of Mexico before us. "Now Jack we're leaving everything behind us and entering a new and unknown phase of things. All the years and troubles and kicks---and now <u>this</u>! so that we can safely think of nothing else and just go on ahead with our faces stuck out like this, you see, and <u>understand</u> the world as, really and genuinely speaking, other Americans haven't done before us---they were here weren't they? The Mexican war. Cutting across here with cannon." "This road" I told him "is also the route of old American outlaws who used to skip over the border and go down to old Monterrey, so if you'll look out on that graying desert and picture the ghost of an old Tombstone hellcat making his lonely exile gallop into the unknown you'll see further..." "It's the world" said Neal. "My God!" he cried slapping the wheel. "It's the world! We can go right on to South America if the road goes. Think of it! Sonofabitch---Gawd-<u>damn</u>!" We rushed on. The dawn spread immediately and we began to see the white sand of the desert and occasional huts in the distance off the road. Neal slowed down to peer at them. "Real beat huts, man, the kind you only find in Death Valley and much worse. These people don't <u>bother</u> with appearances." The first town ahead that had any consequence on the map was called Sabinas Hidalgo. We looked forward to it eagerly. "And the road don't look any different than the American road" cried Neal "except one mad thing and if you'll notice, right here, the mileposts are written in kilometers and they click off the distance to Mexico City. See, it's the only city in the entire land, everything points to it." There were only 767 more miles to that metropolis; in kilometers the figure was over a thousand. "Damn! I gotta go!" cried Neal. For awhile I closed my eyes in utter exhaustion and kept hearing Neal pound the wheel with his fists and say "Damn" and "God what kicks!" and "Oh what a land!" and "Yes!" We arrived at Sabinas Hidalgo across the desert at about seven o'clock in the morning. We slowed down completely to see this. We woke up Frank in the backseat. We sat up straight to dig. The main street was muddy and full of holes. On each side were dirty brokendown dobe fronts. Burros walked in the street with packs. Barefooted women watched us from dark doorways. It was incredible. The street was completely crowded with people on foot beginning a new day in the Mexican countryside. Old men with handlebar mustaches stared at us. The sight of three bearded bedraggled American youths instead of the usual welldressed tourists was of unusual interest to them. We bounced along over Main Street at ten miles an hour taking everything in. A group of girls walked directly in front of us. As we bounced by one of them said "Where you going man?" I turned to Neal amazed. "Did you hear what she said?" Neal was so astounded he kept on driving slowly and saying "Yes I heard what she said, I certainly gawd-damn well did, Oh me, Oh my, I don't know what to do I'm so excited and sweetened in this morning world. We've finally got to heaven. It couldn't be cooler, it couldn't be grander, it couldn't be any-<u>thing</u>." "Well let's go back and pick them up!" I said. "Yes" said Neal and drove right on at five miles an hour. He was knocked-out he didn't have to do the usual things he would have done in America. "There's millions of them all along the road by gawd!" he said. Nevertheless he U-turned and came by the girls again. They were headed for work in the fields; they smiled at us. Neal stared at them with rocky eyes. "Damn" he said under his breath "OOh! This is too great to be true. Gurls, gurls. And particuarly right now in my stage and condition Jack I am digging the interiors of these homes as we pass them---these gone doorways and you look inside and see beds of straw and little brown kids sleeping and stirring to wake, and the mothers cooking up breakfast in iron pots and dig them shutters they have for windows and the old men, the old men are so cool and grand and not bothered by anything. There's no suspicion here, nothing like that. Everybody's cool, everybody looks at you with such straight brown eyes and they don't say anything, just look and in that look all of the human qualities are soft and subdued and still there. Dig all the foolish stories you read about Mexico and the humble peasant and all that crap---and crap about greasers and so on---and all it is, people here are straight and kind and don't put down any bullshit. I'm so amazed by this." Schooled in the raw road night Neal was come into the world to see it. He bent over the wheel and looked both ways and rolled along slowly. We stopped for gas the other side of Sabinas Hidalgo. Here a congregation of local strawhatted ranchers with handlebar mustaches growled and whooped in front of antique gaspumps. Across the fields an old man plodded with a burro in front of his switch stick. The sun rose pure on pure & ancient activities of human life. Now we resumed to Monterrey. The great mountains rose snowcapped before us; we bowled right for them. A gap widened and wound up a pass and we went with it. In a matter of minutes we were out of the mesquite desert and climbing among cool airs in a road with a stonewall along the precipice side and great whitewashed names of presidents on the cliffsides---"Aleman!" We met nobody on this high road. It wound among the clouds and took us to the great plateau on top. Across this plateau the big manufacturing town of Monterrey sent smoke to the blue skies with their enormous Gulf clouds written across the bowl of day like fleece. Entering Monterrey was like entering Detroit, among great long walls of factories, except for the burros that sunned in the grass before them, and the barefoot girls that cut along with groceries. And downtown Monterrey was our first sight of thick city dobe neighborhoods with thousands of shifty hipsters hanging around doorways and whores looking out of windows and strange shops that might have sold anything and narrow sidewalkscrowded with Hongkong-like humanity. "Yow!" yelled Neal. "And all in that sun. Have you dug this Mexican sun, Jack? It makes you high. Whoo! I want to get on and on--this road drives me!" We wanted to stop in the excitements of Monterrey but Neal wanted to make extra-special time to get to see Bill Burroughs as quickly as possible and Mexico City and besides he knew the road would get more interesting, especially ahead, always ahead. He drove like a fiend and never rested. Frank and I were completely bushed and gave it up and had to sleep. I looked up outside Monterrey and saw enormous weird twin peaks shaped like a wild saddle cutting clouds high up in the sky. Now we were going beyond Old Monterrey, beyond where the outlaws went. Montemorelos was ahead, a descent again to hotter altitudes. It grew exceedingly hot and strange. Neal absolutely had to wake me up to see this. "Look Jack, you must not miss." I looked. We were going through swamps and alongside the road at ragged intervals strange Mexicans in tattered rags walked along with bolo knives hanging from their rope belts and some of them cut at the bushes. They all stopped to watch us without expression. Through the tangled bush we occasionally saw thatched huts with African like bamboo walls. Strange young girls dark as the moon stared from mysterious verdant doorways. "Oh man I want to stop and twiddle thumbs with the little darlings" cried Neal "but notice the old lady or the old man is always somewhere around---in the back usually, sometimes a hundred yards gathering twigs and wood or tending animals. They're never alone. Nobody's ever alone in this country. While you've been sleeping I've been digging this road and this country and if I could only tell you all the thoughts I've had man!" He was sweating. His eyes were red-streaked and mad and also subdued and tender---he had found a people like himself. We bowled right through the endless swamp country at a steady forty five. "Jack I think the country won't change for a long time. If you'll drive I'll sleep now." I took the wheel and drove among reveries of my own, through Linares, through hot flat swamp country, across the steaming Rio Soto la Marina near Hidalgo, and on. A great verdant jungle valley with long fields of greencrops opened before me. Groups of men watched us pass from a narrow oldfashioned bridge. The hot river flowed. Then we rose in altitude till a kind of desert country began reappearing. The city of Victoria was ahead. The boys were sleeping and I was alone in my eternity at the wheel and the road ran straight as an arrow. Not like driving across Carolina, or Texas, or Arizona, or Illinois; but like driving across the world and into the places where we would finally learn ourselves among the worldwide fellaheen people of the world, the Indians that stretch in a belt around the world from Malaya to India to Arabia to Morocco to Mexico and over to Polynesia. For these people were unmistakably Indians and were not at all like the Pedros and Panchos of silly American lore---they had high cheekbones, and slanted eyes, and soft ways---they were not fools, they were not clowns---they were great grave Indians and they were the source of mankind and the fathers of it. And they knew this when we passed, ostensibly self-important moneybag Americans on a lark in their land, they knew who was the father and who was the son of antique life on earth, and made no comment. For when destruction comes to the world people will still stare with the same eyes from the caves of Mexico as well as from the caves of Bali, where it all began and where Adam was suckled and taught to know. These were my growing thoughts as I drove the car into the hot sunbaked town of Victoria where we were destined to spend the maddest afternoon of our entire lives. Earlier, back at San Antonio, I had promised Neal, as a joke, that I would get him laid. It was a bet and a challenge. As I pulled up the car at the gas station near the gates of sunny Victoria a kid came across the road on tattered feet carrying an enormous windshield-shade and wanted to know if I'd buy. "You like? Sixty pesos. Habla Mexicano. Sesenta peso. My name Gregor." "Nah" I said jokingly "buy senorita." "Sure sure!" he cried excitedly. "I get you gurls, anytime.

Twenty pesos, thirty pesos." "You serious? True? Now?" "Now mon, ennytime. Too hot now" he added with distaste. "No like gurls when hot day. Wait tonight. You like shade." I didn't want the shade but I wanted the girls. I woke up Neal. "Hey Man I told you in Texas I'd get you laid---allright, stretch your bones and wake up boy, we've got girls waiting for us." "What? what?" he cried leaping up haggard. "Where? where?" "This boy Gregor's going to show us where." "Well lessgo, lessgo!" Neal leaped out of the car and clasped Gregor's hand. There was a group of other boys hanging around the station and grinning, half of them barefoot, all wearing floppy strawhats. "Man" said Neal to me "ain't this a nice way to spend an afternoon. It's so much cooler than Denver poolhalls. Gregor, you got gurls? Where? A donday?" he cried in Spanish. "Dig that Jack, I'm speaking Spanish." "Ask him if we can get any tea. Hey kid, you got mari-ju-a-na?" The kid nodded gravely. "Sho, ennytime mon. Come with me." "Hee! Whee! Hoo!" yelled Neal. He was wide awake and jumping up and down in that drowsy Mexican street. "Let's all go!" I was passing Lucky Strikes to the other boys. They were getting a great pleasure out of us and especially Neal. They turned to each other with cupped hands and rattled off comments about the mad American cat. "Dig them Jack talking about us and digging. Oh my goodness what a world!" We all got in the car and lurched off. Frank Jeffries had been sleeping soundly and woke up to this incredible madness. We drove way out to the desert the other side of town and turned on a rutty dirt road that made the car bounce as it never bounced before. Up ahead was Gregor's house. It sat on the edge of cactus flats overtopped by a few trees, just a dobe crackerbox, with a few men lounging around in the yard. "Who that?" cried Neal all excited. "Those my brothers. My mother there too. My sister too. That my family. I married, I live downtown." "What about your mother?" flinched Neal. "What she say about marijuana." "Oh she get it for me." And as we waited in the car Gregor got out and loped over to the house and said a few words to an old lady, who promptly turned and went to the garden in back and began pulling marijuana plants out of the earth. Meanwhile

Gregor's brothers grinned from under a tree. They were coming over to meet us but it would take a while for them to get up and walk over. Gregor came back grinning sweetly. "Man" said Neal "that Gregor is the sweetest gonest little cat I've ever met all my life. Just look at him, look at his cool slow walk. There's no need to hurry around here." A steady insistent desert breeze blew into the car. It was very hot. "You see how hot?" said Gregor sitting down with Neal in the front seat and pointing up at the burning roof of the Ford. "You have marijuana and it no hot no more. You wait." "Yes" said Neal adjusting his dark glasses "I wait. For sure Gregor m'boy." Presently Gregor's tall brother came ambling along with some weed wrapped in a newspaper. He dumped it on Gregor's lap and leaned casually on the door of the car to nod and smile at us and say "hallo." Neal nodded and smiled pleasantly at <u>him</u>. Nobody talked; it was fine. Gregor proceeded to roll the biggest bomber anybody ever saw. He rolled (using brown paper bag) what amounted to a tremendous Optimo cigar of tea. It was huge. Neal stared at it popeyed. Gregor casually lit it and passed around. To drag on this thing was like leaning over a chimney and inhaling. It blew into your throat in one great blast of heat. We held our breaths and all let out simultaneously. Instantly we were all high. The sweat froze on our foreheads and it was suddenly like the beach at Acapulco. I looked out the backwindow of the car and another and strangest of Gregor's brothers---a tall Peruvian of an Indian---leaned grinning on a post too bashful to come up and shake hands. It also seemed the car was surrounded by brothers for another one appeared on Neal's side. Then the strangest thing happened. Everybody became so high that usual formalities were dispensed with and the things of immediate interest were concentrated on, and what it was now, was the strangeness of Americans and Mexicans blasting together on the desert and more than that, the strangeness of seeing one another up close. So the Mexican brothers began talking about us in low voices and commenting, while Neal Frank and I commented on them. "Will you d-i-g that weird brother in the back." "Yes, and the one to my left here, he's like a gawddamn Egyptian king. These guys are real CATS. Ain't never seen anything like it. And they're talking and wondering about us just like we are but with a difference of their own, their interest probably resolving around how we're dressed---same as ours---but the strangeness of the things we have in the car and the strange ways that WE laugh so different from them, and maybe even the way we smell compared to them. Nevertheless I'd give my eye-teeth to know what they're saying about us." And Neal tried. "Hey Gregor, man...what your brother say just then?" Gregor turned mournful high brown eyes on Neal. "Yeah, yeah." "No you didn't understand my question. What you boys talking about?" "Oh" said Gregor with great perturbation "you no like this mariguana?" "Oh yes, yes fine! What you TALK about?" "Talk? Yes, we talk. How you like Mexico." It was hard to come around without a common language. And everybody grew quiet and cool and high again and just enjoyed the breeze from the desert and mused separate national thoughts. It was time for the gurls. The brothers eased back to their station under the tree, the mother watched from her sunny doorway, and we slowly bounced back to town. But now the bouncing was no longer unpleasant, it was the most pleasant and graceful billowy trip in the world, as over a blue sea, and Neal's face was suffused with an unnatural glow that was like gold as he told us to understand the springs of the car now for the first time and dig the ride. Up and down we bounced and even Gregor understood and laughed. Then he pointed left to show which way to go for the girls, and Neal, looking left with indescribable delight and leaning that way, pulled the wheel around and rolled us smoothly and surely to the goal, meanwhile listening to Gregor's attempt to speak and saying grandly and magniloquently "Yes, of course! There's not a doubt in my mind! Decidedly, man! Oh indeed! Why, pish, posh, you say the dearest things to me! Of course! Yes! Please go on!" To this Gregor talked gravely and with magnificent Spanish eloquence. For a mad moment I thought Neal was understanding everything he said by sheer wild insight and sudden revelatory genius inspired by his supreme and glowing happiness. In that moment, too, he looked so exactly like

Franklin Delano Roosevelt---some delusion in my flaming eyes and floating soul----that I drew up in my seat and gasped with amazement. I saw streams of gold pouring through the sky, and sensed God in the light just outside the car in the hot sunny streets. I looked out the window and saw a woman in a doorway and I thought she was listening to every word we said and nodding to herself---routine paranoiac visions of tea. But the stream of gold continued. For a long time I lost consciousness of what we were doing and only came around sometime later when we were parked outside Gregor's house and he was already at the door of the car with his little baby son in his arms showing him to us. "You see my baby? Hees name Perez, he six month age." "Why" said Neal, his face still transfigured into a shower of supreme pleasure and even bliss "he is the prettiest child I have ever seen. Look at those eyes. Now Jack and Frank" he said turning to us with a serious and tender air "I want you part-ti-cu-lar-ly to see the eyes of this little Mexican boy who is the son of our wonderful friend Gregor, and notice how he will come to manhood with his own particular soul bespeaking itself through the windows which are his eyes, and such lovely eyes surely must belie the loveliest of souls." It was a beautiful speech. And it was a beautiful baby. Gregor mournfully looked down at his angel. We all wished we had a little son like that. So great was our intensity over the child's soul that he sensed something and began a grimace which led to bitter tears and some unknown bitter sorrow that we had no means to soothe. We tried everything, Gregor smothered him in his neck and rocked; Neal cooed; I reached over and stroked the baby's little arms. His bawls grew louder. "Ah" said Neal "I'm awful sorry gregor that we've made him sad." "He is not sad, baby cry." In the doorway in back of Gregor, too bashful to come out, was his little barefoot wife with anxious tenderness waiting for the babe to be put back in her arms so brown and soft. Gregor having showed us his child, he climbed back into the car and proudly pointed to the right. "Yes" said Neal, and swung the car over and directed it through narrow Algerian streets with faces on all sides watching us with gentle wonder and secret fancy. We came to the whorehouse. It was a magnificent establishment of stucco in the golden sun. On it were written the words "Sale de Baile" which means dancehall, in proud official letters that seemed to me in their dignity and simplicity like the letterings on stone friezes around the Post offices of the United States. In the street, and leaning on the window-sills that opened into the whorehouse, were two cops, saggy-trousered, drowsy, bored, who gave us brief interested looks as we walked in and stayed there the entire three hours that we cavorted under their noses, until we came out at dusk and at Gregor's bidding gave them the equivalent of twenty four cents each just for the sake of form. And in there we found the girls. Some of them were reclined on couches across the dancefloor, some of them were boozing at the long bar to the right. In the center an arch led into small cubicle shacks that looked like the places where you put on your bathingsuit at public municipal beaches or bathhouses. These shacks were in the sun of the court. Behind the bar was the proprietor, a young fellow who instantly ran out when we told him we wanted to hear mambo music and came back with a stack of records, mostly by Perez Prado, and put them on over the public address system. In an instant all of the city of Victoria could hear the goodtimes going on at the Sale de Baile. In the hall itself the din of the music---for this is the real way to play a jukebox and what it was originally born for---was so tremendous that it shattered Neal and Frank and I for a moment in the realization that we had never dared to play music as loud as we wanted and this was how loud we wanted. It blew and shuddered directly at us. In a few minutes half that portion of town was at the windows watching the Americanos dance with the gals. They all stood, side by side with the cops, on the dirt sidewalk leaning in with indifference and casualness. "More Mambo Jambo," "Chattanooga de Mambo," "Mambo Numero Ocho," all these tremendous numbers resounded & flared in the golden mysterious afternoon like the sounds you expect to hear on the last day of the world and the Second Coming. The trumpets seemed so loud I thought they could hear it clear out in the desert, where the trumpets had originated anyway. The drums were mad.

The piano montunos showered down on us from the speaker. The cries of the leader were like great gasps in the air. The final trumpet choruses that came with drum climaxes on conga and bongo drums, on the great mad Chattanooga record, froze Neal in his tracks for a moment till he shuddered and sweated, then when the trumpets bit the drowsy air with their quivering echoes like a cavern's or a cave's his eyes grew large and round as tho seeing the Devil and he closed them tight. I myself was shook like a puppet by it; I heard the trumpets flail the light I had seen and trembled in my boots. On the fast Mambo Jambo we danced frantically with the girls. Through our deliriums we began to discern their varying personalities. They were great girls. Strangely the wildest one was half Indian, half white and came from Venezuala, and only eighteen. She looked like she came from a good family. What she was doing whoring in Mexico at that age and with that tender cheek and fair aspect God knows. Some awful grief had driven her to it. She drank beyond all bounds. She threw down drinks when it seemed she was about to chuck up the last. She overturned glasses continually, the idea also being to make us spend as much money as possible. Wearing her flimsy housecoat in broad afternoon she frantically danced with Neal and clung about his neck and begged and begged for everything. Neal was so stoned he didn't know what to start with, girls or mambo. They ran off to the lockers. I was set upon by a fat and uninteresting girl with a puppy dog who got sore at me when I took a dislike to it because it kept trying to bite me. She compromised by putting it away in the back, but by the time she returned I had been hooked by another gal, better looking but not the best, who clung to my neck like a leech. I was trying to break loose to get at a 16 year old colored girl who sat gloomily inspecting her navel through an opening in her flimsy dress across the hall. I couldn't do it. Frank had a 15 year old girl with an almond colored skin and a dress that was buttoned halfway down and halfway up. It was mad. A good twenty men leaned in that window watching. At one point the mother of the little colored girl---not colored but dark---came in to hold a brief and mournful convocation with her daughter. When I saw that I was too ashamed to try for the one I really wanted. I let the leech take me off to the back, where as in a dream, to the din and roar of further loudspeakers inside, we made the bed bounce a half hour. It was just a square room with wooden slats and no ceiling, a bulb hanging from the hall roof, and ikon in the corner, a washbasin in another. All up and down the dark hall the girls were calling "Aqua, aqua caliente!" which means hot water. Frank and Neal were also out of sight. My girl charged thirty pesos, or about three dollars and a half, and begged for an extra ten pesos and gave a long story about something. I didn't know the value of Mexican money, for all I knew I had a million pesos, I threw money at her. We rushed back to dance. A greater crowd was gathered in the street. The cops looked as bored as usual. Neal's pretty Venezualan dragged me through a door and into another strange bar that apparently belonged to the whore house. Here a young bartender was talking and wiping glasses and an old man with handlebar mustache sat discussing something earnestly. And here too the mambo roared over another loudspeaker. It seemed the whole world was turned on. Venezuala clung about my neck and begged for drinks. The bartender wouldn't give her one. She begged and begged, and when he gave it to her she spilled it and this time not on purpose for I saw the chagrin in her poor sunken lost eyes. "Take it easy baby." I told her. I had to support her on the stool, she kept slipping off. I've never seen a drunkener woman, and only eighteen. I bought her another drink, she was tugging at my pants for mercy. She gulped it up. I didn't have the heart to try her either. My own girl was about thirty and took care of herself better. Still with Venezuala writhing and suffering in my arms I had a longing to take her in the back and undress her and only talk to her---this I told myself. I was delirious with want of her and the other little dark girl. Poor Gregor, all this time he stood on the brassrail of the bar with his back to the counter and jumped up and down gladly to see his three American friends cavort. We bought him drinks. His eyes gleamed for a woman but he wouldn't accept any, being faithful to his wife. Neal thrust money at him. In this swelter of madness I had an opportunity to see what Neal was up to. He was so out of his mind he didn't know who I was when I peered at his face. "Yeah, yeah!" is all he said. It seemed it would never end. Again I rushed off with my girl to her room; Neal and Frank switched the girls they'd had before; and we were out of sight a moment and the spectators had to wait for the show to go on. The afternoon grew long and cool; soon it would be mysterious night in old gone Victoria. The mambo never let up for a moment. I couldn't take my eyes off the little dark girl, even after the second time, and the way, like a Queen, she walked around and was even reduced by the sullen bartender to menial tasks such as bringing us drinks. Of all the girls in there she needed the money most; maybe her mother had come to get money from her for her little infant sisters and brothers. It never, never occurred to me to just approach her and give her some money. I have a feeling she would have taken it with a degree of scorn and scorn from the likes of her made me flinch. In my madness I was actually in love with her for the few hours it all lasted; it was the same unmistakable ache and stab across the breast, the same sighs, the same pain, and above all the same reluctance and fear to approach. Strange that Neal and Frank also failed to approach her; her unimpeachable dignity was the thing that made her poor in a wild old whorehouse, and think of that. At one point I saw Neal leaning like a statue toward her, ready to fly, and befuddlement cross his face as she glanced coolly and imperiously his way and he stopped rubbing his belly and gaped and finally bowed his head. For she was the queen. Now Gregor suddenly clutched at our arms in the furor and made frantic signs. "What's the matter?" He tried everything to make us understand. Then he ran to the bar and grabbed the check from the bartender who scowled at him and took it to us to see. The bill was over 300 pesos, or thirty-six American dollars, which is a lot of money in any whore house. Still we couldn't sober up and didn't want to leave and tho we were all fussed-out we still wanted to hang around with our lovely girls in this strange Arabian paradise we had finally found at the end of the hard, hard road. But night was coming and we had to get on to the end; and

Neal saw that, and began frowning and thinking and trying to straighten himself out, and finally I broached the idea of leaving once and for all. "So much ahead of us man it won't make any difference." "That's right!" cried Neal glassy eyed and turned to his Venezualan. She had finally passed out and lay on a wooden bench with her white legs protruding from the silk. The gallery in the window took advantage of the show; behind them red shadows were beginning to creep, and somewhere I heard a baby wail in a sudden lull, remembering I was in Mexico after all and not in a sweet and orgiastic final dream. We staggered out; we had forgotten Frank; we ran back in to get him, like the boys run to get Ollie the seaman in Long Voyage Home, and found him charmingly bowing to the new evening whores that had just come in for nightshift. He wanted to start all over again. When he is drunk he lumbers like a man ten feet tall and when he is drunk he can't be dragged away from women. Moreover women cling to him like ivy. He insisted on staying and trying some of the newer, stranger, more proficient senoritas. Neal and I pounded him on the back and dragged him out. He waved profuse goodbyes to everybody, the girls, the cops, the crowds, the children in the street outside, he blew kisses in all directions of Victoria and staggered proudly among the gangs and tried to speak to them and communicate his joy and love of everything this fine afternoon of life. Everybody laughed; some slapped him on the back. Neal rushed over and paid the policemen the four pesos and shook hands and grinned with them. Then he jumped in the car, and the girls we had known, even Venzuala who was wakened for the farewell gathered around the car huddling in their flimsy duds and chattered goodbyes and kissed us and Venezuala even began to weep--- tho not for us, we knew, not altogether for us, yet enough and good enough. My dusky darling love had disappeared in the shadows inside. It was all over. We pulled out and left joys and celebrations over hundreds of pesos behind us and it didn't seem like a bad day's work. The haunting mambo followed us a few blocks. It was all over. "Goodbye Victoria!" cried Neal blowing it a kiss. Gregor was proud of us and proud of himself. "Now you like bath?" he asked. Yes, we all wanted wonderful bath. And he directed us to the strangest thing in the world: it was an ordinary American type bathhouse one mile out of town on the hiway, full of kids splashing in a pool and showers inside a stone building for a few centavos a crack, with soap and towel from the attendant. Besides this it was also a sad kiddy park with swings and a brokendown merrygoround and in the fading red sun it seemed so strange and so beautiful. Frank and I got towels and jumped right into ice-cold showers inside and came out refreshed and new. Neal didn't bother with a shower and we saw him far across the sad park strolling arm in arm with good Gregor and chatting volubly and pleasantly and even leaning excitedly towards him to make a point and pounding his fist. Then they resumed arm-in-arm and strolled. The time was coming to say goodbye to Gregor so Neal was taking the opportunity to have moments alone with him and to inspect the park and get his views on things in general and in-all dig him as only Neal could do and does. Gregor was very sad now that we had to go. "You come back Victoria, see me?" "Sure man!" said Neal. He even promised to take Gregor back to the states if he so wished it. Gregor said he would have to mull over this. "I got wife and kid--ain't got a money---I see." His sweet smile glowed in the redness as we waved to him from the car. Behind him was the sad park and the children. Suddenly he jumped after us and asked for a ride home. Neal was so bent on the road he was momentarily annoyed by this and brusquely told him to get in. And we went back to Victoria and dropped Gregor a block from his house. He didn't understand this sudden businesslike grimness on the part of Neal and Neal realizing it began talking and pointing what he could to him, and finally they were straight again and Gregor walked down the streets of his life. And off we bowled for the jungle, the mad mad jungle that we never expected. And after all this what more could we take in? Immediately outside Victoria the road began to drop, great trees arose on each side, and in the trees as it grew dark we heard the great roar of billions of insects that sounded like one continuous high-screeching cry. "Whoo!" said Neal, and he turned on his headlights and they weren't working.

"What! what! damn now what?" And he punched and fumed at his dashboard. "Oh my, we'll have to drive through the jungle without lights, think of the horror of that, the only time I'll see is when another comes by and there just <u>aren't</u> any cars! And of course no lights? Oh what'll we do Jack?" "Let's just drive. Maybe we ought to go back tho?" "No never-never! Let's go on. I can barely see the road. We'll make it." And now we shot in inky darkness through the scream of insects and the great rank almost rotten smell descended and we remembered and realized that the map indicated just after Victoria the beginning of the tropic of Cancer. "We're in a new tropic! Nowonder the smell! Smell it!" I stuck my head out the window; bugs smashed at my face; a great screech rose the moment I cocked my ear to the wind. Suddenly our lights were working again and they poked ahead illuminating the lonely road that ran between solid walls of great drooping snaky trees as high as a hundred feet. "Son-of-a-BITCH!" yelled Frank in the back. "Hot-DAMN!" He was still high. We suddenly realized he was still high and the jungle and troubles made no difference to his happy soul. We began laughing all of us. "To hell with it!- -we'll just throw ourselves on the gawd-damn jungle, we'll sleep in it tonight, let's go!" yelled Neal. "Old Frank is right, Old Frank don't care! He's so high on those women and that tea and that crazy out-of-this-world impossible-to-absorb mambo blasting so loud that my eardrums still beat to it - -whee! he's so high he know's what he's doing!" We took off our T shirts and roared through the jungle barechested. No towns, nothing, just jungle, miles and miles, and down-going, getting hotter, the insects screaming louder, the vegetation growing higher, the smell ranker and hotter until we began to get used to it and like it and love it. "I'd just like to get naked and roll and roll in that jungle" said Neal- -"No hell, man, that's what I'm going to do soon's I find a good spot." And suddenly Limon appeared before us, a jungle town, a few brown lights, dark shadows, enormous and unimaginable skies overhead and a cluster of men in front of a jumble of woodshacks---a tropical crossroads. We stopped in the unimaginable softness. It was as hot as the inside of a baker's oven on a June night in New Orleans. All up and down the street whole families were sitting around in the dark chatting; occasional girls came by, but extremely young and only curious to see what we looked like. They were barefooted and dirty. We leaned on the wooden porch of a brokendown general store with sacks of flour and fresh pineapple rotting on the counter with flies. There was one oil lamp in here, and outside a few more brown lights, and the rest all black, black, black. Now of course we were so tired we had to sleep at once and moved the car a few yards down a dirtroad to the backside of town and flopped off to sleep. It was so incredibly hot it was impossible to sleep. So Neal took a blanket and laid it out on the soft hot sand in the road and stretched out. Frank was stretched on the front seat of the Ford with both doors open for a draft but there wasn't even the faintest puff of a wind. I in the backseat suffered in a pool of sweat. I got out of the car and stood swaying in the blackness. The whole town had instantly gone to bed, the only noise now was barking dogs. How could I ever sleep? Thousands of mosquitos had already bitten all of us on chest and arms and ankles, there was nothing to do but give in to it and even enjoy. Then a bright idea came to me: I jumped up on the steel roof of the car and stretched out flat on my back. Still there was no breeze but the steel had an element of coolness left in it and dried my back of sweat, clotting up thousands of dead bugs into the cakes of my skin and I realized the jungle takes you over and you become it. Lying on the top of the car with my face to the black sky was like lying in a closed trunk on a summernight. For the first time in my life the weather was not something that touched me, that caressed me, froze or sweated me, but became me. The atmosphere and I became the same. Soft infinitesimal showers of microscopic bugs fanned down on my face as I slept and they were extremely pleasant and soothing. The sky was starless, utterly unseen and heavy. I could lie there all night long with my face exposed to the heavens and it would do me no more harm than a velvet drape drawn over me. The dead bugs mingled with my blood, the live mosquitoes exchanged further portions, I began to tingle all over and smell of the rank, hot and rotten jungle all over from hair and face to feet and toes. Of course I was barefoot. To minimize the sweat I put on my bug-smeared T-shirt and lay back again. A huddle of darkness on the blacker road showed where Neal was sleeping. I could hear him snoring. Frank was snoring too. Occasionally a dim light flashed in town and this was the sheriff making his rounds with a weak battery and mumbling to himself in the junglenight. Then I saw his light jiggling towards us and heard his footfalls coming soft on the mats of sand and vegetation. He stopped and flashed the car. I sat up and looked at him. In a quivering almost querulous and extremely tender voice he said "Dormiendo?" indicating Neal in the road. I knew this meant sleep. "Si, dormiendo." "Bueno, bueno" he said to himself and with reluctance and sadness turned away and went back to his lonely rounds. Such lovely policemen God hath never wrought in America. No suspicions, no fuss, no bother: he was the guardian of the sleeping town, period. I went back to my bed of steel and stretched out with my arms outspread. I didn't even know if branches or open sky was directly above me, and it made no difference. I opened my mouth to it and drew deep breaths of jungle atmosphere. It was not air, never air, but the palpable and living emanation of trees and swamp. I stayed awake. Roosters began to crow the dawn across the brakes somewhere. Still no air, no breeze, no dew, but the same Tropic of Cancer heaviness held us all pinned to earth where we belonged and tingled. There was no sign of dawn in the skies. Suddenly I heard the dogs barking furiously across the dark and then I heard the faint clip clop of a horse's hooves. It came closer and closer. What kind of mad rider in the night would this be? Then I saw an apparition: a wild-horse, white as a ghost, came trotting down the road directly towards Neal. Behind him the dogs yammered and contended. I couldn't see them, they were dirty old jungle dogs, but the horse was white as snow and immense and almost phosphorescent and easy to see. I felt no panic for Neal. The horse saw him and trotted right by his head, passed the car like a ship, whinnied softly, and continued on through town bedevilled by the dogs and clipclopped back to the jungle on the other side and all I heard was the faint hoofbeat fading away in the woods. The dogs subsided and sat to lick themselves. What was this horse? What myth and ghost, and what spirit? I told Neal about it when he waked up. He thought I'd been dreaming. Then he recalled faintly dreaming of a white horse and I told him it had been no dream. Frank Jeffries slowly woke up. The faintest movements and we were sweating profusely again. It was still pitchdark. "Let's start the car and blow some air!" I cried. "I'm dying of heat." "Right!" We roared out of town and continued along the mad highway. Dawn came rapidly in a gray haze revealing dense swamps sunk on both sides, with tall forlorn viney trees leaning and bowing over tangled bottoms. We bowled right along the railroad tracks for awhile. The strange radio station antenna of Ciudad Mante appeared ahead, as if we were in Nebraska. We found a filling station and loaded the tank just as the last of the junglenight bugs hurled themselves in a black mass against the bulbs and fell fluttering at our feet in huge wriggly groups, some of them waterbugs with wings a good four inches in spread, others frightful dragonflies big enough to eat a bird, and thousands of immense mosquitoes and unnamable spidery insects of all sorts. I hopped up and down on the pavement for fear of them; I finally ended up in the car with my feet in my hands looking fearfully at the ground where they swarmed around our wheels. "Lessgo!" I yelled. Neal and Frank weren't perturbed at all by the bugs; they calmly drank a couple of bottles of Mission Orange and kicked them away from the watercooler. Their shirts and pants like mine were soaked in the blood and black of thousands of dead bugs. We smelled our clothes deeply. "You know I'm beginning to like this smell" said Frank "I can't smell myself anymore." "It's a strange good smell" said Neal "I'm not going to change my shirt till Mexico City, I want to take it all in and remember it." So off we roared again, creating air for our hot caked faces, and went to Valles and on towards the great foothill town of Tamazunchale. This town is at an elevation of 682 feet and still in the jungle heat. Mudhuts leaned brownly on both sides of the road; great groups of children stood in front of the only gas station. We loaded up for the climb into the mountains that loomed ahead all green. After this climb we would be on the great central plateau again and ready to roll ahead to Mexico City. In no time at all we soared to an elevation of 5,000 feet among misty passes that overlooked steaming yellow rivers a mile below. It was the great River Moctezuma. The Indians along the road began to grow extremely weird. "Don't you see, this is a nation in itself, these people are mountain Indians and shut off from everything else!" cried Neal. They were short and squat, and dark, with bad teeth; they carried immense loads on their backs. Across enormous vegetated ravines we saw patchworks of agriculture on steep slopes. "The bastards walk up and down those slopes and work the crop!" yelled Neal. He drove the car five miles an hour. "Whooee, this I never thought existed!" High on the highest peak, as great a peak as any Rocky Mountain peak, we saw bananas growing. Neal got out of the car to point. We stopped on a ledge where a little thatched hut suspended itself over the precipice of the world. The sun created golden hazes that obscured the Moctezuma now more than a mile below. In the yard in front of the hut, for there was no back to it, only a chasm, a little three year old Indian girl stood with her finger in her mouth watching us with big brown eyes. "She's probably never seen anybody parked here before in her entire life!" breathed Neal. "Hel-lo little girl...how are You?...do you like us?" The little girl looked away bashfully and pouted. We began to talk and she again examined us with finger in mouth. "Gee I wish there was something I could give her! Think of it being born and living on this ledge---this ledge representing all you know of life---her father is probably groping down the ravine with a rope and getting his pineapples out of a cave and hacking wood at eighty degree angle with all the bottom below. She'll never never leave here and know anything about the outside world. It's a nation. They probably have a chief. Off the road, over that bluff, miles back they must be even wilder and stranger because the Pan American hiway partially civilizes this nation on this road. Notice the beads of sweat on her brow" Neal pointed out "It's not the kind of sweat we have, it's oily and it's ALWAYS

THERE because it's ALWAYS hot the year round and she knows nothing of non-sweat, she was born with sweat and dies with sweat." The sweat on her little brow was heavy, sluggish, it didn't run, it just stood there and gleamed like a fine olive oil. "What that must do to their souls? How different they must be in their evaluations and wishes!" Neal drove on with his mouth hanging in awe, ten miles an hour, desirous to see every possible human being on the road. We climbed and climbed. The vegetation grew more riotous and dense. A woman sold pineapples in front of her roadhut. We stopped and bought some at the fraction of a penny; she sliced them with a bolo knife. They were delicious and juicy. Neal gave the woman an entire peso which must have been a month's satisfaction for her. She gave no sign of joy but merely accepted the money. We realized there were no stores to buy anything in. "Damn, I wish I could give somebody something!" As we climbed the air finally grew cooler and the Indian girls on the road wore shawls over their heads and shoulders. They hailed us desperately; we stopped to see. They wanted to sell us little pieces of rock crystal. Their great brown innocent eyes looked into ours with such soulful intensity that not one of us had the slightest sexual thought about them; moreover they were very young, some of them eleven and looking almost thirty. "Look at those eyes!" breathed Neal. They were like the eyes of the Virgin Mother must have been when she was a child. We saw in them the tender and forgiving gaze of Jesus. And they stared unflinching into ours. We rubbed our nervous blue eyes and looked again. Still they penetrated us with sorrowful and hypnotic gleam. When they talked they suddenly became frantic and almost silly. In their silence they were themselves. "They've only <u>recently</u> learned to sell these crystals, since the hiway was about ten years back---up until that time this entire nation must have been <u>silent</u>." The girls yammered around our doors. One particuarly soulful child gripped at Neal's sweaty arm. She yammered in Indian. "Ah yes, ah yes dear one" said Neal tenderly and almost sadly and he got out of the car and went fishing around the battered trunk in the back---the same old tortured American trunk---and pulled out a wristwatch. He showed it to the child. She whimpered with glee. The others crowded around with amazement. Then Neal poked in the little girl's hand for "the sweetest and purest and smallest crystal she has personally picked from the mountain for us." He found one no bigger than a berry. And he handed her the wristwatch dangling. Their mouths rounded like the mouths of chorister children. The lucky little girl squeezed it to her ragged breastrobes. They stroked Neal and thanked him. He stood among them with his ragged face to the sky looking for the next and highest and final pass and seemed like the Prophet that had come to them. He got back in the car. They hated to see us go. For the longest time, as we mounted a long straight pass, they waved and ran after us like dogs that follow the family car from the farm until they loll exhausted by the side of the road. We made a turn and never saw them again, and they were still running after us. "Ah this breaks my heart!" cried Neal punching his chest. "How far do they carry out these loyalties and wonders! What's going to happen to them? Would they try to follow the car all the way to Mexico City if we drove slow enough?" "Yes" I said, for I knew. We came into the dizzying heights of the Sierra Madre Oriental. The banana trees gleamed golden in the haze. Great fogs yawned beyond stonewalls along the precipice. Below the Moctezuma was a thin golden thread in a green jungle mat. Steams rose from down there and mingled with the upper airs and great atmospheres like white heaven propelled among the bushy peaks. Strange crossroad towns on top of the world rolled by, with shawled Indians watching us from under hatbrims and rebozos. All had their hands outstretched. They had come down from the backmountains and higher places to hold forth their hands for something they thought civilization could offer and they never dreamed the sadness and the poor broken delusion of it. They didn't know that a bomb had come that could crack all our bridges and banks and reduce them to jumbles like the avalanche heap, and we would be as poor as them someday and stretching out our hands in the samesame way. Our broken Ford, old Thirties upgoing America Ford, rattled through them and vanished in dust. At Zimapan, or

Ixmiquilpan, or Actopan, I don't know which, we had reached the approaches of the last plateau. Now the sun was golden, the air keen blue, and the desert with its occasional rivers a riot of sandy hot space and sudden Biblical treeshade. The shepherds appeared. Now Neal was sleeping and Frank driving. We went through an entire belt of the ascent to the last plateau where the Indians were dressed as in first times, in long flowing robes, the women carrying golden bundles of flax, the men staves. Across the shimmering desert we saw great trees, and under these great trees the shepherds sat and convened, and the sheep moiled in the sun and raised dust beyond. Great maguey plants showered out of the strange Judean earth. "Man, man" I yelled to Neal "wake up and see the shepherds, wake up and see the golden world that Jesus came from, with your own eyes tell!" But he was unconscious. I went out of my mind when we passed suddenly through a ruined dusty dobe town in which hundreds of shepherds were gathered by the shade of a battered wall, their long robes trailing in the dust, their dogs leaping, their children running, their women with head lowered gazing sorrowfully, the men with high staves watching us pass with noble and chieflike miens, as though they had been interrupted in their communal meditations in the living sun by the sudden clanking folly from America with its three broken bozos inside. I yelled to Neal to look. He shot his head up from the seat, saw one glimpse of it all in the fading red sun, and dropped back to sleep. When he woke up he described it to me in detail and said "Yes, man, I'm glad you told me to look. Oh Lord, what shall I do? Where will I go?" He rubbed his belly, he looked to heaven with red eyes, he almost wept. At Colonia we reached the final level of the great Mexican plateau and zoomed straight ahead on an arrow road towards Zumpango and Mexico City. Here of course the air was tremendously cool and dry and pleasant. The end of our journey impended. Great fields stretched on both sides of us; a noble wind blew across the occasional immense trees and groves and over old missions turning salmon in the late sun. The clouds were close and huge and pink. "Mexico City by dusk!" We'd made it. When we stopped for pisscall I got out and walked across a field to the big trees and sat awhile thinking on the plain. Frank and Neal sat in the car gesticulating. Poor fellows, their flesh mingled with mine had been carried now a total of nineteen hundred miles from the afternoon yards of Denver to these vast and Biblical areas of the world and now were about to reach the end of the road and though I didn't know it I was about to reach the end of my road with Neal. And my road with Neal had been considerably longer than nineteen hundred miles. "Shall we change our insect T-shirts?" "Naw, let's wear them into town, hell's bells." And we drove into Mexico City. A brief mountain pass took us suddenly to a height from which we saw all of Mexico City stretched out in its volcanic crater below and spewing city smokes and early dusklights. Down to it we zoomed, down Insurgentes boulevard, straight to the heart of town at Reforma. Kids played soccer in enormous sad fields and threw up dust. Taxi drivers overtook us and wanted to know if we wanted girls. No, we didn't want girls now. Long ragged dobe slums stretched out on the plain; we saw lonely figures in the dimming alleys. Soon night would come. Then the city roared in and suddenly we were passing crowded cafes and theaters and many lights. Newsboys yelled at us. Mechanics slouched by barefoot with a wrench and a rag. Mad barefoot Indian drivers cut across us and surrounded us and tooted and made frantic traffic. The noise was incredible. No mufflers are used on Mexican cars. Horns are batted with glee continual. "Whee!" yelled Neal. "Lookout!" He staggered the car through the traffic and played with everybody. He drove like an Indian. He got on a circular drive on Reforma Boulevard and rolled around it with its eight spokes shooting cars at us from all directions, left, right, dead ahead, and yelled and jumped with joy. "This is traffic I've always dreamed of! Everybody GOES!" An ambulance came balling through. American ambulances dart and weave through traffic with siren blowing; the great worldwide fellaheen Indian ambulances merely come through at eighty miles an hour in the city streets and everybody has to get out of the way, and it does not pause for an instant

APPENDIX

The last few feet of the scroll manuscript are lost. According to a handwritten note at the end of the scroll reading "DOG ATE [Potchky-a-dog]," Potchky, a dog belonging to Lucien Carr, chewed up the ending. Kerouac told John Holmes about the accident, and in later years Carr confirmed the story. After Kerouac's marriage to Joan Haverty had collapsed Kerouac stayed at Carr's West Twenty-first Street apartment for a brief time in mid-June 1951 before he traveled to join his family in North Carolina. Kerouac's letters to Neal Cassady in May and June and a July 6 letter to Kerouac from his then agent Rae Everitt show that Kerouac had typed a revised version of the novel to be sent out for consideration by Harcourt, Brace and other publishers before he left New York, and so Kerouac may have left the scroll at Carr's apartment before heading south. Working backward from Kerouac's post-April 1951 drafts and the published novel, here's what the lost ending might have looked like.

Howard Cunnell
Brixton, London, 2007

An ambulance came balling through. American ambulances dart and weave through traffic with siren blowing; the great worldwide fellaheen Indian ambulances merely come through at eighty miles an hour in the city streets and everybody has to get out of the way, and it does not pause for an instant or any circumstance and flies straight through there. We saw it reeling out of sight. The drivers were Indians. People, even old ladies ran for buses that never stopped. Young Mexico City businessmen made bets and ran by squads for buses and barely jumped them. The busdrivers were barefoot and sat low and squat in T-shirts at the low enormous wheel. Ikons burned over them. The lights in the buses were brown and greenish and dark faces were lined on wooden benches. Downtown Mexico City thousands of hipsters in floppy strawhats and longlapeled jackets over barechests padded along the main drag, some of them selling crucifixes and weed in the alleys, some of them kneeling in beat chapels next to Mexican burlesque shows in sheds. Some alleys were rubble, with open sewers, little doors that led to closet-size bars stuck in dobe walls. You had to jump over a ditch to get your drink. You came out of the bar with your back to the wall and edged back to the street. They served coffee mixed with rum and nutmeg. Mambo blared from everywhere. Hundreds of whores lined themselves along the fronts of dark and narrow streets and their sorrowful eyes gleamed at us in the night. We wandered in a frenzy and a dream. We ate beautiful steaks for 48 cents in strange tiled Mexican cafeterias with marimba musicians and wandering guitars. Nothing stopped; the streets were alive all night. Beggars slept wrapped in advertising posters. Whole families sat on the sidewalk playing little flutes and chuckling in the night. Their bare feet stuck out. On corners old women cut up the boiled heads of cows and served it on newspaper. This was the great and final city that we knew we would find at the end of the road. Neal walked through with his arms hanging zombie-like at his sides, his mouth open, his eyes gleaming, and conducted a ragged and holy tour that lasted till dawn in a field with a boy in a strawhat who laughed and chatted with us and wanted to play catch, for nothing ever ended. We tried to find Bill Burroughs too, and learned that he had just left for South America with his family, so Bill Burroughs had finally sunken from our sight and was gone. Then I got fever and became delirious and unconscious. I looked up out of the dark swirl of my mind and I knew I was on a bed eight thousand feet above sea level, on a roof of the world, and I knew that I had lived a whole life and many others in the poor atomistic husk of my flesh, and I had all the dreams. And I saw Neal bending over the kitchen table. It was several nights later and he was leaving Mexico City. "What you doing man?" I moaned. "Poor Jack, poor Jack you're sick. Frank'll take care of you. Now listen if you can in your sickness---I got my divorce from Carolyn down here and I'm driving back to Diane in NY if the car holds out." "All that again?" I cried. "All that again, good buddy. Gotta get back to my life. Wish I could stay with you. Pray I can come back." I grabbed the cramps in my belly and groaned. When I looked up again Neal was standing with his old broken trunk and looking down at me. I didn't know who he was anymore, and he knew this, and sympathized, and pulled the blanket over my shoulders. "Yes, yes, yes, I've got to go now." And he was gone. Twelve hours later in my sorrowful fever I finally came to understand that he was gone. By this time he was driving back alone through those banana mountains, this time at night, black night, secret night, holy night. BOOK FIVE:- A week later the Korean War began. Neal drove from Mexico City and saw Gregor again in Victoria and pushed that old car all the way to Lake Charles La. before the rear-end finally dropped on the road as he always knew it would and he wired Diane for $32 airplane fare and flew the rest of the way. Arriving in NY with the divorce papers in his hands he and Diane immediately went to Newark and got married; and that night, telling her everything was all right and not to worry, and making logics where there was nothing but inestimable sorrowful sweats, he jumped on a bus and roared off again across the awful continent to San Francisco to rejoin Carolyn and the two baby girls. So now he was thrice-married, twice-divorced, and living with his second wife. In the Fall I myself started back from Mexico City and one night just over

Laredo border in Dilley, Texas, I was standing on the hot road underneath an arclamp with the summermoths smashing into it when I heard the sound of footsteps from the darkness beyond and lo, a tall old man with flowing white hair came clomping by with a pack on his back, and when he saw me as he passed, he said "<u>Go</u> <u>moan</u> <u>for</u> <u>man</u>" and clomped on back to his dark. Did this mean that I should at last go on my pilgrimage on foot on the dark roads around America? I struggled and hurried to NY, and one night I was standing in a dark street in Manhattan and called up to the window of a loft where I thought my friends were having a party. But a pretty girl stuck her head out of the window and said "Yes? Who is it?" "Jack Kerouac" I said, and heard my name resound in the sad and empty street. "Come on up" she called "I'm making hot chocolate." So I went up and there she was, the girl with the pure and innocent dear eyes that I had always searched for and for so long. That night I asked her to marry me and she accepted and agreed. Five days later we were married. Then in the winter we planned to migrate to San Francisco bringing all our beat furnitures and broken belongings with us in a jaloppy truck. I wrote to Neal and told him what I had done. He wrote back a huge letter 18,000 words long and said he was coming to get me and personally select the old truck himself and drive us home. We had six weeks to save up the money for the truck so we began working and counting every cent. And suddenly Neal arrived anyway, five and a half weeks in advance, and nobody had any money to go through with the plan. I was taking a walk and came back to my wife to tell her what I thought about during my walk. She stood in the dark parlor with a strange smile. I told her a number of things and suddenly I noticed the hush in the room and looked around and saw a battered book on the television set. I knew it was Neal's book. As in a dream I saw him tiptoe in from the dark kitchen in his stockinged feet. He couldn't talk any more. He hopped and laughed, he stuttered and fluttered his hands and said "Ah---ah---you must listen to hear." We listened. But he forgot what he wanted to say. "Really listen---ahem... look dear Jack...sweet Joan...I've come...I'm gone...but wait...Ah yes." And he stared with rocky sorrow into his hands. "Can't talk no more...do you understand that it is...or might be...but listen!" We all listened. He was listening to sounds in the night. "Yes!" he whispered in awe. "But you see...no need to talk any more...and further." "But why did you come so soon Neal?" "Ah," he said looking at me for the first time "so soon, yes. We...we'll know...that is I don't know. I came on the railroad pass...cabooses...brakeman pass...played flute and wooden sweetpotato all the way." He took out his new wooden flute. He played a few squeaky notes on it and jumped up and down in his stockinged feet. "See?" he said. "But of course Jack I can talk as soon as ever and have many things to say to you in fact I've been reading and reading all the way across the country and digging a great number of things I'll never have TIME to tell you about and we STILL haven't talked of Mexico and our parting there in fever...but no need to talk. Absolutely, now, yes?" "All right we won't talk." And he started telling the story of what he did in L.A. on the way over in every possible detail, how he visited a family, had dinner, talked to the father, the sons, the sisters (they were cousins)---what they looked like, what they ate, their furnishings, their thoughts, their interests, their very souls, and having concluded this he said "Ah, but you see what I wanted to REALLY tell you...much later...Arkansas, crossing on train...playing flute...playing cards with boys, my dirty deck...won money, wooden sweetpotato...Long long awful trip five days and five nights just to SEE you Jack." "What about Carolyn?" "Gave permission of course...waiting for me...Carolyn and I all straight forever-and-ever..." "And Diane?" "I...I...I want her to come back to Frisco with me live other side of town...don't you think? Don't know why I came." Later he said in a sudden moment of gaping wonder "Well and yes, of course, I wanted to see your sweet wife and you...gone and done it, old man...glad of you...love you as ever." He stayed in NY three days and hastily made preparations to get back on the train with his railroad passes and again re-cross the groaning continent, five days and five nights in dusty coaches and hardbench cabooses and still he didn't know why he had come, and of course we had no money for a truck and couldn't go back with him at all now. He simply had no idea why he had come, beyond the fact that he wanted to see me and my sweet wife, and we agreed she was. With pregnant Diane he spent one night fighting and she threw him out. A letter came for him care of me and I deliberately opened it to see what was up. It was from Carolyn. "My heart broke when I saw you go across the tracks with your bag. I pray and pray you get back safe...I do want Jack and his new wife to come and live on the same street...I know you'll make it but I can't help worrying---now that we've decided everything...Dear Neal, it's the end of the first half of the century. Welcome with love and kisses to spend the other half with us. We all wait for you. (signed) Carolyn, Cathy, and Little Jami." So Neal's life was settled with his most constant, most embittered and best-knowing wife Carolyn and I thanked God for him. The last time I saw him it was under sad and strange circumstances. Henri Cru had arrived in New York after having gone around the world several times in ships. I wanted him to meet and know Neal. They did meet but Neal couldn't talk any more and said nothing, and Henri turned away. Henri had gotten tickets for the Duke Ellington concert at the Metropolitan Opera and insisted Joan and I come with him and his girl. Henri was fat and sad but still the eager and formal gentleman and he wanted to do things the right way as he emphasized. So he got his bookie to drive us to the concert in a Cadillac. It was a cold winter night. The Cadillac was parked and ready to go. Neal stood outside the windows with his bag ready to go to Penn Station and on across the land. "Goodbye Neal" I said. "I sure wish I didn't have to go to the concert." "D'you think I can ride to 40th St. with you?" he whispered. "Want to be with you as much as possible, m'boy and besides it's so durned cold in this here New Yawk..." I whispered to Henri. No, he wouldn't have it, he liked me but he didn't like my friends. I wasn't going to start all over again ruining his planned evenings as I had done at Alfred's in San Francisco in 1947 with Allan Temko. "Absolutely out of the question Jack!" Poor Henri, he had a special necktie made for this evening; on it was painted a replica of the concert tickets, and the names Jack and Joan and Henri and Vicki, the girl, together with a series of sad jokes and some of his favorite sayings such as 'You can't teach the old maestro a new tune.' So Neal couldn't ride uptown with us and the only thing I could do was sit in the back of the Cadillac and wave at him. The bookie at the wheel also wanted nothing to do with Neal. Neal, ragged in a motheaten overcoat he brought specially for the freezing temperature of the East, walked off alone and the last I saw of him he rounded the corner of 7th Ave., eyes on the street ahead, and bent to it again. Poor little Joan my wife to whom I'd told everything about Neal began almost to cry. "Oh we shouldn't let him go like this. What'll we do?" Old Neal's gone I thought, and out loud I said "He'll be all right." And off we went to the sad and disinclined concert for which I had no stomach whatever and all the time I was thinking of Neal and how he got back on the train and rode over 3,000 miles over that awful land and never knew why he had come anyway, except to see me and my sweet wife. And he was gone. If I hadn't been married I would have gone with him again. So in America when the sun goes down and I sit on the old brokendown river pier watching the long, long skies over New Jersey and sense all that raw land that rolls in one unbelievable huge bulge over to the West Coast, all that road going, all the people dreaming in the immensity of it, and in Iowa I know by now the evening-star must be drooping and shedding her sparkler dims on the prairie, which is just before the coming of complete night that blesses the earth, darkens all rivers, cups the peaks in the west and folds the last and final shore in, and nobody, just nobody knows what's going to happen to anybody besides the forlorn rags of growing old, I think of Neal Cassady, I even think of Old Neal Cassady the father we never found, I think of Neal Cassady, I think of Neal Cassady.